ETHNIC
AMERICA
1970~1977

ETHNIC AMERICA
1970~1977

updating the ethnic chronology series~with cumulative index

by
MELVIN HECKER

1979 oceana publications, inc., dobbs ferry, new york

Library of Congress Cataloging in Publication Data

Hecker, Melvin, 1946-
    Ethnic America, 1970-1977.

    Bibliography: p.
    1. Minorities—United States—History—Chronology.
I. Title.
    E184.A1H42   973'.04   79-12913
    ISBN 0-379-00710-X

To My Parents, Rose and Leo Hecker

It is only by risking our persons from one hour to another that we live at all. And often enough our faith beforehand in an uncertified result is the only thing that makes the result come true.

William James
The Will to Believe, 1897

TABLE OF CONTENTS

PREFACE

The Ethnics in America series describes the history and development of thirty ethnic groups within American society. *The American Indian* launched the series in 1971; the last volume, *The Arabs In America,* was published in 1977.

Oceana Publications initially intended the series to be a record of significant ethnic events that would introduce high school and community college students to social studies reference materials and sources. But because of the growing interest of many Americans, both old and young, in their ethnic heritage, the books have achieved a broader appeal. The constant evolution of ethnic America and this heightened interest in its cultural diversity have called for the publication of a *Yearbook* to relate the significant events occuring each year and thereby keeping the series up to date.

In addition to reporting on the latest developments within each ethnic group, the *Yearbook* will explore a subject of concern shared by most, if not all, the groups. Topics may include the effects of World War II on the flow of immigrants to the United States; the reasons for ethnic communities settling where they have; the ethnic background of prominent political leaders or of notable figures in the sciences.

Ethnic America, 1970 to 1977 updates to the end of 1977 all the books in the series, providing a bridge that will permit the publication of a *Yearbook.* It covers the activities and trends within each of the thirty ethnic groups during the 1970s. In addition, a cumulative index for the entire series has been included which provides an invaluable tool for researching the historical and other personalities featured in the Ethnics in America series.

It is the publishers' belief that to ignore ethnic culture is to distort American history. For this reason, Oceana Publications will continue in its effort to uncover the rich pluralism of the American people and to inform them of the virtues of their heritage.

INTRODUCTION

America, its land and its people; a remarkable diversity comprising a coherent whole. Its people have come from the fjords of Scandinavia, the shores of the African coast, the mountains of Japan, the valleys of the Rhine and the plains of the Russian Steppes. They have come from all lands to make the United States their home.

Throughout American history, external social forces and often intragroup pressure combined to push immigrants to assimilate, to give up those customs and traditions which separated them from the American mainstream. The immigrant was told, sometimes brutally and at other times through more subtle means, to blend into the majority culture as swiftly and as completely as possible. After World War II, however, a new emphasis on ethnic values and activities became evident. This surge of ethnic pride strengthened throughout the decades that followed and appeared to culminate in the Bicentennial celebrations, which revealed a somewhat paradoxical phenomenon. At the same time that the ethnic communities proclaimed their allegiance to the United States, many took the opportunity to assert the distinctiveness of their group's heritage. A large proportion of the secular and religious Bicentennial celebrations were flavored by the history and cultural traditions of America's ethnic groups.

The growth of ethnicity, an ethnic group's desire to preserve its cultural history and revive its best traditions, can be traced to a spreading sense of the individual's alienation coupled with a new freedom of self-expression. Trends that have aggravated this feeling of isolation include the increased mobility of American society; the flow of people from rural to urban areas; the decline in family stability; and the growth of technology with the unsettling emphasis on novelty and change. Americans, confronted by all this, are reaching out for things that are familiar, whether customs, values or artifacts, to provide them with a form of continuity and security. The self-expression movement, sometimes referred to as the 'ME-generation', has resulted in a glorification of the individual and hence of the diversity of American life. In addition, legislation and popular liberal sentiment have given minorities a new sense of their political and social importance. Cooperative power, it is realized, is stronger than the sum of its parts.

Membership of an ethnic group or organization, whether social, economic or political, provides a scale that is comprehensible to most people, and supplies a mechanism through which the individual can achieve some action. Furthermore, the group reinforces the member's sense of identity and individuality in relation to the American masses, and supports the rightness of his or her life-style, preferences and values. The individual is no longer merely a name, address and a nine-digit social security number, but has a position and roots connecting him or her to a long history and a rich cultural background.

The *Ethnic America* chronology presents a survey of important events in American history from the perspective of the ethnic community. The sources of information appearing in the chronology were chosen to impart unbiased facts on the thirty ethnic groups with equal proportions. For the most part, use was made of reference material such as the *New York Times Index*, which reports the significant achievements and activities of all groups. Other primary sources of data were: Wynar's *Encyclopedic Directory of Ethnic Organization in The United States;* Miller's *A Comprehensive Bibliography For The Study of American Minorities; Facts on File, 1970-1977; Who's Who* and *Who Was Who In America* series; and, of course, the individual volumes in the Ethnics in America series. Any resulting imbalance is accounted for because the activities of the larger and better organized groups are more widely publicized. In addition, the wealth of data tends to favor foreign-born Americans; facts specific to second and third generation Americans are reported more sporadically.

The author is indebted to a small number of people who either helped get the project underway, or aided in the research, or helped shape the volume into its final form. I must first thank Philip F. Cohen, the president of Oceana Publications, who conceived of an Ethnic Yearbook and worked with me in shaping this volume. The staff at Mercy College Library in Dobbs Ferry, New York was most helpful in locating useful source material. Monica Gerard-Sharp made an invaluable contribution in the copy-editing of the manuscript. I am grateful to Joan Silver for the design of the title page and for her production expertise, as well as to Michael Schwartz for his help. Lastly, thanks to Anna Knecht who patiently typed the seemingly interminable index.

CHRONOLOGIES

THE AMERICAN INDIAN

1970   JANUARY 1. The California Indian tribes of the San Diego
        area completed a proposal under the auspices of the Wright
        Institute at Grossmont College which requested financing
        from the federal government for a research and development
program to uncover and implement solutions for minority and low income peoples in that area. The proposal was sent to the Special
Services Office of the Department of Health, Education and Welfare.

FEBRUARY. The Indians of All Tribes issued a statement calling for renewed support of their November 1969 occupation of Alcatraz
Island.

MARCH 23. The first Convocation of American Indian Scholars
convened at Princeton University under the chairmanship of Dr. Alfonso Ortiz, a San Juan Pueblo Indian. The meeting was held under the
auspices of the American Indian Historical Society with the purpose
of bringing together Indian students.

MARCH. A research and development office for the Native American Centre for Living Arts was opened in New York City. The project
was conceived by the internationally known Cree folk singer, Buffy
Sainte Marie.

APRIL 17. The Tesque Pueblo governor signed a ninety-nine
year lease with Santos E. Campos and the Sangre de Cristo Development Company for 5,400 acres of pueblo land for the creation of a
resort city north of Santa Fe, New Mexico.

JULY 8. In his message to Congress on new policies and goals
for American Indians, President Nixon presented a new Indian doctrine.
He stated that "it is long past time that Indian policies of the
federal government began to recognize and build upon the capacities
and insights of the Indian people."

JULY. Commissioner of Indian Affairs Louis R. Bruce signed
a contract with the Ramah Navajo School Board to provide $368,000 a
year for the next three years to help them start their own high
school.

*The author is indebted to Henry C. Dennis, the editor of THE AMERICAN INDIAN, 2nd Ed.,
for his research covering the period 1970 to 1976.*

AUGUST. The Ford Foundation announced that the California Indian Legal Service had been awarded a grant to establish a nationwide demonstration program known as the Native American Rights Fund which would engage in major litigation involving Indian rights.'

AUGUST. A five day seminar held at Fort Collins, Colorado marked the first national gathering of American Indian women. The new group elected Marie Cox, a Comanche from Midwest, Oklahoma as executive director.

SEPTEMBER 18. A suit on behalf of treaty fishing rights of Indian tribes in the state of Washington was filed by the Department of Justice at the request of the Department of the Interior. The action was brought on behalf of seven tribes: the Payallup, Nisqually, Skokomish, Makah, Quileute, Hoh and Muckleshoot.

SEPTEMBER 19. Laguna pueblo, the youngest Indian pueblo in New Mexico, held its annual fiesta and harvest dance. The pueblo was formally established in 1699 by Don Pedro de Cubero, governor of New Mexico, on a land grant given the Indians by the king of Spain.

SEPTEMBER. Interior Secretary Walter J. Hickel, acting as trustee for the Rincon, La Jolla and San Pascual bands of Mission Indians, filed a petition with the Federal Power Commission to revoke the license of the Escondido Mutual Water Company. The petition claimed that the company had trespassed on the Indian reservations without authority.

OCTOBER 18. Secretary of the Interior Hickel announced the appointment of fifteen American Indians to key executive posts in the Washington, D.C. headquarters of the Bureau of Indian Affairs.

OCTOBER 21. Secretary Hickel attended the National Congress of American Indians Annual Convention in Anchorage, Alaska.

NOVEMBER 1. The Indian Claims Commission announced that it had finished work on 327 of 609 dockets, or sub-petitions of Indian claims, since it was created in 1946. Thus far, Congress had appropriated more than 330 million dollars to Indians as a result of commission awards. The commission is a judicial body set up to adjudicate tribal claims against the United States so as to obtain payment for lands taken from them in the eighteenth and nineteenth centuries.

NOVEMBER 19. The world premiere of the new Anthony Quinn movie *Flap*, which was filmed in Albuquerque, New Mexico, was held as a benefit performance for the new Indian studies program at the University of New Mexico.

DECEMBER 15. After receiving the bipartisan bill passed by the Senate, President Nixon signed the long sought legislation that returned to the Taos Indians 48,000 acres of land they claimed was an intrinsic part of their religious observances.

The United Indian Development Association (UIDA) was organized in order to assist Indian-owned businesses and profit enterprises.

The National Indian Educational Association (NIEA) was founded in St. Paul, Minnesota. The NIEA sponsors lectures, panel discussions and seminars and produces a monthly publication entitled *Indian Education.*

1971   JANUARY 12.   The NAACP Legal Defense and Educational Fund, Inc. charged that federal funds appropriated for the education of Indian children were being used for "every conceivable school need except aiding the 177,000 Indian children in public schools."

JANUARY 14.   The United States Government gave custody of an old Davis, California army base to Indians who had occupied the 640-acre site in November 1970. Jack Forbes, a Powhatan Indian, stated that a university for Indians and Mexican-Americans would be developed on the land.

FEBRUARY.   The Commissioner of Indian Affairs, Louis R. Bruce, announced an environmental awareness award program for Indian schools and communities.

MARCH 25.   A Blackfoot Vietnam veteran, William J. Gobert, was selected Outstanding Handicapped Worker of the Year by the Department of Health, Education and Welfare.

APRIL.   The Economic Development Administration of the Department of Commerce made twelve grants and one loan that amounted to over six million dollars to Indian tribes and Indian-related development groups.

APRIL.   During a three-day Tribal Chairmen's Conference held in Pierre, South Dakota, eighteen Indian tribal leaders voted to form the National Tribal Chairmen's Association. The group was formed to ensure that federally recognized tribes had proper representation.

MAY 1.   The start of a movement among western Indians of the United States "to give the Indians of small tribes a voice equal to the strength exercised presently by the largest Indian tribes in the nation" took place in Federal-Way, Washington, at the headquarters of the Small Tribes Organization of Western Washington (STOWW).

MAY.   An innovative public-interest law firm, the Institute for the Development of Indian Law, opened its office in Washington, D.C. The group's executive director, a Kiowa attorney, was Kirke Kickingbird.

MAY.   Fleming D. Begay, a Navajo Indian, was honored by the

Bureau of Indian Affairs (BIA) as Indian Businessman of the Year.

MAY 4. The noted anthropology and linguistics professor, Dr. Edward P. Dozier, died at the age of fifty-five. Dr. Dozier, who specialized in the American Indian, was a Santa Clara Indian of international repute.

MAY 5. Official dedication ceremonies took place for the Kicking Horse Regional Manpower Center, the country's first all-Indian Job Corps Center which was located near Ronan, Montana.

MAY 14. Residents of the San Carlos Apache Indian reservation in Arizona dedicated their own radio station, SCCR, which was said to be the first station on an Indian reservation in the country.

MAY 12. Included in the announced selection of sixteen young men and women as White House Fellows was Martin Seneca, a Seneca Indian.

JUNE 6. Some of the Indians that had set up camp on top of the Mount Rushmore National Memorial were arrested. The protestors demanded that the government honor an 1868 Sioux treaty declaring that all the land in South Dakota west of the Missouri River belonged to the Indians.

JUNE 11. Thirty-five United States marshalls removed fifteen Indians from Alcatraz Island, thereby ending a nineteen-month occupation of the former federal prison.

JUNE. The commissioner of Indian affairs announced the appointment of John Artichocker, a Sioux, as area director of the bureau's office in Phoenix.

JULY 1. Approximately 100 Indians who had taken over several buildings at a one-time Nike missile site near Chicago on June 14 were removed by 150 armed policemen. The occupation took place as a protest against the lack of housing available in the area.

JULY 12. Dr. James J. Wilson III assumed his new duties as executive director of the Southwestern Cooperative Educational Laboratory.

JULY 16. The commissioner of Indian affairs announced that over the past year American Indians had started 241 new businesses and expanded 143 Indian-owned businesses through the Indian Business Development Fund program of the BIA. Mr. Bruce estimated that the new developments would create nearly three thousand new jobs for Indians, with an annual payroll of about twelve million dollars.

JULY 23. Secretary of the Interior, Rogers C. B. Morton, announced the appointment of John O. Crow as commissioner of the Bureau of Indian Affairs.

AUGUST 21. The newest and most advanced polytechnic institute in the United States, Southwestern Indian Polytechnic Institute (SIPI), opened in Albuquerque, New Mexico with the dedication of the BIA's new $14 million, 164-acre facility. The institute was planned to offer unique post-secondary training to the members of more than sixty Indian tribes.

SEPTEMBER 1. A National Indian Training Center opened on the campus of Intermountain School, a BIA facility located in Brigham Center, Utah.

SEPTEMBER. The School of Public Health at the University of California in Berkeley offered ten traineeships to American Indians for the graduate degree of Master of Public Health.

DECEMBER 16. An unprecedented union of Native Americans, the Coalition of Organized Indians and Natives (COINS), was formed in Washington, D.C. to set a strategy for Indians in the 1970s. Included in COINS were the National Congress of American Indians (NCAI), the American Indian Movement (AIM) and the National Indian Youth Council (NIYC) together with many other Indian organizations.

DECEMBER 18. In a history-making act, President Nixon signed into law an Alaska native land settlement bill, following the approval vote of the Federation of Alaskan Natives. The signing of the bill into law meant that a freeze on Alaska state land acquisition from the previous administration had been lifted.

In order to organize the Alaskan American Indians on health, education and other such issues, the Tanana Chiefs Conference, Inc. was founded in Fairbanks.

1972   JANUARY 11. The Reverend Harold Stephen Jones, a Sioux, was consecrated as suffragan bishop of the Episcopal diocese of South Dakota. One thousand people attended the ceremony in which the South Dakota-born clergyman became the first American Indian elevated to the office of bishop.

JANUARY. Charles Trimble, executive director of the NCAI, addressed three hundred Indian leaders gathered in Denver. In regard to the proposed redesigning of the BIA, he claimed that no Indian organization had been involved in these actions; despite offers of cooperation, they had been ignored.

JULY 17. The director of Navajo affairs for the BIA, Anthony Lincoln, offered the Navajo self-rule, which would give them control of all BIA operations in their area. The offer was seen as a victory for the self-determination forces that operated within the bureau. Only two tribes had previously acquired complete control of all programs affecting their resevations, the Miccosukee of Florida and the Zuni of New Mexico. Neither of these compared in size with the twenty-five thousand square-mile Navajo reservation, which covers parts of

Arizona, New Mexico and Utah, and which has a population of 134,000.

AUGUST. A calm AIM national meeting was held in White Oak, Oklahoma. Carter Camp was elected national chairman of the group, with John Trudell being elected co-chairman.

NOVEMBER 2. A group of approximately five hundred Indians arrived in Washington, D.C. after a trek across the country. The event, a Trail of Broken Treaties, called for a week of demonstrations to promote public demands for reform in the BIA and to get congressional action on a program of twenty demands. These demands included treaty adjustments, land policy changes and social and economic programs. The protestors were headed by activists in AIM.

DECEMBER 2. Public reaction to the occupation of the BIA offices in Washington, D.C. and other factors led Secretary Morton to take away "all present authority for Indian Affairs" from Commissioner Bruce, Assistant Secretary Harrison A. Loesch and Deputy BIA Commissioner John. All three submitted official resignations which were announced to the press six days later.

The United Indian Development Association began publishing the annual *American Indian Business Directory*.

The Coalition of Eastern Native Americans (CENA) was founded in Washington, D.C. Its objective is to help in the economic, cultural and social advancement of the native American people inhabiting eighteen states in the East, from Maine to Florida.

1973   JANUARY 9. The administration officially refused to accept the twenty demands submitted by the Trial of Broken Promises, a group of about one thousand "militant" Indians who had occupied the Bureau of Indian Affairs headquarters in Washington, D.C. for seven day in November of the previous year. In a letter delivered to Hank Adams, a leader of the group, the Nixon administration stated that the demands had been found either unacceptable or had already been acted upon.

FEBRUARY. FBI agents in the nation's capital arrested Hank Adams and Les Whitten as they were loading boxes of government papers into the latter's car. They were preparing to return the documents to the BIA.

FEBRUARY 27. Members of the American Indian Movement and some activist supporters seized and occupied the tiny place of Wounded Knee, located on the Ogalala Sioux Reservation in South Dakota. They remained there until May 8.

MARCH. The Wounded Knee Legal Defense-Offense Committee was founded with the purpose of protecting and defending the 445 people arrested in the occupation of and activities related to Wounded Knee.

JULY 17. The United States Census Bureau released a report which revealed that an analysis of the 1970 data showed that Indians continued to bring up the rear in most economic and social areas, in spite of significant advances in education since the 1960 census.

JULY 30. Dennis Banks, speaking to members of AIM in Tulsa, said that a massive effort was needed to influence legislation which was seeking to repeal the 1934 Indian Reorganization Act and the abolishment of the BIA.

AUGUST 5. Governor Richard Kneep of South Dakota, bending to public pressure, announced that the sacred religious Sun Dance Ceremony had been cancelled at the long publicized site on an eight hundred acre parcel of private land adjoining the Crazy Horse Mountain. The ceremony was held on the Rosebud Reservation.

AUGUST 13. The creation of an Office of Indian Rights was announced by the United States Department of Justice.

SEPTEMBER 29. The United States House Interior Committee approved a bill to restore federal services to the Menominees who had lost their status under a 1961 Act of Congress during a termination-minded administration.

DECEMBER 3. Morris Thompson, an Athabascan Indian, was apapointed commissioner of Indian Affairs. As his first official act, the new BIA commissioner appointed the first Indian woman superintendent. Mrs. Shirley Plume, an Oglala Sioux, was named to head the Standing Rock, North Dakota agency.

DECEMBER 28. President Nixon signed a comprehensive manpower training and jobs act. One important provision of the bill was the authorization of special assistance for certain hard-hit segments of the labor market, including Indians.

1974   FEBRUARY. Richard Wilson was reelected to the position of Oglala Sioux Indian tribe president. Russell C. Means, the leader of AIM, who ran against Mr. Wilson, was defeated.

APRIL. President Nixon signed the Indian Financing Act of 1974. The law consolidated existing revolving loan funds already administered by the BIA and authorized the appropriation of an additional fifty million dollars.

MAY. Mohawks seized a 612-acre site in the Adirondack State Park of Big Moose, New York, using an old girl's camp buildings for shelter.

MAY. Clarence Antioquia, a Tlingit Indian, was named director of the Juneau, Alaska Area Office of the BIA.

JUNE. Jose A. Zuni, an Isleta Pueblo Indian, was named director of administration of the BIA.

JUNE.   The BIA published *A History of Indian Policy* by Dr. S. Lyman Tyler, head of the American West Center at the University of Utah.

JULY.   Francis E. Briscoe, a member of the Caddo tribe, was named BIA area director of the Portland Area Office.

AUGUST.   A decision was announced which ended the long dispute and gave the Chemehuevi tribe equitable title to eighteen miles of shoreline along Lake Havasu, a portion of the Colorado River.

SEPTEMBER 16.   Charges against AIM Wounded Knee defendants Dennis Banks and Russel Means were dismissed by United States Judge Fred J. Nichols. The judge said that during the trial the FBI had been shown to lie and suborn perjury.

SEPTEMBER 19.   At midnight, the sixty-seven member Bonners Ferry Kootenais band of Indians in Idaho declared war against the United States government. After making their demands known, they emphasized that theirs was a war against the government and not against the "suyapi", or white people.

OCTOBER.   Thomas J. Ellison, an Oklahoma Choctaw, was named area director of the BIA's Muskogee, Oklahoma Area Office.

OCTOBER.   The Crow Indian tribe of Montana honored Secretary of the Interior Morton as an "Advocate of the American Indian" for his leadership in promoting Indian self-determination and his role in the Alaska Native Claims Settlement.

DECEMBER.   The United States Senate in a 70 to 0 vote passed a bill designed to settle a ninety-two year old land dispute over 1.8 million acres in Arizona between the Navajo and the Hopi Indian tribes. The dispute began in 1882 when President Chester A. Arthur gave the Hopis land located in the Navajo Reservation. The Senate bill provided for thirty-seven million dollars in federal funds for relocation expenses and the purchase of dwellings by the Indians forced to move from the divided land.

DECEMBER.   Harley M. Frankel was appointed new deputy commissioner of the Bureau of Indian Affairs.

1975   JANUARY 1.   A group of armed Menominee Indians took over the

abandoned Alexian Brothers Noviciary in Gresham, Wisconsin. They seized the Roman Catholic monastery, demanding that it be turned over to the tribe for conversion into a health center.

JANUARY 5.   President Ford signed into law a bill which provided for a policy of self-government for American Indians on reservations. The services which the Indians could now contract on their own included the operation of reservation schools, police forces, welfare programs and road maintenance.

JANUARY 6. The last full-blooded member of the Mandan tribe, Mrs. Mattie Grinnell, died at the age of 108.

JANUARY. A legislative bill nearly doubling the size of Grand Canyon National Park from 673,000 to 1.2 million acres, while ceding 185,000 acres to the Havasupai Indian Reservation in Arizona, was signed into law by President Ford.

JANUARY. The International Indian Treaty Council, an organization representing 103 American Indian tribes as well as other Indian groups in Canada and South America, opened an office in New York City near the United Nations in an effort to draw attention to their long-standing territorial claims and demands for sovereignty.

FEBRUARY 3. The thirty-four day seizure of the Alexian Brothers Novitiate by the Menominee War Society ended when the Indians voluntarily turned themselves over to the Wisconsin National Guard.

MARCH. Senator James G. Abourezk, who was born and raised on South Dakota's Rosebud Sioux Reservations, was named chairman of the American Indian Policy Review Commission.

MARCH. Indian leaders throughout the country met in March, April and May in Washington, D.C. with representatives of the BIA and the Indian Health Service to plan implementation of the Indian Self-Determination and Education Assistance Act.

APRIL 2. Nearly two hundred tribal representatives met in Washington, D.C. for the National Conference on Indian Water Rights, jointly sponsored by the National Tribal Chairmen's Association (NTCA) and the National Congress of American Indians (NCAI).

APRIL 2. The Omaha tribe reclaimed 3,190 acres of rich crop land by moving houses into the area.

APRIL. It was announced that the new American Indian Institute, established by a grant from the Department of Health, Education and Welfare (HEW) at Brooklyn College, would collect information on Indians in New York City and the Northeast areas overlooked by most contemporary studies, which concentrate on Indians in the West.

APRIL. The president of the Oglala Sioux announced the formation of the Indian Nation Restoration Committee to counteract the American Indian Movement.

MAY 22. The BIA bowed to months of pressure and announced a decision to keep open for an additional year the Intermountain Boarding School at Brigham City, Utah.

JULY.   A fifteen million dollar luxury tourist and recreation complex opened on the Mescalero Apache Reservation. The tourist project was conceived in 1970 when the tribe was given 2.2 million dollars in federal grants from the economic development branch of the Commerce Department.

JULY.   About three hundred Indians spontaneously decided to occupy the Interior Department building in Portland, Oregon, during a protest march. They only stayed twenty-four hours and left peacefully.

JULY.   Approximately three thousand American Indians attended the forty-fourth annual American Indian Exposition in Anadarko, Oklahoma.

AUGUST.   Ross Swinner, banker and former Cherokee tribal attorney, won the election for Cherokee tribal chief.

SEPTEMBER 5.   Chief Frank Fools Crow, holy man of his tribe and guest chaplain of the United States Senate for the day, delivered a prayer before the Senate in the Oglala Sioux language, calling for peace and understanding.

SEPTEMBER 15.   The Department of Housing and Urban Development (HUD) announced the creation of a HUD Task Force on Indian Housing Programs which would recommend "policy alternatives" and "field organization to best support Indian programs."

SEPTEMBER 15.   The Ute tribe in Utah set up a tribal code claiming civil and criminal jurisdiction over all lands, including exterior boundaries.

SEPTEMBER.   The Goshute Indians, one of the poorest tribes in the United States, voted to accept a 7.1 million dollar settlement over a 100-year land dispute with the federal government involving approximately five million acres in Utah and Nevada.

OCTOBER.   The Fund for the Improvement of Post-Secondary Education (FIPSE) awarded the Mississippi band of Choctaw Indians in Philadelphia, Mississippi $29,341 to extend their educational services by providing accredited college courses on the reservation.

OCTOBER.   A seven-hour series entitled *Tribal Eye*, produced by the BBC in association with Warner Brothers TV, made its debut on public television.

NOVEMBER.   Dr. Frank Clarke, a Hopi and Hualapai Indian, joined the Albuquerque, New Mexico Indian Hospital. He was a past president of the American Indian Physicians.

DECEMBER.   A study made by the Federal Indian Domestic Assistance Program revealed that of 1,200 federal domestic assistance programs in 1974, Indian tribes took part in only 78. Phil Lujan, of the Indian Law Center, said: "Of all the money appropriated, only .004 percent of it went to Indian programs."

1976 JANUARY 9. The ABC television network presented *I Will Fight No More Forever*, the story of the last tribe of American Indians to fight confinement on a reservation.

JANUARY. The Museum of Contemporary Crafts in New York City opened a special show called *The American Indian and the American Flag*. The exhibition of various crafts from thirty-three tribes, dating from 1857 to the present, was organized by the Flint, Michigan Institute of Art under a grant from the National Endowment for the Arts. All two hundred exhibits revealed the American Flag, incorporated as a motif in one respect or another.

JANUARY. Fugitive AIM leader Dennis Banks was arrested by FBI agents in San Francisco. Banks was wanted on a federal flight charge and other charges stemming from the much-publicized South Dakota courthouse melee.

MARCH 1. William Red Fox, a Sioux Indian Chief, died at the age of 105. His memoirs recalling the 1876 Battle of Little Big Horn and the 1890 Massacre of Wounded Knee had led to a publishing controversy in 1972.

APRIL. The United States Supreme Court unanimously upheld the rights of Indian tribes to go to the federal court rather than a state court to challenge state taxes on Indians and Indian-owned property within an Indian reservation. This decision was made in the case of *Salish-Kootenai Tribes of Flathead Reservation* v. *The State of Montana*.

JUNE. Senator Warren G. Magnuson was joined by Indian shaman Willie Sam at the opening of the Seattle, Washington health clinic for Indians.

JUNE. The United States Supreme Court unanimously decided that the 1953 federal law that gave certain states criminal and civil jurisdiction over reservations did not give those states any power over reservation Indians.

JUNE. Indians Robert Robideau and Darrelle Butler went on trial in Cedar Rapids, Iowa on charges of taking part in the murder of FBI agents Jack Coler and Ronald Williams in the shootout of June 1975 at Pine Ridge Reservation in South Dakota.

AUGUST. The Indian Pueblo Cultural Center was dedicated in Albuquerque, New Mexico. The museum and research center was established in order to help preserve the Pueblo Indian culture, and was expected to become a major tourist attraction.

SEPTEMBER. The United States Senate passed a bill appropriating 475 million dollars over a three-year period to provide health care for American Indians.

OCTOBER 10.   President Ford signed a proclamation designating the week of October 10 as Native American Awareness Week.

OCTOBER.   The federal government awarded the Mesquakie Indians 6.6 million dollars for land in Iowa, Missouri, Illinois and Kansas that was ceded to the government in ten treaties between 1804 and 1867.

OCTOBER.   The Puyallup Indian Tribal Council occupied the Cascadia Juvenile Diagnostic Center in Tacoma, Washington contending that the building legally belonged to the tribe.

DECEMBER 13.   The Navajo radio network began broadcasting news and information programs in the Navajo language to Navajo Reservations in Arizona, New Mexico and Utah.

The town of Mashpee, Massachusetts retained lawyer James St. Clair to defend it in a federal suit being brought against it by the Wampanoag Indians.   The suit contended that sixteen thousand acres of land were seized by the state during the nineteenth century despite the fact that the 1790 Indian Non-Intercourse Act prevented the state from doing so without Congressional approval.

1977   JANUARY.   Dennis Banks, the leader of AIM, called for a national boycott of the Holiday Inn chain in an effort to dissuade them from excavating an Indian burial ground in San Jose, California.

FEBRUARY.   An exhibition of some five hundred pieces was displayed in the Monmouth Museum in New Jersey.   The show was entitled *Indian Art of the Americas*.

MARCH.   Maine Indians' elected officials and lawyers met at the White House with President Carter's mediator, Justice William B. Gunter, to discuss the land claims issue.   No compromise was reached, however.

APRIL.   Sioux Indians living on the Pine Ridge Reservation voted down a government proposal to move their headquarters from a remote village near the Nebraska border to a more central location on the reservation.   Fifty-eight million dollars would have been provided for the construction of a town at the new site.

APRIL.   Congress was asked to settle a land claim involving 144,000 acres of York and Lancaster counties in South Carolina that the Catawba Indians claimed was rightfully theirs.   Several other claims were already before Congress including those made by the Penobscot and Passamaquiddy Indians and the Wampanoag Indians in Maine.

JULY. The Interior Department agreed to sue New York state and thirty thousand individual property owners in order to recover 262,500 acres of land claimed by the Oneida, Cayuga and St. Regis Mohawk Indian tribes.

JULY. Leaders of forty Ute nations and Comanche tribes entered a ceremonial teepee and ended a two-century year-old conflict over hunting rights. About two thousand people attended the ceremony, which took place in Ignacio, Colorado.

AUGUST. A ceremonial opening attended by five hundred visitors took place in Salamanca, New York. The Seneca Nation opened its new $265,000 museum, which was designed and constructed by tribe members. The museum would exhibit artifacts of the Seneca Nation and Iroquis Confederacy.

OCTOBER. Forrest Gerard, a Blackfoot Indian, was sworn in as assistant secretary of Indian Affairs in a ceremony which took place in Washington, D.C.

NOVEMBER. American Indian Movement leader Russell Means began his prison term for violating bail. He was charged with bail violation because of his continued activities with the movement.

NOVEMBER. Wampanoag Indians rested their case in the first step of their land claim concerning sixteen thousand acres in Maine.

NOVEMBER. Frank James, president of the United American Indians of New England, announced plans to hold a day-long fast on Thanksgiving Day at Plymouth, Massachusetts.

DECEMBER. The federal government announced its plan to have 3,500 Navajos relocate, leaving the land that had been promised to the Hopis in 1882.

DECEMBER. It was reported that the federal government had awarded 160 grants amounting to 20.6 million dollars for furthering the education of Indian children and adults.

The Federal Economic Development Association approved plans for the construction of a 4.9 million dollar Indian Culture Center in Niagra Falls, New York.

THE ARABS IN AMERICA

1970   Under the leadership of the Reverend Archimandrite Gregory Abboud, St. Nicholas Cathedral in Brooklyn, New York, purchased land on Staten Island and instituted plans for the construction of a home for the aged. The home would be dedicated to all of the Arabic-speaking people in North America and those related to them, regardless of their religious beliefs.

A thirteen-year-old Arab-American boy from Ramsey, New Jersey, received the "In the Name of God Award" for the Islamic faith in an Eagle Scout ceremony. It was the first time the award had been presented to a Moslem scout in the Eastern United States.

Dr. William A. Small of Geneseo, New York, was reelected president of the Federated American-Arab Organizations at its annual three-day conference in New York City.

Jerrier Abdo Haddad, son of journalist Abdul Massih Haddad, led the engineering team that developed the first IBM electronic calculator which was mass produced.

All religious segments of the Arab-American community, Christian and Moslem, joined together at Washington Cathedral, Washington, D.C., in a "Plea for Justice for People of the Holy Land." Dr. Frank Maria, chairman of the Department of Near East and Arab Refugee Problems for the Antiochian Orthodox Church of North America, was program director of the meeting.

Yusuf A. Najem, Arab-American writer, died.

The American University of Beirut (the Syrian Protestant College until 1921) celebrated its one hundredth anniversary.

A delegation from the Federated Organizations on American-Arab Relations met with the legislative staff of Senator Mark Hatfield, a Republican from Oregon, at the Senate Office Building. The delegates wanted to express their appreciation to the Senator for his statement on the floor of the Senate concerning the Middle East. Senator Hatfield had stated that the Palestinians must be

The author is indebted to Beverlee Mehdi, the editor of THE ARABS IN AMERICA, for her research covering the period 1970 to 1977.

considered in any solution to the Mid-East conflict. Memebers of the delegation included: M. G. Sadak, president of the Washington Chapter of the World Lebanese Union; Nabil Awad; Joe Samaha and M. T. Mehdi.

St. Nicholas Antiochian Orthodox Cathedral in Brooklyn, New York, celebrated its fiftieth anniversary. Father Gregory Abboud, pastor of St. Nicholas presided, while Richard Zraick served as chairman of the souvenir journal and the banquet.

William Nahas of New London, Connecticut, was elected mayor of the city.

1971 AUGUST. Dr. Muhsin Mahdi, president of the Society for the Study of Islamic Philosophy and Science, addressed the first world-wide meeting of the society, which was held at Columbia University. Dr. Mahdi, a native of Iraq, was the director of the Harvard Middle East Studies Center.

SEPTEMBER. The Forum for Arab Art and Culture sponsored a much-heralded tour of the United States for famed Lebanese singer Feyrouz and her troupe of sixty Dabke dancers and musicians from Baalbeck.

The *Palestine Digest*, a weekly magazine, was first published by the League of Arab States in Washington, D.C.

Michael Nackel, president of the American-Arabic Association of Boston, Massachusetts, submitted a three-page statement on the question of the Holy City of Jerusalem at the request of the House of Representatives Foreign Relations Committee.

Fouad Al Akl, noted Arab-American surgeon and poet, died. Dr. Al Akl, who wrote a number of definitive texts in the field of surgery, was a founder of the Salaam Club, American Middle East Relief Organization, and the American Academy of Poetry. His autobiographical insights are collected in *Until Summer Comes*.

Dr. Alexander A. Kirkish was elected by the Western Federation of Syrian-Lebanese Clubs as "Man of the Year."

Marlo Thomas of *That Girl* television fame spurred efforts of the American Lebanese Syrian Association Charities (ALSAC) to raise money for St. Jude Hospital in Memphis, Tennessee, the philanthropic creation of her father, Arab-American comedian Danny Thomas. Working with Ms. Thomas was ALSAC vice president Major Al Toler.

It appeared as if *Al-Hoda* the oldest Arabic language newspaper in the United States would have to close. However, Fares Stephan purchased the paper and pledged to continue publication with the dean of Arab journalism, Fred Khouri, still active as editor.

The "Baylor College of Medicine-Dr. Michael DeBakey Fund" was established with a grant from the southern Federation of Syrian Lebanese American Clubs.

George Alexander Doumani reached the South Pole and had a mountain peak there named after him. Mr. Doumani is a staff member of the Science Policy Research Division of the Congressional Research Service of the Library of Congress.

William Peter Blatty published *The Exorcist*, the screenplay of which won him an Academy Award.

1972 The *Al-Islah* Arabic newspaper celebrated its fortieth anniversary. Its editor and publisher, Dr. J. Alphonse Chaurize, said that he, as well as the editors of other Arabic papers, had been serving the Arabic language and preserving it in Al-Mahjar, the land of the immigrants.

Dr. M. T. Mehdi appeared on the *Dick Cavett Show* to respond to anti-Arab remarks made on a previous show by Senator Jacob Javits and film producer and director, Otto Preminger.

The International Arab Federation which was founded in 1967 in Toledo, Ohio first published its monthly, the *Arab Tribune*.

Four hundred members of the American Arab Society and several representatives of the American Arab Chamber of Commerce gathered at "Gleannloch" which is owned by Douglas B. Marshall, the founder and life-time honorary president of the society. The occasion was the seventh anniversary of the American Arab Society. The president of this group, Ahmed Rahman, reviewed the activities of the society which in 1968 established the American Arab Chamber of Commerce as an independent affiliate.

Toby Moffett was elected United States Congressman from Connecticut.

George R. Simon, Chicago businessman, and Phyllis Joseph, Cleveland schoolteacher, were honored as the Man and Woman of the year by the Midwest Federation of American Syrian-Lebanese Clubs, at their annual convention in Milwaukee, Wisconsin.

The Moslem community of Cedar Rapids, Iowa dedicated a new mosque and Islamic Center. The new center contained, in addition to a prayer hall, a small school and library. Abdullah Igram was chairman of the dedication committee.

The Arab American Social Cultural Club opened its headquarters on Atlantic Avenue in Brooklyn. Officers of the newly formed group included: Amin Awad, president; Subhi Al Waddi, vice president; Mohammad Massoud, treasurer; Naif Hassan Hamdan, assistant treasurer and Dr. Omar Ghobashi, legal advisor.

The American Association of Teachers of Arabic published its spring journal *An Nashra,* in which it was reported that the enrollment in Arabic language cources in the United States had risen from 541 in 1960 to 1,669 in 1972.

Salah Mourad began publication of *Mougaz-El-Anbaa* (The News in Brief). The weekly magazine aimed primarily at covering the news of Egypt and serving the Egyptian-American community.

Metropolitan Michael Shaheen of Toledo announced plans to break grounds for the new St. George Antiochian Orthodox Cathedral of Toledo, Ohio. This was to be phase one of the proposed million dollar Orthodox Center for Toledo. Groundbreaking ceremonies were held with the co-chairmen of the project, Richard O. Joseph and Michael Damas in attendance, as were the president of the board of trustees, George M. Saba and the pastor of the Cathedral, the Reverend Mark Pemberton.

Abraham Kazen, Jr., of Laredo, Texas was reelected to his fourth term in the United States House of Representatives. Mr. Kazen commented that his district in Texas covered 17,384 square miles, about four times the area of Lebanon, the birthplace of his father.

Arabesque Radio, under the guidance of producer and director Ghazi Khankan, celebrated its fifth year on WHBI New York.

The Arab-American Association located in Cincinnati, Ohio began publication of its newsletter, proposing to publish ten issues each year.

1973 James Abdnor was elected United States Congressman from South Dakota. Prior to holding this office, Mr. Abdnor had served as State Senator and as Lieutenant Governor of the state.

Samuel Hazo's book of poetry, *Once for the Last Bandit,* was nominated by the National Book Award Committee for being one of the best books of 1973.

The American-Ramallah Federation held its fifteenth annual convention, with some two thousand members in attendance. Members of the federation are immigrants from the village of Ramallah and their descendants.

When war broke out in the Middle East, the Arab-American workers in Detroit's automobile industry held a demonstration supported by a coalition of Arab organizations in the city. Nearly two thousand workers took the day off to protest the United Auto Workers Union purchase of Israeli bonds.

The seventy-fifth anniversary celebration of the Arabic language newspaper, *Al-Hoda,* was held at the Waldorf Astoria Hotel in New York City.   Edward A. Zraick served as chairman of the jubilee committee.

The National Association of Arab-Americans (NAAA) was founded to act as a political lobby in Washington, D.C. on behalf of Arab-Americans. The goals of the organization were to encourage Arab-Americans' political participation and to promote a more "even-handed" Middle East policy. The first president of the NAAA was Dr. Peter Tanous.

1974   The Arab American Medical Association was founded. The objectives of the group are: to provide medical aid to the needy in the Middle East and to Arab-Americans; to provide scholarships for needy medical students of Arabic heritage; to enhance medical knowledge; to promote medical relations between its members who share a common background; to perpetuate the pride of heritage; to be a medical host unit; and to help newly graduated medical students.

Dr. Philip Habib became assistant secretary of state for east Asian and Pacific affairs.

Arab Speaking Communities in American Cities, edited by Barbara C. Aswad, was published by the Center for Migration Studies of New York, in cooperation with the Association of Arab-American University Graduates, Inc.

Michael J. Thomas, sports writer for the Providence, Rhode Island *Journal Bulletin*, died. Mr. Thomas was generally credited with "discovering" boxer Rocky Marciano, former heavyweight champion.

James Abourezk was elected United States Senator from South Dakota. In 1970, Mr. Abourezk was the first Democrat in thirty-six years to be elected from South Dakota's second congressional district. During his years in the House of Representatives, he authorized the Family Farm Act of 1972, the National Power Grid Act and Amendments to the 1970 Disaster Relief Act.

.Helen Thomas was designated by United Press International as its White House reporter. Ms. Thomas was the first woman to head the presidential reporting team of a major news service.

The third annual Arab World Festival held in Detroit brought together a quarter of a million Arab-Americans to enjoy Arabic food; listen and dance to Arabic music; watch Alex Acie, at sixty-four, perform the ritual Arab sword dance; and enjoy the comraderie of some twenty-eight Arab clubs in Detroit.

Joseph Robbie, managing general partner of the Miami Dolphins, cheered his team on as they won the second Super Bowl in a row.

Edward Hanna was elected mayor of Utica, New York. Mr. Hanna, who had lived in Utica all his life, became New York's first Independent mayor since 1885. Prior to his election as mayor, he had served a term in the New York Assembly.

Gamal El-Zoghby, Egyptian-born interior 'architect, was voted one of the top ten designers in the United States by *Progressive Architecture Magazine*.

The Arabic-speaking community of Detroit, Michigan was judged to be sufficiently large for Town Pride, Associated Food Distributors, Inc. to begin printing their canned food labels in Arabic as well as English.

The monthly newsletter of the National Association of Arab-Americans, *The Voice*, was first published.

Joseph J. Rookis of Birmingham, Alabama, was cited as being instrumental in the establishment of the only Diabetes Research and Education Hospital in the entire world. The hospital is located in Birmingham.

Stage and screen star, Paul Jabara, appeared on the Movie of the Week, *The Last Angry Man*, on ABC-TV.

The American Arabic Speaking Community Almanac for 1974 was published by Joseph R. Hayek, editor and publisher of *The News Circle*.

The Federated Arab American Organizations commemorated the twenty-fifth anniversary of the Dier Yassin Massacre with a memorial service at the Church Center for the United Nations, New York City. Dr. William A. Small, president of the federation, presided.

Richard Kotite was promoted to the rank of general in the United States Army. For his distinguished service, he had received the Purple Heart, the Bronze Star, the Commanding Ribbon and the Service Cross.

Khalid S. M. Al-Najdi, known in the entertainment world as Ali Baba, was the first Kuwaiti to become an American citizen.

The American Syrian Lebanese community honored Bill George, the one-time middle linebacker of the Chicago Bears. The testimonial was held just one day after Mr. George's induction into the Pro Football Hall of Fame.

The memory of World War II hero Corporal Raymond A. L. Saquet was honored by the dedication of a square to his name in Boston, Massachusetts.

Three Arab-Americans were named by *Time* magazine in a feature article entitled "200 Faces of the Future." The three leaders mentioned were: James Abourezk, United States Senator; A. Robert Abboud, deputy chairman of the First Chicago Corporation and Ralph Nader, consumer advocate.

The Michael Berry International Terminal, servicing all international carriers through Detroit, was the first such edifice to be named after a person of Arab heritage. Mr. Berry, a Dearborn attorney, had worked zealously for a multi-million dollar airport expansion program.

Richard C. Shadyac, president of the National Association of Arab Americans, was joined by the group's past president, Peter S. Tanous and its vice president, Edmond Howar at a State Department dinner hosted by Secretary of State, Henry Kissinger.

Samira Zara Al-Quazzaz was elected president of U.S. OMEN for 1975, thus becoming the first woman to hold that position.

Over 1,700 delegates from over twenty-five cities across the the United States and Canada rallied in Manhattan on November 13 to welcome the Palestine Liberation Organization (PLO) to the United Nations. The invitation to Yassir Arafat to address the General Assembly of the United Nations brought an outpouring of support from Arab-American communities across the country.

Arab Report, a biweekly newsletter, was first published by the Arab Information Center in Washington, D.C.

1975   The Board of Directors of the Arab Cultural Center of San Francisco announced the purchase of a twelve-room mansion that would be used to house the various Arab-American organizations in the Bay Area. The San Francisco Arab Cultural Center was the first of its kind in the United States.

SEPTEMBER. The Metropolitan Museum of Art opened eighteen permanent galleries that would be devoted to their Islamic collection. Pieces of jewelry, glass, pottery tiles, carpets, mosque lamps and manuscripts dating from a pre-Islamic period (but styles pertinent to Islam) would be on permanent display, many of them in two period rooms. One room, from seventeenth century Damascus, was donated to the museum by the Kevorkian Foundation. The second room, acquired in the 1930s, includes an Hispano-Moorish wooden ceiling of the late fifteenth century.

OCTOBER 26. President Anwar el-Sadat of Egypt arrived in the United States for an official ten-day visit, the first such visit ever by an Egyptian president. Although President Nasser did come to New York in 1960 to attend the United Nations General Assembly, he did not make an official visit to Washington, D.C.

NOVEMBER 5. President Sadat addressed a joint session of Congress.

Adel Assad Yunis, M.D., chief of hematology at the Univer-

sity of Miami School of Medicine, isolated a substance in cancer
cells that destroys fibrin, the protein that makes possible the
clotting of blood.

Thomas L. Hazouri, at thirty-one, became the second Arab-
American to be elected to the Florida State Legislature.

James J. Tayoun was elected to the Pennsylvania House of
Representatives. He also represented his Philadelphia district in
the House in 1969-70 and 1973-74.

The American-Arab Association for Commerce and Industry, Inc.
reported that combined United States-Arab trade for the year amounted
to twelve billion dollars. The organization was founded by a group
of American businessmen in 1951, when total trade was $440 million.

Mansour Alwan was elected mayor of Chesilhurst, New Jersey.

The two Syrian Orthodox archdioceses joined to become the
Antiochian Archdicese of North America.

The Islamic Council was established as the umbrella organization for all Moslems in New England.

The Columbia Broadcasting System (CBS) presented its first
documentary on Arab-Americans, featuring the Arab-American community
in Southern California.

Raji Daher, editor and publisher of *Al-Bayan* retired to
Phoenix, Arizona. *Al-Bayan* had maintained the reputation as an Arab-
American newspaper of the very highest intellectual and literary
quality throughout its long history.

1976   FEBRUARY 19. The Justice Department charged the Arab Infor-
mation Center based in New York City and its director, Amin
Hilmy II, with violation of the Foreign Agents Registration
Act by means of its propaganda on behalf of the League of Arab States.

FEBRUARY. After a closure of twenty months as the result of
a fire at its offices, the Arab-American newspaper *Action* once again
began publication. M. T. Mehdi, the weekly newspaper's executive
editor, announced that *Action* would be the Arab-American "challenge
to *Commentary.*"

APRIL. Bhazi al-Gosaibi, Saudi Arabia's Minister of Industry and Electricity, presented the University of Southern California,
on behalf of his government, with one million dollars. It was given
to establish a King Faisal Chair of Islamic and Arab Studies. The
first holder of the professorship was to be Willard A. Beling, head
of the University's Middle East-North African program. It was reported that more than 150 Saudi Arabian students were enrolled at
the University.

JUNE 8. About thirty Arab demonstrators took over the Arab Information Center in Chicago. The members of the group planned to occupy the office for forty-eight hours as a protest against the Syrian invasion of Lebanon.

AUGUST 2. Addressing a businessman's conference at the University of Maine at Orono, Ruddick C. Lawrence, president of the United States-Arab Chamber of Commerce, stated that "American know-how and Middle East dollars are a good partnership."

The *Treasures of Tutankhamun* was exhibited in the United States and was expected to be on display at various galleries across the country until 1979. The exhibition, on loan from the Cairo Museum, was to be shown at the National Gallery of Art in Washington, D.C., the Field Museum of Natural History and the Oriental Institute of the University of Chicago, the New Orleans Museum of Art, the Los Angeles County Museum of Art, the Seattle Art Museum and the Metropolitan Museum of Art, New York.

Dr. George E. Assousa, staff member in astrophysics at the Department of Terrestrial Magnetism of the Carnegie Institution of Washington, D.C., coordinated the first meeting of Arab physicists in the United States and Canada, which was held in Washington, D.C.

Tewfiq Zayyad, mayor of Nazareth, Dr. Emile Touma, editor of the largest Arab-Israeli daily, *al-Ittihad* (Unity) and Mrs. Felicia Langer, Israeli lawyer and author of *With My Own Eyes* were featured speakers at the ninth annual convention of the Association of Arab-American University Graduates in New York City.

Vance Bourjaily published *Now Playing at Canterbury*. He had also written *Confessions of a Spent Youth* and *The Man Who Knew Kennedy*.

Mary Rose Oakar from Cleveland, Ohio became the first Arab American Congresswoman.

Herb Macol was elected mayor of Mankato, Minnesota.

Mustafa Akkad, a Los Angeles film producer, completed his epic film *Mohammad, Messenger of God*. Included among its roster of stars was Arab American Michael Ansara.

The Action Committee on American-Arab Relations changed its name to the American-Arab Relations Committee (AARC).

The civil war in Lebanon divided the Arab community in America. There were "right wing" Lebanese demonstrations against the United Nations and "left wing" demonstrations against Syrian intervention in Lebanon.

The United State Information Agency made a feature film about five Arab Americans and their success in the United States.

The five people chosen to be so honored were: Raymond Jallow, vice president of United California Bank; Farouk El-Baz, geologist for the Apollo Moon Landing; Joseph Robbie, principal owner of the Miami Dolphins; Abdulmunim Shakir, director of Muslim-World Studies at Ricker College in Houston, Maine; and George Simon, builder of factories in Latin America from his base in Detroit.

Robert Rahall was elected to the United States Congress, becoming a representative of West Virginia.

Abe Gibron, the former pro-football star, served as head coach of the Chicago Bears.

Dr. M. T. Mehdi authored *Peace in Palestine* which was published by the New World Press in New York. The book proposed new directions for American foreign policy in the Middle East.

1977   APRIL 13. President Anwar el-Sadat of Egypt, who arrived in the United States for meetings with President Carter, was greeted by an official delegation headed by Secretary of State Vance and was cheered by two hundred Arab Americans.

APRIL 14. Over five hundred Egyptian immigrants crowded into the Coptic Orthodox Church in Jersey City to receive the blessings of His Holiness Pope Shenouda III, the reigning Coptic pope. The fifty-three year old Pontiff, spiritual leader of more than twenty-two million Coptic Christians in Egypt, Ethiopia and the Middle East, was the first reigning Coptic pope to visit the North American continent. The pontiff's official title is Pope of Alexandria and Patriarch of the See of St. Mark. He is the 117th successor to St. Mark the Apostle who is credited with founding the First African Christian Church in Egypt around 42A.D.

MAY 23. Pope Shenouda III ended his month-long visit to the 85,000 Copts in the United States and Canada. Fouad el-Kassas, the editor and publisher of *The Egyptian*, a biweekly newspaper printed in Los Angeles, remarked that "His Holiness will probably need a long rest when he gets back to Cairo. From the beginning to the end of the trip, he has been called upon to solve the problems our people have found in America. The Egyptian immigrants are torn between the poverty at home and the lose of identity and culture in America. They are said to have an ironic saying: 'Better the hell of America than the paradise of Egypt.'"

JULY 2. The United States Department of State and Senate sources reported that the Carter administration was considering providing military aid to the Lebanese government to help rebuild its army to maintain order in the country.

NOVEMBER. The majority of Arabs living in the United States expressed dismay after hearing that President Sadat had scheduled a visit to Israel. M. Cherif Bassiouni, professor of law at De Paul University in Chicago and president of the Mid-America Arab Chamber of Commerce said; "If it goes through it will be a one-man mission, a sort of messianic endeavor." The most vehement condemnations came, however, from some of the approximately fifty thousand Palestinians who live and work in the United States. Joseph Hayek, the editor and publisher of the yearly *Arab Almanac* based in Los Angeles said: "This visit tells the Israelis that we accept them without withdrawal from our lands and without recognition of Palestinian rights."

Isa Sabbagh, an American of Palestinian origin, traveled as interpreter with President Carter to his meeting with Syrian President Hafez al-Assad in Geneva.

Arab American attorney Robert W. Thabit defended the United States-Arab Chamber of Commerce in a hearing before the New York State Human Rights Commission.

THE
ARMENIANS
IN AMERICA

1970   A new wave of Armenian immigrants to the United States began. The immigrants came from the Soviet Union and Middle Eastern countries, especially from Lebanon, where the civil war between the Moslems and the Christians gravely affected the Armenian community.

Dr. Vaharn Norair Dadrian was appointed professor of philosophy at the State University of New York at Geneseo, New York. He had previously taught at several other universities and colleges, contributed to professional journals and received several awards and grants.

1971   The Western Armenian Athletic Association (WAAA) was founded in Oakland, California. Its purpose was to unite the various segments within the Armenian community by sponsoring atheletic competitions.

A thirty-minute 16mm color and sound film entitled *The Heart of a Nation* by Toukhanian was released. The film describes the history and present-day activities of the Armenian Relief Society.

1972   APRIL. An evening of Armenian entertainment was organized by the Armenian General Benevolent Union, a sixty-year-old philanthropic organization that supports a number of schools and health and research centers for citizens of Armenian origin. Over 150 Armenians sang and danced at the Felt Forum at Madison Square Garden, New York City, before an audience of five thousand people, mostly Armenians.

The Armenian Assembly Charitable Trust was founded in Washington, D.C. It was formed in order to provide a common meeting place for all the Armenian-American organizations and institutions.

According to the official statistics, the diocese of the Armenian Church of America had under its jurisdiction fifty-eight Armenian American churches with a membership of about 375,000, while

The author is indebted to Vladimir Wertsman, the editor of THE ARMENIANS IN AMERICA, for his research covering the period 1970 to 1976.

the Armenian Apostolic Church of America had twenty-nine churches and 125,000 members. The Armenian Catholic membership was estimated to be around eight thousand, concentrated mainly in six churches under the jurisdiction of local bishops. The Armenian Evangelical membership encompassed about five thousand members.

A noted movie actor, Akim Tamiroff, died at the age of seventy-three. Mr. Tamiroff had appeared in several dozen movies, often playing a key character part.

1973   SEPTEMBER. The city's forty thousand residents of Armenian descent invited people of all ethnic backgrounds to attend their One World Festival at St. Vartan's Cathedral in New York City. The festivities were in celebration of the diamond jubilee of the expansion of New York City to its present five boroughs and the founding of the first Armenian Orthodox Church in the city. Archbishop Torkom Manoogian, primate of the Armenian Church of America, stated: "We have struggled to preserve ourselves and to build our own churches and cultural centers, now we are settled and ready to enjoy ourselves and share our joy with others."
Two exhibitions were held during the fair, one of paintings by Armenian artists and another of jewelry, pottery and sculpture from around the world on loan from the Metropolitan Museum of Art.

Armen Tashdinian was named director of planning and analysis at the National Foundation of Arts and Humanities in Washington, D.C.

Koren Der Harootian, noted sculptor, completed his twenty-foot bronze sculpture with four relief panels for the Armenian Bicentennial Commemorative Commission in Fairmont, Pennsylvania. Harootian is represented in the permanent collections of the Metropolitan Museum of Art and the Whitney Art Museum in New York City, as well as in the Worcester Art Museum in Massachusetts.

John K. Najarian was named probate judge in Johnston, Rhode Island.

1974   Margo Terzian Lang exhibited her paintings at the Corcoran Museum in Washington, D.C., one of the finest and oldest museums in the United States. Her watercolors enhance American embassies all over the world, and some of her works were acquired for the permanent collection of the Smithsonian Institution in Washington, D.C.

William Saroyan's latest play, *Armenians*, was presented in the Armenian General Benevolent Union's auditorium in New York City. The play is about a cross-section of Armenian emigres to the United States, their problems in losing their national heritage and the Americanization of their children.

Armais Artunoff, nationally prominent engineer, was inducted into the Oklahoma Hall of Fame for his most outstanding achievements in the fields of electro-mechanics and hydraulic engineering, as well as for his invention of the famous electro-motor submergible multi-stage centrifugal oil and water pumping units.

The Armenian Literary Society honored the late Zarouhi Kalemkarian with a literary program devoted to her works.

Suren Saroyan, an attorney from San Francisco, received the Man of the Year Award from the American National Committee to Aid the Homeless Armenians. Mr. Saroyan is credited with the repatriation of 18,500 Armenians.

1975 APRIL 15. Congressman B. F. Sisk of California read into the *Congressional Record* the proclamation issued by Mayor Wills of Fresno, California, officially designating the week of April 20, 1975, as Armenian Heritage Week. The last sentence of the proclamation read: "Now, therefore, I, Ted C. Wills, Mayor of the City of Fresno, do hereby proclaim the week of April 20-26, 1975, as Armenian Heritage Week and Thursday, April 24th as Day of Remembrance of Man's Inhumanity to Man, and urge all the citizens of Fresno to render proper recognition to this solemn occasion and commemoration of the 60th Anniversary of the martyrdom of the Armenian people, and to participate in the activities of Armenian Heritage week."

APRIL 23. A procession of several thousand Armenians, organized by Samuel Azadian, marched from St. Vartan Cathedral to St. Patrick's Cathedral in New York City, marking the sixtieth anniversary since the Turks massacred the Armenians of eastern Anatolia. This observance was held the evening before the anniversary of the actual atrocity which occured on Arpil 24, 1915, when the Turks rounded up and killed over two hundred Armenian leaders in Constantinople as a prelude to a general extermination. In a proclamation delivered at St. Patrick's, Mayor Beame declared the anniversary as a "day of memory and dedication to human rights." Archbishop Manoogian, in a sermon, referred to the genocide as a victory because "we are here and we were not supposed to be."

APRIL 24. Armenian Americans all over the United States observed the sixtieth anniversary of the Turkish massacre of Armenians during World War I.

APRIL 24. Both Governor Hugh Carey of New York and Governor Brendan Byrne of New Jersey declared the day to be Armenian Martyr's Day in their respective states in memory of the more than 1,500,000 Armenians living in Turkey who were exterminated between 1915 and 1918.

APRIL 24. Haik Kavookjian of New York City, probably the oldest living Armenian American, celebrated his 100th birthday at a gala party attended by prominent Armenian American community leaders.

APRIL. St. Nerses Shnorhale Library was opened in New York City at the headquarters of the Armenian Apostolic Church of America. The library, which contains about 2,500 volumes, was built mainly from donations.

NOVEMBER. Lucine Amara, a soprano member of the Metropolitan Opera with a repertoire of over thirty major operetic roles, celebrated her twenty-fifth anniversary of association with that distinguished institution.

The *Armenian Observer,* a weekly covering the major events in the life of Armenian Americans living in California, was first published in Hollywood, California.

Dr. Winston L. Sarafian was named head of the library and director of the Learning Resources Center at Oxnard College in California.

The Armenian Sisters Academy of Radnor, Pennsylvania, a Montessori school, completed the constuction of a new building.

The United Armenian Commemorative Film Committee of Los Angeles, California, produced two films devoted to the massacre of the Armenians during World War I. The films, directed by Dr. Michael Hagopian, who was assisted by Salpi Ghazarian, were: *The Armenian Case* and *The Forgotten Genocide.*

The Armenian American community and Armenian American organizations showed a deep concern for the fate of Armenians in Lebanon, a country profoundly divided and gravely affected by the civil war between the Moslems and the Christians. The Armenian American organizations and chuch groups started a relief campaign to aid the Armenians in Lebanon, and to help resettle those Armenians who were admitted as immigrants to the United States. Many of the newly arrived immigrants settled in California.

1976 FEBRUARY 26. The day was proclaimed as St. Vartan's Day in the city of New York. St. Vartan, whose real name was Vartan Mamoolian, fought against Persian invaders and gave his life for the Armenian national and religious couse in 451 A.D.

APRIL 5. President Ford sent a special message to the Armenian American community of Massachusetts, stressing the contributions made by Armenian Americans during the two centuries of America's existence.

APRIL 24. The Ararat Dance Ensemble performed at the Philadelphia Folk Fair. The dance group had fifty members under the direction of John Samelian and Tom Torkomian.

APRIL 25. The Statue of Meher, an ancient Armenian legendary hero, was unveiled near the Philadelphia Museum of Fine Arts. The statue, by Khoren Der Harootian, was a symbol of the gratitude Armenian Americans expressed for the United States during the country's Bicentennial year.

MAY 10. A delegation of Soviet clergymen, including Bishop Nereses Bozabalian of the Armenian Apostolic Church, arrived in New York on a ten-day visit during which they hoped to observe religious life in the United States.

SEPTEMBER. People from a variety of ethnic backgrounds participated in the fourth annual One World Festival sponsored by the Armenian Church in America. The weekend of festivities took place at St. Vartan Cathedral in New York City. The highlight of the celebration was the ecumenical service presided over by Archbishop Manoogian.

SEPTEMBER. The first Armenian college in the United States opened in La Verne, California.

NOVEMBER 5. The city of Stamford, Connecticut paid homage to Reuben Nakian, a noted sculptor, venerated by art lovers in the United States and abroad. In the presence of the eighty-year-old sculptor, a slide program surveyed the artist's major works during the past five decades.

NOVEMBER 12. George Mardikian of San Francisco, California received the Horatio Alger Award, aimed at encouraging young people to realize that success in the United States can be achieved by any man or woman regardless of race, creed or origin. Mr. Mardikian was the first Armenian American to be honored with this award.

NOVEMBER 16. The Armenian Evangelical Church of New York celebrated the eightieth anniversary of its founding. Reverend Vartan Hartunian, pastor of the First Armenian Church of Belmont, Massachusetts, was the principal speaker.

NOVEMBER 26. More than one thousand Armenian Americans, many of whom had come to the United States in the past few years, attended a meeting of solidarity with Lebanese Armenians gravely affected by the civil war in Lebanon. The rally was held at St. Paul the Apostle Church in New York City.

NOVEMBER 28. A gala banquet, entitled Thank You, America, was held at the Waldorf Astoria Hotel in New York City. The event was attended by 1,300 guests representing the Armenian American community from coast-to-coast, and acknowledged the gratitude Armenian Americans feel toward the United States.

DECEMBER 12. The 300th anniversary of the birth of Mekhitar of Sebastia was celebrated in New York City at the Hotel Statler-Hilton. The event was sponsored by six cultural associations, including the Armenian Literary Society. Mekhitar (1676-1749) was a Catholic priest who promoted the idea of uniting the Armenian Church

with Rome. He built a monastery on the Island of San Lazaro in Ven-
ice, Italy which contained a large library and printing press. The
output of this press -Armenian religious, language, literary, historical, scientific and other publications- played a very important role,
in the development of the Armenian spiritual life all over the world.

DECEMBER. William Saroyan's latest play, *Across the Board
on Tomorrow Morning*, was presented in Los Angeles. Mr. Saroyan recently published a new autobiographical work called *Sons Come and Go,
Mothers Hang in Forever*.

The Armenian Assembly published a *Directory of Armenian American Academic Personnel in the United States*. The work, based on a
three-year study, revealed that there were about 1,500 Armenian aca-
demics in America.

Congressman George E. Danielson, a Democrat from California,
was named deputy majority whip of the House of Representatives. He
served as assistant majority whip in the 92nd, 93rd and 94th Congress,
and often came out as a strong spokesman for the Armenian American
community and its achievements.

George Deukmejian, noted Armenian American politician and
statesman from California, was reelected state senator.

Anne Avakian-Bishop of Los Angeles distinguished herself by
being appointed to the Bicentennial Committee of the Los Angeles
Press Council.

The Armenian Missionary Association of America (AMAA) started
publishing the *AMAA News*, which combined the former *A.M.A.A. Newsletter* and the *Armenian American Outlook*.

Levon Chaloukian of Los Angles purchased Ryder Sound Services, Inc., and thus became the president and general manager of
the largest leading independent motion picture and television sound
recording company.

Under a grant from the Alex and Marie Manoogian Foundation,
the University of Michigan introduced a two-year program in the
Armenian language. The course was to be taught by James Garabedian.

An exhibition of watercolors, oils and graphics by Armenian
American artists from the East coast and Canada opened at the head-
quarters of the Armenian General Benevolent Union, Inc. in New York
City.

Prominent Armenian American leaders led by Set C. Momjian,
chairman of the Thank You, America committee, presented a series of
twenty-one tapestries to the United States as a gift to the city of
New York. The tapestries, the work of Albert Herter, depict different episodes in the history of New York City during the last three
centuries, and were deposited with the Metropolitan Museum of Art.

The Fourth Armenian Book Fair was held in Providence, Rhode Island, under the auspices of the Knights of Vartan, Arax Lodge. The fair presented 250 books in English on Armenian history, culture, language and related subjects. The fair was entitled *Armenia: Its Legacy to the World.*

Thirty-one portraits, some in black and white and others in color, by Christopher Der Manuelian of San Francisco were selected by Harvard University for inclusion in its Carpenter Visual Arts permanent collection.

The Armenian Masons of Pennsylvania started preparations to celebrate the twenty-fifth anniversary of the Ararat Square Club.

1977 JUNE. A special issue of *Ararat*, the Armenian American quarterly, entitled *Armenians in America*, was published. Growing ethnic pride and a new wave of Armenian immigrants had led to a greater feeling among Armenians of a link with their history.

SEPTEMBER 10. The fifth One World Festival, sponsored by the Armenian Church of America, took place with its usual multi-ethnic burst of food and entertainment. It was said that 150,000 people had attended the festival the previous year and at least that number were expected in 1977.

NOVEMBER 6. An exhibition of the cultural heritage of the Armenian people opened at Columbia University's Low Memorial Library. The exhibition included illuminated manuscripts, ceramics and metal objects, maps, coins and costumes.

NOVEMBER. Reuben Nakian's *Descent From the Cross*, a bronze sculpture ten feet high and weighing over three tons, was unveiled at St. Vartan Cathedral. The piece was accepted by Archbishop Manoogian as part of a campaign to establish an Armenian Museum of Art and Antiquity in New York.

DECEMBER 10. Stephan G. Svajian, a dentist, writer and major supporter of the construction of St. Vartan Cathedral, died at the age of seventy-one. Earlier that year, his book *A Trip Through Historic Armenia* was published. The 643-page book described areas in Turkish Armenia in ancient times, as they were in his youth and as they are now. Mr. Svajian came to the United States in 1923 and was educated in New York.

A retrospective exhibition of the works of Edmund Yaghjian was held at the Harold Decker Galleries in Norfolk and Richmond, Virginia. Mr. Yaghjian, who was born in Harpoot, Armenia in 1904, came to the United States in 1907 and became a citizen in 1930. As a teacher of art, he had been associated with the University of South Carolina from 1945.

THE BLACKS IN AMERICA

1970   JANUARY 10. Four Southern governors, Lester Maddox of Geor-
        gia, John J. McKethen of Louisiana, Albert P. Brewer of Ala-
        bama and Claude R. Kirk of Florida, vowed to defy the fed-
eral government's plan to implement student busing arrangements in
their home states. The government's action was aimed at the desegregation of school systems.

        JANUARY 13. William B. Robertson, a public school supervi-
sor, was appointed by Governor Linwood Holton of Virginia as a key
member of his executive staff. This was the first time that a Black
served in a Virginia governor's office.

        JANUARY 14. The Supreme Court ruled that integration of
school districts in six deep South states had to take place no later
than February first.

        JANUARY 15. Some cities closed their schools, some gover-
nors declared a special day, and many churches held services on the
forty-first anniversary of the birth of the Reverend Dr. Martin
Luther King, Jr., the assassinated civil rights leader.

        JANUARY 22. The National Institute of National Health pre-
sented a study on civil disorders, *A Study of Arrest Patterns in the
1960s Riots*, which showed that armed white civilians were more widely involved in civil disorders during the last decade than were
Blacks.

        JANUARY 25. Col. Daniel Jones, Jr., a fighter-pilot who
served as commander of the United States forces at Wheelers Air
Force Base in Libya, was nominated for the rank of brigadier general.

        JANUARY 30. Joseph L. Searles III was the first Black man
to be proposed for membership on the New York Stock Exchange.

        FEBRUARY 19. The Senate and the House approved education
appropriation bills containing amendments introduced by Southern
opponents of school desegregation. The House bill contained three
antibusing and "freedom of choice" amendments designed to restrict

---

*The author is indebted to Irving J. Sloan, the editor of THE BLACKS IN AMERICA, 4th Ed.,
for his research covering the period 1970 to 1977.*

federal power to enforce desegregation. The Senate bill contained an amendment which would halt busing of children to achieve racial balance.

MARCH 3. School buses bringing Black children to a newly integrated school in Lamar, South Carolina, were attacked by a mob of raging whites.

MARCH 23. William Warfield, the world-famous singer, celebrated the twentieth anniversary of his debut in New York City concert halls at a recital at Alice Tully Hall in Lincoln Center.

MARCH 24. President Nixon pledged that he would help to eliminate officially imposed segregation in Southern schools and announced plans to allocate 1.5 billion dollars to assist local schools in overcoming the effects of residentially caused segregation.

APRIL 27. Allison Davis was appointed as **John Dewey** Distinguished Professor of Education at the University of Chicago, the first Black to hold a major endowed chair in this or any of the great universities in the United States.

MAY 1. James H. Hubert, the first executive director of the New York Urban League, died.

MAY 8. The criminal charges against seven Black Panthers who survived a Chicago police raid in December of 1969, in which two Black Panthers were killed, were dropped after the prosecution decided that there was insufficient evidence that any of the defendants had fired at the police.

MAY 12. A dusk-to-dawn curfew was imposed in Atlanta, Georgia, after a night of rioting that left six Blacks dead from police fire and at least seventy-five people injured.

MAY 14. The NAACP donated fifty thousand dollars to save a commission set up in December 1969 to undertake a national study of clashes between the police and the Black Panthers.

JUNE 11. Earl Grant, entertainer and organist, who was best known for his instrumental version of *Ebb Tide*, died.

JUNE 15. Federal Judge A. Leon Higginbotham, Jr., was elected a trustee of Yale University, the first Black to be chosen for the institution's governing board since it was founded in 1701.

JUNE 16. Kenneth A. Gibson was elected Mayor of Newark, New Jersey, thus becoming the first Black to be elected mayor of a major city in the East.

JUNE 16. The Reverend Henry Jogner, Jr. became the minister of the Cavalry Methodist Church in Atlanta, Georgia, thus becoming the first Black minister to take the pulpit of an all-white Southern parish of the United Methodist Church.

JULY 1. Dr. Felton G. Clark, retired president of Southern University, one of the nation's leading Black educators and a controversial figure in early efforts to integrate lunch counters in Louisiana, died.

AUGUST 1. Louis E. Lomax, a nationally-known Black writer and member of the faculty of Hofstra University in Long Island, New York, was killed in an automobile accident. He was known as one of the major interpreters of the integration movement.

AUGUST 31. There was no reported violence as most Southern children returned to school, many returning to newly-integrated classrooms.

SEPTEMBER 1. Dr. Hugh S. Scott was appointed Superintendent of Schools by the District of Columbia Board of Education. Dr. Scott thus became the first Black school superintendent of a major American city.

OCTOBER 22. Dr. Ralph J. Bunche, Under-Secretary of the United Nations, received the eighth Annual Family of Man Award for excellence from the Council of Churches of the City of New York.

NOVEMBER 4. Wilson Riles was elected Superintendent of Public Instruction and became the first Black ever to hold statewide office in California.

NOVEMBER 4. A record number of Blacks were elected to the United States House of Representatives. The newly elected members of the House were: George W. Collins (IL), Ronald V. Dellums (CA), Ralph Metcalfe (IL), Parren J. Mitchell (MD), and Charles B. Rangle (NY). All the Representatives were Democrats.

DECEMBER 14. Louis Mason, Jr. was the first Black elected president of Pittsburgh's City Council.

1971 JANUARY 4. Dr. Melvin H. Evans, a Black physician, was installed as the first elected governor of the Virgin Islands.

JANUARY 4. Dr. Leon H. Sullivan, a Black minister from Philadelphia, was elected to the Board of Directors of the General Motors Corporation. He was the first Black to be appointed to such a position.

JANUARY 22. United States Black congressmen boycotted President Nixon's State of the Union message because of his "consistent refusal" to listen and respond to the needs and concerns of the Blacks in America.

JANUARY 22. The United States Navy announced that it would name a destroyer escort in honor of Ensign Jesse Leroy Brown, the first Black American aviator and the first naval officer of his ethnic background to be killed in the Korean War.

MARCH 23. In the richest single sports event in world history, Joe Frazier won a fifteen-round decision against challenger Muhammad Ali.

APRIL 15. Samuel Lee Gravely, Jr. was promoted to admiral, thus becoming the first Black admiral in the history of the United States Navy.

JUNE 15. Vernon E. Jordan, Jr., former executive director of the United Negro Fund, was appointed executive director of the National Urban League, succeeding Whitney M. Young, Jr.

JULY 7. The NAACP bestowed the Spingarn Medal upon Dr. Leon Sullivan, "clergyman, activist and prophet, in admiration of the singular steadfastness with which he had melded religious leadership and social vision for the advancement of Black folk."

AUGUST 7. George W. Crockett, Jr. of Detroit was elected head of the Judicial Council, the first formal organization of Black judges in the United States.

AUGUST 21. Althea Gibson Darden, former winner of the United States and Wimbledon championships, was elected to the National Lawn Tennis Hall of Fame in Newport, Rhode Island.

AUGUST. Ralph Bunche, Under-Secretary-General of the United Nations, died.

OCTOBER 9. The Ford Foundation announced that it would award one hundred million dollars to private Black colleges over a six-year period to help them improve their academic and fiscal conditions.

The Coalition of Concerned Black Americans was founded in New York. The primary purpose of this organization was the study of criminal justice practices with respect to Black Americans.

The Congressional Black Caucus which was founded in 1969 (under the name of the Democratic Select Committee) began publication of a semi-annual newsletter.

1972   JANUARY 11. A federal court removed the special tax status
 and concomitant tax benefits granted to fraternal organizations that exclude Blacks from membership.

JANUARY 25. Representative Shirley Chisholm of New York announced that she would seriously seek the Democratic nomination

for president of the United States. Ms. Chisholm was the first Black woman to do so.

JANUARY 30. Huey P. Newton, co-founder of the Black Panther Party, announced that the party had given up the "pick up the gun" approach in favor of community work and voter registration.

FEBRUARY 8. The Congressional Black Caucus elected Congressman Stokes of Ohio as chairman of the organization.

APRIL 4. Adam Clayton Powell, Jr., minister and former congressman and protest leader, died.

APRIL 11. Benjamin L. Hooks, Black Memphis attorney and Baptist minister, was named by President Nixon to the Federal Communications Commission thereby becoming the first Black to serve on the commission.

APRIL 24. Robert Wedgeworth was named director of the American Library Association, thus becoming the first Black chosen to head this major organization.

APRIL 25. Major General Frederick E. Davidson, the highest ranking Black officer in the United States Army, was assigned to command the Eighth Infantry Division in Europe thus becoming the first Black officer to lead an army division.

JUNE 26. The United States Senate confirmed the appointment of W. Berverly Carter as ambassador to the Republic of Tanzania.

JUNE 29. The NAACP reported that more school segregation took place in 1971 than in any year since the 1954 Supreme Court decision of *Brown v. Board of Education.*

JULY 3. The United States Department of Housing and Urban Development (HUD) secretary, George Romney, announced that Floyd McKissick's new town, Soul City, to be located in North Carolina, would have fourteen million dollars in land development bonds guaranteed by HUD. Soul City would be the first federally funded guaranteed plan with a Black sponsor and the first of such plans to be located outside a metropolitan region.

OCTOBER 21. The Black National Assembly met in Chicago and established itself as a permanent organizational structure. Representative Charles C. Diggs, Jr. of Michigan was chosen president.

OCTOBER 24. Jackie R. Robinson, the first Black to play in a major league baseball team, the Brooklyn Dodgers, died.

OCTOBER. Gordon Parks, photographer, writer, film producer and composer, received the Spingarn Medal for his multifaceted creative achievements.

NOVEMBER 7.   Barbara Jordan was elected to the House of Representatives as a Democrat from the eighteenth district in Texas.

DECEMBER 1.   Theodore Berry was elected the first Black mayor of Cincinnati, Ohio.

The Council of Independent Black Institutions (CIBI) was formed as an educational and cultural organization aimed at establishing an independent national Black educational system.   In addition to the quarterly *C.I.B.I. Newsletter*, the organization sponsors research, seminars, teacher training workshops, and it maintains a library devoted to Black education.

1973   According to the United States Census Bureau, only fifty-two percent of the eligible Black voters participated in the 1972 presidential elections.   Nationally, sixty-two percent of the voting population participated.

JANUARY 17.   The United States Supreme Court ruled unanimously that a defendant had the right to demand that potential jurors be questioned about possible racial prejudice.

FEBRUARY 5.   Stanley Scott was appointed the President's liason with minority groups, making him the highest-ranking Black in the Nixon administration.

FEBRUARY 27.   The American Federation of Teachers presented its first Civil Rights Award to Roy Wilkins, executive director of the NAACP.

MARCH 3.   The National Black Assembly met in Detroit and set up the first practical program aimed at the group's objective of greater Black political power.

MARCH 8.   H. R. Crawford was named assistant secretary of Housing and Urban Development, thereby becoming the highest-ranking Black in the Nixon administration.

MAY 23.   The number of Blacks holding the rank of admiral or general in the United States armed services rose to sixteen with the promotion of three Black colonels.   Charles C. Rogers, Fred C. Sheffy and Roscoe Robinson were raised to the rank of brigadier general.

MAY 29.   Thomas Bradley was elected mayor of Los Angeles in a nonpartisan election.   He was the city's first Black mayor.

JUNE 1.   Claude W. B. Holman, one of Chicago's most powerful politicians, a staunch supporter of Mayor Daley, and president pro tempore of the City Council, died at the age of sixty-nine.

JUNE 4.   Arna Bontemps, Black poet, author and critic, a leader of the 1920s movement known as "Harlem Renaissance", died.

JUNE 5. Cardess R. Collins was elected the first Black woman to serve in Congress from the state of Illinois. She was elected to succeed her husband who was killed in an airplane crash.

JULY 20. The National Black Network, the nation's first Black-owned and operated news network, began operation with hourly news releases being sent to forty affiliated stations. The network, based in New York City, was scheduled to provide news reports of interest to Black listeners on a daily basis.

The nation's first Bicentennial exhibition opened at the National Portrait Gallery in Washington, D.C. Entitled *The Black Presence in the Era of the American Revolution: 1770 - 1800*, the show was considered a scholarly documentation of the Black participation in the American Revolution.

AUGUST 8. Dr. George A. Wiley, leader of the National Welfare Rights Organization, who sparked radical reform in the welfare system, and who served as coordinator for the Movement for Economic Justice, died at the age of forty-two.

AUGUST 14. *Soul at the Center '73*, held at Lincoln Center, New York City, was comprised of twenty-two events celebrating Black theater, dance, music, poetry, photography and fashion.

SEPTEMBER 17. Governor Daniel Walker of Illinois signed a bill legalizing January fifteenth as a holiday in honor of the birth of the Reverend Dr. Martin Luther King, Jr. Illinois was the first state to take this action.

OCTOBER. Wilson C. Riles, the Superintendent of Public Instruction in California, was awarded the Spingarn Medal for his outstanding contributions in the field of education.

NOVEMBER. Clarence Lighter was elected the first Black mayor of Raleigh, North Carolina.

The CIBI began publication of the *Black Education Annual*.

Duke Ellington was presented with the Legion of Honor decoration. In the same year, his book *Music is My Mistress* was published.

1974   JANUARY 2. The United States Bureau of Labor Statistics reported that 166,000 Blacks moved from the Southern states to the North, and that 247,000 Blacks returned to the South from the North.

JANUARY 11. A group of sixteen Black mayors and civil rights leaders met with Vice President Ford. Among those who attended the session were: Roy Wilkins, executive director of the NAACP; Rev. Jesse L. Jackson, leader of Operation Push; Vernon E. Jordan, Jr., executive director of the National Urban League; John H. Johnson, publisher of *Ebony* magazine; as well as Mayors Thomas Bradley, Coleman Young and Maynard H. Jackson, Jr.

FEBRUARY 2.   The first Black priest in the Episcopal diocese of New York elevated to the rank of bishop, the Right Rev. Harold L. Wright, was consecrated in a ceremony at the Cathedral Church of St. John the Devine.   Of the 140 active bishops in the Episcopal church, six were Black.

FEBRUARY 4.   The Voter Education Project, a private organization based in Atlanta, reported that 363 Blacks had won office in the South in the 1973 off-year elections.   According to the group's study, 253 victories were in elections for municipal councils and commissions.   There were sixty-three school board victories, nineteen new Black mayors, fourteen election commissioners and two state legislators.

FEBRUARY 13.   James "Cool Papa" Bell was named to the Hall of Fame by the Negro Baseball Selection Committee.   Mr. Bell was a renowned base stealer and hitter, whose twenty-six year career was spent in the Negro Leagues during the 1920s, 30s and 40s.

FEBRUARY 15.   About 1,700 delegates to the second National Black Political Convention met in Little Rock, Arkansas, in an atmosphere of conflict between Black nationalist leaders advocating a separatist approach to political action, and the more conservative leaders who favored operating within the traditional political structure.

APRIL 12.   Lee Elder became the first Black pro golfer to qualify for the Masters Tournament when he defeated Peter Oosterhuis of England in a sudden-death playoff to win the Monsanto Open in Pensacola, Florida.

MAY 5.   Governor George C. Wallace won twenty-five percent of the Black vote in his victorious nomination for a fourth term in Alabama.

MAY 28.   The *Autobiography of Miss Jane Pitman*, a televised dramatization of the life of a woman born into slavery, who survives to see the unfurling of the civil rights movement, was awarded an Emmy.   It was recognized as the best special television program of 1973.   The award for best actress in a special was given to Cicely Tyson for her portrayal of Jane Pitman.

MAY.   Edward Kennedy "Duke" Ellington, pioneer in the wordless use of the voice as an orchestral instument, in the use of the miniature concerto from in building jazz arrangements around a soloist as well as in extended orchestral jazz compositions and suites, died.

JUNE 6.   The Rev. Dr. Lawrence W. Bottoms, a minister in Decatur, Georgia, was elected to be the first Black moderator of the

Presbyterian church in the United States.

JUNE 24. The Boston National Center of Afro-American Artists received an award of $750,000 from the Ford Foundation.

JULY 29. Vice President Ford addressed the National Urban League convention in San Francisco. His speech marked the first time during the five-year Nixon administration that one of its top officials addressed a major Black organization, civil rights or otherwise.

AUGUST 23. Henry "Hank" Aaron broke Ty Cobb's major league baseball record by playing in his 3,034th game. He also hit 715 homeruns, breaking the record set by Babe Ruth.

SEPTEMBER 18. An exhibition of one hundred works by contemporary Black artists throughout the United States opened at the H. F. Johnson Museum of Art at Cornell University. The show was entitled *Directions in Afro-American Art*.

OCTOBER 9. Frank L. Stanley, civil rights leader and publisher of the Louisville *Defender* for forty years, died at the age of sixty-nine.

NOVEMBER 7. Simon Gourdine, an attorney, became the highest ranking Black administrator in professional sports when the Board of Governors of the National Basketball Association (NBA) named him deputy commissioner.

NOVEMBER. Black members of the United States House of Representatives increased their number by one in the November elections, with all fifteen incumbents winning and with an upset victory for Harold E. Ford, a twenty-nine year old Democratic state representative, over four-term Republican Dan Kuykendall in the eighth District of Tennessee. Blacks made no gains in the Senate, where the only Black member, Edward W. Brooke, a Republican from Massachusetts, was reelected to a second term in 1972. The fifteen reelected Black Representatives, all Democrats, were: Yvonne Brathwaite Burke (CA), Shirley Chisholm (NY), William Clay (MO), Cardess Collins (IL), John Conyers, Jr. (MI), Ronald V. Dellums (CA), Charles C. Diggs, Jr. (MI), Augustus F. Hawkins (CA), Barbara C. Jordan (TX), Ralph Metcalfe (IL), Parren J. Mitchell (MD), Robert N. C. Nix (PA), Charles B. Rangel (NY), Louis Stokes (OH) and Andrew Young (GA).

NOVEMBER 24. Raymond P. Alexander, a figure in the civil rights movement for fifty years and senior Philadelphia judge, died at the age of seventy-six.

1975   JANUARY 14. President Ford appointed William T. Coleman, a Philadelphia attorney and specialist in transportation law, to be transportation secretary in his cabinet. Mr. Coleman was the second Black to hold a cabinet position in history.

FEBRUARY 21. In a White House ceremony to illustrate the progress made by Black Americans, Vice President Nelson Rockefeller presented the first annual Black Enterprise awards to seven business and professional leaders. Those honored were: Ray Dones, Dempsey J. Travis, Mildren Montgomery, Gaston Cannon, Freddye Scarborough Henderson, Herbert H. Britton and Naylor Fitzhugh.

FEBRUARY 25. Elijah Muhammed died.

FEBRUARY 26. Leaders of the Nation of Islam proclaimed Wallace D. Muhammed their new leader and messenger.

APRIL 10. Josephine Baker, an American singer and dancer who became one of France's great music hall stars, died at the age of sixty-eight.

APRIL 11. Dr. Max Yergan, a Black leader and educator who also worked for civil rights in Africa, died at the age of eighty-two.

APRIL 14. Stevie Wonder, blind singer-musician-composer, won four Grammy Awards.

APRIL 19. Dr. Percy L. Julian, research chemist who held more than 130 chemical patents, isolated soya protein, was an early synthesizer of cortisone drugs, and was active in the civil rights movement, died at the age of seventy-six.

APRIL 19. James B. Parsons was named as the first Black chief judge of a federal court. He was appointed to the United States District Court in Chicago.

MAY 5. Kivie Kaplan, past president of the NAACP, died at the age of seventy-one.

MAY 21. The United States Senate confirmed Lowell W. Perry as a member and chairman of the Equal Employment Opportunity Commission.

MAY 23. Jackie "Moms" Mabley, a Black commedienne who worked in vaudeville, nightclubs, radio and theater, died at the age of seventy-eight.

JULY. Leigh Whipper, Sr., the first Black member of the Actors Equity Association and a founder of the Negro Actors Guild, died at the age of ninety-eight.

SEPTEMBER 2. Joseph W. Hatchett was sworn in as the first Black State Supreme Court Justice in the post-reconstruction South. Governor Rubin Askew of Florida was present at the ceremony.

SEPTEMBER 7. Violence erupted on the second day of the first court-ordered busing of Black and white school children between a major city, Louisville, Kentucky, and its suburb, Jefferson County.

SEPTEMBER. Black Americans to Support Israel Committee (BASIC), an organization to support Israel and counter anti-Semitism, was formed by a group of prominent Black leaders in the United States. Among those affiliated with BASIC were: Bayard Rustin, A. Philip Randolph, Roy Wilkins, Percy C. Sutton and Eleanor H. Norton.

NOVEMBER. NAACP director, Roy Wilkins, was presented with the Joseph Prize for Human Rights by Seymour Groubard, chairman of the Anti-Defamation League of B'nai Brith.

DECEMBER. Black Americans met for three days of conferences held in Montgomery, Alabama to commemorate the twentieth anniversary of the Montgomery bus boycott. Among those in attendance were: Representative Andrew Young, Mrs. Coretta Scott King, Representative John Conyers, Montgomery Mayor Jim Robinson, Mrs. Rosa Parks and Mr. Leon Hall, the conference coordinator.

John Hope Franklin, historian of the Black's experience in America, was elected by the National Council on Humanities to give its fifth annual lecture.

1976 JANUARY 24. Paul Robeson, the singer, actor and Black activist, died at the age of seventy-seven. His death was described by Clayton Riley, the American cultural historian, as the loss of "one of the nation's greatest men, an individual whose time on earth has been spent in the pursuit of justice for all human beings and toward the enlightenment of men and women the world over."

FEBRUARY. President Ford issued a statement urging all Americans to join in observing February as Black History Month.

MARCH 16. Ruby S. Murchison received a crystal apple from President Ford at the White House ceremony honoring the seventh grade teacher from Fayetteville, North Carolina as the 1976 Teacher of the Year. Mrs. Murchison, who had taught for twenty-two years, declared that her credo was: "I don't teach subjects, I teach children."

APRIL 5. Roy Wilkins, executive director of the NAACP, was the recipient of the 1976 Civil Rights Award presented by the American Jewish Congress in recognition of his work for racial equality.

MAY 14. Transportation Secretary William E. Simon was the guest speaker at the Black Lawyer and American Justice Seminar, held to commemorate the twenty-second anniversary of the United States Supreme Court decision of May 17, 1954, outlawing segregation in public schools.

MAY 19. Ground-breaking ceremonies took place at Lincoln

Center for the Richard Allen Center for Culture and Arts, a Black
arts center intended to house the Ira Aldridge Playhouse, the Paul
Robeson Concert Hall, the Henry O. Tanner Gallery, the Oscar Micheaux
Media Center and the James Baldwin Library. James R. Doman, Jr. was
appointed to design the space and Hazel J. Bryant was to be the center's director.

MAY. As part of its Bicentennial contribution, the National
Urban League announced that it would distribute 4,500 copies of *The
Black American* to political leaders, schools, colleges and churches.
In addition, the organization would give out three hundred thousand
pamphlets on the involvement of Blacks in politics, economics, edu-
cation and wars as well as a pamphlet on the Black family.

MAY. The executive director of the Voter Education Project,
John Lewis, announced that Blacks had gained 356 elected offices in
the South during 1975. Black officeholders in the eleven Southern
States region thus reached 1,944 positions. This represented only
2.5 percent of the total positions, however, in a region where Blacks
make up 20.4 percent of the population.

JUNE. Joseph Segars assumed his duties as the first American
Black to be assigned to the position of consul in South Africa.

JUNE. An exhibition of the work of nineteenth century Black
artists opened at the Metropolitan Museum of Art, New York City. The
show, organized as a Bicentennial celebration, was said to include
ninety-two "outstanding examples" of works by such well-known artists
as Joshua Johnston, Robert S. Duncanson, Edmonia Lewis, Edward M.
Bannister and Henry O. Tanner.

JUNE. The United States Supreme Court, in a seven to two decision, ruled that private nonsectarian schools may not exclude Black
children because of race. This decision was lauded by the general
counsel for the NAACP, Nathaniel R. Jones.

JUNE. The Reverend Joseph A. Francis was the fourth Black
American to be made a Roman Catholic bishop. His ordination took
place at the Sacred Heart Cathedral, Newark, New Jersey, and was presided over by the retired Newark archbishop, Thomas A. Boland; Newark
archbishop, Peter L. Gerety; and the auxiliary bishop of New Orleans,
Harold Perry.

AUGUST 25. Lewis H. Michaux, a bookseller who contributed
greatly over four decades to encourage Blacks to read about themselves and about Africa, died at the age of ninety-two. Since opening the National Memorial African Bookstore in Harlem, New York City
forty-four years ago, he had turned it into the largest in the nation
devoted solely to Black and African subjects.

AUGUST. Reverend Ralph Abernathy was reelected president of
the Southern Christian Leadership Conference.

SEPTEMBER 10. Mordecai Wyatt Johnson, the first Black president of Howard University, died at the age of eighty-six. During his thirty-four-year tenure as president of Howard, he built it into a major university which had a law school, a fully accredited medical school and a prestigious dental school.

SEPTEMBER 20. *I Have a Dream*, a play based on the words of the Rev. Dr. Martin Luther King, Jr., opened at the Ambassador Theater in New York. Mrs. Coretta Scott King and Martin Luther King, Sr. attended the theatrical tribute to the Black militant pacifist preacher who became a Nobel Peace Prize winner.

NOVEMBER. It was announced that the American Broadcasting Corporation (ABC) would broadcast a twelve-hour dramatization of Alex Haley's book *Roots: The Saga of an American Family*. The television presentation would be produced by David Wolper and was scheduled to appear over eight consecutive nights.

DECEMBER. The Schomburg Library and Cultural Center, New York City, the world's most comprehensive collection of Black history, literature and art, was awarded a federal grant of $3,700,000.

The National Institute of Arts and Letters named Gwendolyn Brooks a member. Ms. Brooks thus became the first Black woman to be elected to the institute.

Mehary Medical College, the nation's only privately financed medical college established for Blacks, celebrated its one hundredth anniversary.

Clara Jones was installed as the first Black president of the American Library Association.

Texas Southern University named its law school the Thurgood Marshall School of Law in honor of the nation's first Black Supreme Court justice.

Singer Natalie Cole, daughter of Nat "King" Cole, received two Grammy Awards, one for the Best Artist of the Year and the other for the Best Female Rhythm and Blues Vocalist.

Federal Communications Commissioner Benjamin L. Hooks was elected by the NAACP Board to succeed Roy Wilkins as executive director of the country's oldest and largest Black organization.

The Reverend Dr. Joseph H. Evans of New York was elected president of the predominantly white United Church of Christ and thus became the first Black president of the denomination.

Mayor Kenneth A. Gibson became the first Black president in the forty-three year history of the Conference of Mayors.

Rear Admiral Samuel L. Gravely was promoted to the rank of

vice-admiral and assigned to command the United States Third Fleet, thereby becoming the first Black commander of a Navy fleet.

The National Association of Black journalists was organized in Washington, D.C.

Dr. Henry A. Hill was named president of the American Chemical Society and became the first Black to head the society.

The largest biographical reference book about Blacks ever compiled was published. The volume, entitled *Who's Who Among Black Americans*, edited by William C. Matney, contains references to ten thousand living Blacks.

1977   JANUARY 1. Roland Hayes, the son of a Georgia slave who became an internationally acclaimed concert tenor, died at the age of eighty-nine. Mr. Hayes had received many awards and citations during his lifetime, including the Spingarn Medal for the most outstanding achievement among Blacks in 1925.

JANUARY. President Carter installed two Blacks in important positions with his new administration: Patricia Harris would serve in his cabinet as secretary of Housing and Urban Development, and Representative Andrew Young would be the chief United States representative at the United Nations.

JANUARY. Attorney General Griffin Bell chose NAACP aide Drew Days to be the assistant attorney general in charge of civil rights. This would make Mr. Day the first Black chief of civil rights enforcement and the first Black ever to be appointed assistant attorney general.

FEBRUARY 19. Stevie Wonder was presented with four Grammy Awards at the nineteenth annual awards ceremony of the National Academy of Recording Arts and Sciences. In past years, the composer-producer-performer had been presented with ten other Grammy Awards. This year he won them for Best Album of the Year, Best Male Pop Performer, Best Male Rythm and Blues Performer and Best Producer.

FEBRUARY. A televison documentary entitled *This Far by Faith*, produced by AT&T and narrated by Brock Peters, was broadcast. It analysed the Black church and its impact on American culture.

FEBRUARY. The largest television audience in history, eighty million people, watched the final episode of *Roots*.

FEBRUARY. In honor of Black History Month, an exhibition of over three hundred photographs, playbills, programs and artifacts entitled *Dixie to Broadway: An Exhibition of Black America on Stage, 1800 - 1939* was held at the Metropolitan Museum of Art. The show, designed by Don Vlack, was mounted from an unusual collection of Black theatrical memorabilia from the Helen Armstead-Johnson Foundation.

FEBRUARY. A television documentary was presented on James Van Der Zee, the Harlem photographer.

MARCH. *Other Than White: Towards a Whole Answer*, a multi-arts series which attempted to explore the history and culture of American Blacks, was presented for the third time at the Nassau County Center for Fine Arts on Long Island, New York.

MARCH. The Volunteers of America reported that it would present its Ballington and Maud Booth Award to retiring NAACP executive director and Black activist, Roy Wilkins.

APRIL 18. Alex Haley was awarded a special Pulitzer Prize for his controversial best seller *Roots*, the book which he said was based on a twelve-year, three-continent search for his African and American ancestors. The week before, Mr. Haley was paid special recognition for his book by the National Book Awards committee.

APRIL. Dick Gregory, the entertainer and civil rights activist, attended a ceremony in St. Louis where a street was named "Dick Gregory Place" in his honor.

JUNE 25. *Two Centuries of Black American Art*, an exhibition of two hundred works by sixty-three artists, opened at the Brooklyn Museum.

JULY 4. President Carter announced that he would posthumously award the Medal of Freedom, the government's highest civil award for meritorious contributions to the nation, to the Rev. Dr. Martin Luther King, Jr. The beginning of the citation read: "Martin Luther King, Jr. was the conscience of his generation. A Southerner, a black man, he gazed upon the great wall of segregation and saw that the power of love could bring it down." The citation ended with: "His life informed us, his dreams sustain us yet."

AUGUST. The Southern Christian Leadership Conference held its annual convention in Atlanta with scheduled speakers including: Mrs. Coretta Scott King, Dr. Benjamin Hooks, Rev. Jesse Jackson and Vernon Jordan. The results of their elections saw Dr. Joseph Lowery as president; Hosea Williams as executive director; Walter Fauntroy as board chairman; and Rev. Ralph Abernathy as president-emeritus for life.

AUGUST. The Interfaith Black Theological Project sponsored a conference which brought together the leaders of Black churches in order to plan an open drive to increase goods, services and human rights for the poor.

AUGUST. The United States Postal Service announced that it would issue a commemorative series of stamps to be called *Black Heritage U.S.A.*

SEPTEMBER 1. Ethel Waters, the singer and actress who performed in more than a dozen Broadway productions and nine motion pictures, died at the age of eighty.

The first Paul Robeson Medal of Distinction was presented to Alice Childress, the author, at the fourth annual Oscar Micheaux Awards ceremony of the Black Film Makers Hall of Fame.

Karen B. Farmer became the first Black member of the Daughters of the American Revolution.

THE BRITISH IN AMERICA

1970   JULY 16. Prince Charles and Princess Anne arrived in the
United States for an informal two-day visit as the invited
guests of Julie and Tricia Nixon.

NOVEMBER 13. Arthur Stanley Maxwell died. He was the author of such books as: *War of the Worlds*(1941), *You and Your Future*(1959), *Man the World Needs Most*(1970) , *Uncle Arthur's Bed Time Stories* (forty-eight volumes published from 1924 to 1971) and *The Children's Hour* (five volumes published between 1945 and 1949). This prolific writer of over eighty volumes was born in London in 1896 and emigrated to the United States in 1936.

Arthur T. Ippen, who emigrated to the United States in 1932 and has been associated with the Massachusetts Institute of Technology since 1945, was appointed director of the Ralph M. Parsons Laboratory for Water Resources and Hydrodynamics.

Does It Matter? and *Erotic Spirituality*, both by Alan W. Watts, were published. It was in 1943 that Professor Watts, born in Chislehurst, England became a citizen of the United States. This widely-read philosopher began his career as an author with the publication of *The Spirit of Zen* in 1936 and subsequently wrote many volumes such as: *The Meaning of Happiness*(1940), *The Wisdom of Insecurity*(1951), *Nature, Man and Woman*(1958), *Psychotherapy East and West*(1961) and *Beyond Theology*(1964).

London-born and educated William Matthews, who was a professor at the University of California at Los Angeles from 1939, was made Director of the Center for Medieval and Renaissance Studies at that institution. His written work includes: *Diary of Dudley Ryder*(1939), *British Autobiographies*(1955) and *The Ill-Famed Knight*(1966).

Harold B. Robinson, who was ordained a priest of the Episcopal Church in 1946, was elevated to the rank of bishop. Bishop Robinson was born in Nelson, England, came to the United States in 1922 and became a citizen of his adopted country in 1945.

The British Military Historical Society of the United States was founded in Bayport, New York, for collectors and researchers. It publishes a bimonthly newsletter entitled *The Broad Arrow*.

1971 FEBRUARY. An exhibition entitled *British Art 1890-1928*
  opened at the Gallery of Fine Arts in Columbus, Ohio. That
period was chosen because it marked "the apogee of British power" according to the organizer of the show, and, at the same time, the most neglected period in British art.

JUNE 10. Michael Rennie, the actor who was born in Bradford, Yorkshire and who became a United States citizen in 1960, died at the age of sixty-two. Although he appeared in over fifty major motion pictures, Mr. Rennie was probably best known for his portrayal of Harry Lime, the romantic international spy, in one of the most popular television series ever made, *The Third Man*.

JUNE 25. An exhibition entitled *English Landscape Artists: Drawings and Prints* opened at the Metropolitan Museum of Art in New York City.

The Kate Greenaway Society (KGS) was founded in Folsom, Pennsylvania under the directorship of James L. Lowe. The new organization announced that it would publish a quarterly entitled *Under the Window*.

Alan Powell was made chairman of the Undersea Warfare Research and Development Council based in Bethesda, Maryland. Professor Powell was born in Buxton, England in 1928. He earned a Doctor of Philosophy degree from the University of Southampton in 1953 and came to the United States in 1956.

Arthur C. Turner, a Scottish-born professor of political science at the University of California, Riverside, published *The Unique Partnership: Britain and the United States*. Professor Turner became a naturalized American citizen in 1958.

Wilfred S. G. Pope, English-born music publishing company executive, was made president of the Music Publishers Association of the United States.

Terence A. Rogers was made dean of the University of Hawaii School of Medicine. Dr. Rogers, who was born in London in 1924, arrived in the United States in 1952 and became a citizen six years later. He is the author of *Elementary Human Physiology*, published in 1961, and in the same year was elected president of the Hawaiian Academy of Science.

Arthur E. Satherley, an English-born pioneer in the record producing business, was elected to the Country Music Hall of Fame.

Christopher Isherwood published *Kathleen and Frank*.

1972 JANUARY. The one hundredth Archbishop of Canterbury, the
 Most Reverend Michael Ramsey, arrived in New York for a
series of ecumenical sermons and conferences.

*Invisible Immigrants: The Adaptation of English and Scottish
Immigrants in 19th Century America,* by Charlotte Erickson, was published by the University of Miami Press. Letters written by English
and Scottish immigrants are arranged with introductory notes exploring questions of motives for emigration, networks of migration and
the economic and social adjustment of the immigrants. The volume
itself is broken down into three sections: part I deals with immigrants in agriculture; part II covers immigrants in industry; and
part III explores immigrants in professional, commercial and cler-
ical occupations.

Cecily C. Selby, a London-born biologist, was named national
executive director of the Girl Scouts of America, based in New York
City.

Claude Marks, the artist born in London in 1915 who became
a United States citizen in 1942, had a one-man show at the Dimitria
Gallery in Princeton, New Jersey. In the same year he published
From the Sketchbooks of the Great Artists.

1973 APRIL. "Her Majesty Queen Elizabeth II", announced the British Information Services, "has been pleased to confer upon
Mr. Alfred Alistair Cooke Membership of the Most Excellent
Order of the British Empire in the rank of Honorary Knight
Commander (KBE), in recognition of his outstanding contribution over
many years to Anglo-American mutual understanding." Because English-
born Mr. Cooke, who is one of Britain's most respected correspondents,
became a United States citizen in 1941 he will not be called Sir
Alfred or Sir Alistair.

SEPTEMBER 28. The British-born poet and essayist, W. H.
Auden, one of the major literary figures of the century, died at the
age of sixty-six. He was the recipient of the Pulitzer Prize in
1948.

The renowned British-American author and philosopher, Alan
W. Watts, died at the age of fifty-eight.

It was a year of acclaim for London-born author Hugh Calling-
ham Wheeler: he was the recipient of the Edgar Allen Poe award, the
Antoinette Perry award, the Drama Critic Circle award and the Drama
Desk award. The playwright, who became a citizen of the United
States in 1942, received all of these honors for *A Little Night Music.*

William J. Porter, the British-born public official, was made
under-secretary of state specializing in political affairs.

Michael V. Korda published *Male Chauvinism: How It Works.*

1974   JANUARY 9. Henry L. Williams, a British-born author who
came to the United States in 1923 and later became an American citizen, died at the age of seventy-nine. Mr. Williams
wrote more than seventy books covering a wide range of subjects, both fiction and non-fiction.

MARCH 21. Kenneth Chorley, who was born in Bournemouth,
England in 1893 and came to the United States seven years later,
died at the age of eighty. He was involved in the restoration of
Colonial Williamsburg from its beginning in 1926. Mr. Chorley became vice president of Colonial Williamsburg in 1929, and president
in 1935, only retiring from that post in 1958. Among his honors
was being made a Commander of the Order of the British Empire by
Queen Elizabeth II in 1959 for his promotion of British-American
friendship.

MAY 25. Donald Crisp, who came to the United States from
England in 1906, died. As an actor, he appeared in such memorable
movies as: *Birth of a Nation, Mutiny on the Bounty, Charge of the
Light Brigade, The Life of Emil Zola, Jezebel, Wurthering Heights*
and *National Velvet.*

JULY. *New British Printmakers*, an exhibition of seventy-
six graphic works by eighteen young artists, was held at the Brooklyn Museum in New York City.

OCTOBER 15. Olivia Newton-John was the recipient of the
Country Music Association's top female vocalist award.

NOVEMBER 15. Nathaniel B. Wales, physicist and inventor
who received patents on electric refrigerators and other household
appliances, died at the age of ninety-one. He was a descendant of
the Nathaniel Wales who came to the United States in 1630 from Idle,
England on his own ship, *The James.*

Hugh C. Wheeler again received the Drama Desk award as outstanding book writer, this time for *Candide*, which also received an
Antoinette Perry award for the best book of a musical. *Candide* was
futher chosen by the New York Drama Critics Circle and the Outer
Circle as best musical.

Alex Wyton, a British-born composer and organist who became
a citizen of the United States in 1968, became the organist for St.
James's Church in New York City. He had previously been the organist for the Cathedral of St. John the Divine in New York City for
twenty years.

James B. Reston, the journalist who was born in Clyde-bank
in Scotland, was the recipient of the Elijah Parrish Lovejoy award.
He had previously received two Pulitzer Prizes, three Overseas Press
Club awards, a George Polk Memorial award, a University of Missouri
medal and the John Peter Zenger award.

Ralph P. Hudson, a British-born physicist, was made president of the Philosophy Society of Washington, D.C. Dr. Hudson, who was born in Wellingborough, England and came to the United States in 1949, became an American citizen in 1960.

Myer M. Lubran, an educator and pathologist who was born in London and who came to the United States in 1964, was named president of the Association of Clinical Scientists.

William Hedley J. Summerskill was made the chairman of the Federal Drug Administration-Drug Evaluation Committee and the same year became president of the American Association for the Study of Liver Diseases. The London-born physician came to the United States in 1958 and became a citizen in 1965.

1975   JANUARY 1. P. G. Wodehouse, the ninety-three year old Brit-
 ish-born humorist who wrote more than eighty novels, three hundred short stories, five hundred essays and articles, the scenarios of half a dozen movies and the lyrics of twenty-three musical comedies, was knighted. The writer was named Knight Commander of the Order of the British Empire in the Queen's New Year's honors list.

FEBRUARY 14. P. G. Wodehouse, who had recently adopted the title of Sir Pelham Grenville Wodehouse, died. He was best known for creating such familiar characters as Jeeves and Bertie Wooster. According to Evelyn Waugh: "The first thing to remark about Mr. Wodehouse's art is its universality; he satisfies the most sophisticated taste and the simplest."

MARCH. Alfred C. Berol's collection of Lewis Carroll's writings, photographs, letters and memorabilia was donated to New York University.

MAY 29. Charles Collingwood, the news commentator, was decorated with the Order of the British Empire at the British Embassy in Washington, D.C.

JUNE 14. John Russell, the art critic, and Clive Barnes, the theater and dance critic, both of the *New York Times*, were made Commanders of the Order of the British Empire in the honors list published on the eve of Queen Elizabeth's official birthday.

JUNE 27. It was announced that Queen Elizabeth II and the Duke of Edinbourgh would make a state visit to the former Colonies shortly following the 200th anniversary of the Declaration of Independence in 1976.

JUNE 30. J. W. Fulbright, the seventy year old Democratic Senator from Arkansas, was awarded an honorary knighthood in the Order of the British Empire. A student at Oxford in the 1920s, he was honored in particular for his part in establishing the Fulbright Scholarships program under which twenty-five thousand American students have studied abroad and twice that number from overseas have studied in the United States.

JULY 4. Prince Charles opened an exhibition on *The American War of Independence, 1775-1783* at the British Museum. Lord Eccles, chairman of the Library of George III, which was staging the show, remarked that: "Only the British would take so much trouble over the bicentenary of an humiliating defeat."

JULY. The British government announced that they planned to send one of the original copies of the Magna Carta to the United States to commemorate the Bicentennial. In addition, they were to send a bell "presented to the people of America from the people of Britain." The Bicentennial Bell, which was to be cast by the White-chapel Bell Foundary, casters of the Liberty Bell in 1752, would be placed in a new belltower in Independence National Historical Park in Philadelphia. Also, a joint United States-British fellowship program was announced as part of the Bicentennial celebration. Five fellowships each year for five years would be awarded in the crea⁺tive or performing arts.

AUGUST. Wales Week in New York was celebrated by Welsh men and women from all over the United States and Canada. Craft fairs, art exhibitions and lectures coincided with the forty-fourth annual North American Welsh choral, called the National Gymanfa Ganu. The Welsh in the United States are centered in Ohio, Wisconsin, upstate New York and parts of Pennsylvania. It was estimated that only five thousand people of Welsh descent resided in the New York City area.

AUGUST. Queen Elizabeth II made Lewis Mumford, the American architect and urban planner, an honorary Knight Commander in the Order of the British Empire for the influence his writings have had on city planning in Britain. On learning of this honor, Mr. Mumford commented ruefully, "If I'd really had any influence, the cities of the world would be in better condition."

Marjorie Lynch was named under-secretary of the Department of Health, Education and Welfare. A native of England, in 1974 she had been appointed deputy administrator of the American Revolution Bicentennial Commission by President Ford. The Daughters of the Revolution protested because they contended the position should not go to an Englishwoman.

1976   JANUARY. In honor of the American Bicentennial, both the
    Royal Marines and the Black Watch, two of Britain's most cel-
ebrated military units, started a ten-week tour in Philadel-
phia. Performances were also scheduled for Boston, Houston, Pittsburgh, Chicago, New York, Baltimore, San Francisco, Los Angeles and Washington, D.C.

APRIL. A group of members of the House of Lords and other land-owners came to the United States to visit American historic places and to persuade Americans to visit their castles. In the words of Lord Montagu of Beaulieu, one purpose of the visit was "a desire to make Americans aware of the more than one thousand historic homes there are to see in England."

JUNE 3. A Parliamentary delegation headed by Lord Elwyn-Jones, Britain's Lord Chancellor, presented the oldest copy of the four remaining original copies of the Magna Carta to the American people as a Bicentennial loan. Although the 761 year old document would only remain on display in the Rotunda for one year, the gold facsimile of the Magna Carta and its massive gold and silver presentation case was to remain as a permanent fixture in the Capitol. Carl Albert, the Speaker of the House, accepted the document and commented that the occasion was "the most significant part of our Bicentennial celebration, because it means that our Capitol will house, out of the generosity of the British Parliament, the most important single political document in the long history of the English-speaking nation."

JUNE. In honor of the Bicentennial and Queen Elizabeth II's forthcoming visit, it was announced that fourteen Americans would be awarded honorary British titles for their contributions to Anglo-American friendship. Among those who would receive the honorary Knight Commander of the British Empire were: Eugene Ormandy, the conductor of the Philadelphia Orchestra; Dean Rusk, the former United States secretary of state; and Walter H. Annenberg, the Philadelphia publisher who was ambassador to Britain from 1969 to 1974. Sir Peter Ramsbotham would also present Bob Hope, the English-born entertainer, with the honorary Commander of the Order of the British Empire. The ceremony took place at the British Embassy in Washington, D.C.

1977   MARCH 10. E. Power Biggs, the British-born organ virtuoso who popularized the instrument and baroque music through weekly recitals over the CBS radio network from 1942 to 1958, died at the age of seventy.

MARCH 28. For the first time in its forty-nine year history, the Academy of Motion Picture Arts and Sciences made a posthumous award. The award was for best actor and was given to Peter Finch who died on January 14 at the age of sixty. He won the award for his role as a mad television news anchorman in *Network*.

MAY 4. Lillian Kemble Cooper, the English-born Broadway singer and actress who starred in the 1920s and 1930s, died at the age of eighty-five. She was from a well-known British theatrical family and came to the United States in 1918.

JUNE 17. In honor of the Silver Jubilee, Princess Anne was

on hand for the annual Queen's birthday garden party on the lawns of the British Embassy in Washington, D.C.

JUNE 22.   Ending his three years as Her Britannic Majesty's Ambassador to Washington, D.C., Sir Peter Ramsbotham said that the basis of his faith in President Carter's administration and in American youth, he felt optimistic about the future of the United States.

JULY 11.   George B. Barbour, the Scottish-born internationally-known geologist, died at the age of eighty-six.   Professor Barbour had served on many geological expeditions around the world and was associated with the discovery of Peking Man who was believed to have flourished 650,000 years ago in China.

SEPTEMBER 8.   Margaret Thatcher, the leader of the Conservative opposition in the British Parliament, addressed a meeting of the British American Chamber of Commerce in New York.

OCTOBER 19.   Charles, the Prince of Wales, began a ten-day goodwill tour of America in Chicago.   During a discussion with students at the University of Chicago, Prince Charles remarked that his ancestor, King George III, who ruled England and her colonies at the time of the American Revolution, "got a raw deal in history."   The Prince was scheduled to visit St. Louis, Atlanta, Athens (GA), Keensville (TX), Houston, San Antonio, Los Angeles and San Francisco.

OCTOBER 24.   Princess Margaret arrived in New York.   It was expected that she would attend a dinner-dance sponsored by the Anglo-American Contemporary Dance Foundation later in the week.

NOVEMBER 10.   A British educator, Frank H. T. Rhodes, was sworn in as the ninth president of Cornell University.

Jack Gwillim, who was born in Canterbury in 1915 and made his Broadway debut in 1956 in *Macbeth*, played the part of Friar Laurence in a production of *Romeo and Juliet* at the Circle in the Square Theatre in New York City.

Bob Hope, the stage, radio, film and television actor/comedian who was born in Eltham, England, published the *Road to Hollywood*. Among Mr. Hope's other books are: *They Got Me Covered* (1941), *Five Women I Love* (1966) and *The Last Christmas Show*.   During his career as an entertainer, he received many awards, including: the Congressional Gold medal, presented to him by President Kennedy; the Medal of Freedom, presented by President Johnson; and the People to People Award, presented by President Eisenhower.

Norman Ellis Isaacs, the British-born educator and editor, was made the chairman of the National News Council.

THE CHICANOS IN AMERICA

1970   MARCH 30. During the five-day second annual Chicano Youth
Liberation conference, young Hispanic Americans from more
than a dozen states decided to call for the formation of a
new nation to be called Aztlan. The name was taken from an
Indian word for a stretch of land which was formerly Mexican and
which is presently a part of the United States.

MARCH. McGeorge Bundy, president of the Ford Foundation,
announced that the Southwest Council of La Raza with its headquarters
in Phoenix, Arizona had been awarded a two-year grant of $1,300,000.
The Council, which was established in 1968, served as a source of
information about Mexican Americans both to its own people and to the
community at large.

JUNE. Coachella and San Joaquin Valley growers in California
signed contracts with Chavez's union. By the end of the year, the
majority of the table grape industry had signed contracts with the
union. Having completed this task, Chavez then moved on to organize
the lettuce workers.

AUGUST 29. The Chicano Moratorium was organized in Los Angeles. Thirty thousand Chicanos of all ages protested the war in
Vietnam. To date, this was the largest protest of its kind by any
minority group. Violence ensued resulting in several Chicanos losing
their lives, including Ruben Salazar, a popular writer and journalist.

SEPTEMBER 16. Chicanos in California celebrated Mexico's
Independence Day by organizing a demonstration to protest against
the violence and police brutality following the Chicano Moritorium.
The two to three hundred protesters were heard to cry out Chicano
Power, Viva La Raza and Who Killed Ruben Salazar?

The Chicano Studies Library Projects was initiated at the
Hayden Library at Arizona State University in Tempe. The library
was designed to serve as a storehouse for Chicano material, both by
and about Mexican Americans, and as a research center producing an
annual Chicano bibliography.

The author is indebted to Richard A. Garcia, the editor of THE CHICANOS IN AMERICA, for his research covering the period 1970 to 1974.

The Catholic church established the Fund for Human Development, a nationwide collection taken up on a yearly basis in Catholic churches throughout the United States. The money was to be distributed to Chicano grassroots organizations.

Ricardo Romo, a Chicano, ran for governor of California on the Peace and Freedom Party ticket.

Patrick Fernandes Flores became the first Chicano priest to be elevated to a major church post. He was appointed to the post of auxiliary bishop and subsequently invited Chicano activists to the ceremony.

1971 MARCH. The Los Angeles Superior Court ruled against the challenge of lawyer Oscar Zeta Acosta that Chicanos were systematically excluded from grand jury duty in Los Angeles County. The Court decided that this was not the case "because in each of the last ten years at least one Mexican American was nominated for grand jury duty."

APRIL 3. La Raza Unida candidates ran for election in Crystal City, Texas. The organization swept the board of education and city council elections, gaining a majority on both boards. Crystal City's population was over eighty percent Chicano.

JUNE. The First Chicana's Conference was held in Houston, Texas. Chicano women from around the United States gathered in Texas to analyze their role in the Chicano movement.

The Chicano Cultural Center, founded in 1969, began publication of *El Calendario* (The Calendar), a monthly publication.

The National Committee to Defend Los Tres was established. It sought to defend three Chicano activists accused of killing a police officer who was posing as a drug pusher.

The United Farmworkers Organizing Committee signed a pact with the Teamsters that gave them jurisdiction over the food processing workers and gave the UFWOC jurisdiction over the field workers.

In order to advance the social, economic and educational opportunities of members of the Mexican American community, El Congreso Nacional de Asuntos Colegiales was established in Washington, D.C.

The Chicano Training Center in Houston, Texas was founded. It serves primarily as a consulting agency to institutions, organizations and agencies that work with the Mexican American community. It also sponsors the publication of a bimonthly newsletter, *Mano a Mano*.

Abogados (Lawyers) of Aztlan, an organization of Chicago lawyers whose express purpose was to help the people of El Barrio, was funded by the Catholic church's Fund for Human Development.

The Mid-West Conference of La Raza met in Muskegan, Michigan. The main purpose of the meeting was to organize Raza United Party chapters in the Midwest.

Jim Plunkett, the Mexican American football star, was named rookie of the year at the American Football Conference by United Press International.

1972   AUGUST. Members of the Brown Berets occupied Catalina Island off the coast of California. The demonstration, according to the Brown Berets, symbolized the takeover of Mexican lands by the United States during the last century.

SEPTEMBER. La Raza Unida Party held its first national convention in El Paso, Texas. The representatives at the convention decided not to have a La Raza Unida Party ticket and not to give their full support to either of the major American political parties. Nevertheless, a National Committee was established.

SEPTEMBER. Mayor John Lindsay proclaimed the period from September 11 through September 15 to be Mexico Week in New York City.

OCTOBER. Reies Lopez Tijerina called for a National Land and Culture Conference to be held in Albuquerque, New Mexico.

DECEMBER 2. Jose Arcadia Limon, concert dancer and choreographer, died at the age of sixty-four. A native of Mexico, Mr. Limon came to the United States in 1915 at the age of seven. In 1964 the State Department awarded him the Capezio Award for his dance tours abroad. That same year he was named artistic director by the New York State Council on the Arts of the American Dance Theater.

El Centro de Accion Social Autonoma (CASA) was organized under the leadership of Bert Corona, a Chicano activist for many years. CASA was established to fight the deportation of Chicano and Mexican workers.

The California state legislature passed the Dixon-Arnett Law which stipulated that employers who knowingly hired undocumented Mexican workers would be fined. The state Supreme Court ruled the law unconstitutional.

Ramsey Muniz, a Chicano lawyer, ran for the position of governor of Texas on the Raza Unida Party ticket.

About four thousand Chicano workers, predominantly women,

struck the Farah pants factories in El Paso, San Antonio and Victoria, Texas. The workers demanded unionization, and after a two-year struggle which gained national attention, the strikers finally won their case.

Ramona Acosta Banuelos, a prominent Mexican American businesswoman from Los Angeles, was appointed and confirmed as the treasurer of the United States.

La Raza National Lawyers' Association (LRNLA), located in San Francisco, California, was established.

1973   DECEMBER 12. A group of Chicanos who had been organizing

cultural and educational centers in the Portland, Oregon area took over the Benedictine Sisters' Mount Angel College. They assumed most of the college's debts and renamed it for the leader of Mexican American farm workers in California, Cesar Chavez.

Entre Vecinos (Among Neighbors), a bimonthly publication, was first produced by the Chicano Cultural Center located in Woodburn, Oregon.

The Chicano Social Scientists' Association was formed at a conference held at the University of California in Irvine.

A Better Life, a thirty-seven minute, 16mm color film produced by the Motion Picture Production Division of the Sandia Corporation, was released. The film examines problems of racial stereotyping as Chicanos and Indians relate their experiences of being raised and educated in America.

1974   FEBRUARY 4. The United States Civil Rights Commission accused five southwestern states, Arizona, California, Colorado, New Mexico and Texas, of not providing Mexican American children with an education equal to that of white students. The Commission blamed federal, state and local governments, as well as institutions of higher learning in the five states, for the alleged failure.

MARCH. An article by Richard Severo entitled "The Flight of the Wetback" was featured in the *New York Times Magazine*. According to the author, the United States Department of Justice estimated that there were between 800,000 and 1,000,000 illegal aliens in the United States, 500,000 of which were Mexican. This figure was substantiated by Dr. Jose Juan de Olloqui, Mexico's ambassador to the United States. Under present immigration laws, only 120,000 people can emigrate to America from all the independent nations of the western Hemisphere. In the fiscal year for 1972, this meant that a little more than 64,000 Mexicans were able to cross into the United States as legal aliens.

AUGUST 31. Over 2,500 Chicanos marched in East Los Angeles, protesting the deportation of undocumented workers. Similar marches were held throughout the United States.

NOVEMBER. Raul Castro became the first Chicano to win election as governor of Arizona. The Raza Unida Party ran partial or complete electorial slates in state and local elections in California, Texas and Colorado. Olga Rodriguez, a Chicana activist and feminist, ran unsuccessfully for governor of California on the Socialist Workers Party ticket.

NOVEMBER. Attorney General William B. Saxbe called for the deportation of one million "illegal aliens, mostly Mexicans, because they constituted a severe national crisis." Angry Chicanos around the United States quickly responded that the government was responsible for the economic ills of the country, not the undocumented workers. Javier Rodriquez, the president of CASA, voiced this opinion when he stated that Attorney General Saxbe's recent recommendation was "declaring open season on all Mexicans" and that he was using the aliens as "scapegoats" for the failure of the administration's economic policies.

NOVEMBER. A referendum which would have led to the incorporation of East Los Angeles, the largest Mexican American community in the United States, was defeated.

DECEMBER. Reies Lopez Tijerina, the founder of the Alianza movement which sought to regain title to public lands that were once Spanish land grants, was released from prison. He had served six months of a two-to-ten-year sentence. Mr. Tijerina was imprisoned after a raid on the Rio Arriba County courthouse.

Chicano Power: The Emergence of Mexican America by Tony Castro was published by the Saturday Review Press.

The Ethnic Heritage Studies Program at Indiana University in South Bend was established through funds provided by the United States Office of Education. Its purpose was to identify, adapt and disseminate culturally pluralistic curriculum materials on Mexican Americans and four other ethnic groups.

It was reported that immigration officers had apprehended 800,000 illegal aliens in 1973, ninety percent of whom had entered the United States from Mexico.

1975   AUGUST 23. It was announced that scores of Mexicans and United States citizens would ride horses, mules and burros to reenact the 1,500-mile trek made two centuries ago by the Mexicans who founded the mission settlement that became today's city of San Francisco. The journey, which was started at Horcasitas, Mexico on September 29 in celebration of the American Bicentennial, was to commemorate the journey made by Juan Bautista de Anza and 177 followers in 1775. De Anza had been authorized by the Mexican Viceroy Antonio Maria de Bucareli to found the California mission.

DECEMBER 7. Representatives from Wisconsin, Iowa, Ohio, Kansas, Washington and California attended a meeting in Lincoln, Nebraska and voted to form a national organization to lobby the federal government on behalf of Spanish-speaking citizens. The group, called the Association of State Officers for Spanish-Speaking Affairs, elected Stan Porras of the Nebraska Mexican American Commission as its first president. The members were particularly concerned about questions dealing with unemployment, migrant labor, voting rights and education.

1976   JANUARY. Manuel D. Fierro, president of the National Congress of Hispanic American Citizens (El Congreso), announced that the members of El Congreso were threatening to quit the Leadership Conference on Civil Rights. Membership comprised 125 major Mexican American, Cuban, Puerto Rican and other Hispanic groups across the country. The Hispanic Congress contended that they were under-represented and that the civil rights coalition had not supported any issues that directly affected the Hispanic community.

DECEMBER 8. It was reported that four Democratic members of Congress and Baltasar Corrada del Rio, the resident commissioner-elect of Puerto Rico, were to form the first Congressional Hispanic caucus. The congressional members of the caucus were: Herman Badillo of the Bronx, E. de la Garza and Henry B. Gonzalez, both of Texas and Edward R. Roybal of California. The caucus members stated: "The fact that we have joined together is a sign of the growing power of our community and we are looking forward to strengthening the federal commitment to Hispanic citizens." They also committed themselves to "work together with other groups both inside and outside Congress to promote the goals of our mutual interests in seeking equality for every Hispanic citizen in this country."

DECEMBER. Colegio Cesar Chavez in Mount Angel, Oregon, the only Chicano college in the United States, was on the brink of dissolution. The Department of Housing and Urban Development announced plans to auction off the college's campus and buildings in order to satisfy a one million dollar mortgage.

DECEMBER. A special task force was created by President Carter to look for solutions to the growing problem of illegal aliens in the United States.

The Chicano Cultural Center, which was founded in Woodburn, Oregon in 1969, reported a membership of about twelve thousand. The basic aim of the center is to provide a vehicle which fosters the realization of a pluralistic community for Chicanos in the economic, educational and social sectors.

1977   FEBRUARY 15. President Carter met with President Jose Lopez
    Portillo of Mexico, the first Chief of State to visit the
        United States after Mr. Carter's inauguration. Following
this visit, a Consultative Mechanism with Mexico was established to deal with economic, social and political matters.

        FEBRUARY 16. At a meeting of the Mexican-American Legal De-
fense and Education Fund, Attorney General Griffin B. Bell, in addressing its members, said that he would support proposed legislation to help decrease the number of aliens entering the United States
but that he would be opposed to any large scale deportation of illegal aliens already in the country.
        The fund was using lawsuits to push for the granting of local
voting rights to permanent resident aliens. Vilma Martinez, a Chicana graduate of Columbia Law School and the president of the fund,
was attempting to redress the political under-representation of
Chicanos. In Los Angeles, for example, Mexican Americans were said
to make up twenty-eight percent of the population yet there was not
one Mexican American on the city council.

        FEBRUARY 17. President Portillo addressed Congress during
his first official visit to Washington, D.C.

        MARCH 10. A Justice Department source confirmed that Leonel
Castillo, the city comptroller of Houston, Texas, was to be named
by President Carter to be commissioner of the Immigration and Naturalization Service. Mr. Castillo, a thirty-eight year old Mexican
American, would oversee the Federal agency that would deal with the
approximately six million undocumented aliens in this country, two-
thirds of whom have been estimated to be Mexican. Legal Mexican
Americans were estimated to number seven million, comprising the
largest group within the twelve million American Latino community.

        APRIL. The special task force appointed by President Carter
last December submitted a report suggesting the following reforms:
(1) passage of legislation providing civil fines for employers who
knowingly hired illegal aliens; (2) stricter enforcement of wage-
and-hour-laws and working condition standards; (3) amnesty for illegal aliens who had lived in the United States for some length of
time; (4) increased monitoring of United States borders and points
of entry; and (5) foreign policy efforts to help improve the econ-
omies of those countries from which the mass of illegal aliens
came.

        AUGUST. The Carter administration expressed its policy and
made proposals for legislation on undocumented aliens. This was
the first attempt by the federal government to provide a comprehensive approach to this issue. It included, among other provisions,
employer sanctions and improved status for most undocumented workers
already living in the United States. The proposal by President Carter would thus grant amnesty to approximately four million Mexican
Americans who had been working without papers in the United States
since before January 1, 1970. Mexican American groups around the

country refused to endorse the proposal, holding that the President's amnesty should also apply to more recent arrivals.

Edward Hidalgo, a lawyer who was born in Mexico City in 1912 and became a United States citizen in 1936, was appointed assistant secretary of the Navy for manpower.

THE CHINESE
IN AMERICA

1970 FEBRUARY. A bilingual newspaper, *Getting Together*, was first issued by I Wor Kuen in New York. This new organization, set up in 1969 by a group of young Chinese, began to challenge the authority of older establishments in Chinatown.

NOVEMBER. Senator Hiram Fong of Hawaii was reelected for a third term.

It was reported that 17,956 Chinese would emigrate to the United States by the end of June, and that 5,899 Chinese already in the United States had established their status as permanent residents.

Shih Hsun Ngai, a physician and educator who was born in Wuchang, China, was made chairman of the Department of Anesthesiology at the Columbia College of Physicians and Surgeons. Dr. Ngai came to the United States in 1946 and became a citizen in 1953.

The 1970 census report revealed that the total number of Chinese in the United States was 435,062, which indicated an increase of 83.32 percent over the figure which appeared in the 1960 census report. The Chinese Americans were no longer concentrated on the West Coast, even though California still had the highest number with a Chinese population of 170,131. Following California were New York (81,378), Hawaii (52,039), Illinois (14,474), Massachusetts (14,012), Washington (9,201), New Jersey (9,233), Texas (7,635), Pennsylvania (7,635), Maryland (6,520), Michigan (6,407) and Ohio (5,305).
According to the same census, the Chinese constituted only one-fifth of one percent of the 1970 population in the United States, making it one of the smallest minority groups in the country.

1971 The Hawaii Chinese History Center (HCHC) was established in Honolulu, Hawaii. Its primary function is to promote interest in and research on the Chinese in Hawaii.

Scores of Chinese Americans were permitted to visit mainland China, among those so honored were: Dr. Chen-ning Yang, professor of physics at the State University of New York at Stony Brook; Dr.

The author is indebted to William L. Tung, the editor of THE CHINESE IN AMERICA, for his research covering the period 1970 to 1974.

Chun-tu Hsueh, professor of political science at the University of
Maryland; Way Dong Woo, a Boston industrialist; and Tommy Lee, a
businessman in New York City.

In a ceremony at City Hall, Charles Kee was sworn in as as-
sistant commissioner of the Rent and Housing Maintenance Department.
It was an histroic moment, as Mr. Kee became the highest-ranking New
York City official of Oriental extraction.

Irving Chin, education chairman of the Chinatown Advisory
Council, was awarded a grant of $150,000 by the Department of Health
Education and Welfare in order to establish a language laboratory in
Chinatown, New York City. The facility when opened would have twenty-
three bilingual teachers operating a program of basic "survival"
English which would accommodate 650 Chinese.

Chen Chung Chang, a mathematician who was born in Tientsin,
China and who became a citizen of the United States in 1959, became
the editor of the scholarly journal *Algebra Universalis*.

There were 17,622 Chinese scheduled to come to the United
States by the end of June, and 6,747 Chinese already in the United
States who changed their status from a temporary basis to one of permanent resident. From the effective date of the 1965 immigration and
nationality act to the middle of 1971, there were as many as 115,509
Chinese who came to the United States, with almost equal distribution
between males and females. During the same period, 42,392 Chinese
already in the United States on a temporary basis were able to read-
just their status to permanent residents with the intention of becoming American citizens through naturalization.

1972   MARCH 6. Henry Chung was inaugurated as the president of the
    Chinese Consolidated Benevolent Association, thus becoming
        the head of some fifty-nine community groups in Chinatown,
        New York City. The presidency of this organization alter-
nates every two-year term between the Ning Young and the Lin Sing
Associations.

MARCH. An exhibition entitled *Chinese Calligraphy* opened at
the Metropolitan Museum of Art, New York City.

SEPTEMBER 23. Mayor John Lindsay of New York City declared
this to be *Chinese Arts Day* and Chinatown residents celebrated the
occasion by organizing an exhibition of oils, watercolors, acrylics,
crayons, photographs and sculptures by more than seventy-five Chinese
American artists.

The visit of President Nixon to Peking on February 21st
marked a new era of Sino-American relations, as well as creating
much excitement among the Chinese in the United States. The meeting
of President Nixon with Premier Chou En-lai of the People's Republic
of China culminated in the two leaders signing the Shanghai com-

muniqué on February 25. Many of the Chinese in America, particularly businessmen who were sentimentally inclined to the Republic of China in Taiwan, expressed dismay at the sudden change of American policy.

The University of Pennsylvania conferred an honorary degree of doctor of law upon Dr. Yu-hsiu Ku, professor of electrical engineering from 1952 to 1972, in recognition of his outstanding contributions to the analysis of the transit behavior of a/c machines and systems. A renowned educator in China, Dr. Ku came to the United States in 1950, first teaching at M.I.T. and then joining the faculty at the University of Pennsylvania. Author of several books in his field as well as Chinese poems and songs, Dr. Ku has also been active in a number of cultural organizations sponsored by the Chinese in the United States.

In spite of the downward trend in demand for foreign-language daily newspapers in the United States, the number of Chinese dailies in New York City increased to six, these being: *The Chinese Journal*, *The United Journal*, *The China Tribune*, *The China Times*, *Sing Tao Jih Pao* and *The China Post*. In addition, there were two Chinese dailies in San Francisco, *The Young China* and *The Chinese Times*, and two others in Honolulu, *The United Chinese Press* and *The New Chinese Daily News*.

Irving Chin, a member of the New York City Human Rights Commission, reported that New York's Chinatown population had swelled to some sixty thousand after a yearly infux of eight thousand immigrants since the mid-1960s.

The Chinese Amateur Musicians Association (CAMA) was founded in Houston, Texas.

"Chink!" A Documentary History of Anti-Chinese Prejudice in America edited by Cheng-tsu Wu was published by the World Publishing Company.

1973　　FEBRUARY 3. The Chinese New Year's Day of the Year of the Ox was celebrated according to the Chinese traditional calendar. Both President Nixon and Vice President Agnew sent congratulatory messages to many Chinese Americans.

MARCH. There were two major exhibitions of Chinese works of art on view in New York City. At the China Institute a show called *Ceramics in the Liao Dynasty* displayed sixty ancient pots, bottles, dishes and other vessels dating from the tenth to the eleventh centuries. The show at the New York Cultural Center entitled *Chu Ta: Selected Painting and Calligraphy* displayed paintings of the mid-seventeenth century artist Chu Ta.

JUNE 9. The Organization of Chinese-Americans (OCA) was established in Washington, D.C. A non-partisan coalition of many Chinese Americans, it is designed to help solve various problems confronting the Chinese who have become citizens or permanent residents of the United States.

SEPTEMBER 1. At the annual convention for Chinese students, alumni and their friends, sponsored by the China Institute of America, a special panel was arranged to examine the social and personal problems of the Chinese in America. Among the participants were: David Fung, instructor of Chinese at the China Institute; Dr. Richard P. Wang, staff psychiatrist of the Neuro-psychiatric Institute in New Jersey; and Dr. William L. Tung, professor of political science at the City University of New York's Queens College. Several important topics were discussed, including discrimination, assimilation and diversified interests among Chinese Americans.

SEPTEMBER 8. Over one thousand people attended the dedication ceremony of the Sun Yat Sen Memorial Hall at St. John's University in New York. The construction of this unique building of Oriental architecture, named in honor of the founder of the Chinese republic, was made possible through generous contributions of many Americans and Chinese in the United States and abroad. The hall houses the Center of Asian Studies, which is under the directorship of Dr. Paul K. T. Sih.

Anna Chennault, widow of General Claire Lee Chennault, was named to a three-year term on the Women's Advisory Committee of the Federal Aviation Administration.

The Chinese Professionals Association (CPA) based in Elmhurst, Illinois was established. The primary function of this organization is to promote better communications among Chinese professionals in the United States.

The Chinese-American Cultural Association (CACA), which was founded in 1964, began publication of *Pamir*, its monthly newsletter.

Two twenty minute 16mm color and sound films dealing with the history of Chinese immigration to the United States and special problems which developed were released by the Handel Film Corporation. The first of these two films in their Americana Series was entitled *The Chinese American-The Early Immigrants*, while the second was entitled *The Chinese American-The Twentieth Century*.

It was reported that a new expressway planned for the downtown area in Philadelphia would go through Chinatown. The residents of the small community feared that the new road would not only sweep aside the major Chinese church, school and cultural center, but that it would also lead to the demise of their recent prosperity. The thaw in relations with China and particularly President Nixon's visit to that country had created a new interest in Chinese food which was demonstrated by the recent opening of five new restaurants in Philadelphia's Chinatown. This brought the number of Chinese restaurants in the area to fifteen.

1974 JANUARY 21. The San Francisco Board of Education was ordered by a federal court to offer a special English language class to Chinese students who were disadvantaged because of their lack of proficiency in the English language.

JANUARY. An exhibition of forty-seven Chinese paintings entitled *The Colors of Ink* together with nineteen related black and white ceramics, from the collection of the Cleveland Museum of Art, opened at Asia House in New York City.

JANUARY. To celebrate the coming of the Year of the Tiger, San Francisco's Chinese residents decided to conduct walking tours through Chinatown that would include a visit to a fortune-cookie factory, a dragon temple, Chinese food markets, a Chinese newspaper plant and a Chinese art studio. This was in response to the counseling of Chinese sages of old who advised that the best way to start the new year was to take a long walk ("Hung dai woon") for it would put opportunities in your path.

FEBRUARY 6. In celebration of the Chinese new year in New York, on this the fifteenth day of the festivities, a procession of three thousand children aged eight to twelve years old carried lighted lanterns through Chinatown to City Hall Park.

FEBRUARY. After ten years' work, *Modern Chinese Society*, the first comprehensive bibliography covering works about China from the beginning of the Manchu dynasty in 1644, was published. The three volume set containing 31,441 entries involving 90,000 titles was edited by G. William Skinner aided by Winston Hsieh and Shigeaki Tomita.

APRIL. The first foreign-language paper in New York City devoted to horse racing, *The Chinese Racing Daily*, published by Bongung Dong, did not last a fortnight.

MAY. An exhibition of *Tantric Buddhist Art*, comprised of fifty-four paintings and sculptures, was held at the China House Gallery.

OCTOBER 10. Hundreds of Chinese Americans marched through Chinatown, New York City in celebration of the sixty-third anniversary of the 1911 Nationalist revolution that ousted the Manchu Dynasty and led to the founding of the Republic of China under Sun Yat-sen. The festivities were sponsored by the Chinese Consolidated Benevolent Association, a group of business and family organizations.

DECEMBER. *The Friends of Wen Cheng-ming: A View from the Crawford Collection* was on view at the China House Gallery. The exhibition was comprised of paintings from the sixteenth century.

An Anthology of Asian-American Writers edited by Jeffery Chan, Frank Chin, Lawson Fusao Inada and Shawn Hsu Wong was published. In its preface, the editors warn the reader that "The Asian-American writers here are elegant or repulsive, angry and bitter, militantly anti-white or not, not out of any sense of perversity or revenge but of honesty." The collection of short stories, excerpts from novels and a short play met with good reviews.

1975 MAY 12. More than 2,500 residents of Chinatown, New York City, angered by alleged police brutality, demonstrated outside City Hall. The rally was sponsored by the Asian Americans for Equal Employment.

MAY 19. Another demonstration, this one sponsored by the Chinese Consolidated Benevolent Association, saw thousands of Chinese and Chinese Americans march through Chinatown to City Hall. The rally was called to protest alleged police brutality and to ask for an end to discrimination.

AUGUST 24. A week-long Bicentennial celebration was held in Chinatown, New York City, which featured dancers, films, art exhibitions, music and sports competitions.

Kwang-Chih Chang, an anthropologist who was born in Peking and who came to the United States in 1955, authored *Studies in Ancient China*.

The China Institute in America, under a $320,000 federal grant, sponsored a bilingual vocational training program whereby one hundred newcomers (citizens, permanent residents or refugees) would be taught American English and Chinese restaurant cooking. It was estimated that there were over one thousand Chinese restaurants in New York City alone.

1976 JANUARY 30. Governor Carey of New York saluted the state's 450,000 Chinese Americans on the approach of the Year of the Dragon, the lunar year 4674. The governor proclaimed January 31 as Chinese New Year's Day.

FEBRUARY. Evanston, Wyoming had its first Chinese New Year celebration in over fifty years. It was a weekend attraction which was enjoyed by more than nine thousand people. Evanston is a town of 5,700 located in southwest Wyoming which once boasted an area population of 1,500 Chinese, but which today only has thirteen Chinese American residents.

FEBRUARY. Two different television programs on the archeological discoveries from China that recently toured United States museums were broadcast on two consecutive days. Both *The Red Flower and the Green Horse* on CBS and *Six Hundred Millennia: China's History Unearthed* produced by WNET cover the full range of objects from the Paleolithic period to the fourteenth century.

MAY 28. Dr. V. K. Wellington Koo presented Columbia University president William J. McGill with his oral-history memoirs. The five hundred hours of tape recordings were a result of seventeen years of collaboration with the Chinese Oral History Project directed by C. Martin Wilbur of Columbia's East Asian Institute. This material, representing eleven thousand transcribed pages was believed to be the longest oral-history project ever produced.

SEPTEMBER 10. An article in the *New York Times* reported that the people of Chinatown reacted with "intense but mixed emotions" upon hearing that Chairman Mao Tse-tung had died.

SEPTEMBER 26. The first annual Asian American Festival was held in Columbus Park in Chinatown, New York. The director of the Asian American Caucus, reflecting on the festival, said that although there were cultural differences among the Asian groups, they had to learn to live and work together and that this celebration would "show people the wealth and richness of talent among Asian Americans."

OCTOBER. Dr. Samuel C. C. Ting was informed that he had been chosen, along with Dr. Burton Richter, to receive the Nobel Prize in Physics for his work in discovering subnuclear particles.

OCTOBER. The Wong Family Association of New York honored Richard Wong, a third-generation American Chinese lawyer, for his recent appointment as a commissioner on the New York State Human Rights Appeals Board. It was the highest official position achieved by an American Chinese in New York. During the ceremony, Mr. Wong was presented with a scroll by I-chen Wa, poet and calligrapher.

NOVEMBER 30. The highlight of the fiftieth anniversary celebration of the China Institute was a pageant of two thousand years of Chinese costumes ranging through five dynasties from the Han period to the Ch'ing period. The China Institute, which was organized to encourage greater understanding between the peoples of the United States and China, also sponsors language classes, art courses and other programs. The president of the institute was F. Richard Hsu.

DECEMBER 25. Ginffa Lee, the Chinese-born poet, sculptor and diplomat, described as a founder of the symbolism school of Chinese poetry, died at the age of seventy-six. Mr. Lee emigrated to the United States in 1951.

The Asian American Women's Caucus, a Chinatown-based multi-partisan organization, was formed. The group attempts to encourage women to get involved in the political process, emphasizes job opportunities for Asian women, bilingual and bicultural education and expansion of social services.

 1977 FEBRUARY. According to leading Chinese art experts, the 170 objects spanning a period of some 4,000 years which were on display at Long Island University's C. W. Post Art Gallery amounted to a most important exhibition. F. Richard Hsu, the president of the China Institute, commented: "We are delighted that a university museum and Americans are showing a stronger and stronger interest in Chinese culture. Such a show reflects the fact that Americans have gone beyond superficial involvement with Chinese exotica and have developed a more serious involvement in a more important segment of Chinese history." In addition to the art objects, thirteen twenty-minute films on the history of Chinese art, produced by Wango Weng for the China Institute, were shown in conjunction with the exhibition.

FEBRUARY 27. The National Association of Chinese Americans sponsored an open letter to President Carter asking for the immediate establishment of full diplomatic relations between the United States and the People's Republic of China.

MARCH. The National Committee on United States–China Relations reported that Peking had agreed to an increase in the number of exchange visits with the United States. The committee announced that it would dispatch four delegations to China during 1977, and that China would send three groups to the United States. In the previous three years, China had accepted only two American groups and had sent just one.

APRIL 9. An eleven member United States congressional delegation arrived in China on the start of a goodwill visit.

APRIL 13. The American Academy and Institute of Arts and Letters, at the twenty-eighth annual National Book Awards ceremony, presented Li Li Chen with an award for the translation *Master Tung's Western Chamber Romance.*

OCTOBER 1. In an attempt to attract people back to Chinatown after the Golden Dragon killings of September 4, the Chinese American community in San Francisco began the Mid Autumn Festival or Moon Festival which celebrates the year's harvest. The festival conveniently covered the dates of two important Chinese political anniversaries: October 2 which marks the twenty-eighth anniversary of the Chinese takeover of mainland China, and October 10 which marks the sixty-sixth anniversary of Sun Yat-sen's declaration of the Republic of China.

OCTOBER. Chou-Liang Lin, a violinist who came to the United States from Taiwan, won the first prize in the first Queen Sofia Competition in Madrid.

NOVEMBER. Goldie Chu of Chinatown, New York, represented the Asian American Women's Caucus at the First National Women's Conference in Houston, Texas.

DECEMBER 19. Anthony A. Bliss, executive director of the Metropolitan Opera, and Arthur H. Rosen, president of the National Committee on United States–China Relations, announced that the 150 member Ballet Troupe of the People's Republic of China, based in Peking, would tour the United States during the summer of 1978.

DECEMBER 19. Wing F. Ong, the first Chinese American to be elected as a state legislator in the United States, died at the age of seventy-three. Mr. Ong served two years in the Arizona House before being elected to the State Senate.

THE CZECHS
IN AMERICA

1970   The Czechs in America joined in with Czechs around the world in commemorating the 300th anniversary cf the death of Jan Amos Komensky (Comenius, 1592-1670). The exiled bishop of the Czech Brethren and the father of modern education Professor Komensky, who recommended universal education for both sexes, was once invited to become the president of Harvard College.

Henry G. Mautner became chairman of the departments of biochemistry and pharmacology at Tufts University School of Medicine. Dr. Mautner, who was born in Prague in 1925, came to the United States in 1941 and became a citizen of his adopted country five years later.

George J. Biskup was elevated to the rank of archbishop of Indianapolis. Archbishop Biskup was ordained a priest in the Roman Catholic church in 1937.

1971   Leopold J. Pospisil, a professor of anthropology at Yale University, published *The Anthropology of Law*. Professor Pospisil was born in Olomouc, Czechoslovakia and emigrated to the United States in 1949. He became a naturalized citizen in 1954 and two years later began his association with Yale University.

Jan H. Pokorny, the architect who was born in Brno, Czechoslovakia in 1914 and came to the United States in 1940, was made chairman of the board of directors of the American Fund for Czechoslovak Refugees. Mr. Pokorny had been a member of the organization since 1959.

1972   DECEMBER 7. Apollo 17 carried Eugene Cernan of Chicago who is of Czech descent toward a lunar landing. With this, his third mission, he logged close to five hundred hours of space travel.

Lubomir Kavalek became a member of the American chess team.

The author is indebted to Vera Laska, the editor of THE CZECHS IN AMERICA, for her research covering the period 1970 to 1977.

1973   SEPTEMBER 27. Stefan Osusky, a former Czechoslovakian dip-
    lomat who was a leader in various efforts to free his coun-
try from Nazi and Communist domination, died in the United
States, in exile. Dr. Osusky, who had lived in this country
since the late forties, was elected chairman of the Central Committee
of the Council of Free Czechoslovakia in America in 1952.

        Peter H. Adler was made director of the Juilliard American
Opera Center. Mr. Adler, who was born in Jablonec, Czechoslovakia
and studied at the Conservatory of Music in Prague, became an American citizen in 1944.

1974   DECEMBER 12. Karl Arnstein, a designer of airships who em-
    igrated from Czechoslovakia in 1924, died. Among other
achievements, he was known for designing and directing the
construction of the *U.S.S. Akron* and the *U.S.S. Macon*.

        Julius H. Hlavaty, a Czechoslovakian-born professor of math-
ematics, was made chairman of the United States Commission Mathematics Institution. Professor Hlavaty, who was born in the town of
Piestany, emigrated to the United States in 1921 and became a citizen eight years later.

        Harold K. Ticho, an educator and physicist who was born in
Brno, Czechoslovakia, became dean of the division of physical sciences at the University of California at Los Angeles. Professor
Ticho came to the United States in 1939 and became an American citizen in 1944.

        Bruno Nettl, the Prague-born musicologist and chairman of
the division of musicology at the University of Illinois at Urbana,
was made editor of the *Yearbook of the International Folk Music
Council*.

        The Bohemian Opera House, which opened in 1885 in Manitowak,
Wisconsin and which had been maintained over the years by the Slo-
vanska Lipa and the Sokols, was closed.

        Mojmir Povolny was made chairman of the executive committee
of the Council for a Free Czechoslovakia based in Washington, D.C.
Professor Povolny, who taught government at Lawrence University in
Wisconsin, was born in Menin, Czechoslovakia in 1921. He emigrated
to the United States in 1950 and became a naturalized citizen six
years later.

        Zenske Listy (Women's Gazette), which was started as a weekly
in Chicago by Josephina Humpal-Zeman in 1894 and which became the
Hlas Jednoty (Voice of Unity) in 1947, became a quarterly.

        The Czechoslovak Society of America (CSA), which was founded
in 1854 and which has branches in twenty-two states, reported a membership of approximately 45,000.

1975   AUGUST 20. Koloman Lehotsky, who was born in Spissaka Nova

Ves, Czechoslovakia in 1906 and came to the United States
in 1929, died. He was a professor of forestry at Clemson
University in South Carolina from 1947, and from 1968 to
1972 had served as the director-at-large for the Czechoslovak Society
of Arts and Sciences in America.

SEPTEMBER 6. Martina Navratilova, the eighteen year old
tennis star from Czechoslovakia, asked for political asylum in the
United States and was granted a temporary residence visa while the
Department of Justice considered her request.

OCTOBER 7. The United States Immigration and Naturalization
Service announced that it had granted Martina Navratilova permanent
residency status.

DECEMBER 19. The last issue of *Katolik* (the Catholic), a
weekly published by the Chicago Benedictine Press for over eighty
years, was published. The publisher's other weekly, *Narod* (Nation)
also ceased publication that month.

It was reported that over twenty-seven thousand Czechoslovak
refugees were admitted to the United States over the past thirty
fiscal years. During the past fiscal year, 118 Czechs were permitted to enter the United States as permanent residents.

1976   JANUARY 1. The weekly *Hlas Naroda* (Voice of the Nation) was
launched, edited by Father Vojtech Vit and published in
Chicago by the Czech-American Heritage Center.

JANUARY 5. Jana Hlavaty, a native of Czechoslovakia who
came to the United States in 1969, became an American citizen although she was two months short of the four year residency requirement. A special bill passed by Congress and signed by President
Ford on December 26, 1975, thus made her eligible to compete for the
United States in the Winter Olympics at Innsbruck in Austria.

AUGUST 12. An assertion of the need to intensify the pursuit of free inquiry and exchange of ideas was approved by the General Assembly of the Czechoslovak society of Arts and Sciences in
America. In honor of the Bicentennial the Society which is primarily
a "cultural organization dedicated to the principles of free search
for truth and knowledge, free contacts among peoples and free dissemination of ideas" reaffirmed its members' "allegiance to the fundamental rights invested in the Declaration of Independence and the
United States Constitution." The members also resolved "to urge all
scientists, scholars, artists and writers throughout the world to
ask and work for reestablishing these fundamental rights in Czechoslovakia as well as elsewhere in the world."

The American Bicentennial was celebrated in Czech centers

around the United States, with speeches, lectures and musical performances. The Council in Chicago, for example, honored the event
with a gala concert, and the theme of the Washington, D.C. congress
of the Czechoslovak Society of Arts and Sciences in America was the
Czech and Slovak contributions to the United States.

1977 JANUARY. The United States Department of State issued a
 statement charging Czechoslovakia with violating the 1975
Helsinki agreement by harassing members of Charter 77, a
group that had signed a manifesto calling for the protection
of human rights in Czechoslovakia.

APRIL. The ailing Masaryk Club in Boston, Massachusetts
co-sponsored the opera *Bartered Bride* which was performed at Tufts
University. The event was a great success and brought Czechs from
neighboring states to see it.

JUNE 19. John Nepomucene Neumann, who was born Prachatice,
Czechoslovakia and emigrated to the United States in 1836, was canonized in Rome, the first male saint from America. A month after
he arrived in the United States, he was ordained a Catholic priest
in the old St. Patrick's Cathedral. He served in New York, Maryland
and Pennsylvania, becoming the fourth bishop of Philadelphia in 1852.
He was the founder of the American parochial school system and was
beatified in 1963.

JUNE 26. In honor of the first American male saint, St.
John Neumann, tens of thousands of Philadelphians attended an outdoor mass and concert. The concert and mass were celebrated by John
Cardinal Krol, the Archbishop of Philadelphia and fifty other priests
who participated in a spectacle of religion, music and pagentry.

Henry Kucera, a professor of Slavic languages and linguistics
who was born in Trebarov, Czechoslovakia, was appointed to the executive committee of the Center for Neural Studies. Professor Kucera,
who had been associated with Brown University since 1955, came to
the United States in 1949 and became an American citizen in 1953.

George Liska, author and professor of political science who
was born in Pardubice, Czechoslovakia, published *Quest for Equilib-
rium.* Among his other works are: *Nations in Alliance*(1962), *War
and Order*(1968), *America and the World*(1970) and *States in Evolution*(1973).

THE DUTCH
IN AMERICA

1970 The Dutch Immigrant Society (DIS), which was established
in 1950 in Grand Rapids, Michigan, began publication of its
quarterly entitled *D.I.S.* The organization functions primarily as a socio-cultural institution which sponsors charter flights and tours, cultural events and religious, social and
recreational activities.

Harm Jan De Blij, a Dutch-born geographer and educator, was
made the editor of the *Journal of Geography*. Professor De Blij,
chairman of the department of geography at the University of Miami
in Coral Gables, was born in Schiedam, the Netherlands.

1971 DECEMBER. An exhibition of a series of seven lithographs
by the Dutch-born American artist, Willem de Kooning, opened
at the Museum of Modern Art in New York City.

Nina Foch, the actress, who was born Nina Consuelo Maud Fock
in Leyden, the Netherlands, appeared in the Paramount Studios' production of *Such Good Friends*.

The Dutch-born writer Erik Barnouw was presented with the
Bancroft prize for his three-volume set *A History of Broadcasting
in the United States*. Volume I, *A Tower in Babel*, was published in
1966, with volume II, *The Golden Web*, being published in 1968 and
volume III, *The Image Empire*, appearing in 1970. Mr. Barnouw, who
emigrated to the United States in 1919, became an American citizen
in 1928.

The Princess Beatrix Lectureship for the teaching of Dutch
language and literature was founded at the University of California
in Berkeley.

Arend Bouhuys, a physician and educator who was born in De-
venter, the Netherlands, was made the director of the Yale Lung Research Center. Dr. Bouhuys, who came to the United States in 1962,
received his M.D. at the University of Utrecht in 1948 and his D.M.S.
from the University of Amsterdam.

Jan De Hartog published *The Peaceable Kingdom*. The writer, who was born in Haarlem, Holland, is the author of other volumes including: *This Time Tomorrow*(1947), *The Distant Shore*(1952), *The Inspector*(1960), *The Call of the Sea*(1966) and *The Children*(1968).

1972   FEBRUARY. An exhibition entitled *Dutch Masterpieces from the Eighteenth Century* opened at the Philadelphia Museum of Art.

JUNE 23. A group of young people conducted services in the Dutch Reformed Church in Rhinebeck, New York for fifty-six consecutive hours. They reported that this feat broke the previous church marathon record by eight hours.

Gerrit DeJong, the Dutch-born professor of modern languages, was the recipient of the David O. McKay Humanities award.

Nicolaas Bloembergen, the physicist who was born in Dordrecht, the Netherlands, was the recipient of the Half Moon trophy awarded by the Netherlands Club of New York. He became an American citizen in 1958.

Bart Jan Bok, a Dutch-born professor of astronomy at the University of Arizona in Tucson, was made president of the American Astronomy Society. Professor Bok was born in Hoorn in 1906 and educated at the University of Leiden and the University of Groningen. He came to the United States in 1929 and became a citizen of his adopted country in 1938.

1973   APRIL. The Albert Einstein College of Medicine of Yeshiva University in New York announced that Willem de Kooning was to receive one of the 1973 Albert Einstein Commemorative Awards. The painter and major figure in abstract expressionism was awarded this distinction "for his great influence on contemporary painting and modern art."

DECEMBER 24. Peter Gerard Kuiper, who was born in Harencarspel, the Netherlands in 1905 and became a United States citizen in 1937, died. He had been the head of the Lunar and Planetary Laboratory at the University of Arizona since 1960, and had previously been a professor of astronomy at the University of Chicago.

1974   FEBRUARY. On the occasion of the thirtieth anniversary since the Dutch painter Piet Modrian died, an exhibition of his work was held at the Sidney Janis Gallery in New York City. In addition to his paintings, photographs, documents, objects, sketches and unfinished pieces by and of the artist were displayed

AUGUST 16. Saco Rienk de Boer, Dutch-born city planner and landscape architect who became a citizen of his adopted country in 1914, died. He was a member of a handful of planning societies including the Netherlands Institute for City Planning and Housing.

AUGUST 23. Jan Otto M. Broek, professor of geography at the University of Minnesota from 1948 to 1970 and professor emeritus from 1970, died. Born in Utrecht in 1904, he emigrated to the United States in 1936 and became a naturalized citizen in 1942. He is the author of *Geography, Its Scope and Spirit*(1965) and *Compass of Geography*(1966) as well as other volumes.

SEPTEMBER. A large-scale exhibition of Willem de Kooning's drawings and sculptures was held at the Phillips Memorial Gallery in Washington, D.C. After the show closed on October 27, the exhibition moved on to the Albright-Knox Art Gallery in Buffalo and then to the Museum of Fine Arts in Houston.

Hugo E. R. Uyterhoeven was made Timkin professor of business administration of the Harvard University Graduate School of Business. Professor Uyterhoeven, who was born in Eindhoven, the Netherlands in 1931 and received his doctorate in law from the University of Ghent in 1955, became an American citizen in 1967.

Psychoanalyst Hendrik M. Ruitenbeek published *The New Sexuality*. The Dutch-born physician received his training in Holland and emigrated to the United States in 1955. Among his other works are: *Freud and America*(1966), *The Male Myth*(1967) and *The New Group Therapies*(1970).

1975   MAY. President Ford met with Premier Joop M. den Uyl of the Netherland in Washington, D.C.

JUNE 28. Princess Christina of the Netherlands married Jorge Guillermo of New York. After their marriage in Holland, the couple were to return to the United States.

Dutch-American Bibliography, 1693-1794: A Descriptive Catalog of Dutch Language Books, Pamphlets and Almanacs Printed in America by Hendrik Edelman was published by the Spoken Language Service.

Heiman Van Dam, a Dutch-born psychoanalyst, was made president of the board of directors of the Child Development and Psychotherapy Training Program in Los Angeles.

1976   APRIL 7. It was announced that thirty Dutch athletes who would arrive in New York on April 20 would carry an Olympic-style torch on a five-state relay run commemorating America's Bicentennial and "symbolizing the friendship between Dutch and American people". The 266-mile run through New York, New Jersey, Pennsylvania, Maryland and Delaware, would conclude with a reception by President Ford at the White House.

MAY.   Jan Willem de Waal, the Netherlands vice consul in
New York City, was the guest of honor at the dedication of the Van
Riper-Hopper Museum complex in Wayne, New Jersey. The Netherlands
government had donated three thousand hyacinth bulbs to the people
of the town rich in Dutch history which were planted around the
three-buliding museum complex.

DECEMBER 27.   Ella Dutcher Romig, former president of the
Women's Board of Foreign Missions of the Reformed Church in America,
died at the age of eighty-four. During World War II, Mrs. Romig and
her husband made the West End Collegiate Church in New York City
into a center for Dutch relief and refugee work, for which they received an award from the Dutch government.

DECEMBER.   An exhibition entitled *The Dutch Republic in the
Days of John Adams, 1775-1795* opened at the New York Historical Society. Although it was a Bicentennial show, it did not focus on
what happened in this country during the American Revolution, but
rather explored its effect abroad, especially in the Netherlands.

Cornelis H. van Schooneveld, chairman of the department of
Slavic languages and literature at Indiana University in Bloomington,
published *Semantic Transmutations*. Professor van Schooneveld, who
was born in the Hague, came to the United States in 1949 and became
an American citizen in 1961.

1977   NOVEMBER 23.   Henry Heinemann, a physiologist known for his
    research into kidney and pulmonary diseases, died at the age
         of fifty-seven. Dr. Heinemann, who was born in Sumatra,
         came to the United States in 1951. During World War II, he
was active in the Dutch resistance in the Netherlands.

Jack Vanderryn was made director of the Office of International Programs for the Department of Energy. Professor Vanderryn,
who was born in Groningen, the Netherlands in 1930, emigrated to
the United States in 1939.

THE
ESTONIANS
IN AMERICA

1970   MARCH 7.   The Parent-Teachers Association of the Estonian
    Supplementary School in New York City confirmed a plan ad-
vocated by Victor Obet and Alfred Joks to establish a fund
which would provide centralized financial assistance to the
network of Estonian American Supplementary Schools.

APRIL. The oldest Estonian organization continually in existence, Eesti Uliopilaste Selts (the Estonian Students Association),
celebrated its 100th anniversary.

JUNE 15. Calling the June 15, 1940 invasion of the Baltic
states by Russia "an outrage", Governor Nelson Rockefeller proclaimed
the day "Commemoration Day of the Mass Deportation to Siberia of
Lithuanians, Latvians and Estonians" in New York.

OCTOBER. The Estonian academic fraternity Rotalia sponsored
a special public discussion on issues of assimilation in the Estonian American community. Estonian academic fraternities have been
active in the United States since 1949, and in 1950, twelve of these
groups united to form the League of Estonian Fraternities in the
United States (Eesti Korporatsioonide Liit).

The Center for Estonian Schools in the United States, a society to promote the teaching of the Estonian language, history, geography, literature and music, was founded in Willimantic, Connecticut.

The United States census indicated that there were 20,507
first and second generation Estonians in the United States. In 1950
the figure was 10,085 and in 1960 it was 19,938. The major change
to be noted between the 1960 and the 1970 report was the decreasing
number of the first, or foreign born, generation. In 1960, seventy
percent of the group was foreign born, while in 1970 this group accounted for only fifty-nine percent of the population.

The census report revealed that no major changes had occurred in Estonian American settlement patterns during the past ten
years. About one-half of the population still lived in the densely
populated corridor between Boston and Washington, D.C. There had
been a significant decline in the Estonian population in New York,

---

*The author is indebted to Jaan Pennar et.al., the editors of THE ESTONIANS IN AMERICA,
for their research covering the period 1970 to 1975.*

Connecticut and Ohio during the past decade and an increase of Estonians living in California, Florida, Oregon, Maryland and Massachusetts.

Younger generation Estonian American activists in New York City decided to organize an annual cultural symposium to be called Kultuuripaevad (Cultural Days). The program was to include concerts, theater, films and art displays as well as scholarly lectures, panel discussions and seminars.

Valvo Raag, an Estonian-born electrical engineer, developed a new and unique battery with a life of ten to twenty years. The battery was especially important for use in heart pacemakers.

Endel Tulving was appointed a full professor of psychology at Yale University. The Estonian-born educator specialized in experimental psychology and is considered an expert in the field of storage and retrieval processes in human memory.

1971 APRIL. The first Estonian play in English translation performed in the United States on the legitimate stage premiered at the off-Broadway La Mama E.T.C. theater. Entitled *The Cinderella Game* (originally *Tuhkatriinu Mang*), the play was authored by the young Soviet Estonian playwright Paul-Eerik Rummo. It was translated into English by Andres Mannik and Mardi Valgemae.

MAY. The Voice of America's Estonian Service entered its twentieth year of broadcast activities in the Estonian language. The service was initially headed by Kaarel R. Pusta, Jr. (1951-1957), and thereafter by Jaan Kitzberg (1957-1974) and Voldermar Veedam (from 1975). The service beams two half-hour broadcasts to Soviet Estonia daily.

JULY. The American Chamber Music Festival at Thiel College in Greenville, Pennsylvania, was organized by an Estonian-born member of the music faculty, Ivan Romanenko. Mr. Romanenko came to the United States in 1949 and was concert master of the National Symphony Orchestra in Washington, D.C. for sixteen years.

One part of the lunar vehicle remaining on the moon bore the inscription: "Harald Oliver - Estonian." Mr. Oliver, born in the United States of Estonian parents, was an engineer who helped construct the moon vehicle.

Juri Kaude who was born in Estonia in 1921 was appointed a professor of radiology at the University of Florida, Gainesville.

Alan Tomson, born in the United States of Estonian parents and probably the first Estonian American to have attended the United States Military Academy at West Point, set two new academy records. Mr. Tomson broke the 200-yard swim mark by twenty-four seconds and the record for combined competition (marksmanship, running and swimming) by two seconds.

1972   JUNE 16. The University of Maryland conducted a special
    assembly during which Dr. Ernst Opik presented a lecture on
the moon's morphology and evolution. The purpose of the
assembly was to award Dr. Opik a special gold medal "for distinguished achievements and important contributions to the understanding of the origin of the solar system and the planets." Only
six such gold medals were struck jointly by the American Association
for the Advancement of Science and the Meteoritic Society to commemorate the 400th anniversary of the birth of Johannes Kepler.

NOVEMBER 18. The presidents of the following three organizations, the Estonian World Council, the Supreme Committee for the
Liberation of Lithuania and the World Federation of Free Latvians,
issued a declaration of principles in New York City which subsequently led to the formation of a Baltic World Conference. Alfred Anderson signed the declaration on behalf of the Estonians.

NOVEMBER. Estonian Americans took an active part in the
national elections and, in some cases, in local elections. Estonians
headed the state-wide Republican effort among ethnic groups in four
key electoral states: Arne Kalm in California, Ilo Johanson in
Indiana, Ilmar Pleer in New Jersey and Mati Koiva in Connecticut.
Anne Treumuth, one of the very few Estonian Americans to actually
run for office, was elected as a Republican to the Jackson Township
Municipal Council in New Jersey.

William S. Hein and Company of Buffalo reprinted the 537-
page congressional report entitled *Baltic States: A Study of Their
Origin and National Development; Their Seizure and Incorporation
into the U.S.S.R.* which was originally published in 1954 as the third
interim report of the Select Committee on Communist Aggression in
the House of Representatives. This group is more popularly known as
the Kersten Committee.

The Estonian Centre of the International P.E.N. Club, the
world-wide organization of creative writers, essayists and publi-
cists, transferred its operations from Sweden to the United States.
Founded in Estonia in 1928, the centre has existed outside the country since 1944.

The Estonian American National Council received a letter
from Senator Charles H. Percy of Illinois which stated: "The Department of State has assured me that the flags of free Lithuania, Latvia
and Estonia, among others, will be implanted on the moon during the
flight of Apollo XVI.

Mardi Valgemae, an Estonian-born professor of English, authored *Accelerated Grimace: Expressionism in the American Drama of the
1920s.*

August E. Komendant, who was born in Estonia and who came to

the United States after World War II, authored a 640-page volume
entitled *Contemporary Concrete Structures*.

1973   SEPTEMBER. Nineteen year old Toomas Edur, who is of Estonian
    descent, became a member of the Cleveland Crusaders hockey
        team.

SEPTEMBER. Hardu Keck's first showing in New York City took
place at the Warren Gallery in Greenwich Village. Mr. Keck, who was
born in Estonia in 1940, received his Master of Fine Arts degree
from the Rhode Island School of Design.

Alvine Kingo, who emigrated to the United States in 1949,
celebrated her 100th birthday. She is believed to be the first Estonian to have lived to such a great age in the United States.

The international literary quarterly, *Books Abroad*, published
by the University of Oklahoma, devoted an issue to Baltic literature.
It contained four essays on Estonian topics.

1974   JANUARY. A report issued by the coordinating organization,
    Estonian Schools Center (Eesti Koolide Keskus), revealed
        that there were fifteen Estonian Supplementary Schools in
        the United States. These schools were located from coast
to coast and employed nearly one hundred teachers.

MARCH 17. Louis Kahn, the "humble titan of world architecture," died. Professor Kahn was born on the Estonian island of
Saaremaa (which was at that time called Osel) in 1901 and was brought
to the United States four years later. He designed buildings in relation to the inner order by which he believed people interact. He
had a reverence for natural light and brought the workday metabolics
of buildings, the mechanical equipment, stair towers and other elements which architecture had hidden for centuries, into the open.
Among his most famous architectural landmarks are the library at the
Phillips Exeter Academy, the Kimball Art Museum in Fort Worth, Texas,
the Yale Art Gallery, the Institute of Management at Ahmedabad and
the Capitol of Bangladesh at Dacca.

JUNE. Estonian academic fraternities, sororities and student associations held their third joint Summer Days in Lakewood,
New Jersey.

JUNE. Anton Mannik, who emigrated to the United States from
Estonia in 1944, dedicated a new building-block factory at his Lakewood Super Block Company in New Jersey.

JULY. The twentieth annual Estonian Athletic Games on the
East coast were held at Lakewood, New Jersey, under the traditional
sponsorship of the local Estonian community and the Estonian Athletic
League in the United States (Eesti Spordiliit Uhendriikides). Simi-

lar events have been held on the West Coast and Estonian, Latvian
and Lithuanian athletic organizations in the United States and Canada have periodically held Baltic Olympics.

JULY. Under Estonian leadership, exiled boy and girl scout
units of Estonian, Latvian, Lithuanian, Polish, Ukrainian and Hungarian ancestry held a joint camp, Unity-74, at the Estonian Scouting
Reservation in Jackson, New Jersey. The camp was headed by Estonian
scoutmaster Harry Tarmo, and girl scout leader Anu-Irja Parming was
program director.

AUGUST. Tonu Kalam, a twenty-seven year old Estonian-born
musician on the faculty of the University of Nevada at Reno, conducted the closing number at the Marlboro Musical Festival in Massachusetts.

SEPTEMBER. An Estonian American developer, Rudolf Susi, with
the participation of local dignitaries, dedicated Lake Endla in New
York State near the village of Modena. The lake, situated on a 240-
acre tract, was named for a similar lake located in central Estonia,
and was said to be the third American lake to carry an Estonian name.

DECEMBER. The Estonian language weekly newspaper *New Yorgi
Postimees* (The New York Courier), published and edited by August
Karsna, completed its tenth year with a circulation of eight hundred.
New York City had two other Estonian language newspapers and one per-
iodical to serve the Estonian community. The *Uus Ilm* was founded in
1909, the *Vaba Eesti Sona* in 1949, and the magazine *Meie Tee* in 1931.

Rein Ise, born in Estonia in 1935, was named director of the
Skylab project. He had previously headed the Apollo Telescope Mount
project at the Marshall Space Flight Center in Alabama.

Ilse Lehiste became the elected president of the Association
for the Advancement of Baltic Studies, an international scholarly
organization based in the United States. Professor Lehiste, a teacher of linguistics at Ohio State University, was the first woman to
head the seven hundred member association.

Victor Terras' *Belinsky and Russian Literary Criticism* was
published. Estonian-born Professor Terras, who is the chairman of
the department of Slavic languages and literature at Brown University, also authored *The Young Dostoevsky* (1969).

A *Bibliograhy of English-Language Sources on Estonia: Periodicals, Bibliographies, Pamphlets and Books* by Marju Rink and Tonu
Parming was published by the Estonian Learned Society in America.

1975   JANUARY. The annual Valiseestlase kalender (Calendar for
        the Estonian abroad), published for over two decades by Nord-
        ic Press in New York City and edited by Erich Ernits, report-
        ed that there were at least 106 Estonian medical doctors and

dentists in the United States. This is approximately one doctor for every two hundred first and second generation Estonian Americans. The 1975 calendar also listed five veterinary doctors, ten lawyers and twenty-three architects.

JANUARY. A newly elected Representative Assembly of the Estonian American National Council convened in New York City for its annual meeting. The fifty-delegate assembly has been elected every three years by the Estonian American community, with about four thousand people voting in each of the elections since 1952. The assembly elected Ilmar Pleer of New Jersey to a second term as president of the council. The organization's 1975 budget revealed an important shift in priorities. For the first time, the council budgeted more money for programs dealing with Estonian culture and youth activities than for those programs dealing with political affairs.

JULY 25. President Ford declared that the agreement that he would sign at the Conference on Security and Cooperation in Europe to be held in Helsinki would provide a "yardstick" to guage advances in human rights for subjects of Communist rule in Eastern Europe. Meeting with members of Congress and leaders of emigre organizations, the President asserted that after World War II the United States had not recognized the Soviet annexation of Estonia, Lithuania and Latvia, and "is not doing so now."

JULY 29. Two American citizens of Baltic descent were detained by the Finnish police at the Helsinki airport. The Finns were afraid that Uldis Grava, head of the Baltic World Conference, and Joseph Valiunas had come to their country to protest the Soviet take-over of Estonia, Lithuania and Latvia. Mr. Grava called for the signers of the European security charter to recognize "the rights and aspirations of the Baltic peoples."

AUGUST 1. It was reported that thousands of Americans of Estonian descent believed that President Ford's signature on a multinational agreement in Helsinki formalized forever the incorporation of their homeland, Estonia, in the Soviet Union.

1976   The second Estonian World Festival was held in Baltimore, with the preparatory work being done by the members of the Baltimore Estonian Society. Participants from as far away as Australia and Sweden enjoyed the festivities which included all types of cultural events, social gatherings and political rallies. The first such festival was held in Toronto in 1972 and attracted 25,000 Estonians from around the world.

The Estonian American National Council, which was founded in 1952, reported a membership of approximately ten thousand. The association, which is based in New York City, has branches in ten states and aims to coordinate all political and cultural activities of other Estonian organizations. In addition, the council encourages the retention of the Estonian language, culture and heritage and maintains a six hundred-volume collection of Estonian titles as well as an archival collection pertaining to Estonian American life.

1977   A reprint of the 1935 edition of *Estonia: Population, Cultural and Economic Life,* was published.

    According to the *Annual Report* of the Department of Justice, Immigration and Naturalization Service, only one Estonian-born person emigrated to the United States during 1977. The records also showed that during the period from 1820 to 1977 a total of 1,122 Estonians came to the United States as immigrant aliens.

THE FILIPINOS IN AMERICA

1970 MAY 8. Governor Reagan of California appointed a Filipino judge to the Los Angeles bench. Ms. Marion Lacadia Obera thus became the first judge of Filipino descent to sit on a judicial bench in the continental United States.

MAY. Construction began on the Filipino Cultural Center being built in San Luis Obispo, California.

OCTOBER. Dr. F. A. Gonzales, a noted Filipino physician and surgeon from Salinas, California, was one of the few Filipinos, if not the only one, listed in *Who's Who in America*.

Government statistics revealed that the most dramatic result of the 1965 change in the United States immigration policies was the increase in the number of Filipinos coming to the United States. From 2,545 in the fiscal year in 1965, the number jumped to 25,417 during the 1970 fiscal year.

1971 MARCH. Abbott Laboratories, one of the largest pharmaceutical companies in the United States, awarded F. A. Gonzales, M.D., a research grant to evaluate a new psychotropic drug.

APRIL. The Seattle Executive Department's Youth Division awarded a grant to Filipino Youth Activities of Seattle. The grant was to be used for expanded cultural enrichment programs and to further student job opportunities,

DECEMBER. Ernest Escutron won twelve thousand dollars in scholarships. A resident of San Francisco, Mr. Escutron won a ten thousand dollar scholarship from the National Maritime Union and also received a two thousand dollar scholarship for being the most outstanding American high school student.

The *Annual Report* of the United States Immigration and Naturalization Service revealed that during the previous year 30,507 residents of the Philippine Islands had emigrated to America.

The author is indebted to Hyung-chan Kim & Wayne Patterson, the editors of THE FILIPINOS IN AMERICA, for their research covering the period 1970 to 1974.

1972   JANUARY. Dion V. Corsilles, the managing editor of *Todd*
    News, was one of the five winners of the Orchid Award given
by the Pacific Northwest Industrial editors at a conference
held at the Seattle-Tacoma Hilton.

JANUARY. The former Philippine ambassador to Portugal, Es-
tela Romualdez Sulit, died in Seattle at the age of seventy.

MARCH 25. The Filipino-American Council named four council
representatives in Washington to serve on Governor Daniel Evans' advisory board. Those chosen were Jose Prudencio, Vincent Barrios,
Tony Baruso and Juanito Umipig, one of whom would be named to serve
as a representative on minority ethnic groups.

JULY. A new organization composed mostly of professionals
and civic leaders from the Western Visayas was formed at the residence of Mr. and Mrs. A. Reyes in Monterey Park, California. The
new association was called the Greater Hiligaynon of Southern California.

JULY. The Washington State Council on Aging approved the
International Drop-In Center's application for a project grant for
$25,370.

SEPTEMBER 28. A national organization of United States Filipino American citizens was established during a conference held in
Seattle. Professor Manuel S. Rustia was named general chairman of
the newly-formed group.

OCTOBER. Dr. Dulzura, president of the Filipino American
Community of Los Angeles, was invited to speak at the International
Minority Business seminar that was held at the Los Angeles Conven-
tion Center.

NOVEMBER 18. Joan Mendoza Kis was named Mrs. Filipino Community for 1972 at the final contest held at the Seattle Filipino
Community Center.

Jose Bejar Cruz, a professor of engineering, was the recipient of the Curtis W. McGraw Research award presented by the American Society for Engineering Education. Professor Cruz, who was born
in Bacolod City, the Philippines, came to the United States in 1954
and became a citizen in 1969.

The Philippine Cultural and Trade Center, Inc. was founded
in San Francisco by a group of Filipinos who emigrated to the United
States. Their purpose was to promote the cultural heritage and products of the Philippines.

Alfonso A. Ossorio, an artist who was born in Manila and
who came to the United States in 1930, had a one-man show at the
Cordier and Ekstrom Gallery in New York City.

1973   JANUARY 7.   Silvestre A. Tangalan was reelected president of

the Filipino Community of Seattle, Inc.

FEBRUARY 9.   Julius B. Ruiz, contributing editor of Seattle's
Filipino-American Herald, died at the age of sixty-five.

FEBRUARY 18.   Seattle Mayor Wes Uhlman proclaimed the week
of February 18 to 25 as Filipino Youth Week in Seattle.

MARCH.   The American College of Cardiology awarded Dr. M.
Alimurung, a prominent Filipino cardiologist from Manila, its highest award.   The award, which is given annually to one cardiologist,
was presented during the organization's annual convention in San
Francisco.   Dr. Alimurung, who was the founding president of the
Philippine Heart Association, was the first non-American to receive
this award.

APRIL 12.   Jack Anderson's column in the *Seattle Post-Intel-
ligencer* reported that there were approximately 120 Filipino stewards
stationed in the Washington, D.C. area.   Of these, thirty-two were
assigned to Headquarters of the Naval District.   Another fifty-eight
were assigned to the Navy Administration Unit which is the official
designation for those stewards on the White House staff.

APRIL 16.   The Filipino Community Council decided to establish a community blood bank.   The goal was to reach two hundred units
for use by contributing community members.

MAY.   Filipinos abroad who were holding or hoarding Philippine currency were advised to exchange it for new currency for
after the end of the year, when the demonetization took place, the
money would become worthless.

MAY.   It was reported that the proposed closing of nine can-
neries by operators of the Alaska salmon industry would put many
Filipinos out of work.

JULY 16.   Nemesio Domingo was named Father of the Year by
the Filipino Community of Seattle.

JULY.   The Philippine Cultural Foundation of Santa Clara,
California was incorporated.   The main purpose of the Philippine
cultural center, which is sponsored by the foundation and is
the only one in California, is to provide funds to educate the Filipino Americans in the culture of their homeland.

AUGUST.   Twelve Filipino generals were included in the new
Allied Officer Hall of Fame at the United States Army Command and
General Staff College at Fort Leavenworth, Kansas.

OCTOBER.   President of the Philippines, Ferdinand Marcos, approved the right of dual citizenship for natural-born Filipinos who
had acquired American citizenship.   This move was intended to en-

able older Filipino Americans who retire in the Philippines to acquire land and enjoy the same rights as any other citizen.

NOVEMBER 26. Lamberto Aledia, a Filipino sailor in the United States Navy, won a one million dollar prize in the Massachusetts
State lottery.

Pablo A. Morales, who was born in Manila, was made editor-
in-chief of the *Urology Journal*. Dr. Morales had been associated
with the New York University School of Medicine since 1953, and was
made chairman of the Department of Urology in 1972.

Assemblyman Willie L. Brown, Jr. announced the signing into
law of his bill that would enable foreign-trained pharmacists to
practice their profession in California without completing courses
in the United States. He said that he introduced the bill because
of his concern for the highly experienced Filipinos who were forced
to return to school in order to obtain a license to practice their
skills in California.

Foreign Secretary Carlos Romulo of the Philippines arrived
in the United States for two weeks of talks with businessmen and
especially tour group operators to tell them about the Philippines
of 1973.

The Department of Justice of the Philippines, in response to
an inquiry by their embassy in Washington, D.C., stated that Filipino Americans who owned land in the Philippines could legally continue to do so. However, according to both the 1935 Philippine Constitution and the new constitution (which went into effect in January of this year), these properties "may be transferred or conveyed
only to citizens of the Philippines or to corporations or associations at least 60 percent of the capital of which is owned by such
citizens, save in cases of hereditary succession."

Philippine citizens across the United States were unduly
jarred by the news of President Marcos' Decree No. 174, which stated
that they would have to pay taxes to his government on a flat per-
centage of total income earned. Filipinos residing outside the
Philippines who had a net taxable income of more than $13,000 in
1971 and prior years could take advantage of the new decree by fil-
ing the corresponding return and paying ten percent of any excess
over the $13,000.

The first Filipino American commercial bank in the United
States opened in Los Angeles, California. The bank, the Internation-
al Bank of California, was the first and only bank in the United
States that involved Filipinos in its management and control. Four
Filipinos served on the board, Dr. B. Tan, A. Holigores, J. Licuanan
and Dr. R. Navarro.

The Philippine Consul General in San Francisco announced that
on the basis of information and instructions received, all Filipino

citizens living in the United States who desired to go to the Philippines might do so without jeopardizing the possibility of their returning to the United States.

President Marcos announced a "Balikbayan", an open invitation to all overseas Filipinos to visit the Philippines. A special low-rate tour was offered to the Filipinos in America.

1974   JANUARY 21. Well over three hundred members of the Caballeros de Dimas Alang, Inc. attended a conference held by the group in San Francisco.

FEBRUARY. Casino Cafe, the oldest Philippine restaurant in Seattle, established in 1949, celebrated its twenty-fifth anniversary. The proprietor, Ignacio Navarette, headed the festivities.

FEBRUARY. Max Callao of Boise, Idaho was promoted to the rank of associate professor of psychology at Boise State College. In 1973 he was recognized in the twelfth edition of *American Men and Women of Science: The Social and Behavioral Sciences.*

MARCH. It was reported that there were approximately 120,-000 residents of Philippine descent in Hawaii and that new immigrants were being admitted to that state at a rate of almost 4,000 a year.

APRIL. Juneau's three hundred Filipinos were praised by officials upon the occasion of the National Bank of Alaska's lending the group forty thousand dollars to build a new Filipino Community Center.

JUNE 8. The Filipino War Brides Association of Seattle celebrated its twenty-fifth anniversary. Mariano Angeles, the founder of the association, was the guest speaker.

AUGUST. A Filipino American Association was organized on the naval base at Lemore, California.

SEPTEMBER 30. About seven thousand Filipino teachers registered with the United States embassy were not given immigration visas to enter the United States because employment prospects in their field were extremely limited.

OCTOBER 1. Fred and Dorothy Cordova founders of Filipino Youth Activities of Seattle, Inc., were presented with the Wing Luke Award for 1972.

OCTOBER 4. Luis Taruc, former leader of the Hukbalahap (Communists), lectured at the University of Washington in Seattle. His lecture was sponsored by the Filipino Youth Activities, Inc. and the University of Washington Institute for Comparative and Foreign Area Studies.

A Filipino architect, Richard Galvez, was appointed to the

Planning Commission of Fremont, California. He was the architect of the proposed ten-acre cultural park for the cultural center project of the Filipino Community of Santa Clara.

The Philippines were second, after Mexico, in the number of its citizens who emigrated to the United States. It was reported that 25,696 Filipinos had come to the United States as permanent residents in 1973.

An Hawaiian of Filipino ancestry, Ben Banoy, was named to the Hawaii Supreme Court. He is the elder brother of state Representative Barney Banoy.

Runy M. Sarda, Jr., who came to the United States in 1959, was named senior vice president of Manufacturers Hanover Leasing Corporation.

According to the Immigration and Naturalization Service, about 155,000 Filipinos had entered the United States as immigrants in the past six years. California gets the largest proportion of these new residents, last year receiving more than one-third the United States total.

1976 SEPTEMBER 26. The first annual Asian American Festival was held in Columbus Park in Chinatown, New York City. The director of the Asian American Caucus, reflecting on the festival, said that although there were cultural differences among the Asian groups, they had to learn to live and work together and that this celebration would "show people the wealth and richness of talent among Asian Americans."

Ronnie Alejando of the Philippine Dance Company performed at the first annual Asian American Festival. He had choreographed a special dance for the festival that he called *Sulyap* which means glimpse. What he hoped to do was "give the people a glimpse into Philippine culture."

Libertito Pelayo, publisher and editor of the *Filipino Reporter*, a weekly with a national circulation of 7,500, stated that he believed that there were 35,000 people of Philippine Islands origin living in New York City alone, and perhaps as many as 75,000 living in the tri-state metropolitan area.

1977 Official records of the Philippine government showed that 1.4 million Filipinos were working overseas, some two-thirds of whom were in the United States. Although most of these people lived on the West Coast, there were more than twenty thousand living in New York. Several hundred thousand Filipinos had applied for visas at the American embassy in Manila, but the waiting list could last ten years or more since only twenty thousand of them could legally be accepted each year.

Severino Legarda Koh, a mechanical engineer and educator who was born in Manila in 1927 and emigrated to the United States in 1954, was made assistant head of the division of interdisciplinary engineering at Purdue University in Indiana. Professor Koh, who had been associated with the university since 1957, became an American citizen in 1972.

Domingo M. Aviado, a pharmacologist who was born in Manila in 1924, was made senior director of biomedical research for the Allied Chemical Corporation.

THE FRENCH IN AMERICA

1970   Francis I. P. Plimpton was elected president of the Feder-

ation of French Alliances in the United States.

France in the American Revolution by James B. Perkins was
published by the Corner House Publishers of Williamstown, Massachusetts.

Louis Boudreau was elected to the Baseball Hall of Fame.

1971   The Alliance Francaise de New York which was founded in 1898

merged with the French Institute in the United States which
was established in 1911. The resulting organization has as
its main purpose the dissemination of French culture in the
United States and the study of French language and history.

John de Menil, a French-born businessman and art patron, and
his wife, underwrote the cost of designing and building an important
religious-artistic chapel in Houston, Texas. The centerpiece of the
structure, an octagonal room, was to be used to display fourteen
paintings by the late American abstract artist, Mark Rothko. Mr.
Menil emigrated to the United States in 1941 and became an American
citizen in 1962.

Pierre Boulez, the composer-conductor who was born in Mont-
brison, France in 1925, was made the musical director of the New
York Philharmonic Orchestra.

Jean Morel retired from his conducting position with the
Metropolitan Opera. Born in Abbeville, Somme, France in 1903, he
came to the United States in 1939 and had worked with the Metropolitan Opera since 1956.

Cherilyn La Piere made her television debut on the popular
Sonny and Cher Show.

When a Federal injunction prohibited the *New York Times* from
publishing the *Pentagon Papers*, Senator Mike Gravel of Alaska read

The author is indebted to James S. Pula, the editor of THE FRENCH IN AMERICA, for his
research covering the period 1970 to 1974.

portions of the documents into the record of a Senate subcommittee.

1972   Three major books about the French presence in America were
published this year: *Napoleon's Soldiers in America* by
Simone de la Souchere Delery, *France in America* by William
J. Eccles and *The French in America During the War of Independence of the United States, 1777-1783* by Thomas Balch.

Ron Turcotte rode Riva Ridge to victory in the Kentucky Derby and the Belmont Stakes.

Simone de Beauvoir published *The Coming of Age*, an expose of Western neglect of the elderly.

1973   MAY 2. Germaine Blanche Porel Wilson, who was born in Paris
and who in 1946 was named a Chevalier of the Legion of Honor,
died at the age of eighty-six. During World War II Mrs.
Wilson was a director of American Aid to France.

SEPTEMBER 21. A retrospective of the works of Marcel Duchamp opened at the Philadelphia Museum of Art. The show included almost three hundred pieces drawn from public and private collections in the United States and Europe, covering the entire span of Mr. Duchamp's lengthy career.

Claudette Colbert (nee Lily Chauchoin), the Paris-born actress, toured the United States with *A Community of Two*. Ms. Colbert, who was brought to the United States as a child in 1910, was the recipient of the 1934 Oscar award for best actress.

Mario L. Maurin, a professor of French who was born in Neuilly sur Seine, was awarded the Prix de la Langue Francaise by the French Academy. Professor Maurin came to the United States in 1941 and became an American citizen in 1953.

Ron Turcotte rode Secretariat to the Triple Crown in the Kentucky Derby, the Preakness and the Belmont Stakes.

1974   MARCH 12. Paul Mellon presented a rare and complete collection of 761 engraved portraits of the elite in America from
1796 to 1814 by the French artist Saint-Memin to the National Portrait Gallery. The artist, who was born 204 years
earlier in Dijon, fled his native land with his family after the French Revolution.

MARCH. An exhibition of eighty French drawings of the nineteenth and twentieth century was held at the Metropolitan Museum of Art. The show had just returned from the Louvre Museum in Paris, where it was reported to have been a great popular as well as critical success.

JUNE 13. The Museum of Modern Art's department of drawings mounted an exhibition of 184 works on paper called *Seurat to Matisse: Drawing in France*.

JULY 13. Cape Vincent, New York celebrated its sixth annual French Festival to commemorate the town's settlement by refugees from the French Revolution in the early 1880s.

NOVEMBER. A large survey of Yves Tanguy's paintings including fifty-three works dating from 1925 to 1954 was shown at the Acquavella Galleries, New York City. The French-born artist is an established figure of some importance in the history of Surrealist art.

Rene Dubos, a professor of bacteriology who has been associated with Rockefeller Institute of Medical Research and Rockefeller University since 1927, published *Beast or Angel: Choices That Make Us Human*. The 1969 Pulitzer Prize winner, who was born in St. Brice, France in 1901, is also the author of: *The Bacterial Cell* (1945), *Pasteur and Modern Medicine* (1960), *The Unseen World* (1960), *Man Adapting* (1965) and *Reason Awake: Science for Man* (1970).

The French-born actress Joanna Burns Miles was the recipient of the American Women in Radio and Television award. Mrs. Miles, who was born in Nice in 1940, came to the United States in 1941 and became a citizen that same year.

Philippe Petit thrilled spectators by walking on a tightrope between the World Trade Towers in New York City.

President Ford met with French President Giscard d'Estaing on Martinique in an attempt to solve energy problems and improve Franco-American relations.

A special Oscar for lifetime achievement was presented to Jean Renoir by the Academy of Motion Picture Arts and Sciences.

Pierre Robert Graham, who was born in Saint-Nazaire, France, became the United States ambassador to Upper Volta.

Roger C. L. Guillemin, a physiologist who was born in Dijon and became a citizen of the United States in 1965, was the recipient of the Gairdner International award and during the same year was decorated with the Legion of Honor by the Republic of France.

1975 MARCH. David Rockefeller was presented with the insignia of Commander of the Legion of Honor at the French Embassy in Washington, D.C. Ambassador Jacques Kosciusko-Morizet praised the generosity of the Chase Manhattan Bank president, including his contributions toward the restoration of Versailles, and said that this, in conjunction with his economic and technical understanding, made him "an outstanding example of humanism" in this century.

MARCH. The United States Postal Service issued a set of stamps honoring four people chosen to be symbolic of the many who aided the colonies in their fight for independence. One of the "Contributors to the Cause" was Peter Francisco who joined the Continental Army at the age of fifteen and who took part in seven major battles, including the British surrender at Yorktown.

APRIL 14. Jean Morel, who had been awarded the Chevalier of the Legion of Honor in recognition of his conducting career in the United States and abroad, died.

APRIL. The French ambassador was in Lafayette, Louisiana to present the Legion of Honor to James Domengeaux for his "French in Louisiana" campaign. Mr. Domengeaux, a sixty-seven year old lawyer and former Congressman, won his attempt to make French the official second language of the state.

APRIL. In a ceremony honoring the seventy-four year old lawyer, the French consul general, Gerard Gaussen, made Francis I. P. Plimpton a Chevalier of the Legion of Honor. Mr. Plimpton was a president of the Association of the Bar of the City of New York, has served as deputy United States representative at the United Nations and has been the president of the Federation of French Alliances in the United States since 1970.

MAY 14. During the benefit preview of the New York City Ballet's Ravel Festival, George Balanchine was made an officer of the Legion of Honor. Just before his new ballet *L'Enfant et les Sortileges* was performed, the French ambassador presented Mr. Balanchine with the award. The new ballet was just one of sixteen that he and three other choreographers created for the festival. Each of the ballets was performed to the music of the French composer Ravel.

JUNE 30. Jacques M. May, who was born in Paris in 1896 and received his M.D. from the University of Paris in 1925, died. Dr. May , who became a citizen of the United States in 1954, was chief of the international unit nutrition program for the United States Public Health Service in Bethesda, Maryland from 1966 to 1970. In 1971 he became a consultant to AID.

JULY 14. The French in America celebrated le Quatorze Juillet: Bastille Day, their Day of Independence. In reading a proclamation written by Mayor Beame, Angier B. Duke, city commissioner of civic affairs and public events, declared July 14 to be Bastille Day in New York City. The Proclamation stated: "The principles of French and American democracy were forged in revolution"; and "In spite of separation by an ocean, the devotion to freedom and the understanding between the peoples of the two countries have varied little since the time of our two revolutions." The French consul general, Gerard Gaussen, expressed his thanks to Americans for their help to his country during both World Wars, and announced that his country's Bicentennial gift to the United States would be a sound and light spectacle that would run through the rest of the summer at George Washington's home in Mount Vernon.

JULY. Pierre Szamek, an anthropologist and professor, was
the receipient of the Order of the Academic Palms, a French award
which is presented by the government that was established by Napoleon
in 1808. Professor Szamer was cited for his activities on behalf of
France during World War II.

Marcel Grandjany, a harpist and composer who was born in
Paris in 1891 and emigrated to the United States in 1936, died.
Mr. Grandjany made his debut as a concert artist on the harp in
1924 at Aeolian Hall and later became a soloist with the New York
Symphony Orchestra. From 1938 he was the head of the harp department at Julliard School of Music in New York City, and in 1962 he
founded the American Harp Society.

1976 FEBRUARY 13. Lilly Pons, world-renowned opera singer who
was born in Cannes, but became an American citizen in 1940,
died. Ms. Pons made her opera debut as Lakme at the Mulhouse
Municipal Opera House in France in 1929 and first appeared in
New York as Lucia in 1931, performing with the Metropolitan Opera
Company. In addition to her many stage appearances, she also performed in motion pictures, including *That Girl From Paris* which was
released in 1931. Ms. Pons had received many honors, not the least
of which was the naming of a town in Maryland, Lillypons.

MARCH. It was announced that the French chose New Orleans
as the location for their annual international Bal des Petits Lits
Blancs scheduled for May 21. Ann-Aymone Giscard d'Estaing, wife
of the French President, was to preside at the ball, while her sis-
ter-in-law, the Comtesse Guy de Brantes of New York was to act as the
chairman in this country.

MAY 18. President Valery Giscard d'Estaing arrived in Washington, D.C. on the Concorde. He came in what was said to be a "symbolic visit" for America's Bicentennial. President Ford commented
that the "French American relationship -entering its third century-
stands out as an enduring symbol of common dedication to freedom, to
the rights of Man, and to the increased well-being of our peoples in
a more peaceful and prosperous international environment."
During a reception given in honor of President Giscard
d'Estaing, he was made an honorary member of the Society of Cincinnati, an organization of descendants of Frenchmen who fought in the
American Revolution.

JULY. The journals of the future French King Louis Philippe's
travels to the United States during the period from March to July of
1797 were published for the first time. His accounts comment not only
on the United States, but also on his travelling companions, his
brothers the Duke of Montpensier and the Count of Beaujolais.

AUGUST. Four works by the French American composer Betsey

Jolas were performed at the Festival of Contemporary Music at Tangle-wood, Massachusetts.

1977   JANUARY 14. Anais Nin, the French-born novelist and diarist
 whose work explored the contemporary themes of surrealism,
the subconscious and the feminist viewpoint, died at the age
of seventy-three. Some of Ms. Nin's most well-known works
were: *The Diary of Anais Nin* (four volumes), *Four-Chambered Heart,
House of Incest, Ladders to Fire, Novel of the Future, Seduction of
the Minotaur, Spy in the House of Love* and *Winter of Artifice*.

APRIL. Arthur K. Peters, international trade executive and
scholar in French literature, was named president of the French-
America Foundation. Professor Peters succeeded Nicholas Wahl, a
founder of the organization who was to continue as the chairman of
the board.

SEPTEMBER 6. The highest French cultural award, the order
of Commander of Arts and Letters, was presented to Gregory Peck by
Michael d'Ornano, the French minister of culture who praised the
actor for his film career which has spanned thirty years and included
more than fifty films. Mr. Peck was in France attending a retrospective of his movies at the Deauville Film Festival.

OCTOBER 18. Official sources in Paris announced that Francois Lefebve de Laboulaye would be the new French ambassador to the
United States.

OCTOBER. Roger C. L. Guillemin, who was working as a researcher at the Salk Institute in La Jolla, California, was informed that he had been awarded a share in the Nobel Prize in physiology and medicine. He was chosen to receive the award because
of his invaluable research into the production of peptide hormones
in the brain.

DECEMBER 19. Jacques Tourneur, a French-born Hollywood director known chiefly for his macabre horror films, died at the age
of seventy-three. Mr. Tourneur emigrated to the United States in
1913.

Jacques Barzun, the author who was born in Creteil, France in
1907 and came to the United States in 1920, was made president of the
American Academy and Institute of Arts and Letters.

Dane Rudhyar, the Paris-born and educated author and composer, published *Culture, Orisis and Creativity*.

THE GERMANS IN AMERICA

1970   MARCH 30. Heinrich Bruening, who was forced to flee Germany
 after the Nazi "blood purge" of June 1934 and who had been
a professor of political science at Harvard University since
1950, died at the age of eighty-four. Professor Bruening
had been Germany's chancellor under the Weimar Republic and was a
leader of pre-Nazi Germany's Catholic Center party.

APRIL 4. Chancellor Willy Brandt of West Germany arrived in
the United States for a one-week visit. Mr. Brandt remarked that he
thought that his talks with President Nixon would aid cooperation between the United States and the European Common Market.

Of German Ways by LaVern Rippley was published by the Dillon
Press of Minneapolis.

Gerhard Neubeck, a professor of family social science and
psychology at the University of Minnesota, was made program chairman
of the National Council of Family Relations. Professor Neubeck was
born in Dortmund, Germany and came to the United States in 1940, becoming a citizen five years later.

*Cases and Materials on the Regulation of International Trade
and Investment* by Carl H. Fulda was published. Professor of law at
the University of Texas at Austin since 1965, he had emigrated to
the United States from Germany in 1936.

Wernher von Braun, the German-born scientist and pioneer in
space travel and rocketry was appointed NASA's deputy associate administrator for planning.

The Imperial German Military Collector's Association (IGMCA)
was founded in Shawnee Mission, Kansas. The organization's objective
is to provide information to those interested in doing research on
the pre-1918 German military.

Wolf V. Vishniac, educator and biologist, was the recipient
of the Brooklyn College Distinguished Alumnus award. In the same year,

he was presented with the Apollo Achievement award by NASA. A citizen of the United States since 1946, Professor Vishniac was born in Berlin in 1922 and came to the United States in 1940.

German Political Refugees in the United States During the Period From 1815-1860 by Ernest Bruncken was reprinted from the *Deutsch-Amerikanische Geschichtsblatter* by R&E Research Associates of San Francisco. The book examines the prominent role played by German political exiles in German American communities and their influence on social, political and religious institutions in the United States during the short period of their ascendancy.

1971   Alfred A. H. Keil was made dean of the Massachusetts Insti-
    tute of Technology School of Engineering. Professor Keil was born in Konradswaldau, Germany, and came to the United States in 1947, becoming a naturalized citizen in 1954.

Hans V. Von Leden, German-born surgeon, was made president of the United States section of the International College of Surgeons.

Karl-Ludwig Selig, a professor of romance languages who was born in Wiesbaden, Germany and who became a United States citizen in 1948, was made the general editor of *Revista Hispanica Moderna.*

William H. Hendelson, who emigrated to the United States from Germany in 1930, was appointed editorial director of Funk & Wagnalls, Inc.

1972   JUNE 5. Chancellor Willy Brandt of West Germany announced
    that his country planned to donate forty-seven million dol-
lars to the United States out of gratitude for the Marshall
Plan's heavy contribution to Western Europe's postwar economic recovery. The money would be used to establish and administer an independent American-run educational foundation specializing in European problems. The foundation would be called the German Marshall Fund of the United States.

SEPTEMBER 23. Mayor John V. Lindsay of New York City and Mayor Klaus Schultz of West Berlin watched thousands of German Americans march up Fifth Avenue in the fifteenth annual Steuben Day Parade. The yearly event honors General Friedrich von Steuben, the Prussian-born hero of the American Revolution who helped to train Washington's troops at Valley Forge, Pennsylvania.

A reprint of an 1886 volume concerned with the participation of German Americans in the French and Indian War, the American Revolution, the Mexican War and the Civil War was published by R&E Associates of San Francisco. The title of the volume, by J. G. Rosengarten, is *The German Soldier in the Wars of the United States.*

Judith Malina, who was born in Kiel, Germany and who was co-

director of the Living Theatre which she founded with her husband
Julian Beck in 1947, published *The Enormous Despair*. She had pre-
viously authored a volume entitled *Conversation with Julian Beck and
Judith Malina*, and another written with her husband, called *We, The
Living*.

Ernst W. Bergmann, a German-born orthopedic surgeon who came
to the United States in 1939, was honored by the West German government with the Order of Merit, first class. Dr. Bergmann had received
his medical training at the universities of Munich, Wurzburg and Er-
langen.

Two volumes by the German-born educator/philosopher Herbert
Marcuse, *Counter-revolution and Revolt* and *Studies in Critical Philosophy*, were published. Among the philosopher's most well known
other books are: *Reason and Revolution*(1941), *Eros and Civilization*
(1954) and *One-Dimensional Man*(1965).

Robert F. A. VonNeumann, the German-born artist, was the recipient of the Steuben award. Mr. VonNeumann, who was born in the
town of Rostock, came to the United States in 1926 and became a citizen four years later.

The Hans Neuberger award for excellence in teaching was established at Pennsylvania State University. The award was named for
a German-born professor of meteorology who first became associated
with the university in 1937.

Shimon Wincelberg, the writer who was born in Kiel in 1924,
was the recipient of the Edgar Allen Poe Special Award for Mystery
Writers of America for his book *The Crimson Halo*.

1973   JUNE 10. Fritz Kredel, the illustrator who was born in
    Michelstadt, Germany and who was educated in Darmstadt and
Offenbach, died at the age of seventy-three. The artist,
who won the gold medal for book illustration at the Paris
World Exhibition in 1938, emigrated to the United States that same
year.

SEPTEMBER 23. Henry A. Kissinger took the Constitutional
oath of office, thereby becoming the fifty-sixth United States secretary of state and the first naturalized citizen to gain the office.
Mr. Kissinger was born in Furth, Germany and came to the United
States in 1938. President Nixon had chosen him as "a man who has
the poise and strength and character to serve in this great position."

The German-born professor-philosopher Nicholas Rescher published two books this year, *Conceptual Idealism* and *The Coherence
Theory of Truth*.

The astrophysicist, Rupert Wildt, who was born in Munich
and who emigrated to the United States in 1935, was appointed chair-

man of the board for the Association of Universities for Research in Astronomy.

1974   JANUARY. An exhibition of the more or less representational paintings created by the late Hans Hofmann between 1936 and 1940 was held at the Emmerich Gallery in New York City.

FEBRUARY 1. The Reverend Edmund G. Ryan, executive vice president of Georgetown University, announced that in order to relieve the overcrowding in German universities approximately five hundred German students would be enrolled in the fall of 1975 in a number of American public, private and sectarian colleges in five states across the country. If after five years the program proved itself successful, it was estimated that as many as thirty thousand college-prepared German students who were denied entrance into their own universities each year could cross the Atlantic and earn their bachelor's and masters' degrees in America.

FEBRUARY 3. The world famous child psychologist Charlotte Buhler, who was born in Berlin and emigrated to the United States in 1940, died. She was the author of: *Childhood and Adolescense* (1928), *Die Psychologie im Leben Unserer Zeit* (1962), *The Human Course of Life in its Goal Aspects* (1968) and *Introduction into Humanistic Psychology* (1972) as well as other books and articles.

APRIL. Rudolf Frankel, who was born in Neisse in 1901 and who came to the United States in 1950, died. He had been an industrial architect/city planner in Berlin from 1924 to 1933, in Bucharest from 1933 to 1937 and in London from 1937 to 1950. From 1950, he was a professor of architecture at Miami University in Oxford, Ohio.

AUGUST 25. The German Alps Festival, the annual event that became the Catskills' equivalent to Munich's Oktoberfest, was held in Purling, New York.

SEPTEMBER 4. The United States established formal diplomatic relations with East Germany. Herbert Suss, the East German foreign minister and Arthur A. Hartman, the United States assistant secretary for European affairs signed the documents that provide for the two governments to negotiate trade, consular and cultural relations. John S. Cooper, former Republican senator from Kentucky, was named United States ambassador to East Germany and Rolf Siber, professor of economics, was named East German ambassador to the United States.

SEPTEMBER 21. Germanic folklore and the contributions of German immigrants in America were the primary themes of the seventeenth annual Steuben Day Parade. Approximately twelve thousand German Americans marched up Fifth Avenue as tens of thousands watched along the parade route.

DECEMBER. An exhibition entitled *Twentieth Century German*

Graphics went on view at the New School Art Center in New York City.

Henry C. Wallich, a German-born economist, was made a member of the Board of Governors of the Federal Reserve System. Professor Wallich, who came to the United States in 1935, had been a teacher of economics at Yale University from 1951.

Winfried R. Dallmayr, the political scientist who was born in Ulm, Germany and who became a citizen of the United States in 1961, published *Materials on Knowledge and Human Interests*.

Steven C. Beering, a German-born physician and educator, was made dean of the School of Medicine at Indiana University in Indianapolis. Dr. Beering, who was born in Berlin, came to the United States in 1948 and became an American citizen in 1953.

Stephan G. Kuttner, a professor of history and law who was born in Bonn and came to the United States in 1940, was made president of the Mediaeval Academy of America.

A German-born planetary astronomer, Reinhard Beer, was the recipient of NASA's medal for exceptional scientific achievement.

1975 FEBRUARY. An exhibition of theatrical drawings and watercolors by George Grosz was held at the Neuberger Museum in Purchase, New York.

APRIL 10. In order to mark the one hundredth anniversary of the birth of Thomas Mann, a three-day symposium on the author and his works was held at Rutgers University in New Jersey. The sessions, which included lectures, panel discussions and films, was sponsored by the university's Graduate Division of German and by Goethe House of New York.

JUNE 16. President Ford welcomed President Walter Scheel of West Germany to Washington, D.C., and promised that the United States would continue to stand by its strong commitments to the defense of Western Europe. Mr. Scheel was the first president of West Germany to visit Washington, D.C. in seventeen years, the last being President Theodor Heuss who visited President Eisenhower in June of 1958.
During their meeting, President Scheel announced that his government had decided to present the United States with a one million dollar Bicentennial gift, the funds of which were to be used to establish a scholarship in the name of the first United States high commissioner of Germany after World War II, John J. McCloy. The scholarship was to be employed to further German American exchange visits by leaders of both countries.

JUNE 17. President Scheel addressed a joint session of Congress. He was the first foreign leader to do so in three years.

SEPTEMBER 20. About twelve thousand visitors from Germany

attended the eighteenth annual Steuben Day Parade. There were thirty-one groups from Germany and forty-four groups from the United States that participated in the parade in honor of Baron von Steuben.

DECEMBER 4. Hannah Arendt, who was born in Hanover, Germany in 1906 and came to the United States in 1941, died. A famous author and political scientist, she wrote: *The Origins of Totalitarianism* (1968), *The Human Condition* (1958) and *Crises of the Republic* (1972), as well as other books and many scholarly articles. Professor Arendt, who became an American citizen in 1951, disputed deterministic political philosophies such as Marxism and held that free, individual human action was the key factor in history.

Igor Kipnis, the German-born harpsichordist, was the recipient of the Stereo Review Record of the Year award. He had received the award twice before, once in 1971 and then again in 1972.

A guide listing books, pamphlets, records, photograph collections, dissertations, government documents, newspaper and journal articles concerned with German Americans was published by Scarecrow Press. The title of the volume, which was compiled by Don Heinrich Tolzmann, is *German-Americana: A Bibliography*.

Johannes C. C. Nitsche was the recipient of the Lester R. Ford award for outstanding expository writing. Professor Nitsche, a research mathematician and educator, was born in Olbernhau, Germany and came to the United States in 1956.

1976   JANUARY 9. Rupert Wildt, who was a professor of astronomy at Yale University from 1946 and who in 1966 had been awarded the Eddington Gold Medal by the Royal Astronomers Society in London, died.

MARCH. Hannah Arendt was posthumously awarded Denmark's Sonning Prize for contributions made to European civilization. She was the first American to have ever received this award.

JUNE. A society to preserve, promulgate and perpetuate the music of Ludwig van Beethoven was organized by Robert Becker. Karl Haas was made the artistic director of the New York based organization and an advisory board was established which included Eugene Ormandy, Rudolf Serkin and Işaac Stern.

JULY 16. Chancellor Helmut Schmidt of West Germany was in Washington, D.C. on a two-day Bicentennial visit.

OCTOBER. John D. Ehrlichman, President Nixon's domestic advisor who was convicted of conspiracy, obstruction of justice and perjury because of his part in the Watergate cover-up, began serving his prison term.

DECEMBER 26. Justin Thannhauser, a German-born art dealer,

died at the age of eighty-four. Henry Berg, the deputy director of the Guggenheim Museum in New York, stated: "Through the generosity of Justin Thannhauser, an incomparable collection of seventy-five priceless works have been placed on permanent exhibition at the Guggenheim Museum in a wing named for the donor."

1977   MARCH. A giant jamboree of some one hundred events entitled Berlin Now-Cultural Aspects of a City, sponsored by Goethe House in New York and supported by a number of other German and American institutions, took place in New York. According to Gerd Loffler, a senator who heads Berlin's Department for the Arts and Sciences, the month-long festivity "was the first time since the disaster of the Hitler era that Germany's cultural scene has the chance to show itself in a broad sweep in the United States."

JUNE 16. Wernher von Braun, the master rocket builder and scientific pioneer, died at the age of sixty-five. Dr. von Braun was eulogized as "a man of bold vision" in a statement of President Carter's released by the White House. The President commented: "To millions of Americans, Wernher von Braun's name was inextricably linked to our exploration of space and to the creative application of technology. Not just the people of our nation, but all the people of the world have profited from his work. We will continue to profit from his example." Dr. von Braun was probably best known for the development of the German V-2 rocket, a dreaded weapon of warfare and precursor of the American Saturn 5 moon rocket. He headed the team that was responsible for launching the first United States satellite into orbit in 1958.

JUNE 21. H. R. Haldeman, former President Nixon's White House chief of staff, entered prison, thus beginning to serve a thirty-month to eight-year sentence for his role in the Watergate scandal. He was convicted of conspiracy, obstruction of justice and perjury.

JULY 13. President Carter met with Chancellor Helmut Schmidt of West Germany.

SEPTEMBER 17. As many as twelve thousand marchers participated in the twentieth annual Steuben Day Parade up Fifth Avenue.

NOVEMBER 25. Axel Grosser, a specialist in architectural photography, died at the age of sixty-five. Mr. Grosser was born in Prenzlau, Germany and studied photography in Berlin before emigrating to the United States in 1949.

DECEMBER 30. Alexander Schreiner ended a fifty-three year career as organist for the Mormon Tabernacle in Salt Lake City, Utah with a public recital. Dr. Schreiner, who was born in Nurenberg, Germany, emigrated to Utah with his family sixty-five years ago.

Hans Namuth, the German-born photographer who came to the

United States in 1941, had a one-man exhibition at the Leo Castelli Gallery in New York City.

Georg F. Springer, a German-born scientist and professor of surgery at Northwestern University, was awarded the Abbott Prize in biomedical research and the Jung Prize in medicine.

THE GREEKS IN AMERICA

1970 Archbishop Iakovos was presented with the Clergyman of the Year Award by the Religious Heritage of America Association for "his leadership in community and ecumenical activities at home and abroad and for contributions to American religious life."

The Reverend Dr. Leonidas C. Contos, president of Hellenic College, received the Gold Medallion for "Courageous Leadership in Intercreedal Relations", which was presented to him by the National Conference of Christians and Jews.

The Bureau of the Census reported that there were 177,275 foreign-born Greeks living in the United States. This revealed an increase of more than ten thousand over the 1960 census figures.

George Christopher was installed as the first Orthodox co-chairman of the National Conference of Christians and Jews.

1971 JANUARY. Bishop John (Christodoulos Kallos) was consecrated Titular Bishop of Thermon and was assigned to the Houston diocese, thus becoming the first American-born bishop in the Greek Orthodox Church.

MARCH. The archbishop opened a series of celebrations for the 150th Anniversary of Greek Independence. The festivities took place at the Fordham University Auditorium at Lincoln Center, New York City.

1972 JULY. His Holiness Athenagoras I, archbishop of Constantin-ople - New Rome and Ecumenical Patriarch, died in Istanbul.

JULY. The Greek Orthodox archdiocese of North and South America held its twenty-first Biennial Clergy-Laity Congress in Houston. It was to mark a "Double Jubilee", celebrating Athenagoras's fiftieth year as a bishop and the fiftieth anniversary of the American archdiocese. At the news of His Holiness Athenagoras's death, the congress adjourned in mourning.

SEPTEMBER. The Orthodox Theological Society in the United States sponsored the second International Conference of Orthodox Theologians at St. Vladimir's Seminary in Yonkers, New York.

NOVEMBER 18. A retrospective exhibition of the works of Lucas Samaras opened at the Whitney Museum of American Art. The show included 377 pieces, some of which dated from 1959.

The *Atlantis* ceased publication. It was first published in 1894 by Solon Vlastos.

1973 Theodore Saloutos, the history professor who was a past president of the Hellenic University of Southern California, was made president of the Immigration History Society.

1974 JANUARY. The Very Reverend Timothy Negrepontis, a priest in the Greek Orthodox archdiocese of North and South America and pastor of the Ascension Church, was elevated to the rank of bishop by the Holy Synod of the Ecumenical Patriarchate of Constantinople. The Reverend was formally consecrated at the Hellenic College in Brookline, Massachusetts.

APRIL 6. The new St. George Greek Church was dedicated in Clifton, New Jersey with Archbishop Iakovos officiating at the ceremonies. The church, designed by Dimitri E. Siderakis, was to serve the congregation of the Reverend John P. Orfanakos.

NOVEMBER 17. Archbishop Iakovos was in Maine to help the Holy Trinity Greek Orthodox Church of Portland celebrate its fiftieth anniversary.

John Brademas, United States congressman from Indiana, received the Cross of the Holy Sepulchre from His Eminence Archbishop Iakovos for "his extraordinary efforts and concern on behalf of the Greek Cypriot refugees."

Greek-American organizations began unifying under the leadership of Andrew Athens, first president of the United Hellenic American Congress. The fighting in Cyprus was the event which encouraged many organizations to set aside their differences. Among this group's main supporters can be included New York shipowners George Livanos, Pericles Callimanopulos and the Goulandris family.

The Hellenic Council of America was founded by Columbia University economics professor Phoebus Dhrymes. He formed this organization for the express purpose of enlisting academic and professional people in the campaign to aid Cyprus.

Theoni V. Aldredge (nee Vachlioti) a costume designer who was born in Salonika, received the Academy Award for her designs for the film *The Great Gatsby*.

Because of the situation in Cyprus, Greek-Americans temporarily suppressed their ideological and personal differences to unite either for the purpose of raising funds to help the large Cypriot refugee population or to support lobbying of the United States Congress. The two best known lobby groups that developed were the United Hellenic American Congress and the American Hellenic Institute. The latter organization employed a full-time lobbyist in Washington, D.C., and had as its head Eugene Telemachus Rossides, the son of a Greek mother and a Greek-Cypriot father.

Archbishop Iakovos founded the Philoptochos Foster Parent Project to help orphaned and homeless children in Cyprus. The archbishop also urged all Greek-Americans to write to their congressmen and to let them know that they would not sanction Turkish aggression against Cyprus.

1975 FEBRUARY. The Reverend Dr. Nicon D. Patrinacos was named by Archbishop Iakovos as archdiocesan director of inter-church relations and social concerns.

SEPTEMBER 17. Nicola Moscona, the Athens-born opera star who became a citizen of the United States in 1946, died. Mr. Moscona made his American debut with the Metropolitan Opera Association in 1937 and remained associated with the group as a leading bass-baritone for more than fifteen years.

The Holy Cross Orthodox Press was founded in Brookline, Massachusetts. Reverend N. Michael Vaporis was the managing editor. The press publishes a wide range of materials from popular to scholarly in the sphere of Orthodox religious doctrine, history, ethics, worship and scholarship.

The first Greek Orthodox convent in America was opened at St. Basil's Academy in Garrison, New York. Called the Greek Archdiocese Convent of St. Iakovos, it was officially opened when His Eminence, the archbishop, conducted the Thiranixia Services. The convent welcomes women who want to serve in the church as nuns.

There were seventeen Greek-American day schools in the United States functioning under the Office of Education of the Greek Orthodox archdiocese. Of these, ten were located in the greater New York area, one in Washington, D.C., three in Chicago, and one each in Lowell, Tampa and Houston.

According to the Annual Report of the Immigration and Naturalization Service of 1975, more than 128,500 Greeks came to the United States between 1966 and 1975.

1976   MAY 16. Telly Savalas served as grand marshal of the Fifth Avenue parade in celebration of the 155th anniversary of Greek independence from the Turkish Ottoman Empire. It was estimated that twenty-five thousand of the approximately three hundred thousand Greeks living in New York City attended the parade.

JUNE. The Cathedral of the Holy Trinity in Manhattan had its interior renovated at a cost of half a million dollars. In accordance with ancient Byzantine custom, Archbishop Iakovos officiated over the traditional rites. The renovations were executed by artist and designer Sirio Tonelli.

OCTOBER. In one of his election speeches, President Carter pledged his support for majority rule in Cyprus and stated that as President he "would do everything in his power to see that the conduct of foreign affairs of this nation would be based on the rule of law and the highest standards of morality." The President commented further that: "Just as we believe that there be majority rule of the peoples of Africa, that there also be majority rule for the people of Cyprus." As the governor of Georgia, Mr. Carter protested to Washington, D.C., about the Turkish invasion of Cyprus, requested steps to be taken for the protection of Cypriot refugees, and supported a drive to raise funds for these refugees in Georgia.

OCTOBER. Greek-American journalist Takis Theodorakopoulos was sentenced to fifteen months imprisonment *in absentia* for asserting that the Athens English-language newspaper was on the payroll of the KGB, the USSR intelligence service.

The Maliotis Cultural Center was added to the campus of the Hellenic College and Holy Cross Greek Orthodox School of Theology. The contemporary glass-walled edifice was built in part with white marble from Greece. The center houses a sizable auditorium and numerous exhibition halls for the presentation of cultural and intellectual programs.

1977 FEBRUARY. The press and information office of the Greek Consulate in New York held a reception to publicize its efforts to promote modern Greek studies in the United States. Some of the guests attending this function included: Prof. Athan Anagnostopoulos who is in charge of the Modern Greek Program at Boston University; Prof. Lily Macrakis, president of the Modern Greek Studies Association; Prof. Adamantia Pollis, professor of political science at New York's New School for Social Research; John Nicolopoulos, director of the Greek Press and Information Service; Prof. L. Komitas, professor of education and prominent anthropologist, of Columbia University; Prof. Malefakis, professor of history at Columbia University; and E. Funderburke, senior development officer at Columbia University.

FEBRUARY. *Treasures of Cyprus*, a major exhibition of archaeological and cultural history, was on tour in the United States as a Bicentennial tribute from the government of Cyprus. The exhibition opened in New York and was then shown in other major American cities.

MARCH. During a cermony honoring B. J. Marketos for his thirty years of service to the Greek-American community as publisher of the *National Herald*, it was announced that Eugene T. Rossides would become the new publisher of the newspaper. Among those in attendence at the celebration were: Menelas Alexandrakis, the ambassador of Greece; Zenon Rossides, the United Nations representative from Cyprus; Charalambos Christophorou, the general consul of Cyprus; Germanos, the Metropolitan of Ierapolis; AHEPA's Supreme President Microutsicos; and Harry Stathos, the publisher of the *Hellenic Times*. The president of the United States, the prime minister of Greece and the president of Cyprus each sent a personal message congratulating Mr. Marketos.

MARCH. Under the title *Noemata* (Concepts), the first broad-based exhibit of works by Greek-American artists was shown at the Brooklyn Museum. Fourteen contemporary artists of Greek descent exhibited their work, seven of whom were born in Greece, six in New York and one in Turkey. The artists were: Stephen Antonakas, Tom Boutis, Chryssa, Nassos Daphnis, Christos Gianakos, Steve Gianakos, Mary Grigoriades, Aristodemos Kaldis, Aris Koutroulis, Michael Lekakis, Lucas Samaras, Nicholas Sperakis, Theodoros Stamos and Theo Stavropoulos. The catalogue viewed the exhibition as an indication that "the Greek-American community has begun to find the time and the resources necessary to extend itself into the arts."

MARCH. On the first anniversary of *Greek World* magazine, the first Annual Greek World Awards were presented in New York City. The awards were given to five distinguished Greek-Americans: Athena Dallas-Damis, a well-known journalist and translator of Nikos Kazantzakis, author of *The Island of the Winds*; Dino Anagnost, the widely celebrated conductor of the Metropolitan Greek Chorale; Harry Mark Petrakis, an author whose latest volume was an account of the time of Greece's struggle for independence and which was entitled *The Hour of the Bell*; Dr. Ioannis Vassiliou Yannas of the Massachusetts Institute of Technology, a brilliant scientist who had most recently worked on the development of artificial skin; and Nicholas Gage, the well-known *New York Times* investigative reporter and author of *The Bourlotas Fortune*.

MAY 15. Thousands of Greek-Americans celebrated the 156th anniversary of Greek independence from the Ottoman Empire by marching in or watching the parade up Fifth Avenue. The theme of the parade was concern for human rights which for the Greek community meant a call for an end to the Turkish military occupation of Cyprus.

DECEMBER 22. Bishop Timotheos, head of the Greek Orthodox archdiocese that includes six Middle Western states, died at the age of sixty. The Bishop, who was born in Attica, Greece, came to the United States in 1957 when he was transferred to the St. Eleftherios parish in New York City.

A new Greek-American daily newspaper, *Proini*, began publication.

George Kotzias, the much-decorated and courageous scientist, died in New York. Dr. Kotzias achieved world-wide fame for his discovery of the most effective drug against Parkinson's Disease. More recently, he was responsible for establishing a chain of cooperation between the leading American and Greek institutions concerned with cancer research.

A chair in memory of the illustrious Greek-born conductor Dimitri Mitropoulos, who died in 1960, was established at the New England Conservatory of Music in Boston. Mr. Mitropoulos's American debut as a conductor was with the Boston Symphony in 1936.

H. Haralambopoulos, the director of the Greek National Tourism Organization for North and South America, stated that the 1977 increase in tourist traffic from the United States to Greece was liable to be as high as twenty to twenty-five percent. On the basis of present calculations, Mr. Haralambopoulos considered that the year 1978 would produce a further increase of twenty percent.

George E. Mylonas, an archaeologist who was born in Smyrna, published *Mycenaean Religion*. Professor Mylonas was decorated by King Paul of Greece for his archaeological discoveries in 1955 and was made a grand commander in the Order of the Phoenix.

Alexander J. Kondonassis, the Greek-born professor of economics, published two volumes: *The European Economic Community and Greece: Toward a Full Membership?* and *The Greek Inflation and the Flight from the Drachma: 1940-1948.*

Nicolas Roussakis, a composer and professor in the music department of the New Brunswick campus of Rutgers University, was the co-founder of the American Composers Orchestra. Professor Roussakis, who was born in Athens, came to the United States in 1950 and became a citizen six years later.

THE
HUNGARIANS
IN AMERICA

1970 The first Hungarian Native Language Congress was held in Debrecen, Hungary. The aim of the conference was to upgrade Hungarian language education abroad and to encourage cultural exchange between Hungary and Hungarian communities outside Hungary. But the congress did not include representatives of Hungarians living in the neighboring countries, i.e., Czechoslovakia, the Soviet Union, Romania and Yugoslavia, where there are some 3,300,000 native Hungarians. The Hungarian American press was constantly concerned about the lack of involvement of Hungarians in these countries and about the one-sided cultural exchange offered by the congress. Approximately thirty Hungarian American delegates attended the congress.

Lili Darvas, the Hungarian-born actress, returned to her native country to film *Love* which was made in Budapest. For her part in *Love* she was given Hungary's prestigious Red Star medal, and later received the Cannes Festival Critics' Award.

1971 JUNE 26. Charles Szechenyi, a member of a noble Hungarian family who formerly served in the Upper House of the Hungarian Parliament, died at the age of sixty-five. Mr. Szechenyi emigrated to the United States in 1946 and became a naturalized citizen in 1951.

The American Hungarian Cultural Center of Washington, D.C. together with the Departments of Language and Linguistics, Music and History of the American University, sponsored a lecture series in Washington, D.C. Those who participated in the project were: Antal Dorati, conductor; C. A. Macartney, professor at the University of Edinburgh; Eleanor Lansing Dulles, professor at Georgetown University; and Frenc Nagy, former Prime Minister of Hungary.

It became publicly known that the United States Department of State was using the Crown of St. Stephen and the concomitant crown jewels in American custody as a bargaining factor in negotiating with the Hungarian Government. Hungarian American associations and individuals protested against the tactic.

The author is indebted to Joseph Szeplaki, the editor of THE HUNGARIANS IN AMERICA, for his research covering the period 1970 to 1974.

Denis Gabor, a Hungarian-born physicist, received the Nobel Prize for physics.

After voluntarily imprisoning himself for fifteen years at the American Legation in Hungary, Cardinal Mindszenty left Hungary because of pressure from the United States government and the Vatican, both of which were trying to reach an accommodation with the present government of Hungary.

Ralph Fabri, the artist, published his *Artist's Guide to Composition*. He was born in Budapest in 1894 and became a naturalized United States citizen in 1927. Other books by Mr. Fabri are: *Learn to Draw* (1945), *Oil Painting* (1966), *Color, A Complete Guide for Artists* (1967) and *Painting Cityscapes* (1969).

1972   MAY 14. Dr. Sandor Rado, the Hungarian-born physician who

was one of Freud's first disciples, died at the age of eighty-two. He was a leader of the psychoanalytic movement, assisting in the establishment of the first school of psychoanalysis at Columbia University in 1944. From 1958 to 1967 he helped to organize, and then presided over the New York School of Psychiatry.

JUNE 13. Dr. Georg von Bekesy, an immigrant in the United States in 1947 who won the Nobel Prize for medicine in 1961 for his research into hearing and the human ear, died in Honolulu at the age of seventy-three. He had been a professor at the University of Hawaii since 1966.

JUNE. Ten years after Lazlo Ispansky arrived in the United States as a Hungarian refugee in 1956, he opened his own porcelain studio in Trenton, New Jersey. His success led from a converted garage to the present twelve thousand square-foot building in Hopewell, New Jersey.

OCTOBER 14. A news release reported that the State Department had signed a preliminary agreement with the Hungarian government to settle $58.1 million in United States citizens' claims for interests taken over by the state and for war-damaged property in Hungary.

Hungarian librarians in the United States and Canada established a forum at the Annual Hungarian Congress in Cleveland, Ohio to discuss Hungarian-related library topics, and to survey Hungarian collections in America.

Hungarian communities throughout the United States and the Hungarian press celebrated the 750th anniversary of the *Golden Bull*, frequently called the *Magna Carta* of Hungary.

Stephen Csoka, an artist who was born in Gardony, Hungary and who came to the United States in 1934, received the Gold Medal award by the Arpad Academy.

The approximately eight hundred Hungarian university professors in the United States attending the Annual Hungarian Congress established an informal organization to survey and to encourage Hungarian studies at American universities.

1973 MARCH 29. On the 125th anniversary of the Hungarian War of Independence and the 150th anniversary of the birth of Sandor Petofi, Hungary's greatest lyric poet, Bishop Zoltan Beky opened a session of the House of Representatives with a prayer.

SEPTEMBER 30. Jozsef Cardinal Mindszenty, the eight-one year old exiled Primate of Hungary, blessed the newly-renovated Church of St. Ladislaus in New Brunswick, New Jersey. More than five thousand people attended an address delivered by the cardinal, the loudest applause being heard when he urged his listeners to keep the Hungarian language and spirit alive.

OCTOBER. A. Raymond Katz, the muralist and painter of religious art born in Hungary in 1895, had a one-man show at the Barney Weinger Gallery in New York City. Mr. Katz, who studied at the American Institute of Chicago and the Chicago Academy of Arts, won his first art prize at the Century of Progress world's fair in Chicago in 1934.

OCTOBER. An exhibition of photographic works by Laszlo Moholy-Nagy was held at the Sonnabend Gallery in New York City. It displayed his works in three categories: straight photographs; photograms, in which the image is printed directly on the sensitized paper without a negative; and "Fotoplastiken," a form of photomontage.

NOVEMBER. An exhibition of several of the larger pieces executed by Turku Trajan, the Hungarian-born sculptor and painter, opened at the Zabriskie Gallery in New York City.

DECEMBER 11. Janos Scholz, Hungarian-born cellist and art collector, celebrated his seventieth birthday and the fortieth anniversary of his arrival in the United States by giving a concert at the Pierpont Morgan Library in New York City. After his recital, Mr. Scholz announced that he would donate his collection of Italian drawings and reference books to the Morgan Library. The collection of more than fifteen hundred works, including drawings by such masters as Leonardo, Raphael, Titian and Bellini, was described by the Morgan Library's director as "certainly the finest private collection of Italian drawings in America and one of the finest in the world."

A park was named after Charles Zagonyi in Springfield, Missouri to commemorate his heroic conduct during the Union soldiers' cavalry charge near Springfield.

A book exhibition, commemorating five hundred years of Hungarian printing, was held at the Chicago Public Library. The show was made possible through the support of Louis Szathmary.

The Harvard Circle for Hungarian Studies was formed by students and faculty interested in Hungarian culture. Since its inception, the group has sponsored several lectures and meetings with guest speakers such as Bela Bartok, Jr., W. D. Snodgrass, Tibor Szasz, and Tibor Ham.

Patria, a fraternal organization for eighteen to thirty year old Hungarian Americans, was established in Cleveland, Ohio. Its purpose is to train leaders within the Hungarian community.

Bishop Zoltan Beky was honored for his forty-five years of devoted service to the American Hungarian Reformed Church by Hungarian communities all over the United States. The city of Trenton, New Jersey named a street, Beky Drive, in his honor.

Ralph Fabri, the Hungarian-born artist, was made president of Allied Artists of America.

A retrospective exhibition of the works of Gyorgi Kepes, who was born in Selyp, Hungary, was held at the Museum of Science in Boston.

1974 MAY. Cardinal Mindszenty began his third visit to the United States while on a world mission tour of Hungarian communities During his tour he visited most of the large Hungarian American communities and met with several high American officials. In view of the reaction of the news media, the cardinal had a great impact on the American people. His memoirs, which were published in an English edition, became a best seller.

OCTOBER 23. John J. Gilligan, governor of Ohio, designated this day as Hungarian Freedom Fighters' Day in Ohio, in memory of the Hungarian Revolution of 1956.

DECEMBER 13. A bill was passed in the Senate, in response to energetic lobbying by the American Hungarian Federation, on the basis of a text drafted by Szabolcs Mesterhazy. The bill provided that any country desiring to acquire the status of "most favored nation" in the United States must agree to allow the free emigration of its citizens who wish to join their relatives in this country. The bill was submitted by Republican Jesse Helms of North Carolina and is wryly referred to as "the Hungarian Amendment."

In the spirit of the coming Bicentennial, the Hungarian Americans and Congress commemorated the 250th anniversary of the birth of the Hungarian-born American hero of the Revolutionary War, Colonel Michael de Kovats.

The American Hungarian Federation published a two-volume set containing the speeches and correspondence of various distinguished members of the United States Senate and House of Representatives with reference to the Hungarian question.

An exhibition of forty photographs by three artists who worked during the 1920s and 1930s was held at the Museum of Modern Art in New York City. Of the three photographers, two were Hungarian-born Americans, Andre Kertesz and Laszlo Moholy-Nagy.

A survey of publications revealed that there were sixty-two Hungarian-language newspapers, periodicals, bulletins and newsletters supported by the Hungarian communities in the United States. Seventeen of these publications were established more than fifty years ago, the oldest including: *Szabadsag* (Liberty) founded in Cleveland eighty-three years ago; *Katolikus Magyarok Vasarnapja* (Catholic Hungarians' Sunday) first published in Youngstown eighty years ago; and *Amerikai Magyar Nepszava* (American Hungarian People's Voice) which first appeared in Cleveland seventy-three years ago.

Thomas S. Szasz, the psychiatrist, born in Budapest and made a United States citizen in 1944, was named Humanist of the Year by the American Humanist Association.

Daniel Szabo was appointed a senior advisor to the Inter-American Development Bank. Mr. Szabo, who was born in Budapest, came to the United States in 1950 and became a naturalized citizen four years later.

Lili Darvas, the celebrated stage and screen actress, appeared in the television production of *Rachel, La Cubana*, a WNET Opera Theater production.

A quarterly, *Patria - The Newspaper of Young Hungarians*, was first published.

The Ethnic Heritage Studies Program at Indiana University at South Bend was established with financial aid made available by the United States Office of Education. Its primary purpose was to identify, adapt and disseminate culturally pluralistic curriculum materials for Hungarian Americans and four other ethnic groups.

The United Hungarian Fund reported that in 1973 their capital was $24,988. The United Hungarian Fund was organized in 1970 by Lorant Pallos to help needy Hungarians and support Hungarian publications in the United States.

The American Hungarian Federation (AHF), which was founded in 1906, reported that its forty-nine chapters located in sixteen states had a membership of almost 120,000. The organization, which represents the interests of American Hungarians in Congress and government agencies, is based in Washington, D.C. and is headed by the Honorable Albert A. Fiok.

1975 George G. Lorinczi, a Hungarian-born lawyer who came tc the United States in 1948, was appointed to the US–USSR Trade and Economics Council.

The Hungarian-born philosopher, Julius M. E. Moravcsik, published *Understanding Language*. Professor Moravcsik, who had been professor of philosophy at Stanford University since 1968, became a naturalized United States citizen in 1953.

 1976 AUGUST 6. Lajos I. von Micsky, the Hungarian-born physician, died at the age of fifty-eight. Dr. von Micsky was a pioneer in the development of ultrasonic diagnosis in gynecology and obstetrics. He emigrated to the United States in 1959.

OCTOBER. Dr. Daniel Carleton Gajdusek, a pediatrician and virologist with a wide-ranging research career, was awarded the Nobel Prize in medicine along with Dr. Baruch S. Blumberg. The Royal Caroline Institute announced that the award was for their discoveries concerning new mechanisms for the origin and dissemination of infectious diseases.

OCTOBER. President Ford met with a dozen Hungarian Americans on the twentieth anniversary of the abortive Hungarian revolution. The President told the group that he shared their wish for freedom. The Hungarian Americans, some of whom had fought in the revolt, presented the President with a book entitled *Remember Hungary*.

Thomas S. Szasz, the Hungarian-born psychiatrist, published *Heresies*. Among his other works are: *Pain and Pleasure*(1957), *The Myth of Mental Illness*(1961), *Psychiatric Justice*(1965), *Ideology and Insanity*(1970), *The Manufacture of Madness*(1970) and *The Second Sin*(1973). Dr. Szasz emigrated to the United States in 1938.

 1977 APRIL 6. The United States and Hungary signed a cultural and scientific exchange agreement.

AUGUST. Laszlo N. Tauber, the Hungarian-born neurosurgeon, donated one million dollars to Brandeis University in Massachusetts. The endowment was to be used for the establishment of two professorships and to set up a scholarship fund.

NOVEMBER 3. Administration and congressional sources reported that in an effort to improve relations with Hungary, the United States would return to Budapest the crown of St. Stephen, the symbol of Hungarian nationhood that had been in American custody since the last days of World War II. The crown was originally sent to Stephen, Hungary's first king in the year 1000, by Pope Sylvester II. It had been used in the coronation of more than fifty Hungarian kings and no state ceremony was considered legitimate without it.

Representative Mary Rose Oaker, a Democrat from Ohio, representing the largest concentration of Hungarians in the United States, expressed strong opposition to the return of the crown.

NOVEMBER 29. Hundreds of Hungarian Americans marched to the White House to protest the planned return of the Crown of St. Stephen to Hungary. Dr. Tibor Bodi of Philadelphia, one of the leaders of the march said: "As a Christian president, it is incomprehensible that President Carter hands over the holiest symbol of a nation to its Communist invaders." President Carter's decision brought protests from organizations representing many of the three million people in the United States of Hungarian descent.

DECEMBER 15. The State Department announced that Hungary's crown jewels including the Crown of St. Stephen would be returned to Budapest by an American delegation in a two-day ceremony which would take place on January 6 and 7. The crown jewels would then be put on permanent public display.

DECEMBER 15. Representatives of the Cardinal Mindszenty Foundation, a national educational organization, reported that they would file a law suit to try to prevent President Carter from returning the Crown of St. Stephen to Hungary. Thousands of Hungarian Americans had already protested the issue, urging the President not to return the jewels to a communist-run government.

DECEMBER 22. Francis S. Juhasz, chairman of the American language program at Columbia University, died at the age of fifty-two. Professor Juhasz was born in Budapest and attended the University there before emigrating to the United States in 1948.

Andre Kertesz, the Hungarian-born photographer who became an American citzen in 1944, was presented with the City of New York Mayor's award of honor for arts and culture.

John A. Lukacs, an historian who emigrated to the United States in 1946 and became an American citizen in 1953, was made president of the American Catholic History Association.

Andor C. Klay was made Washington, D.C. bureau chief of the American Hungarian Associated Press.

It was a successful year for Hungarian-born sculptor Laci Anthony De Gerenday who received an award from the Council of American Artists, the Dr. Radding award from the Academy of Artists Association, and the silver medal of honor from Allied Artists.

THE IRISH IN AMERICA

1970   John Dempsey, the governor of Connecticut from 1961, was the recipient of the John F. Kennedy Memorial award. Mr. Dempsey, who was born in Cahir, Ireland in 1915, came to the United States in 1925 and became an American citizen in 1931.

Michael F. Kennelly became president of Loyola University in New Orleans, Louisiana.

Violence in Northern Ireland continued and the Irish Republican Army revived its guerrilla campaign to end Partition and unite Ireland. Numerous committees and organizations were formed among Irish Americans to work on behalf of civil rights in Ulster and for Irish unification.

1971   MAY 6. Some 2,383 people of Gaelic extraction attended the thirty-ninth annual feis sponsored by the United Irish Counties Association of New York. Most of the people came to compete in one of the 179 contests of dancing, music and declamation, a tradition which is said to go back thousands of years to the time when the kings of Tara convened minstrels and poets in yearly contests. According to Peter J. O'Neill, who was born in Sligoe and who was the president of the Association, "the primary purpose of the feis is to encourage the Irish arts and culture."

MAY 21. A celebration of some six hundred Irish Americans marked the centennial of *The Irish World*, the country's oldest Irish American weekly newspaper. According to Maureen P. Ford, the editor and publisher (and granddaughter of its founder, Patrick Ford) of the one hundred year old newspaper, "We've always reported the activities of the Irish, but we've not always endorsed the Irishman. The paper has traditionally stood for justice for all. That's what we believe." The newspaper has a circulation of about one hundred thousand, one-quarter of which goes to Ireland.

AUGUST. The internment without trial of hundreds of Catholics in Northern Ireland lead to intensified fighting between the IRA and British troops. This action led to protests and demonstrations

The author is indebted to William D. Griffin, the editor of THE IRISH IN AMERICA, for his research covering the period 1970 to 1972.

held by Irish Americans who demanded that the United States government exert pressure on Britain to reach a settlement.

The Irish American Cultural Institute (IACI), which was
founded in 1962 in St. Paul, Minnesota, first published its monthly
Duchas.

Two public affairs organizations composed primarily of Americans of Irish descent were founded. The American Committee for
Ulster Justice and the National Association for Irish Freedom were
both established in New York City.

1972   JANUARY 30. Thirteen demonstrators were killed by British
soldiers in Londonderry in what was to become known as
"Bloody Sunday." There was an expression of outrage in the
United States and demands were made in Congress for concessions by Britain on the Irish question. These turbulent events
in Ulster led to a marked revival of Irish American unity and cultural identity.

MARCH 17. Members of the St. Brendan's League, the New York
Gaelic Society, the Bronx Gaelic League, the Philo-Celtic Society,
the New Jersey Gaelic League and the An Fainna Society attended an
annual Gaelic mass held in honor of St. Patrick's Day. Father Keo-
hane of the Saints Faith, Hope and Charity Chapel delivered the entire mass in Gaelic, including a long sermon on St. Patrick and his
work.

MARCH 17. It was estimated that over one hundred thousand
people marched in the St. Patrick's Day Parade up Fifth Avenue. Pa-
trolman Patrick B. Sheehy, who was born in County Kerry, blew the
whistle which signaled the opening of the festivities. Some of the
participants wore armbands in memory of the thirteen people who were
killed during a civil rights demonstration that resulted in "Bloody
Sunday" in Northern Ireland.

MARCH. The House of Representatives passed a bill which had
been pushed primarily by Representatives Peter W. Rodino of New Jersey and William F. Ryan of Manhattan. The bill would permit, over
a four-year period, additional immigrant visas for about ten thousand
Irishmen and about twenty-eight thousand Italians. Mr. Ryan, who
first proposed a version of the bill five years ago, said that the
differential was needed in order to correct inequalities that had
developed after the immigration laws were revised in 1965.

OCTOBER 14. Mrs. Patricia Nixon, whose father was the son
of Irish immigrants, was presented with the American Irish Historical
Society gold medal by New York State Lieutenant Governor Malcolm
Wilson. Mrs. Nixon was the second woman among thirty-five people
to have received this honor.

NOVEMBER. The New Jersey Gaelic Hall of Fame sponsored by

the Friendly Sons of the Shillelagh, inducted four new members: Dr.
E. McKiernan, Paul O'Dwyer, P. W. Doherty and Representative Peter
Rodino.

NOVEMBER. Brian Heron and a group of some fifty prominent
Americans of Irish descent organized An Claidheamh Soluis, which is
Gaelic for Irish Arts Center, which opened this month. The center
was comprised of the 255-seat Abbey Theater and three floors of office space on 13th Street in New York City.

*That Most Distressful Nation: The Taming of the American
Irish* by Andrew M. Greeley and *Going to America* by Terry Coleman
were published. Both books recount the historic events that led to
the great wave of Irish emigration and the experiences of the Irish
on their arrival in the United States.

Father Patrick J. Peyton, the originator of the slogan "The
Family That Prays Together Stays Together", became the producer of
the television series *A Matter of Faith*. Father Peyton, who was
born in Carracastle, County Mayo in 1909, came to the United States
in 1928 and became a citizen ten years later.

1973   OCTOBER 11. Mrs. Patricia Nixon presented Peter J. Brennan,
        the secretary of labor, with the American Irish Historical
        Society gold medal as "the outstanding American of Irish
        lineage of 1973."

Bishop Timothy Manning was consecrated a cardinal. The new
cardinal, who was born in Cork, Ireland, came to the United States
in 1928 and became a citizen of his adopted country in 1945.

The Chicago Gaelic Society, a socio-cultural educational organization, was founded. The group's primary function is to preserve
the Irish heritage in America.

Daniel Patrick Moynihan was named United States ambassador
to India, and during the same year published *The Politics of a Guaranteed Income*.

Real Lace by Stephen Birmingham was published. The author
presents the story of the rich Irish American Catholics in a narrative form rather than through statistics and sociological theory.

The American Irish Historical Society located on Fifth Avenue
in New York City began publication of its semiannual *Bulletin*.

The Irish Institute (II), which was founded in 1950, reported
a membership of nearly two thousand United States citizens of Irish
descent. The primary purpose of the New York City based organization
is to preserve the Irish customs, arts and culture in America. The
institute also sponsors competitions in the fields of music, drama
and the arts.

1974   JANUARY. An exhibition of abstract drawings by Patrick
    Ireland was held at the Parsons Gallery in New York City.
        Patrick Ireland is the pseudonym of Brian O'Doherty, the
        critic, who wanted to identify himself with the Irish cause
and to separate his work as a creative artist from the business of
merely writing about it.

        MARCH. *Aspects of Irish Art*, an exhibition with the major-
ity of paintings on loan from the National Gallery of Ireland, was
organized by the Gallery of Fine Arts in Columbus, Ohio. Photographs of Irish architecture and a small collection of Irish silver
were also displayed.

        JUNE 30. A mass was celebrated by the newly-appointed Arch-
bishop Peter L. Garety of Newark at the opening of the fourth annual
Irish Festival in Holmdel, New Jersey's Garden State Arts Center.
About seven thousand Irish Americans attended the festival and offered a prayer for peace "and an end to the bloodshed and bitterness
now staining Northern Ireland."

        AUGUST. The Kilkenny-born playwright and novelist Thomas
Kilroy was chosen to receive the 1974 American Irish Foundation Literary Award. For this year the award, which includes a grant of
seven thousand dollars, was sponsored by Thomas F. O'Neil, the New
York City businessman. Other recipients of the award have been:
Austin Clarke, Seamus Heaney and Padraic Colum. Mr. Kilroy's first
novel *The Big Chapel* was published in 1971.

        The Society for the Preservation of Irish Music in America
was established in Bloomington, Indiana.

        Sean Griffin, who was born in Limerick, Ireland in 1942,
made his Broadway debut in *The National Health*.

        A Bridge Too Far, the last book by Cornelius John Ryan, was
published. Mr. Ryan, who was born in Dublin in 1920, emigrated to
the United States in 1947.

1975   JANUARY 1. Hugh Carey began his first term as New York's
        fifty-first governor.

        JANUARY 18. Princess Grace of Monaco joined Governor Bren-
dan Byrne of New Jersey in honoring Irish Americans who participated
in the American Revolutionary War. Princess Grace later presented
a silver medallion for Irish American philanthropy to Patrick Mott
Butler, the mining executive, and his wife Aimmee Mott Butler, at
the first annual awards dinner of the Irish-American Institute.

        JANUARY. The Chicago Gaelic Society began publication of
its monthly *An Mheitheal*.

        AUGUST 29. Eamon de Valera, a chief strategist and fighter

in the cause of Irish Independence who became prime minister and
then president, died in Dublin at the age of ninety-two. Mr. de
Valera was born in New York City, but was taken to Ireland at the
age of two, after the death of his father. President Ford expressed
his sympathy at the death of this elder statesman whom he said had
been "a symbol of Ireland's ideals and aspirations for more than
half a century. He served the Irish people devotedly and unstinting-
ly as parliamentarian, prime minister and as president for fourteen
years." President Ford continued, adding: "Mr. de Valera also per-
sonified the ties of kinship and friendship between Ireland and the
United States. Together with the Irish people, we mourn his passing."
   John Thornton, editor of the *Irish Echo*, was quoted as saying: "He [de Valera] was probably the single Irishman who influenced
history the most in this century."

   OCTOBER 15. New York City Council President Paul O'Dwyer
along with officials from the A.F.L.-C.I.O. and groups representing
pro-Catholic Irish opinion testified before an *ad hoc* Congressional
forum. Mr. O'Dwyer warned the representatives that unless the United
States intervened, a full-scale civil war would sweep Northern Ireland. He stated that he believed that the region "will be in chaos
and the militant majority, armed to the teeth, will descend on the
minority to drive them to their death. The last and only hope lies
in American intervention." Matt Higgins, speaking for the Irish
Northern Aid group, was on hand to answer questions as was Seamas
Naughton who represented the National Association of Irish Freedom.

   NOVEMBER 25. The Duke of Leinster, Ireland's eighty-three
year old ranking peer, arrived in New York with his wife to raise
funds for victims of terrorism in Northern Ireland.

   DECEMBER 22. The Justice Department announced that five
Irish Americans were being indicted on charges of smuggling guns and
ammunition to the Irish Republic Army in Northern Ireland. The five
naturalized citizens of Irish descent were charged with shipping
378 rifles and 140,000 rounds of ammunition to the IRA from August
1970 to date. Previously, there had been eleven indictments and ten
convictions of Americans in connection with shipments of arms to
Ireland.

   Art Carney, star of stage, screen and television, received
the Academy Award for best actor for his performance in *Harry and
Tonto*.

   Jimmy Breslin, newspaper columnist and author, published *How
the Good Guys Finally Won*. Among his other books are: *The Gang
That Couldn't Shoot Straight*(1969) and *World Without End, Amen*(1973).

   Edmund G. Brown, Jr. was elected Governor of California.

   After two years in India, Daniel P. Moynihan returned to the
United States to take up his new position as the United States permanent representative to the United Nations.

1976   JANUARY. The granddaughter of the Irish poet William Butler
    Yeats, Caitriona Yeats, who was living in Brookline, Mass-
achusetts, appeared in a performance entitled *The Best of
Ireland* at Carnegie Hall in New York City. Ms. Yeats is a
professional harpist.

MARCH 1. A memorial mass for Francis Stagg, a thirty-four
year old Irish republican prisoner who died after a sixty-one day
hunger strike, took place in New York City and eight other cities in
the United States and Canada. In Manhattan, one thousand people
attended a memorial mass at the Carmelite church and over three
thousand marched up Third Avenue and rallied at the United Nations.

MARCH 14. A feature article entitled "The Last Hurrah"
written by William V. Shannon appeared in the *New York Times Magazine*. The catch line of the article read "Irish-Americans have become so assimilated that few feel personally involved in the Ulster
crisis. Still, through their gifts for politics and controversy,
they retain a distinctive identity." Mr. Shannon was a member of
the *New York Times* editorial board and the author of *The American
Irish*.

MARCH 17. The annual St. Patrick's Day Parade in New York
City began with the blowing of a whistle by Police Officer Patrick
Skelly who was born in Ballyjamesduff in County Cavan, Ireland. Mr.
Skelly was followed up Fifth Avenue by Governor Carey who was the
grand marshal of the parade leading the 193 bands and 240 Irish or-
ganizations and what was estimated to be 119,000 marchers.

MARCH 17. In a St. Patrick's Day speech to a joint session
of Congress, Prime Minister Liam Cosgrave of the Irish Republic
strongly urged Americans to stop sending aid to extremist groups in
the troubled island.

JUNE 13. The forty-fourth annual feis of the United Irish
Counties Association took place at St. Joseph's Seminary in Yonkers,
New York.

It was a successful year for Jimmy Connors who was ranked
number one male tennis player in the United States and the world.
During the year he won the Cologne Cup, the United States Clay
Court Championship-Men's Singles, the United States Open-Men's Sin-
gles, the Pro Indoor Men's Singles and was a member of the Davis
Cup Team and the World Cup Team.

The New York senatorial race was won by Daniel Moynihan. Although a freshman Senator, he was quick to take a place on the powerful Finance Committee and on the Environment and Public Works Committee.

James T. Farrell published *The Dunne Family*. The following
is only a sample of the author's many books, which include: *Gas
House McGinty* (1933), *A World I Never Made* (1936), *Tommy Gallagher's
Crusade* (1939), *The Life Adventurous* (1947), *It Has Come to Pass* (1958),

The Silence of History (1963) and *Judith and Other Stories* (1974).

1977   JANUARY 4. Representative Thomas P. O'Neill, a Democrat from Massachusetts, was elected Speaker of the House on a 290 to 142 party-line vote thereby defeating Representative John Rhodes, a Republican from Arizona.

MARCH 16. On the eve of St. Patrick's Day, four prominent politicians of Irish descent voiced an appeal for an end to violence in Northern Ireland. Thomas P. O'Neill, the Speaker of the House of Representatives, Senator Edward M. Kennedy of Massachusetts, Senator Daniel P. Moynihan of New York and Governor Hugh Carey of New York pleaded their cause that violence could not help achieve a just and peaceful settlement. The four Democrats urged Americans to embrace the goal of peace and "to renounce any action that promotes the current violence or provides support or encouragement for organizations engaged in violence."

MARCH 17. The twenty-sixth annual St. Patrick's Day Parade in Chicago was dedicated to Mayor Richard J. Daley who died the previous December.

MARCH 17. About 120,000 people marched in the 215th annual St. Patrick's Day Parade up Fifth Avenue, while an estimated one million others stood by watching the spectacle.

MARCH 19. Ireland's foreign minister, Garret FitzGerald, ended a four-day visit to Washington, D.C. Dr. FitzGerald was happy to report that he had found the Carter administration to be "totally in line" with Dublin's views on Northern Ireland.

MAY 18. Senator Edward Kennedy delivered a speech at the Ireland Fund dinner in New York City. He addressed his remarks to "the violence of both sides, Protestant as well as Catholic, U.D.A. (Ulster Defense Association) as well as I.R.A." He urged that while the killing continued in Northern Ireland "let no American have it on his conscience that his efforts or his dollars helped to make the violence worse."

AUGUST 30. President Carter promised that if Roman Catholics and Protestants in Northern Ireland settled their differences peacefully, "the United States government would be prepared to join with others to see how additional job-creating investments could be encouraged, to the benefit of all the people of Northern Ireland."

SEPTEMBER. Lord O'Neill of Shane's Castle, County Antrim, the chairman of the North Ireland Tourist Board, was in New York City to express his conviction that it was once again safe for Americans to travel to the six counties of Ulster.

OCTOBER 14. Bing (Harry Lillis) Crosby, the popular singer and screen actor, died at the age of seventy-three. During his fifty-year career, he made more than 850 recordings and sold over three hundred million records including the biggest-selling single ever produced, *White Christmas*. Mr. Crosby appeared in nearly seventy major motion pictures and won an Academy Award for his performance in *Going My Way*(1944).

OCTOBER 15. Some seventy objects encompassing a three thousand year period beginning with the Bronze Age, from the collections of the National Museum of Ireland, the Royal Irish Academy and Trinity College, Dublin, were displayed at the Metropolitan Museum of Art in New York City in an exhibition entitled *Treasures of Early Irish Art*. The show, which was to travel to San Francisco, Pittsburgh, Boston and Philadelphia, included such important pieces as the Book of Kells and the Ardagh Chalice.

OCTOBER 29. The Irish Arts Center's Celtic New Year Festival was held in New York City. The festival, in celebration of Samhain, the end of harvesting and the beginning of another cycle of planning and hoping for a more productive year ahead, is a rite of ancient Ireland.

DECEMBER 12. Governor Hugh Carey of New York was presented with the United Cerebral Palsey Humanitarian Award.

Michael Harrington, a professor of political science and well-known author, published *The Vast Majority: A Journey to the World's Poor*. Among the other books he has written are: *The Other America*(1963), *The Accidental Century*(1965), *Socialism*(1972) and *Twilight of Capitalism*(1976).

THE ITALIANS IN AMERICA

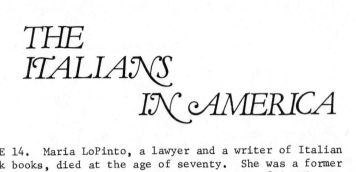

1970 JUNE 14. Maria LoPinto, a lawyer and a writer of Italian cook books, died at the age of seventy. She was a former president of the Italian Professional Women of America.

JUNE. Alfred E. Santangelo was elected president of Americans of Italian Descent, Inc. He succeeded Philip Vitello, a lawyer who held the post for two years.

JULY. Attorney General Mitchell, backed by President Nixon, informed the Justice Department and the FBI that they would have to stop using the terms "Mafia" and "Cosa Nostra" because it offended decent Italian Americans. This action was a result of many complaints and protests which had been voiced by individuals and Italian American organizations across the United States.

OCTOBER 11. Two thousand members and guests of the Columbus Citizens Committee attended a dinner in honor of the Italian navigator. Governor Rockefeller, who appeared at the ceremony, said that the Italian American family "holds up a model for America."

OCTOBER. It was announced that Gian Carlo Menotti had resumed the presidency of Festival Foundation, the organization that raises funds in the United States for the annual Festival of Two Worlds held in Spoleto, Italy.

NOVEMBER. Approximately five thousand people attended an Italian American Civil Rights League benefit in New York City at which time it was announced that the organization planned to build a three and one-half million dollar hospital in Brooklyn. Frank Sinatra entertained the guests who contributed $500,000 to the organization.

Giorgio Cavallon, an Italian-born artist, was presented with an award for painting by the National Institute of Arts and Letters. Mr. Cavallon came to the United States in 1920 and became a citizen in 1929.

Sebastian Leone was the first American of Italian descent to

The author is indebted to Anthony F. LoGatto, the editor of THE ITALIANS IN AMERICA, for his research covering the period 1970 to 1972.

serve as borough president of Brooklyn, New York. Because of its
large population, Brooklyn is often referred to as "the fourth largest city in America."

M. Henry Martuscello was appointed by Governor Rockefeller
as associate justice of the Appellate Division of the New York State
Supreme Court.

Anne Bancroft (nee Anna Maria Luisa Italiano), a star of theater, films and television, was presented with an Emmy Award for her
performance in the CBS television production of *Annie, the Woman in
the Life of a Man.*

Arcangelo W. Salomone, a professor of history who was born
in Guardiagrele, Italy in 1915 and was brought to the United States
in 1927, published *Italy From the Risorgimento to Fascism.* Ten years
earlier he had been decorated by the Italian Republic with the knight-
officer Order of Merit.

The Federation of Italian American Organizations was founded.
Its primary function is to preserve the Italian customs and language
in the United States and to promote political action and social programs that will prove beneficial to the Italian American community.

The winner of the Sculptor of the Year award presented by the
American Numismatic Association was Ralph J. Menconi. Mr. Menconi
has designed many medals among which are included the President Kennedy Campaign medal(1963), the Winston Churchill medal(1965), President Nixon's Inaugural medal and a medal commemorating Man's First
Lunar Landing.

The Ealing Corporation of Cambridge, Massachusetts released
a four-minute super 8mm film entitled *Italian Americans*, as part of
its Ethnic Groups Series. The film included scenes of four genera-
tions of Italian Americans at a traditional Sunday dinner in New
York's Little Italy.

1971   JANUARY. Joseph Colombo was named Man of the Year for 1970
        by the *Tri-Boro Post*, a weekly newspaper regarded in Italian
        American circles as the unofficial voice of the Italian Amer-
        ican Civil Rights League.

JANUARY. An exhibition entitled *The Eighteenth Century in
Italy: Drawings from New York Collections*, which had been in prepara-
tion for three years, opened at the Metropolitan Museum of Art in
New York City.

MARCH. It was announced that at the request of the Italian
American Civil Rights League all references to the Mafia and Cosa
Nostra would be eliminated from the screenplay of *The Godfather*.
The film was based on the book by Mario Puzo who also wrote the
screenplay.

MAY 14. The Urban Coalition and the Congress of Italian American Organizations formed an alliance to be called the New York Project that would be headed by Ralph J. Perrotta. The primary aim of the alliance is to get Italian Americans more involved in dealing with community social problems such as drug addiction, school drop-outs, day-care centers and health care facilities.

JUNE 28. The second annual Unity Day rally in Columbus Circle, sponsored by the Italian American Civil Rights League, was disrupted when Joseph A. Colombo, Sr., the founder of the organization, was shot in the head and critically wounded.

JULY 3. Camp Unity, the summer camp established for children by the Italian American Civil Rights League, was dedicated. The camp was located in Ulster County, New York.

John A. Volpe was appointed by President Nixon to the United States cabinet as secretary of transportation.

Pascal Francis Lucchesi, who was born in Sicily in 1903 and received his M.D. from Jefferson Medical College in Philadelphia in 1926, was appointed consultant to the president of Albert Einstein Medical Center in Philadelphia. Dr. Lucchesi had previously served as the executive vice president and medical director of this institution from 1952 to 1970.

Bruno A. Boley was named Outstanding Educator of America by the New York Academy of Sciences. Professor Boley, an engineer, was born in Gorizia, Italy and came to the United States in 1939, becoming a citizen six years later.

John A. Scali was appointed Special Consultant to the President.

Edward Speno, former lawyer and senator of the New York State legislature, died. He was known for his dedication and struggle to secure legislation providing financial aid to parents and children in private and parochial schools. He was the co-author of the famous Speno-Lerner bill.

 1972   MARCH. The Congress of Italian American Organizations (CIAO) sponsored a symposium attended by Italians, Blacks, Puerto Ricans and Jews in order to explore creative solutions to problems posed by inter-ethnic conflicts. The keynote address was delivered by Monsignor G. Baroni, the director of the National Center for Urban Ethnic Affairs.

APRIL 10. The Academy of Motion Picture Arts and Sciences presented an Oscar for the best foreign film for 1971 to the producers of *The Garden of the Finzi-Continis*.

MAY 10. The Federal grand jury charged the Italian American

Civil Rights League and two of its officers, N. Marcone, president and C. Vitale, secretary-treasurer, with fraudulently obtaining a $6,000 bank loan.

JUNE 11. The first Italian Heritage Cultural Festival, hailing A. Meucci as the inventor of the telephone, was held in New York City's Central Park. The festival was organized by the executive director of the Italian Historical Society of America, J.N. La Corte, who claimed that he had documentation discrediting A. G. Bell and attributing the invention of the telephone to A. Meucci. The festival was held in order to "promote greater appreciation of the basic human values, and to encourage youths to become more meaningfully involved in the enhancement of Man's dignity."

SEPTEMBER 17. President Nixon accompanied by his wife and younger daughter attended the Italian Fall Festival in Mitchellville, Maryland. In addressing the gathering, he stated that Italian Americans had "a strong sense of patriotism" and that they "are proud of their Italian background, but they are proud first of being Americans."

SEPTEMBER 30. The body of F. Concippio, an Italian immigrant murdered in 1911 who had been employed as a carnival worker, was buried. He had been on display in a glass coffin in a funeral home in Laurinburg, North Carolina for sixty years. The burial took place after numerous complaints were made that the mummified corpse was an insult to Italian Americans. Among those who registered protests were Representatives Biaggi and Broyhill and Italian Consul F. Anfuso.

OCTOBER 8. President Nixon addressed a Columbus Day banquet in Washington, D.C. which was sponsored by various Italian American organizations. The President presented the groups' Man of the Year award to Peter Fosco, the general president of the 650,000-member Laborers' International Union of North America, a major affiliate of the A.F.L.-C.I.O.

NOVEMBER. An exhibition entitled *Ottocento Painting in American Collections* opened at the New York Cultural Center. The show included fifty-six works by thirty-one artists and provided a survey of nineteenth century Italian painting.

Michael Pasquale Balzano, Jr., Ph.D., son of Italian immigrants, a high school dropout and former garbageman, was made a White House staff assistant to President Nixon.

Rocco C. Siciliano, a specialist in labor-management relations from California, was appointed by President Nixon as the sole business representative on the Pay Board.

Vince Lombardi, the coach of the Green Bay Packers, was elected to the Football Hall of Fame. He led the Green Bay Packers to win five National Football League titles and the first two Super Bowls.

Alan Alda, actor, director and writer whose real name is Alphonso D'Abruzzo, starred as Hawkeye in the CBS television production *M*A*S*H*. Both he and his father, Robert Alda (Alphonso Giovanni Giusseppe Roberto D'Abruzzo) have had a long career in the entertainment field, playing leading roles in television, motion pictures and the theater.

John P. Lomenzo, secretary of state for New York, was appointed by President Nixon to the National Advisory Council on Supplementary Centers and Services with the Department of Health, Education and Welfare.

The American Committee on Italian Migration (ACIM), which was established in New York in 1952, began publication of its monthly, *The New Way*.

Colonel Ralph D. Albertazzie was assigned to be the pilot of President Nixon's official plane, *Spirit of '76*.

Vincent Gardenia, the actor who was born Vincenzio Scognamiglio in Naples, won the Antoinette Perry (Tony) Award as best supporting actor for his performance as Harry Edison in *The Prisoner of Second Avenue*.

1973   MARCH 2. Guido Nincheri, whose paintings and stained glass windows adorn about one hundred churches in the United States and abroad, died at the age of eighty-six. He was the recipient of four papal awards for his devotional art.

JUNE. It was reported that the restoration of a nineteenth century carriage house on the campus of Seton Hall University in New Jersey was made possible by a $65,000 gift from the Father Monella Center of Italian Culture in Newark and a $60,000 grant from the Kress Foundation. The building was to be converted into an art center that would contain studios, faculty and departmental offices, a lecture hall and an art gallery. The art center was to be named for Father Monella, the founder of the Italian Culture Center which is affiliated with Seton Hall University.

AUGUST. The Feast of St. Anthony at North Hudson County Park began, organized to pay tribute to the Italian Americans who comprise about thirty-seven percent of New Jersey's population. The feast was expected to draw over 300,000 people who would participate in the more than 300 rides and attractions. Some of the proceeds were to be contributed to the Boys Town of Italy.

OCTOBER 7. Former Judge Juvenal Marchisio, who led Italian relief activities in the United States during and after World War II, died at the age of seventy. He was a founder and president of the Boys Republic of Italy and was a national chairman of the American Committee on Italian Migration. For his service to Italy, Mr. Marchisio was decorated by Popes Pius XII and John XXII as well as by the Italian government.

Children of Columbus: An Informal History of the Italians in the New World, by Erik Amfitheatrof, was published. In his book the author writes: "The fact is that Italian-Americans have always been notoriously defensive about their ethnic heritage. A proud people, they have had to struggle - like other minorities - against a debilitating sense of always having to measure themselves by Anglo-Saxon values and standards."

Carlo L. Golino, a professor of Italian who was born in Pescara, Italy, was made chancellor of the University of Massachusetts in Boston. Professor Golino was the editor of the *Italian Quarterly* from 1957. In addition, he was the recipient of the Italian government's Star of Solidarieta in 1958.

Joseph Tusiani, an author and professor of Italian literature, was made a cavaliere of the Italian Republic. Professor Tusiani, who was born in Foggia, Italy and became a citizen of the United States in 1956, has published a number of books, including: *Dante in Licenza*(1952), *The Complete Poems of Michelangelo*(1960), *Envoy from Heaven*(1965) and *From Marino to Marinetti*(1973).

The Federation of Italian American Organizations began publication of its weekly *Avanti*.

Verrazzano College, the first Italian college in the United States, opened in Saratoga Springs in New York, with Mario Procaccino as its first president.

WOP! A Documentary History of Anti-Italian Discrimination in the United States edited by Salvatore J. LaGumina was published as part of the Ethnic Prejudice in America series, by Straight Arrow Books. This volume examines the factors which led to anti-Italian discrimination as manifested in the United States before and after 1880.

1974   FEBRUARY. Representatives of the Italian Historical Society of America congratulated Yale University for admitting that the Vinland Map showing America as discovered by the Vikings hundreds of years before Columbus was a forgery.

MARCH. An exhibition of abstract painting by the seventy-year old Italian-born artist Giorgio Cavallon was held at the Sachs Gallery in New York City.

MARCH. An exhibition entitled *Twilight of the Medici. Late Baroque Art in Florence: 1670-1743* was held at the Detroit Institute of Art. The 310 works being displayed included bronze and marble sculptures, paintings, tapestries, furniture, jewelry, drawings and many kinds of unusual decorative objects.

MAY 28. The consul general of Italy in New York established a vice consulate in Newark, New Jersey. The new office was organized to serve the 345,000 Italian citizens and Italian-Americans living in the surrounding eight northern New Jersey counties.

JUNE 8. An historian of science, Giorgio Diaz de Santillana, who was a professor of history and the philosophy of science at the Massachusetts Institute of Technology from 1941, died. Born in Rome in 1902, he emigrated to the United States in 1936. Among his published works are: *The Crime of Galileo* (1955), *The Origins of Scientific Thought* (1961) and *Reflections and Ideas* (1968).

JUNE 23. The Reverend Charles B. Casale, assisted by an Italian American priest from each of New Jersey's Roman Catholic dioceses, celebrated a mass that would open the festivities of the fourth annual Italian festival at the Garden State Arts Center in Holmdel, New Jersey. A New Jersey State Assembly resolution had declared the week ending that day as Italian-American Heritage Week in the state.

SEPTEMBER 28. The Italian American Labor Council sponsored a dinner in honor of President Giovanni Leone of Italy at which virtually all of the Italian American cultural and political groups in New York City were represented.

SEPTEMBER. A Guglielmo Marconi Award was established to mark the 100th birthday of the radio pioneer. Dr. Joseph Slater of the Aspen Institute for Humanistic Studies said that the purpose of the award would be to "commission creative work by scientists, engineers or other persons who have demonstrated their commitment to the application of science or technology to humanistic goals."

SEPTEMBER. Ernie DiGregorio of the Buffalo Braves, the rookie of the year in the National Basketball Association, was invited to attend a White House dinner in honor of President Leone of Italy.

OCTOBER 14. The longest Columbus Day Parade up Fifth Avenue was said to include 100,000 marchers along with politicians, majorettes, mounted policemen, bands, cheerleaders and floats. Frank Capra, the film director who served as grand marshal, described it as "a knockout production."

NOVEMBER 10. Mario Albi, president of UNICO National, announced that eight literary and journalism awards amounting to ten thousand dollars had been made available to young authors of Italian American descent. Any United States citizen of Italian extraction between the ages of eighteen and thirty-five was eligible to enter the contest sponsored by UNICO (unity, neighborliness, integrity, charity and opportunity).

NOVEMBER. Enrico Donati had an exhibition of his paintings at the Staempfli Gallery in New York City.

Three major books about Americans of Italian descent were published: *A Documentary History of the Italian Americans,* edited by Wayne Moquin and Charles Van Doren; *The Italians: Social Back-gounds of an American Group*, by Francesco Cordasco and Eugene Buc-chioni; and *Ethnic Alienation: The Italian-Americans*, by Patrick J. Gallo. The first two books are of an historical nature and contain a collection of journal articles and other selected readings which illustrate different stages of Italian emigration and community life in the United States. The third book examines a topical problem, alienation, and analyzes both community and family patterns with reference to Italian Americans.

The Italian Historical Society of America observed the twen-ty-fifth anniversary of its founding.

Saverio S. DiFalco, an Italian-born American judge, became president of the American Justinian Society of Jurists.

Funding made available by the United States Office of Educa-tion led to the establishment of the Ethnic Heritage Studies Program at Indiana University's South Bend campus. The organization seeks to encourage mutual awareness and respect among ethnic groups and to eliminate myths, incorrect assumptions and stereotypes by studying and disseminating information on the Italian Americans and four other ethnic groups.

1975   FEBRUARY 4. Frank L. Pandolfi, who was born in Mormanno,

Cosenza and came to the United States in 1912, died. Mr. Pandolfi was the executive director of the Connecticut Opera Association in Hartford from 1942. In 1968, he was decora-ted commendatore dell'Ordine della Stella della Solidarieta Italiana by the Italian Republic.

MARCH 22. An official report released by the Italian govern-ment stated that more than twenty-five million of its citizens had emigrated over the last one hundred years, less than a third of whom had returned to their own country. Of these twenty-five million Italians, eleven million settled in North America with a little over half this number emigrating to the United States (the exact official number was 5,668,947).

APRIL. Attending a meeting of the Italy-America Chamber of Commerce in New York City, Italy's ambassador to the United States, Egidio Ortano, asserted that his country was far from being on the brink of collapse. He felt that the government had made positive moves in reversing the high rate of inflation.

JULY. Mark Clark, the seventy-nine year old retired general who led the Fifth Army into Rome as its liberator from German occu-pation, was presented with Italy's highest award, the Grand Cross of the Order of Merit of the Italian Republic.

The secretary of state of New York, Mario M. Cuomo, was the featured speaker at the two-day session of the annual meeting of the

Italian American Historical Association. Most of the 300 professors and other Italian Americans attending the conference agreed that as a minority group they had to become more organized and involved, thereby increasing their political impact. Among those participating in the conference were: Luciano Iorizzo, president of the organization sponsoring the meetings, the American Italian Historical Association, and Arcangelo D'Amore, a Washington psychiatrist who founded the Group for the Study of Italian Americans.

Professor Luigi Romeo, who was born in Tropea, Italy in 1926 and came to the United States in 1953, published two books in his field of specialization: *Current Trends in Linguistics* and *History of Linguistics*.

The New York Public Library produced an annotated bibliography, *Writings on Italian-Americans*, edited by Carmine Diodati, Jean Coleman and Joseph Valletutti. The selected material covers Italian American artists, business people, laborers, politicians, scholars and writers.

1976   JANUARY 15. Albino Manca, the sculptor born in Sardinia who came to the United States in 1938, died at the age of seventy-eight. He created many pieces, but is best known for his cast bronze busts of Metropolitan Opera stars including Rosa Ponselle, Ezio Pinza and Maria Jeritza.

FEBRUARY 12. Sal Mineo, a young actor who during his career had been twice nominated for an Academy Award, was killed. He appeared in such movie productions as *Rebel Without a Cause*, *Dino*, *Exodus* and *Escape to Zahrian*. In 1969, he directed *Fortune in Men's Eyes* which had a successful run in both Los Angeles and New York theaters and which he later directed as a screen version.

FEBRUARY 26. The Italian Historical Society of America filed a suit with the Federal District Court to prevent the United States Postal Service from issuing a commemorative stamp honoring Alexander Graham Bell as the inventor of the telephone. The organization felt that the issuance of the stamp would "dishonor" Antonio Meucci, whom they described as the real inventor of the telephone.

MARCH. Gian Carlo Menotti, president of the joint Italian American venture, the Festival of Two Worlds in Spoleto, Italy, announced that Charleston, South Carolina had been chosen as the site for the Spoleto Festival, U.S.A. which would take place in 1977.

APRIL. It was reported that Albert P. Schrager, the publisher, was preparing a magazine specifically for Italian Americans that would be called *I-AM*. Marco C. Napoli, who had been with *Il Progresso*, was to be the editor.

MAY. The Boat Jumper, an Italian American social organization in New Jersey, celebrated its twentieth anniversary. The re-

cipients of the annual Boat Jumpers awards were: Judge Benedict E.
Lucchi, Judge John J. Cariddi and Dr. Alfred A. Alessir. Patrick
DiZenzo, president of the club, presided.

MAY. The American Institute of Verdi Studies was established
under the directorship of New York University Professor Martin Chusid
with the assistance of Verdi biographer Mary Jane Matz and *New Yorker*
critic Andrew Porter. The institute, as described by Prof. Chusid,
"will serve as a center for the accumulation and dissemination of all
kinds of information and material relating to Verdi." Andrew Porter
would edit the institute's biannual newsletter.

AUGUST 31. Jimmy Carter met with a gathering of Italian American leaders at Automation House in New York City. The group included
the Reverend Louis F. Gigante, chairman of the Italian American Committee, and Peter Cella, chairman of the Columbian Coalition.

SEPTEMBER 16. The fiftieth annual Feast of San Gennaro opened
when the silver and brass bust of the Italian saint was carried down
Mulberry Street in New York City, where it was placed in a temporary
shrine. It was estimated that over one million visitors attended
the celebration.

OCTOBER 15. Sicilian-born Carlo Gambino, the leader of New
York's largest Mafia "family", died at the age of seventy-four.

OCTOBER. Dr. Francesco Cordasco, a professor of education
at Montclair State College, was awarded the Order of Merit by the
Italian government.

DECEMBER 6. Prime Minister Giulio Andreotti opened a three
day visit to the United States at a White House ceremony prior to
his private talks with President Ford and Secretary of State Kissinger.

Jeno F. Paulucci, the food company executive who was chairman
of the board of Jeno's Inc. and Jeno F. Paulucci Enterprises, was
named chairman of the board of the new Italian American Foundation
in Washington, D.C. He would oversee a nine-member board that included Joseph L. Alioto, mayor of San Francisco; Jack Valenti, president
of the Motion Picture Association of America; and John Volpe, United
States ambassador to Italy. The organization would act as a clearing-
house to spotlight and do research on issues that negatively affect
Italian Americans.

 1977   MARCH 28. The forty-ninth annual awards of the Academy of
Motion Picture Arts and Sciences chose *Rocky*, the story of a
small-time fighter who gets a chance at the big time, as
best picture of the year. The film also won an Oscar for
best director and best editing. The screenplay was written by Sylvester Stallone who also played the leading role.

APRIL 21. Monsignor Geno Baroni was sworn in as assistant secretary of Housing and Urban Development for neighborhoods, non-governmental organizations and consumer protection. As a founder of the Washington-based National Center for Urban Ethnic Affairs, the monsignor helped channel millions of dollars in grants to local community groups.

MAY 26. The Spoleto Arts Festival-U.S.A. opened its twelve days of performances and activities in Charleston, South Carolina.

JULY 22. The Sons of Italy of Baltimore bought a thirty-four foot Venetian gondola named *Gina* to be used as the centerpiece in the city's fifth annual Italian Festival. The gondola was later added to Baltimore's fleet of dockbound vessels.

AUGUST 12. The Holy Rosary Roman Catholic Church in Jersey City, New Jersey sponsored a traditional five-day Italian Village Street Festival, the first to be held there in fifteen years.

AUGUST 23. Governor Michael S. Dukakis of Massachusetts proclaimed the day to be Nicola Sacco and Bartolomeo Vanzetti Memorial Day, marking the fiftieth anniversary of the execution in Boston of these two Italian immigrants. The Governor held that the 1921 trial of Sacco and Vanzetti and the subsequent judicial reviews were "permeated by prejudice" and that the conduct of many officials cast "serious doubt" on their impartiality.

SEPTEMBER 28. Surrounded by dozens of Americans of Italian descent, President Carter in a White House ceremony proclaimed October 10 to be Columbus Day. Speaking of Italian influences on government, the President noted the presence of Federal District Judge John J. Sirica and Representative Peter W. Rodino, Jr., chairman of the House Judiciary Committee.

DECEMBER 6. Alfred Iacuzzi, a past president of the American Association of Teachers of Italian who for twenty years was the chairman of the department of romance languages at Baruch College, New York, died at the age of eighty-one. Professor Iacuzzi was born in Italy but was brought to the United States as a child.

DECEMBER 28. Francis Ford Coppola, the director of *The God-father* and other successful Hollywood films, was presented with Hofstra University's first honorary Doctor of Fine Arts degree. Mr. Coppola received his bachelor's degree in drama at Hofstra in 1959 and was one of the founders of the Spectrum Players, the student drama company.

It was proposed that the old police headquarters on Centre Street in New York City, which had been leased by the Little Italy Restoration Association (LIRA), should not be used solely as a national center for Italian American culture but should rather express the multinational flavor of the area.

THE
JAPANESE
IN AMERICA

1970   JANUARY 28. The National Leadership Conference on Civil
Rights endorsed the Japanese American Citizens League (JACL)
campaign to repeal Title II, the detention camp measure, of
the Internal Security Act.

MARCH 24. Six JACL witnesses testified at the House Internal Security Committee hearing on the Title II repeal bill. Jerry
Enomoto read Justice Earl Warren's letter against Title II into the
record.

APRIL 7. Sgt. Rodney Yano of Hilo, Hawaii was awarded the
Medal of Honor posthumously by President Nixon. Sgt. Yano died in
Vietnam on January 1, 1969.

JUNE 22. The Voting Rights Act Amendment of 1970 eliminated
the literacy test requirement for entrance into the United States.

JULY 13. President Nixon signed an immigration bill to ad-
mit 205 Japanese residents from the Bonin Islands who claimed American sailors as their ancestors.

SEPTEMBER 16. Harry I. Iseki, mayor of Parlier, California,
died.

OCTOBER 24. In New York, the JACL honored eighty year old
Yoneo Arai, the oldest living Nisei in the United States, for his
many contributions.

OCTOBER 28. Kyoichi Sawada, a Pulitzer Prize-winning Issei
photographer for United Press International, died in Cambodia while
on assignment.

NOVEMBER 3. Representatives Spark Matsunaga and Patsy T.
Mink, both of Hawaii, were reelected.

NOVEMBER 4. William Mo Marumoto was appointed a presidential
assistant on executive manpower, thus becoming the first Nisei to
be named to the White House staff.

---

*The author is indebted to Masako Herman, the editor of THE JAPANESE IN AMERICA, for
his research covering the period 1970 to 1973.*

DECEMBER 3.   A new exhibition entitled *Contemporary Japanese Art: Fifth Japan Art Festival* opened at the Guggenheim Museum in New York City, in cooperation with the Japan Art Festival Association.

DECEMBER 7.   George R. Ariyoshi of Honolulu was sworn in as the nation's first lieutenant governor of Japanese descent.   Coincidentally, the ceremony took place on the twenty-ninth anniversary of the Japanese attack on Pearl Harbor.

Dr. Paul K. Kuroda received the Southwest Regional Award of the American Chemistry Society.

The JACL Nisei of the Biennium was Dr. Paul I. Terasaki who had worked in the field of tissue immunology.   Also honored were Dr. S. I. Hayakawa of California State University and Shiro Kashiwa, assistant district attorney from Washington, D.C.

Seiji Ozawa became conductor of the San Francisco Symphony Orchestra.

At a testimonial for Mike Masaoka in Chicago, a trust fund was established in his name.

Dr. Kenichi Nishimoto, Indian Health Service administrator, was elected to the city council in Takoma Park, Maryland, thus becoming the first Nisei councilman on the East coast.

President Nixon signed into law amendments to the 1965 Immigration Act which reflected directly on Asian immigration.

An exhibition of sculptures by Leo Amino was held at the East Hampton Gallery, New York.   Mr. Amino was born in Japan in 1911 and came to the United States in 1929.

1971   SEPTEMBER 23.   President Nixon signed the Title II Repeal bill into Public Law 92-128.

SEPTEMBER.   The Japan Society in New York City moved to its new location, a five-story black cement building at 333 East 47th Street.   It is said to be the first building in New York designed by a Japanese architect, Junzo Yoshimura.   The art gallery on the second floor is open to the public.   The first exhibition held at the new gallery was of Japanese Rimpa art of the seventeenth and eighteenth century.

SEPTEMBER.   Shig Kariya became the first Nisei president of the Japanese American Association of New York.

DECEMBER 13.   The JACL drafted a bill to establish a cabinet committee on Asian Americans which was introduced to the House by Congressmen Spark Matsunaga of Hawaii and Glenn M. Anderson of California.   Twenty-three other representatives acted as cosponsors of the bill.

Norman Y. Mineta was elected mayor of San Jose, California.

Christy Ito, the recipient of the Babbitt Award for five consecutive years (1967-1971), joined the Ice Follies.

Henry Hibino was elected councilman in Salinas, California.

Speaker of the House, Carl Albert, paid tribute to Mike Masaoka on the House floor.

Sculptor Isamu Noguchi was elected to the fifty-member American Academy of Arts and Letters in New York.

1972   JANUARY 6.   Shiro Kashiwa became the first American of Japanese ancestry appointed to a federal court as associate judge of the United States Court of Claims in Washington, D.C.

JANUARY 7.   President Nixon met with Prime Minister Eidsaku Sato in San Clemente, California, and discussed the May 5 Okinawa reversion.

JANUARY.   Asian American groups protested the showing of *Madame Sin*, the ABC television Movie of the Week.

MARCH 22.   Robert Kawaguchi, a veteran of the 100th Infantry Battalion who served as Golden Gate VFW Post Commander in San Francisco, died.

APRIL.   Niseis who were elected in California municipal elections were: Ken Nakaoka, mayor of Gardena; Paul Bannai, councilman of Gardena; Sak Yamamoto, councilman of Carson City; Dr. Tsujio Kato, councilman of Oxnard; Ken J. Nishio, councilman of Hemet City; Tom Kitayama, reelected councilman of Union City and S. Floyd Mori, councilman of Pleasanton.

MAY.   Mike M. Suzuki was appointed director of children and family services with the Department of Health, Education and Welfare.

MAY.   The treaty restoring the Ryukyu Islands (including Okinawa) to Japan formally ended the American occupation of Japan that began in 1945.

MAY.   Harvey A. Itano, M.D., Ph.D., received the first Rev. Dr. Martin Luther King, Jr. Medical Achievement Award for Outstanding Contributions in Research of Sickle Cell Anemia.   It was presented by the Philadelphia chapter of the Southern Christian Leadership Conference.

JUNE 12.   The federal legislature repealed two anti-Oriental laws: the 1872 law prohibiting entry of Orientals without permit, and the 1905 law banning the import of an Oriental woman with intent to force her to live with someone or to sell her.

JUNE. Bill Hosokawa, associate editor of the *Denver Post*, represented the United States communications media at the U.S.-Japan Assembly in Shimoda, Japan.

JUNE. Seiji Ozawa, the conductor, was in Japan to receive a Japan Art Academy Award at a ceremony attended by Emperor Hirohito.

AUGUST 22. The ILGWU's "Don't Buy Made in Japan" posters were denounced by the Asian American group in New York, and a request for their withdrawal was made.

SEPTEMBER 5. The Social and Rehabilitation Service of the Department of Health, Education and Welfare funded five West Coast Asian American programs totalling $524,000.

SEPTEMBER 15. An exhibition of documentary photographs recalling the internment of 110,000 Japanese Americans, native-born citizens and aliens alike, during World War II opened at the Whitney Museum of American Art. The show, organized by Maise and Richard Conrat of the California Historical Society, was called *Executive Order 9066*. The name of the show was taken from the 1942 order, signed by President Roosevelt, which led to many families of Japanese descent living on the West Coast to be sent to "relocation camps."

SEPTEMBER 19. NBC television presented *Guilty by Reason of Race*, a documentary about the Japanese American experience during World War II.

SEPTEMBER 22. Construction began on the Air and Space Museum at the Smithsonian Institution which was designed by Gyo Obata of St. Louis.

OCTOBER 25. The New York Asian American group picketed the ILGWU headquarters protesting the "racist" posters which it had been using in an anti-Japanese advertising campaign.

NOVEMBER. In an effort to better relations between the United States and Japan, the Japanese government endowed the Japan Foundation with sixteen million dollars to be used to support the studies of Americans in their country. Hidemi Kon, the Japanese novelist who was the first president of the foundation, hoped in three to four years that the organization would have an endowment of about $333 million and would be in the position to sponsor various cultural exchanges.

Washington Governor Daniel J. Evans formed the Asian American Advisory Council, which consisted of twenty members.

The National Institute for Mental Health granted $320,000 to the Asian American Drug Abuse Program in Los Angeles.

The JACL honored Dr. Makio Murayama as Nisei of the Biennium for his research dealing with sickle cell anemia.

Dr. Jin Kinoshita was appointed vision research director of the National Eye Institute in Bethesda, Maryland.

Michael Tadao Ito was named assistant district attorney in San Francisco.

Kenzo Takada, a Paris designer from Japan, signed an agreement with the Asian American group in New York City to stop using the anti-Nisei label, JAP. Butterick Patterns subsequently removed the offensive name from their catalogs.

Mitsubishi Corporation of Japan donated one million dollars to Harvard University for a program in Japanese legal studies.

The Japnese Artists Association of New York was organized in order to give Japanese artists a greater opportunity to show their works and to impróve cultural relations between the United States and Japan.

1973 JANUARY 11. An exhibition entitled *Namban Art* opened at the Japan House Gallery. It was the first show of Namban art, the art of the southern Barbarians, in the West.

APRIL. George Ise, a Nisei, was chosen by the city council to be mayor of Monterey Park, California.

MAY 2. Sak Yamamoto became mayor of Carson in Los Angeles county. He was appointed by the city council.

JUNE 18. At the annual dinner of Japan House, Hosai Hyuga, the president of Sumitomo Metal Industries, Ltd., presented John D. Rockefeller III, chairman of the society's board of directors, with a gift of one million dollars. The grant was to be used for policy studies aimed at improving Japanese-American understanding.

JUNE 22. Kingman Brewster, Jr., the president of Yale University, reported that Japan's Sumitomo Group of banking, mining and manufacturing interests had given two million dollars to the university in order to promote better Japanese-American relations. The gift was the largest ever received by the institution from a benefactor outside the country.

JUNE. To celebrate its fiftieth anniversary, the Freer Gallery of Art in Washington, D.C., a branch of the Smithsonian Institution, presented an exhibition of 100 Japanese Ukiyo-e paintings.

JULY. The first Japanese-style hotel in New York opened on Park Avenue. It was named the Kitano Hotel.

JULY. Henry Hibino was elected mayor of Salinas, California.

JULY. Masashi Kawaguchi, president and owner of the Fishking Processors, broke ground for a three million dollar plant in California.

AUGUST 7. The Japanese Government named ten American universities to share in a ten million dollar educational program. Shinsuke Hori, director general of the Cultural Affairs Department of the Foreign Ministry announced the universities chosen, which were: Harvard, Yale, Princeton, Columbia, California at Berkeley, Hawaii, Michigan, Chicago, Stanford and Washington (in Seattle). Each school would receive one million dollars to establish a professorship in Japanese studies and possibly to fund scholarships.

SEPTEMBER 2. Dr. Roy H. Doi, a bacteriologist at the University of California at Davis, presented a paper at the First International Congress of Bacteriology during a week of seminars and lectures in Jerusalem, Israel.

SEPTEMBER 5. William Mo Marumoto, the highest ranking Japanese American in the Nixon administration, resigned.

OCTOBER 23. Dr. Leo Esaki, an Issei in New York, received the Nobel Prize in physics for his electron tunneling theories.

Daniel K. Inouye, a United States senator from Hawaii since 1963, was made a member of the Senate Select Committee on Presidential Campaign Activities.

Richard Yoshikawa became president of the San Joaquin Delta College Board in California.

Dr. Kenneth N. Matsumura of the Immunity Research Laboratory was granted a patent for the world's first artificial liver.

Stanley Uyehara was named deputy city attorney for Los Angeles.

Jena Minako Kobayashi became a member of the New Christy Minstrels, a singing and instrumental group.

The Federal Equal Employment Opportunity Commission awarded $61,000 to Asian, Inc. of San Francisco for research on job discrimination.

Paul T. Bannai of Salinas, California was elected the first Nisei assemblyman.

David Ushio, national director of JACL, urged the prompt recall of offensive license plates bearing JAP or NIP combinations. Governor Ronald Reagan of California signed the necessary legislation authorizing the Department of Motor Vehicles to recall the offensive license plates.

During this year approximately 5,500 Japanese-born immigrants entered the United States.

1974   JANUARY 10. Shizue Iwatsuki, a seventy-seven year old

naturalized United States citizen, was in Japan to attend
the annual poetry-reading party given by Emperor Hirohito.
Mrs. Iwatsuki had entered a thirty-one syllable poem, a tan-
ka, in the competition with the hope that it would be chosen as one
of the ten to be read at the party. Her hopes were realized when
her poem, one of the thirty thousand entered in the yearly contest,
was picked as a winner.

JANUARY 25. An exhibition of Japanese calligraphy entitled
*Nihon Koten Bungei: The Courtly Tradition in Japanese Art and Liter-
ature*, opened at Japan House Gallery. The one hundred pieces included in the show were selected from the private collections of
two Americans and were organized by a committee of Harvard scholars.

SEPTEMBER. The Museum of Modern Art displayed nine lithographs by (Shusaku) Arakawa. They were said to synthesize many of
of the ideas that the artist included in his monumental series *The
Mechanism of Meaning*.

OCTOBER. The Brooklyn Museum in New York City opened four
new galleries devoted to Japanese and Korean art.

NOVEMBER 7. Suzushi Hanayagi gave a performance of four
solo Japanese classical dances at Japan House.

A resolution supporting Iva Toguri D'Aquino, who in 1949 was
convicted of treason for broadcasting Japanese propaganda during
World War II, was passed at a convention of the JACL.

*A Buried Past: An Annotated Bibliography of the Japanese
American Research Project Collection* compiled by Tuji Ichioka and
others was published by the University of California Press. The
volume catalogs the University of California at Los Angeles research
library's collection of approximately fifteen hundred Japanese gov-
government documents and other primary sources pertaining to Japanese
immigrants in the United States.

1975   JANUARY. At a ceremony at the New York Cultural Center, it

was announced that Isamu Nogurhi, whose abstract forms reflect both Oriental and surrealist influences, was chosen as
the second prize winner of a competition held by the Society
of Four Arts in Palm Beach, Florida. Mr. Nogurhi's prize of ten
thousand dollars was made possible by a grant by the Ziuta and Joseph Akston Foundation.

JUNE 18. Secretary of State Kissinger presented a major
United States policy speech at the fifth annual dinner of Japan
Society. In regard to Japanese-American relations, he said, "we
should recognize a higher standard of mutual concern than normally
obtains between states, accepting a greater obligation to consult,
to inform, and to harmonize domestic and external policies that im-

pinge on the interests of each other." The secretary of state continued to express his opinion that United States-Japanese relations
were the best they have been in thirty years.

AUGUST 5. President Ford met with Premier Takeo Miki of
Japan. He assured the prime minister "that the Indochina setback
has not altered the United States intention to continue to play a
major role in the maintenance of peace and stability in Asia."

AUGUST 7. During their White House meeting, President Ford
and Premier Miki agreed to cooperate to prevent the spread of nu-
clear weapons. The occasion marked the thirtieth anniversary of
the detonation of an American atomic bomb at Hiroshima, which was estimated to have killed eighty thousand people.

AUGUST. Leaders of the Los Angeles Japanese American community expressed their displeasure that Premier Miki did not meet
with them or visit the city's Little Tokyo. Apparently, it was
California's Japanese Americans who raised the first twenty thousand dollars that was used for the prime minister's campaign for
parliament.

SEPTEMBER 22. The Japan Foundation in Tokyo announced that
Edwin O. Reischauer, the Harvard professor who served as ambassador
to Japan, would be the recipient of the organization's 1975 prize.
Professor Reischauer, who is an expert on Japan and who is married
to a Japanese, was to be honored for "his outstanding contribution
to the promotion of cultural interchange between Japan and the United States."

SEPTEMBER 23. A special exhibition on the imperial family
of Japan opened at the International Building at Rockefeller Center,
New York City. Included in the display were: ceremonial costumes,
scrolls, instruments, two thrones, books by the emperor and empress,
one hundred photographs and many other objects, some of which had
never been publicly displayed before.

SEPTEMBER 30. Emperor Hirohito and Empress Nagako arrived
in the United States for a fifteen-day visit. Never before had a
reigning Japanese monarch made a formal visit to the United States.

OCTOBER 2. After being greeted at the White House by President and Mrs. Ford, Emperor Hirohito addressed the gathering. He
said that he regreted World War II; but he hoped that his visit
would contribute to "everlasting friendship" between the people of
Japan and the United States. He later said: "Our peoples withstood
the challenges of one tragic interlude when the Pacific Ocean, symbol of tranquility, was instead a rough and stormy sea, and have
built today unchanging ties of friendsip and good will."

The JACL, the national human rights and educational organization founded in 1930, reported a membership of approximately
thirty thousand.

1976   APRIL 9. At the first annual meeting of the newly-formed Southeast United States-Japan Association, representatives of Japan's largest corporations pledged to increase their investments and trade in the Southeast. The states belonging to the association are Alabama, Florida, Georgia, North Carolina, South Carolina, Virginia and Tennessee.

APRIL. A concert directed by Saeko Ichinohe was presented at Japan House. Miss Ichinohe, who has continually sought a meeting ground for traditional Japanese dance and the Western ballet and modern-dance styles, presented a diversified program.

JUNE 2. The Japanese-American Citizens League took a step forward in their efforts to obtain a pardon for Iva Toguri D'Aquino, convicted for treason as Tokyo Rose, the wartime broadcaster. A resolution asking President Ford to grant the pardon and restore her citizenship was passed by a committee of the California Legislature.

JUNE. It was announced that the members of the Nichiren Shoshu organization, the independently incorporated Western Hemisphere affiliate of Soka Gakkai, would participate in New York City's Bicentennial program on the Fourth of July weekend. The members of this lay organization, Soka Gakkai, are adherents of the thirteenth century Buddist saint, Nichiren. The first United States lay organization of this type was established in 1960 and now claims a membership of 250,000.

JULY. Japan's Bicentennial gift of fifty-three dwarf bonsai trees, including a 350 year-old white pine, was installed in a new garden built in the Agriculture Department's National Arboretum. Agriculture Secretary Earl Butz, in a formal dedication ceremony, said the bonsai collection would join Washington's display of Japanese cherry trees as "a living tribute to Japan's friendship."

SEPTEMBER. An exhibition of *Shinto Arts* opened at Japan House Gallery. None of these objects had ever been seen in this country before as they belong to the innermost sanctum of the Shinto shrine.

Mako, the Japanese American actor, director and playwright (nee Makoto Iwamatsu), made his broadway debut as the Reciter in *Pacific Overtures*. In 1966 he founded and was the artistic director of the East West Players and Children's Workshop in Los Angeles. It was a company dedicated to the training and development of Oriental American theatrical artists.

It was reported by the Japanese government that the United States remained the most popular destination for Japanese emigrants, drawing almost half the annual total.

The JACL adopted a resolution calling for a fair trial for Wendy Yoshimura, who was a fugitive from the authorities with Patricia Hearst.

1977 JANUARY 4. Senator Daniel K. Inouye was elected secretary of the Democratic Conference.

JANUARY 20. Wendy Yoshimura, a radical leftist who shared lodgings with Patricia Hearst when both were being sought by law officers, was found guilty on three counts of illegal possession of a machine gun and explosives. During her trial, Ms. Yoshimura was free on $25,000 bail, raised mainly by supporters in the Japanese American community.

MARCH 21. President Carter met with Japanese Premier Takeo Fukuda in Washington, D.C., and discussed a variety of subjects, including atomic energy, Japanese export practices and the presence of United States military forces in the Western Pacific.

MAY 18. The American Academy and Institute of Arts and Letters presented the Gold Medal for Sculpture to Isamu Noguchi at the thirty-seventh annual award ceremony.

JUNE 24. Yoko Ichio was awarded a bronze medal for her performance in the Third International Ballet Competition in Moscow.

OCTOBER 18. A Buddhist ceremony took place at the Kirkpatrick Chapel at Rutgers University in honor of eight Japanese students who died while studying at Rutgers in the late 1800s. The deaths of the nineteenth century Japanese students were attributed to a variety of reasons, from lack of acclimatization to overwork.

NOVEMBER 27. A four-member delegation from the United States Congress was in Tokyo to promote Japanese understanding of the Japan-America Friendship Fund, which was established by Congress to help Americans study the Japanese culture and Japanese study the American culture.

It was estimated that more than 450 Japanese companies were operating in New York City, part of a wave of direct Japanese investment in the United States that approached the one billion dollar mark, a fourfold increase since 1973. There were also some twenty thousand Japanese nationals reported to be working in New York City.

THE JEWS IN AMERICA

1970   Milton J. Shapp was the first Jew to be elected governor of
        Pennsylvania.

The Maryland state legislature elected Marvin Mandel to
succeed Spiro Agnew as governor of the state when Mr. Agnew resigned
to take office as vice president of the United States.

The world's only institution teaching ritual circumcision,
the Brith Milah School at Mt. Sinai Hospital in New York City,
graduated its first class.

The Society for Humanistic Judaism was founded in Farmington,
Massachusetts.

Edward Pringle was elected chief justice of the Colorado
Supreme Court. His elevation made him the third Jew to serve as
the head of the highest court in his state. The other two were:
Justice Joseph Weintraub, chief justice of the New Jersey Supreme
Court, and Chief Justice Stanley Fuld of the New York Court of
Appeals.

The Pulitzer Prize for International Correspondence was
awarded to Seymour Hersh of the *New York Times.*

Dr. William A. Wexler of the B'nai Brith Anti-Defamation
League was elected chairman of the Conference of Presidents of
Major Jewish Organizations.

1971   The American Jewish Historical Society completed documenta-
        tion of hundreds of manuscripts and data dealing with
        general contributions of Jews and Jewish groups to American
civilization. Over three million manuscripts and documents and some
fifty thousand volumes are housed in the social science research
center at Brandeis University.

The United Jewish Appeal opened its 1971 drive with an
announced goal of $150,000,000.

---

*The author is indebted to Irving J. Sloan, the editor of THE JEWS IN AMERICA, 2nd Ed.,
for his research covering the period 1970 to 1977.*

A New York Historical Society exhibit marked the 100th anniversary of the laying of the cornerstone of Central Synagogue in New York City.

Dr. Milton Halpern, chief medical examiner of New York City, was presented with the annual American Medical Association's distinguished service award for 1971.

America's Jews by Marshall Sklare was published.

Mayor Sam Massell of Atlanta was elected president of the National League of China.

Dr. Alfred Gottschalk was named president of Hebrew Union College-Jewish Institute of Religion.

The Medal of Freedom, the nation's highest civilian award, was bestowed on Samuel Goldwyn, the film pioneer, by President Nixon who visited the producer's house in Los Angeles for the presentation.

Touro College, a new Jewish liberal arts college, opened in New York City.

The American Jewish Committee began publication of its monthly, *What's Doing at the Committee*.

Sixteen Jews were among the fifty Americans elected to membership in the National Academy of Science, the nation's leading science organization.

Three Jews were among the nine Americans awarded the 1970 Medal of Science, the country's highest award for scientific achievement. The Jewish recipients of the award were: Albert Sabin, the developer of the Sabin polio vaccine; Richard D. Brauer, professor of mathematics at Harvard University; and the late Saul Winsteen, professor of chemistry at the University of California at Los Angeles.

The Association for the Sociological Study of Jewry (ASSJ) was founded.

Dr. Charles I. Schottland was installed as the third president of Brandeis University, succeeding Acting President Marver Bernstein.

Bennet Cerf, book publisher, humorist, panelist in the long-running television show *What's My Line?* and credited with revolutionizing the publishing industry, died.

An educational foundation, the Research Foundation for Jewish Immigration, was established for the preparation, research, writing, and editing of the history of German-Jewish immigrants of the Nazi period and their resettlement and acculturation.

The first American to receive the silver medal of the University of Liege, Belgium, was the president of the Radio Corporation of America (RCA), Robert W. Sarnoff.

Albert Shanker was elected president of the newly-formed Union of United Teachers of New York State.

President Nixon appointed Ronald S. Berman, professor of English at the University of California at San Diego, as chairman of the National Endowment for the Humanities.

Studies of Mental Disease Among Jews by Benjamin Malzberg was published.

Federal Reserve Board chairman, Dr. Arthur F. Burns, was made a Fellow of the Jewish Theological Seminary of America.

Herbert Stein, a member of the President's Council of Economic Advisors from 1969, was appointed chairman of the council by President Nixon.

Dr. Victor H. Frank of Philadelphia was elected president of the International College of Dentists. He was the first Jew to hold this position.

1972 Michael Rabin, internationally-known violin virtuoso and concert artist, died at the age of thirty-five.

Rabbi Abraham Joshua Heschel, theologician, author and professor at the Jewish Theological Seminary and a leading force in American religion, died.

The American Friends of Israel Museum was established in New York. The organization sponsors programs and development at the Israel Museum in Jerusalem and exhibitions and activities for the museum in the United States.

The first woman rabbi in the United States and the second in the history of Judaism, Sally J. Priesand, was ordained in Cincinnati at the Hebrew Union College-Jewish Institute of Religion.

The United States Census Bureau reported that there were 1,600,000 Jews in the United States who said that their mother tongue was Yiddish.

Fiddler on the Roof closed its Broadway run after 3,242 performances, an all-time record for a Broadway show.

Dr. Gerald M. Edelman, a molecular biologist at Rockefeller University in New York, shared the Nobel Prize for physiology and medicine.

Dr. William H. Stein, of Rockefeller University, shared the Nobel Prize in chemistry.

Artist Louis Lozowick had a one-man show of his paintings at the Whitney Museum in New York City. He has authored such books as: *Treasury of Drawings* (1948), *Modern Russian Art* (1925) and *One Hundred American Jewish Artists* (1948).

1973   NOVEMBER. *A Tribute to Jacques Lipchitz*, an exhibition of sixty-nine of the sculptor's pieces, mostly bronzes, opened at the Marlborough Gallery, New York City. The show, which concentrated on the years of the artist's American production, ranging from the early 1940s until his death, was organized as a benefit for the American Friends of the Israel Museum.

Revival of the American Sephardic Federation to serve the estimated 150,000 American Jews of Sephardic origin began with the election of Dr. Daniel Elazar of Temple University as the chairman of the American branch of the World Sephardic Union.

David Lawrence, one of the country's leading Washington columnists for more than sixty years, founder and editor of the *U.S. News & World Report,* died.

Maurice Rosenberg, professor of law at Columbia Law School, was elected president of the Association of American Law Schools.

Laurence Melchoir, world famous Wagnerian tenor who came from a Danish-Jewish family, died.

Present Tense, a quarterly publication, was first produced by the American Jewish Committee.

David Shub, authority on the Russian Revolution and editor of the *Forward,* died.

Helmut Sonnenfeldthas was confirmed as under-secretary of the Treasury in the administration of President Nixon.

Arthur Freed, the film producer who won Academy Awards for the musicals *Gigi* and *An American in Paris*, and who was twice honored with special awards by the Motion Picture Academy of Arts and Sciences, died.

Five Jews were among the Pulitzer Prize winners for 1973. The recipients of the award were: Max Frankel of *The New York Times,* David S. Brader of the *Washington Post,* James T. Flexner for his four-volume biography of George Washington, Michael Kammen of Cornell University for history, and Maxine Winhour Kumen for poetry.

The 150th anniversary of the American Jewish Press was commemorated at the annual meeting of the American Jewish Historical

Society.

Hyman G. Rickover was elevated to the rank of rear admiral.

American Jewry stood behind Israel in the war with the Arab nations which broke out on Yom Kippur.

Secretary of State Henry A. Kissinger became the first American Jew to receive the Nobel Peace Prize.

The Jewish Publication Society of America published *The Ambivalent American Jew: Politics, Religion, and Family in the American Jewish Life* by Charles S. Liebman. The volume develops the argument that American Jews are torn between two sets of values, integration and acceptance into American society as opposed to Jewish group survival.

1974   JANUARY 28. The American Jewish Committee presented the the Isaiah Award for "Pursuit of Justice" to Senator Henry M. Jackson bacause of his efforts on behalf of Soviet Jews and his support of Israel.

FEBRUARY 18. Members of the American Jewish Congress re-elected Rabbi Arthur Hertzberg as president of the organization. Howard M. Squadron was at the same time elected president of the national governing council and Stanley H. Lowell was elected the national vice president.

Abraham D. Beame took office as the first Jewish mayor of New York City.

Sol Hurok, the world's foremost impressario of international cultural and artistic exchanges, died.

Laurence Silberman, who at the age of thirty-four was the youngest under-secretary of Labor, was believed to be at thirty-eight the youngest person ever named deputy attorney general. He was the first Jew to attain that rank.

Walter Lippman, author and one of the nation's leading political analysts, died.

Two books presenting a description of the history and experience of the Jews in the South were published: *Our Southern Landsman* by Harry Golden and *The Provincials: A Personal History of Jews in the South* by Eli N. Evans.

Allen Ginsberg was the recipient of the National Book Award for *The Fall of America: Poems of These States* published in 1973. Issac B. Singer shared the Fiction Prize for his *A Crown of Feathers and Other Stories*.

A Gallup Poll on religious service attendance showed that Jewish attendance was at nineteen percent in 1973, up from seventeen percent in 1964.

Moses Soyer, artist and educator, died.

Jack Benny, one of the most noted American comedians on radio and televison, died.

The Association for a Progressive Reform Judaism was established as a national organization to reverse the trend of what was considered a serious encroachment of traditionalism within the Central Conference of Rabbis (CCAR), a reform group.

Volume four of the thirteen-volume dictionary of the Yiddish language, being compiled by the Institute for Yiddish Lexicology at the College of the City of New York and at the University of Jerusalem, was published. It was estimated at the outset that the set would take seventeen years to complete at a cost of over one million dollars. The first volume was printed in 1961.

Harry Hershfeld, cartoonist, humorist and columnist who gained widespread recognition in the 1940s with his radio show, *Can You Top This?*, died.

The United States Supreme Court affirmed a lower court ruling upholding the so-called "ritual slaughter" exemption in the Humane Slaughter Act of 1958 which permitted kosher slaughtering methods.

Richard Stone was elected United States senator from Florida, the first professing Jew to serve in the Senate from a Southern state.

1975   MARCH. Haym Salomon was honored as one of the "Contributors to the Cause" by the United States Postal Service in a set of stamps dedicated to those who aided the colonies in their fight for independence.

MARCH. An editorial in the *Novoye Russkoye Slovo*, the New York City Russian newspaper, reported that about three thousand Russian Jews had settled in that city and that many of them were unhappy.

APRIL. The Metropolitan Museum of Art, New York City, presented an exhibition of manuscripts and ritual objects used in the Jewish home during the observance of the Passover holiday. Objects included in *The Passover Story* were lent to the Museum by the Jewish Theological Seminary, the Jewish Museum, Central Synagogue, the General Theological Seminary, the Brooklyn Museum and by Dr. Alfred Moldovan.

MAY. *Moment*, a new magazine for and about Jews in America was founded by author Elie Wiesel and Professor Leonard Fein. Moshe Dworkin was the founding publisher.

JUNE. Barbara Herman, aged twenty-three, was invested as the first woman cantor in the history of American Reform Judaism. The ceremony took place during the annual commencement exercises of the Hebrew Union College-Jewish Institute of Religion.

OCTOBER. The Central Conference of American Rabbis announced the publication of its first new prayer book in eighty years. The book was entitled *Gates of Prayer, The New Union Prayer Book.*

DECEMBER. The United Jewish Appeal presented its first annual David Ben-Gurion Award to Elie Wiesel.

DECEMBER. The American Jewish Congress presented its first annual Beauty Hall of Fame Award to hair stylist Vidal Sassoon who had served with the Israeli army during the first Arab-Israeli war.

Professor Gershon D. Cohen became chancellor of the Jewish Theological Seminary of America.

The Union of American Hebrew Congregations chose Rabbi Alexander M. Schindler as its president.

B'nai Brith Hillel Foundations celebrated its golden jubilee of service to campus communities.

The most influential American Jewish group, the Conference of Presidents of Major Jewish Organizations, representing thirty-one secular and religious bodies, condemned the October sixth attack on Israel by Syria and Egypt and pledged total support and solidarity with their brothers in Israel.

Jacob Adler (Arthur Kober, psued.), playwright, screenwriter and short story writer whose Jewish dialect stories featured a character named Bella Gross, died.

Hannah Arendt, American political philosopher, died.

Mark Spitz won seven gold medals for swimming at the Munich Olympics, the scene of a terrorist attack on Israeli competitors.

Edward H. Levi, dean of the University of Chicago Law School, and president of the University, was appointed by President Ford as attorney general of the United States. He was the first Jew to hold this office.

Charles H. Revson, president and founder of Revlon, Inc., the largest cosmetic and fragrance company in the retail market, who built the multi-million dollar business on a three hundred dollar investment made during the depression years, died.

The Nobel Prize in physiology and medicine was shared by David Baltimore of the Center for Cancer Research at the Massachusetts Institute of Technology and Howard M. Temin, professor of oncology at the University of Wisconsin.

1976 APRIL 30. The House of Representatives unanimously approved a resolution which urged the Soviet Union to permit free emigration of Jews and other citizens wishing to leave.

MAY. A protest voiced by the American Jewish Congress was aimed at the selection of Baghdad, Iraq as the site of the eighth World Congress of the International Association of Art. Among the forty-four artists that signed the statement accusing the Iraqi government of a long history of "racist atrocities" were: Willem de Kooning, Robert Indiana, Jack Levine and Raphael Sawyer.

MAY. Army Secretary Martin R. Hoffmann authorized the construction of a Jewish chapel at the United States Military Academy at West Point. It was estimated that the structure, designed by Max Abramovitz, would cost five million dollars to erect. Academy officials hoped that this might stimulate a larger Jewish enrollment. The current 4,400-member cadet corps included only thirty-three Jews.

JULY. Rabbis Louis C. Gerstein of New York, Theodore Lewis of Newport, Saul J. Rubin of Savannah, Ezekial N. Musleah of Philadelphia, Edward L. Cohen of Charleston and Jack Spiro of Richmond, all rabbis of congregations founded before the American Revolution, presented President Ford with a Bicentennial pledge for "Steadfast loyalty of the American Jewish community to the American dream."

JULY. The Museum of American Jewish History opened in Philadelphia. The first exhibition was entitled *Jews in the Forging of a Nation.* According to the museum's director, Marvin D. Schwartz, the aim of the show was "to tell the story of two thousand Jews among two million colonists."

JULY. An exhibition entitled *Ludwig Yehuda Wolpert: A Retrospective* in honor of the seventy-six year old craftsman, opened at the Jewish Museum, New York City. The show included Torah arks, seder trays, Hanukkah lamps, Sabbath candelabras and kiddush cups.

SEPTEMBER. In commemoration of the Bicentennial, the exhibition *Americana from the Jewish Museum Collection* was mounted at that museum. The show included portraits, silhouettes, miniatures and memorabilia of prominent early American Jews.

OCTOBER. Dr. Baruch S. Blumberg, associate director of the Institute for Cancer Research in Philadelphia, and Dr. Milton Friedman, professor at the University of Chicago, were both awarded Nobel Prizes. Dr. Blumberg was chosen to share the Nobel Prize for physiology and medicine and Dr. Friedman was chosen to receive the economics award.

OCTOBER. Saul Bellow was awarded the Nobel Prize for literature "for the human understanding and subtle analysis of contemporary culture that are combined in his work." Among his works are: *Dangling Man, The Victim, Seize the Day, Herzog* and *Humbolt's Gift.*

OCTOBER. Rabbi Israel Miller assumed his post as chairman of the Conference of Presidents of Major American Jewish Organizations.

DECEMBER. Plans to build a Jewish Cultural Center in the Lincoln Center area in New York City were announced. The complex, to be known as The Abraham D. Goodman House in honor of the New York industrialist and philanthropist who provided most of the funds for the seven-story building, would unite under one roof the twenty-five year old Hebrew Arts School for Music and Dance, the Tarbuth Foundation for the Advancement of Hebrew Culture and five schools belonging to the Lincoln Square Synagogue.

DECEMBER. The Union of American Hebrew Congregations announced its expectation that by 1979 one out of three newly ordained Reform rabbis would be women. According to Matthew H. Ross, chairman of the group's board of trustees, thirty-five of 215 rabbinic students on the four campuses of the Reform movement's Hebrew Union College-Jewish Institute of Religion were women. The union represents 720 Reform synagogues with 1.1 million members in the United States and Canada.

The American Jewish Congress, the American Jewish Committee and the Anti-Defamation League of the B'nai Brith submitted "friend of court" briefs challenging the right of the University of Washington Law School to use race as an admission criterion, as challenged by Marco De Funis.

Richard Tucker, opera singer and cantor, died.

Lionel Trilling, educator, author and critic, and professor of literature at Columbia University since 1948, died.

Samuel Belken, chancellor of Yeshiva University, who supervised its growth from a small Jewish seminary to a large distinguished university, serving as its president for thirty-two years, died.

Alex Rose, prominent New York political and labor leader, died.

Yehudi Menuhin, world-renowned violinist, received an honorary doctorate from the Sorbonne. It was the first time the 719 year-old university awarded an honorary doctorate.

Russian-born cellist Gregor Piatigorsky, who became an American citizen in 1942, died. He was considered one of the three greatest cellists of the twentieth century.

A drive to raise fifteen million dollars for the Harvard
University Center for Jewish Studies was announced by the university's president, Derek C. Bok, and the Fellows of Harvard College.

The first United States Navy chapel to be built for use
specifically as a synagogue was dedicated and consecrated at Pearl
Harbor.

Dr. Jerome Wiesner, president of the Massachusetts Institute
of Technology, was named chairman of the Office of Technology Advisory Council.

Lucy S. Dawidowicz, professor of social history at Stern
College for Women, Yeshiva University, was appointed to the nation's
first endowed chair in Interdisciplinary Holocaust Studies at
Yeshiva University.

1977   JANUARY. Yeshiva University official Rabbi David Mirsky and
        Israeli Bar Ilan University official Aaron M. Schreiber
        announced the establishment of a computer terminal at Yeshiva
for the storage of twelve centuries of religious law and social problems known as "Responsa".

JANUARY. Samuel I. Cohen was named executive vice president
of the Jewish National Fund of America, the part of the World Zionist
movement concerned with afforestation and land reclamation. Dr.
Cohen had previously served as the executive director of the American
Zionist Federation and was a past director of the American Jewish
Congress.

MARCH 10. The National Council of Jewish Women presented
Vice President Mondale with its John F. Kennedy Award for public
service. Mrs. Mondale accepted the award on behalf of her husband.

APRIL 24. A new chamber orchestra, Strings in Exile (also
known as the New Russian Chamber Orchestra), composed of fifteen
Soviet-Jewish emigres, gave its first public performance in New
York. The group was organized in 1976 by its director and conductor,
Joel Spiegelman.

APRIL. To coincide with the exhibition of Russian art being
shown at the Metropolitan Museum of Art, the American Jewish Congress
held a counter-exhibition to display the work of four Jewish emigre
artists from the Soviet Union. The four artists were: Ernst
Neizvestny, Ilya Shenker, Aleksandr Richter and Igor Galinin.

MAY 8. The members of the Society for the Advancement of
Judaism celebrated the fifty-fifth anniversary of the founding of
their synagogue and at the same time marked the fiftieth birthday

of Rabbi Alan W. Miller. The society, based in New York City, is the mother synagogue of the Jewish Reconstructionist Movement, which follows a philosophy of Judaism without requiring a belief in God.

MAY 15. The participants at the seventy-first annual meeting of the American Jewish Committee in New York were addressed by Israel's chief representative to the United Nations, Simcha Dinitz. During their week of meetings, the members of the organization elected Richard Maass, a former mayor of White Plains, New York, as it seventeenth president.

MAY 18. The American Academy and Institute of Arts and Letters awarded the Gold Medal for the Novel to Saul Bellow during the thirty-seventh annual awards ceremony. Mr. Bellow thus became the first American writer to receive both the Gold Medal and the Nobel Prize in the same year.

JUNE 5. The Jewish Museum, which houses one of the largest collections of Jewish ceremonial objects in the world, celebrated its thirtieth anniversary.

JUNE 9. Rabbi Saul I. Teplitz was installed as president of the Synagogue Council of America. The council is the national coordinating body of Orthodox, Conservative and Reform branches of American Judaism.

JULY 22. Jacob Ben-Ami, the actor and a founder of the Jewish Art Theater, died at the age of eighty-six.

JULY. Harry R. Mancher was elected the twenty-third president of the sixty year old Federation of Jewish Philanthropies, succeeding Frederick P. Rose.

AUGUST 9. A symposium of writers, academicians and editors met to commemorate the twenty-fifth anniversary of the execution of some noted Soviet poets and intellectuals. Norman Podhoretz, the editor of *Commentary*, was the chairman of the symposium, which was sponsored by the National Conference on Soviet Jewry.

SEPTEMBER 8. Zero Mostel, the actor whose career spanned nearly four decades, died at the age of sixty-two.

NOVEMBER 2. Members of the World Jewish Congress were addressed by President Carter, who was presented with the Nahum Goldmann award for support of human rights.

NOVEMBER 13. The Stephen Wise Award of the American Jewish Congress was presented to the former Israeli prime minister, Golda Meir, by Henry Kissinger and to Mayor Abraham Beame of New York by Representative Edward Koch.

NOVEMBER. Dr. Gershon D. Cohen, chancellor of the Jewish Theological Seminary of America, announced the appointment of a

thirteen-member committee to study the possibility of admitting women into the rabbinate. Rabbi Gordon Tucker was chosen to serve as
the executive director of the study group.

NOVEMBER. The American Hebrew Congregation Union, in an
effort to achieve formal rights and recognition of Reform Judaism
in Israel, voted to establish a Zionist-affiliated body to seek membership in the World Zionist Organization.

DECEMBER 17. Prime Minister Menachem Begin was in Washington,
D.C., to discuss with President Carter the possibilities of an Is-
raeli-Egyptian peace agreement.

DECEMBER. The Judah L. Magnes Memorial Museum of Berkeley,
California, announced that this year's Jewish-American Hall of Fame
medal would depict the oldest standing house of Jewish worship in
the United States, the Touro Synagogue in Newport, Rhode Island.
The Touro Synagogue was dedicated in 1763.

Rabbi Norman Lamm became president of Yeshiva University.

The growth of "Jews for Jesus" groups and their proselytiz-
ing raised anxieties in the American Jewish community.

The National Association of Jewish State Legislators, made
up of an estimated 200 of the 7,600 state legislators in the fifty
states who are Jewish, was established. The new association planned
to serve as a reference and referral service on issues of concern to
the American Jewish population.

Donald Freeman, a former member of the Federal Power Commission, was named by President Carter to be a director of the Tennessee
Valley Authority (TVA).

President Carter appointed a Jewish woman, Roberta S. Karmel,
as the first woman to serve on the Securities and Exchange Commission.

Dr. Rosalyn S. Yalow became the second woman ever to win a
Nobel Prize in medicine, and only the sixth woman to win in any science category.

A group of about three thousand people attended the dedication ceremony in New Haven, Connecticut of a memorial to the six
million Jews murdered by the Nazis during World War II. The memorial, designed by Augustus Franzoni, was believed to be the first such
memorial in the country to be built under the direction of a city
government.

President Carter spoke to an audience of about eight hundred
Jewish leaders from forty-one countries at a meeting of the General
Council of the World Jewish Congress.

THE KOREANS IN AMERICA

1970 MARCH 29. The Korean American Credit Union was established in San Francisco. The purpose of the organization is to promote the development of the Korean community in America.

APRIL 16. Mrs. Martha Holt brought the five-thousandth orphan from Korea who was adopted into an American family.

MAY 24. The United Association of the Young Korean Christians was organized at the United Korean Presbyterian Church in Los Angeles. Mr. Kim Sang-ki was elected chairman of the association.

JULY 28. A group of eighteen young Koreans met at the Korea House Restaurant to promote the establishment of the Korean Youth Association of Southern California.

OCTOBER 3. The scholarship awarded every year to a Korean student in the United States by the American Korean Civic Organization was presented to Debra Lee.

NOVEMBER 20. The New Korea Restaurant in Los Angeles announced that it would open for business on November 25.

The Korean Community Action Center was organized to help immigrants to adjust to their new country and to make the most of their skills in this country.

The North American Branch Committee of the Hungsa-dan held its delegates' conference and elected Yi Ha-jon as chairman.

Radio Korea reported that it would broadcast between the hours of 9 A.M. and 10 P.M. daily.

The census report indicated that in the course of the year nine thousand immigrants had arrived in the United States from Korea.

The Korean American Wives' Club (KAWC) was founded in Arlington Heights, Illinois. The society promotes cultural exchange between Koreans and Americans.

The author is indebted to Hyung-chan Kim & Wayne Patterson, the editors of THE KOREANS IN AMERICA, for their research covering the period 1970 to 1974.

1971   JANUARY 24. The Kim Ho Scholarship was awarded to five Korean students; each of them received $250.

JANUARY 24. The Korean Association of Southern California
held its annual meeting and elected Sonia Sok as its president.

FEBRUARY 19. The Church of Nazareth was established in Los
Angeles by Han Soo-keun.

MARCH 12. The Korean Temperance Society was organized in
Los Angeles. The purpose of the group is to encourage Koreans not
to smoke, not to drink alcoholic beverages and not to use narcotics.

MARCH 19. The Reverend Chang Si-wha, minister of the Korean
Central Church in Los Angeles, established the Los Angeles Theological Seminary.

APRIL. The Seoul Food Market was opened in Los Angeles.

APRIL. Korean Night was celebrated at the Academy of Motion
Picture Arts in Los Angeles. A Korean film, *Seven Princesses*, was
shown as part of the program.

APRIL. A group of twenty-two Korean scholars in Buffalo,
New York sent a petition to President Park Chung-hee asking him to
guarantee fair play in the coming general election in the Republic
of Korea.

JULY. The federal government made a grant of fifty thousand dollars to the chairman of the Asian American Social Workers
Committee. The grant was to be used for conducting research on social problems in the Asian American community in Southern California.

AUGUST 8. The Korean Women's Patriotic League held its
fifty-second anniversary. Approximately sixty members gathered together to commemorate the event.

SEPTEMBER 12. The Federation of Korean Church Musicians of
Los Angeles was formed. The purpose of the organization is to promote church music. Cho Kwang-hyok was elected chairman of the group.

OCTOBER. The *New Korea* reported that Hobart School in Los
Angeles would offer English classes to Koreans unable to speak English.

NOVEMBER 6. The Korean Ministers' Conference of Chicago
was held at the First Korean Church. The Reverend Kim Yan-guk presented a paper entitled "The Developmental Process of History as
Seen from the History of Salvation."

NOVEMBER 19. The Korean Federation of Scientific and Technical Managerial Personnel in America held a symposium. The members of the group were addressed by Choi Sun-dal whose topic was

the "Present Situation of the Electronic Industry in Korea and Assistance that We Can Offer."

The American-Korean Friendship and Information Center was founded in New York. Its primary function is to promote American Korean relations and disseminate information on Korea in the United States. The center sponsors the publication of the quarterly *Korea Focus*.

1972 JANUARY 8. The Korean Children's Choir of Los Angeles was organized.

JANUARY 30. George Choi was elected chairman of the Korean Association of Southern California.

FEBRUARY 3. The Medical Health Service Center for Koreans was established in Los Angeles.

FEBRUARY 4. The Korean American Youth Foundation was established.

FEBRUARY 5. The Christian Counselling Center for Koreans was founded in Los Angeles.

FEBRUARY 12. Jin Hyong-ki and Yi Kyong-dong were respectively elected chairman and vice chairman of the Board of Directors of the Korean Association of Southern California.

FEBRUARY 17. The Korean American Cultural Association was established.

APRIL 22. The Korean Cultural Center was opened.

MAY 13. Mugung-wha Hakwon, the Rose of Sharon Institute, was established in Los Angeles to teach young children of Korean ancestry the Korean language.

JUNE 27. The Korean Food Products Manufacturers' Association of Southern California was established in Los Angeles.

JUNE 30. It was reported that Korea had sent 1,390 medical doctors to the United States. Korea was ranked third behind the Philippines and India in the number of doctors who came to the United States from foreign nations.

JULY 1. The Korean American Political Association of Southern California was organized in Los Angeles.

JULY 23. The Korean Women's Association of Southern California was established in Los Angeles.

AUGUST. The Korean Philharmonic Orchestra was organized.

The newly-formed group consisted of fifty members, headed by Cho Min-ku, who had once served as conductor for the Hollywood Philharmonic Orchestra.

AUGUST. Korean Americans launched a drive to send money to victims of the floods in Korea.

SEPTEMBER 3. A group of first-generation Korean youths in Hawaii met to establish the Hangkuk Ch'ongnyong Yonhaphoi, the Korean Youth Federation. The purpose of the new organization was to unite all the Korean youth groups that existed in Hawaii.

SEPTEMBER 19. The Korean Restaurant Association of Southern California was organized.

OCTOBER 1. Moon Ch'ung-han was elected president of the Korean Association in San Francisco.

NOVEMBER 4. The Korean Academic Society and the Korean Association of Chicago held a conference to discuss various social and cultural problems which Korean immigrants to America had faced.

NOVEMBER 18. The American T'aekwon-do Association was organized in Los Angeles by thirty T'aekwon-do teachers who gathered in Los Angeles from various parts of the United States. It was reported that seven hundred T'aekwon-do institutes of self-defense existed in the United States.

NOVEMBER 26. The Korean Young Men's Christian Association was organized in Chicago.

DECEMBER. The Athletic Association of Korean Residents in America was established.

1973   JANUARY 7. Kim Chong-sik was elected president of the Korean Association of Southern California.

JANUARY 7. The first Korean Baptist Church was established in San Francisco. A group of eighty people attended the first service officiated by the Reverend Whang Im-ch'un.

JANUARY 9. The governor of Hawaii, John A. Burns, signed a document declaring the period between January 13 and January 17 to be Korean Week. The declaration was made to commemorate the seventieth anniversary of the major era of Korean immigration to Hawaii.

JANUARY 14. The Korean Christian Church was established in San Francisco. A group of sixty people attended the first service delivered by Reverend Ch'on Byong-wook.

JANUARY 28. The first Korean Buddhist temple was established in Carmel, California. Four hundred people attended the dedication ceremony of the Sambo-sa, the Sambo Temple.

FEBRUARY 3. The Dalma Temple was established in Los Angeles.

FEBRUARY 4. A ceremony commemorating the sixty-fourth anniversary of the establishment of the Korean National Association was held with Yi Wha-mok, the president of the group, presiding over the meeting.

FEBRUARY 10. The Korean Book Center opened in Los Angeles. Kim Jin-hyong was the proprietor of the store.

FEBRUARY 15. The Korean Residents Association was established in Santa Clara, California. Kim Seung-un was elected president of the new organization.

FEBRUARY 21. The Korean Town Prosperity Association was established in order to push forward a plan to build a Korean town along Olympic Boulevard in Los Angeles.

FEBRUARY. The One Day Service Center was established to help Koreans in Los Angeles solve their personal and social problems.

MARCH 18. Yi Dal-soon won the American ping-pong championship in Detroit. He was selected to represent the United States in the world ping-pong competition to be held in Yugoslavia in April.

APRIL 17. Noh Seung-jin, a second-generation Korean, was elected to the board of education of Berkeley, California. He was the first person of Asian ancestry to be elected to the Berkeley City Board of Education.

MAY 18. The Los Angeles County authorities appointed the Reverend Kwon Yong-bae as director of the Asian Community Service Center.

MAY 19. The Korean American Education Center was established in San Francisco. Im Yong-bin was appointed as principal of the center, which enrolled a total of seventy-three children of Korean descent who were to receive instruction in Korean history, language and culture.

MAY 20. A public ceremony commemorating the sixtieth anniversary of the establishment of the Hungsa-dan (Corps for the Advancement of Individuals) was held in Los Angeles.

MAY 20. A Korean church was established in Las Vegas. The Reverend Yu Kyong-il presided over the first church service which was attended by one hundred people.

JULY 1. A radio station which would broadcast in Korean was established in Baltimore, Maryland.

JULY 21. A chapter of the Korean Association was established in San Diego, California.

AUGUST 7. Yi Ch'on-yong was appointed by Mayor Bradley of Los Angeles as one of 140 commissioners to serve the city.

SEPTEMBER 8. In Chicago, a group of Korean residents interested in the restoration of a constitutional government in Korea, staged a demonstration led by Choi Myong-sang.

OCTOBER 28. The Korean Opera was organized in Los Angeles. Yi Woo-gun was elected president of the new opera group.

DECEMBER 20. The Korean Chamber of Commerce of Northern California was organized in San Francisco. Ch'u Ki-sok was elected president of the association.

The Berkeley Korean Presbyterian Church was established, with thirty people attending the first church service conducted by Yi Hyon-dal.

The United States gave its full backing to President Park's declaration that his government would no longer oppose the simultaneous admission of South Korea and North Korea to the United Nations. A representative of the United States Department of State said, "We believe this constructive initiative merits careful attention and support of all governments which have an interest in peace and security of the Korean peninsula."

1974 JANUARY 12. Yi Hak-cho was elected chairman of the Korean Chamber of Commerce of Southern California.

JANUARY 21. The Box Sales Company in San Francisco, owned by Ch'u Ki-sok, was burned down.

JANUARY 27. The annual conference of the Korean Association of Southern California, which was held at the Embassy Auditorium, was attended by 350 regular members.

JANUARY. Professor Kim Bok-lim of the University of Illinois received a grant from the National Institute for Mental Health to study the community needs and problems of Asian Americans.

FEBRUARY 5. The California Microfilm Company began the microfilming of *Sinhan Minbo* (the New Korea).

FEBRUARY 17. The Federation of Korean Churches of Southern California held its annual meeting and elected Ahn Su-hun as its chairman.

FEBRUARY 21. The Seoul Choir was organized.

FEBRUARY 24. Yi Min-whui was elected president of the Korean Association of San Francisco.

FEBRUARY 26. The Research Association of the Koreans in America was established. Kuk Young-il was elected chairman of the new organization.

APRIL. The Board of Education of Los Angeles decided to hire several Korean teachers to work with Korean children having language problems.

APRIL. Breed University was established in Los Angeles by Ko Ung-ch'ol, a Korean resident in Japan. The university was founded in order to promote the World Unity Movement. It was reported that the university would offer courses in Korean, English, French, German and Japanese.

MAY 31. The Korean Community Activity Center organized a performance by two young Koreans, Soomi Lee, a pianist, and Young Sun Choi, a violinist, at the Carnegie Recital Hall in New York City.

JULY 3. A twenty-one year old New York pianist, Myung-Whun Chung was the second place winner in the piano section of the quadrennial Tchaikovsky Competition at the Moscow Conservatory. In 1971 Mr. Chung won the Kosciuszko Foundation Award in the United States and in 1973 was a second place winner in the Munich International Competition. He is not the only member of his family to become a recognized musician. In 1967, his sister Kyung-Wha Chung, a violinist, won the Leventritt Competition and in 1971 another sister, Myung-Wha Chung, a cellist, won the Geneva International Competition.

AUGUST. The Hahn Kook Center, representing South Korean interests, bought a twenty-two story building on Park Avenue in New York City. It was reported that at least three floors of the building would be used by Korean organizations, including the consulate and the Korean Traders Association.

The Society to Honor the Old-Aged and the Old People's Association were merged into the Korean Old People's Association. Ahn Min-hong was elected president of the new organization.

The Students' Counseling Center of the Korean Students' Association of Southern California was established to offer free counseling to students in need.

Members of American Scholars for a Democratic Korea sent an open letter to President Park Chung Lee. The text read as follows: "As Americans we are dismayed by your utterly arbitrary acts culminating in your decree in January 8, 1974, which makes mockery of the name of your country, Daehan Minkuk (Great Democratic Country of Korea). We who hailed the birth of your country as a republic and helped to preserve it with money and blood, believing that we were thus contributing to the enjoyment of freedom by your people, cannot remain silent in the face of your flagrant denial to your people of their legitimate rights. In this we believe we express the sentiments of the American people. We urge you to immediately rescind the repressive decree of January 8, 1974, and to enable your people to develop a democratic system of government."

1975   Secretary of State Kissinger delivered the keynote address at the fifth annual dinner of the Japan Society. In presenting a major policy speech on Asia, he said that the United States "will not turn away from Asia" and that we were "resolved to maintain the peace and security of the Korean peninsula, for this is of crucial importance to Japan and to all of Asia."

1976   OCTOBER 28. It was announced by federal authorities that an investigation had been taking place based on a wide range of allegations that Koreans had been harassing and generally violating the civil rights of Korean aliens living in the United States and Korean Americans.

Approximately thirty thousand Koreans with permanent status emigrated to the United States during 1976. The best estimate is that there are about 250,000 Korean immigrants in the United States, thousands of whom have already become naturalized citizens.

1977   JANUARY 11. In testimony at his nomination hearing before the United States Senate Foreign Relations Committee, the proposed secretary of state, Cyrus Vance, termed "objectionable" the lobbying efforts of South Korea among United States Congressmen. Nevertheless, he considered that the allegations were not sufficient to cause the United States to withdraw its troops from South Korea.

FEBRUARY 8. The House of Representatives Rules Committee tabled a resolution (HR 388-0) that allowed the Ethics Committee to commence investigation into allegations that members of Congress had accepted bribes, gifts and kickbacks from agents of the South Korean government.

MARCH 8. The IRS seized two houses, three cars and other personal property belonging to South Korean Tongsun Park, citing the absent bussinessman's refusal to pay tax debts. Some six weeks earlier, the IRS had made the startling announcement that Mr. Park owed some $4.5 million in income taxes and penalties for 1972 to 1975 and that he had spent as much as one million dollars each year on Congressional lobbying.

MARCH 9. President Carter announced that previous restrictions on travel by Americans to Cuba, Vietnam, North Korea and Cambodia would be removed as of March 18.

MARCH 13. The Performing Arts Program of the Asian Society presented the New York debut of Korea's Pongsan Masked Dance Drama at the American Museum of Natural History in New York City.

APRIL 14. The New York City Tax Commission voted to deny the Reverend Sun Myung Moon's Unification Church tax-exempt status for three pieces of church-owned property. The controversy centered on the question of whether the Unification Church's political activities were more than an incidental part of its operation.

APRIL 19. Twelve United States Protestant and Roman Catholic leaders called on President Carter to intervene on behalf of South Korean dissident Christians.

APRIL. Members of the South Korean community in Arlington, Virginia complained of continued harassment by the Korean CIA (K.C.I.A.). Moreover, they were suffering from the effects of an unjustified anti-Korean feeling in the United States stemming from the much-publicized influence-buying scandal which had been dubbed "Koreagate."
At its height, five separate enquiries into South Korean activites were under way. One hundred and fifteen Congressmen were reported to be implicated, and to have received favors from agents of the Park government amounting to millions of dollars. In addition to those Congressmen, businessman Tongsun Park, the Rev. Sun Myong Moon, Sue Park Thomson and several alleged K.C.I.A. agents were under investigation.

JUNE 16. Korean-born physicist, Benjamin W. Lee, was killed in a highway accident. The forty-two year old head of the theoretical group at the Fermi National Accelerator Laboratory (Fermilab) in Batavia, Illinois came to the United States in 1956 and became a naturalized citizen two years later.

AUGUST 25. Sue Park Thomson, South Korean-born American and former secretary to House of Representatives' Speaker Carl Albert, denied in testimony before the House Ethics Committee that she had been an agent of the South Korean government.

SEPTEMBER. Among the important figures from South Korea who defected to the United States since February, giving information on South Korea's covert operations in America, were: the director of the K.C.I.A. from 1963 to 1969, Hyung Wook Kim; Sang Keun Kim, until recently the second-in-command of the K.C.I.A. in the United States; and Young Ho Sohn, K.C.I.A. chief in New York.

According to Reverend Kwon Suk Kim, the second largest Korean Christian community in the United States was to be found in the New York metropolitan area where approximately forty thousand Korean immigrants attended seventy churches. The Korean Christian community in the United States reported that they had more than three hundred churches, a third of which were located in Southern California.

Korean Immigrant Churches Today in Southern California, by Steve S. Skim, was published by R&E Research Association.

THE LATVIANS IN AMERICA

1970   According to the 1970 census data, there were 86,413 Latvian
        Americans residing in the United States. Of these, 41,707
        were foreign-born Latvians, and 44,706 were American nation-
        als of foreign or mixed parentage. The ten states with the
largest number of Americans of Latvian descent were: New York, with
a Latvian population of 16,433; California, with 9,769; Illinois
with 8,318; New Jersey, with 5,164; Massachusetts, with 5,100; Pennsylvania, with 4,946; Michigan, with 4,935; Ohio, with 4,589; Wisconsin, with 2,649 and Maryland, with 2,640, closely followed by
Connecticut, Florida and Minnesota.

The American Latvian Association held its nineteenth annual
congress in Indianapolis, Indiana. The congress elected a new president, Uldis Grava of New York, who succeeded Professor Peter Lejins.

The third Regional Latvian Song Festival of the West Coast
was held in Los Angeles, with over two hundred singers participating.

The Latvian Freedom Fountain, designed by a Latvian artist,
Ansis Berzins, was dedicated in Colorado Springs, Colorado. It
bears the following inscription: "The Latvian Freedom Fountain is
a gift from the Latvian ethnic group to the people of Colorado
Springs, commemorating in 1968 the fiftieth anniversary of the Declaration of Independence of Latvia. Since 1949, thousands of Latvian refugees have found freedom and opportunity in the United States.
This fountain is a symbol of hope for all of the formerly free people
of the world who keep alive in their hearts the hope of self-determination under God for all nations."

Voldemars Korsts of Chicago, Illinois was one of seventeen
Republican leaders appointed to the United States Department of State
Special Advisory Commission on Public Opinion. He was also appointed
chairman of the Policies and Resolutions Committee of the National
Republican Heritage Council.

The Latvian Foundation was established on the initiative of
Dr. Valdis Muiznieks of Kalamazoo, Michigan. The organization was
founded in an attempt to finance the cultural and educational needs

The author is indebted to Maruta Karklis et. al., the editors of THE LATVIANS IN AMERICA,
for their research covering the period 1970 to 1973.

of the Latvian community in the United States. In its second year of operation, the foundation financed two projects, a book for the teaching of Latvian using structural linguistics, by Dr. Jazeps Lelis and Dzidra Liepina, and a dictionary of Latvian phonology by Dr. Velta Ruke-Dravina.

Demonstrations were held at the United Nations in New York City in commemoration of the twenty-fifth anniversary of that organization, and to demand human rights and self-determination for the Baltic nations in the Soviet Union. The Baltic Youth for Freedom, comprised of young Americans of Latvian, Estonian and Lithuanian descent, continued the demonstration for a week, riding a truck through the streets of New York brandishing the slogan "Free the Baltic Three!"

Daina Palena from Soviet Latvia requested political asylum from the United States authorities. An employee aboard a Soviet vessel docked in New York harbor, Palena was brought into the city to receive medical first aid after taking an overdose of aspirin.

The United Baltic Appeal (UBA) and the Baltic Appeal to the United Nations (BATUN) organized a Baltic Folk Festival on the Latvian-owned site of Priedaine (Place of Pines) in New Jersey.

The Latvian Folk Dance Association held a Latvian folk dance seminar at the Latvian Center of Garezers (Long Lake) near Three Rivers, Michigan.

Laimons Eglitis won the top award at the Atlantic City national art exhibit. His drawing *Two Sources* was purchased by the Philadelphia Museum of Art for its permanent collection.

Aldis Lagzdins of New York won the first prize in the Youth Organist Competition in the United States. He was also the recipient of the first prize at the competition of the National Guild of American Organists in Denver, Colorado in 1968, and was the first organist to receive the Erskine Prize at the Julliard School of Music.

1971   The annual congress of the American Latvian Association was held in Grand Rapids, Michigan. The ninety-nine participating delegates commemorated the twentieth anniversary of the founding of the organization. A White House aide addressed the congress on behalf of the president of the United States.

St. Paul's Latvian Evangelical Lutheran Church of Maywood, Illinois constructed a new church.

The American Latvian Theatre, Boston Ensemble, gave four performances of *Nebraus tik Dikti* (Take it Easy! or, Don't Drive so Fast!) by Janis Lejins in Boston, New York, Willimantic (CT) and Toronto.

The Latvian Kokle Ensemble, directed by Andrejs Jansons, toured Western Europe.

Daumants Hazners of New Jersey was appointed to the Highway Safety Commission by President Nixon.

Girts Purins of Pittsburgh, Pennsylvania received a grant from the University of Pittsburgh to study Latvian art in Riga, Latvia.

Gundars J. King, professor and dean of the School of Business Administration at Pacific Lutheran University, became president of the Western Association of Collegiate Schools of Business, a regional affiliate of the ACSB, representing over sixty business school deans.

Marine officer Juris Luzins won the eight hundred meter run in the American Athletic Union track and field championships.

The United States National Volleyball Team included two members of Latvian descent, Ernests Venta and Guntis Baltabols.

Rein Kampersal, a Latvian-born philanthropist and the owner of Kampersal's Dairy in Rolliston, Maryland, died.

1972   The executive board of directors of the World Federation of Free Latvians met for the first time *en toto* in Elka Park, New York. The delegates adapted a new slogan, "Latvia for Latvians and Latvians for Latvia!" and affirmed an ancient Latvian fertility symbol, Jumis, as the representative sign of all Latvians, expressing the demand of modern Latvians to prosper in their own land.

The Latvian Relief Fund of America celebrated its twentieth year of operation.

The twentieth annual congress of the American Latvian Association was held in Cleveland, Ohio, with Dr. Ilgvars J. Spilners of Pittsburgh, Pennsylvania being elected the group's new president.

The UBA-BATUN delegation presented the United States mission to the United Nations with a petition with signatures gathered by the Baltic Youth for Freedom. The petition was in opposition to President Nixon's visit to Moscow.

The eleventh Latvian Press Congress was held in Elka Park, New York. The congress passed a resolution condemning harassments and persecution of writers in Soviet Latvia.

The Latvian Evangelical Lutheran Church of Elizabeth and Newark, New Jersey purchased its own church.

The Latvian Evangelical Lutheran Church in Washington, D.C. purchased two acres in Rockville, Maryland where they planned to build a new church and a social hall.

The American Latvian Theatre of Washington, D.C. toured Latvian communities in the United States and Canada performing *Tagad ir Citadi* (It's Different Now) by Arturs Strautmanis.

Dr. Edgar Andersons, a Latvian historian and professor at San Jose State University, author of twelve books and sixty articles, was named Outstanding Educator of America for 1972.

Dr. Sigurds Grava was commissioned by the City of New York to develop a master plan for its metropolitan transportation system. Dr. Grava heads the City Planning Department at Columbia University and is an advisor to the United Nations on city planning.

The Valley Forge Freedom Foundation awarded the George Washington medal of honor to Dr. Karl Leyasmeyer for his presentation entitled "The Advancing World Menace and How to Meet It."

Dr. Bruno Kalnins, the leader of the Social Democratic party of the Republic of Latvia and an author of numerous books, now living in exile in Sweden, made a speaking tour of the United States Latvian communities. Other speakers touring the United States and addressing Latvian groups during the year were: Imants Freimanis, a leader of the Latvian community in Sweden; Adolfs Silde, the representative of the Latvian Red Cross in West Germany; Dr. Dietrich Loeber, professor of international law at the University of Kiel in West Germany; Janis Andrups, a literary scholar living in Great Britain; Andrejs Eglitis, a noted Latvian poet living in Sweden; and Martins Ziverts, a famous Latvian writer also residing in Sweden.

Dr. Arvids Ziedonis, director of Russian Studies at Muehlenbach College, was a member of a four-man United States delegation to Moscow in preparation for the United States-Russian Citizens and Educational Exchange Convention to be held in Moscow in 1973.

Under the direction of Dr. Ilga Svecha-Zemzare, Case Western Reserve University in Cleveland, Ohio, expanded its sociology department with a new study program dealing with the problems of deprived, emotionally disturbed and physically neglected children.

Andrejs Akermanis, a graduate of Mangali Marine Academy, Latvia, and founder of AOA, Inc., of Florida, patented an underwater scythe designed to mow the proliferating seaweed of Florida's swamp areas. This was the most recent of his numerous inventions for alleviating various water-connected problems.

Architect Eriks Krumins was appointed to the post of Milwaukee county architect.

The architecture firm of Gunnar Birkerts and Associates

started work on the ninth District Federal Reserve Bank in downtown Minneapolis. Professor Birkerts, who was born in Latvia in 1925, is on the architecture faculty at the University of Michigan and is a member of the American Institute of Architects.

The Freedom Foundation at Valley Forge, Pennsylvania awarded its gold medal to Tedis Zierins, who was a recipient of the freedom award in 1970.

Mara Ozolins was selected to serve as a White House social aide.

The Second Conference on Baltic Literature was held at Ohio State University in Columbus, Ohio. Latvian scholars presenting papers at the conference were: Dr. Edgar Andersons, Dr. Vaira Vike-Freibergs, Dr. Juris Silenieks, Gunars Salins, Dr. Valters Nollendorfs, Astrida Ivask and Dr. Valda Melngailis.

The Baltic World Conference was founded in New York. The conference united the highest representatives of the international organization of Latvians, Estonians and Lithuanians in the free world. Its purpose is to facilitate cooperation between the three nationalities, to undertake united political action and to exchange information about circumstances in their occupied lands.

Norberts J. Trepsa, a Roman Catholic priest, author, lawyer, political theorist and social organizer, died in New York. Father Trepsa, who was born in Latvia in 1913, was best known as the founder and first president of BATUN.

1973 JANUARY 19. The Latvian Folk Dance Group of Grand Rapids, Michigan performed at one of President Nixon's inaugural events in Washington, D.C.

JANUARY 20. The Latvian Youth Folk Dance Group and the Youth Kokle Ensemble, directed by Maija Eksteins and Valdis Karklis, performed at the President's inaugural ball in the Kennedy Center for the Performing Arts.

APRIL 13. A conference on the Baltic area in World War II, organized by Dr. Edgar Andersons at Stanford University and California State University, San Jose, attracted forty-two scholars from five countries and one hundred and fifty general participants.

MAY. Dr. Janis Auzins of Michigan, a dentist in the United States Army, was promoted to the rank of full colonel.

MAY. The tenth American Latvian Catholic Association Congress was held in Chicago. Father Baginskis of Chicago was elected to head the organization for a two-year period.

JUNE. Many Latvian Americans participated in demonstrations concerning the Baltic problem during the visit of Leonid Brezhnev, secretary general of the Communist Party of the U.S.S.R., to the United States.

JUNE. Dr. Sigurds Krolls of the United States Air Force in Washington, D.C. was promoted to the rank of full colonel.

JULY 5. Uldis Grava, a citizen of the United States and marketing manager of the Newspaper Advertising Bureau in New York, was placed under arrest on unspecified charges by the Finnish police in Helsinki, Finland. Mr. Grava and eight other representatives of Baltic groups were in Finland to speak for their unrepresented countrymen at the Conference on Security and Cooperation in Europe. Demands by the USSR that the Baltics' protestations be curtailed resulted in the incarceration of these representatives. After a twenty-four hour imprisonment, during which the Balts protested with a hungar strike, they were released and the decision to depart them from Finland cancelled.

SEPTEMBER 17. Dr. Peter P. Lejins, director of the Institute of Criminal Justice and Criminology, took part in the seventh International Congress on Criminology in Belgrade, Yugoslavia. The congress was convened by the International Society for Criminology.

OCTOBER 6. The first Latgallian culture days took place in Toronto, Canada, with participation of distinguished Latgallian personalities from the United States, including the Latvian linguist Dr. Jazeps Lelis of Washington, D.C. and novelist Janis Klidzejs of California. Latgallians, who are an intrinsic part of the Latvian nation, posess a distinctive cultural and religious heritage due to the history of Latgale, which was for centuries politically separated from the rest of Latvia.

NOVEMBER. August Annus, the Latvian master of figurative painting who was born in Liepaja, Latvia in 1893 and who studied and then taught at the Latvian Academy of Art, commemorated his eightieth birthday with a retrospective show of his works. At the same time, his daughter Anna Annus-Hagen, a sculptress, and his son Janis Annus, a painter, held a joint exhibition of their work at the Central Arts Gallery in Manhattan.

NOVEMBER. A series of four one-half hour television programs about Latvians were broadcast over KTCA-2, Minneapolis public television. One of each of the first three programs was devoted to Latvian history, Latvian music and Soviet oppression in Latvia, with the concluding broadcast presenting a Baltic panel of Estonian, Latvian and Lithuanian spokesmen in a political discussion of current East-West relationships.

DECEMBER. For the first time since 1949, a paper concerned with Latvian history was on the agenda of the national conference of the American Historical Association. Dr. Andrejs Plakans, who was born in Latvia in 1940, presented his paper entitled "Peasant Farms and Homesteads in the Baltic Littoral of 1797." At the same conference, Dr. Egils Grislis, a Latvian-born professor of religion and philosophy, chaired a special seminar concerning rhetoric in the history of the Anglican Church.

The fifth Latvian Song Festival commemorating the one hundredth anniversary of the first song festival held in Riga, Latvia in 1873, was held in Cleveland, Ohio. Ralph J. Perk, the mayor of Cleveland, declared a day of Latvian Song Days in the city and presented the keys of Cleveland to Andrejs Eglitis, a Latvian poet from Sweden and Kaspars Svenne, the conductor of the grand concert from Australia. The series of concerts began with an opening ceremony at which a select choir rendered songs from the program of the original festival one hundred years before.

The American Latvian Theatre, Boston Ensemble, toured the United States and Canada with *Minchauzena Precibas* by Martins Ziverts.

Eli Siegal, the founder of the Aesthetic Realism Foundation, and his followers began publishing a newsletter called *The Right of Aesthetic Realism to Be Known.* Mr. Siegal, who was born in Dvinsk, Latvia in 1902, came to the United States with his parents three years later. He described Aesthetic Realism as "the art of liking the world and oneself at the same time, by seeing the world and oneself as aesthetic opposites."

An exhibition of special compositions by Girts Purins opened at the Carnegie Institute Art Museum in Pittsburgh.

The Latvian High School Ensemble from Munster, West Germany made an extensive tour through the United States and Canada.

Professor Martins Straumanis, a world authority on metallurgy and a member of the faculty of the University of Missouri, died.

Peteris Eglitis, an attorney specializing in the laws of Latvia, died in New York. Mr. Eglitis, who was born in Latvia in 1884, was a past president of the Evangelical Lutheran Church of Latvia and, later, the Church in Exile.

A. Liepnieks, the Latvian chess promotor and editor of the Latvian periodical *Sacha Pasaule* (Chess World), died in Lincoln, Nebraska.

Guna Kalmite presented a one-woman show of her paintings in Chicago. She also published a book of reproductions and evaluations of the paintings of her father Janis Kalmite. This was the first professional treatment in English of a Latvian painter's work.

The Joint Latvian Organizations of Los Angeles built a Latvian community center.

Dr. Juris Terauds, who was on the physical education faculty at the University of Maryland, developed a new theory and training method for javelin throwing.

Janis Egils Avots II's short subject film *Skylark and Me* won first place at the Brooks Institute's film festival in Santa Barbara, California.

Father Leons Varna, head of the Latvian Catholic Congregation of Des Moines, Iowa, was appointed coordinator of Latvian Catholic activities in the United States.

Dr. R. Zemjanis, professor of reproductive biology at the School of Veterinary Medicine at the University of Minnesota, received a United States Department of State appointment to Zaria, Nigeria. He was to establish and head a school of veterinary medicine at the Ahmad-Bello University.

Metra Petersons became head librarian of the National Labor Relations Board in Washington, D.C.

The American Latvian Association reported that the number of Latvian scholars and educators serving on the faculties of universities and other institutions of higher learning throughout the United States was between six and seven hundred.

Latvian artist Janis Gailis, who was born in Perkone, Latvia in 1903 and studied at the Latvian Academy of Fine Arts, was commissioned by the 130-nation World Postal Federation to create a painting in honor of its founding in 1874.

Janis Saberts, a prominent actor of the Latvian stage, died in New York City.

Andrejs Karulins, known in Europe as the flamenco guitarist Andre el Letton, returned to the United States and gave a number of concerts for Latvian audiences.

1974   JULY 27. Mikhail Baryshnikov, the twenty-seven year old leading male dancer of the Kirov Ballet Company of Leningrad who
defected in Toronto the previous month, made his United States
debut at the New York State Theater in the American Ballet
Theater's production of *Giselle*. Mr. Baryshnikov was born in Riga, Latvia and was a distinguished pupil of the late Alexander Pushkin. In 1968 he won the Gold Medal in the international ballet competition in Bulgaria, and won again the following year in a similar competition in Moscow.

SEPTEMBER 27. Barnett S. Gruzen, who was born in Riga, Latvia in 1903 and was brought to the United States two years later, died. A well-known architect, his principle works include: the United States Mission to the United Nations(1959), the Albert Einstein College of Medicine(1954), the Veterans Administration Hospital in

Wilkes-Barre, Pennsylvania(1952) and the City Hall building in Canton, Ohio(1960).

Morris Halle, a professor of modern languages and linguistics who was born in Liepaja, Latvia, was made president of the Linguistics Society of America.

1975   JULY 29. Two American citizens of Baltic descent were detained by the Finnish police at the Helsinki airport. The Finns were afraid that Uldis Grava, head of the Baltic World Conference, and Dr. Joseph Valiunas, a past president of the same organization, had come to their country to protest the Soviet take over of Estonia, Latvia and Lithuania. Mr. Grava called for the signers of the European security charter to recognize "the rights and aspirations of the Baltic peoples."

JULY. President Ford declared that the agreement he was to sign at the Conference on Security and Cooperation in Europe would provide a "yardstick" to guage advances in human rights for subjects of Communist rule in Eastern Europe. Meeting with members of Congress and leaders of emigre organizations, the President asserted that after World War II the United States did not recognize the Soviet annexation of the Baltic countries, and "is not doing so now."

AUGUST 1. It was reported that thousands of Americans of Latvian descent believed that President Ford's signature on a multinational agreement in Helsinki formalized forever the incorporation of their homeland, Latvia, into the Soviet Union.

Lipman Bers, a Latvian-born educator who became a citizen of the United States in 1949, was made president of the American Mathematics Society.

Nikolajs Cauna was made chairman of the Department of Anatomy of the University of Pittsburgh School of Medicine. Dr. Cauna was born in Riga in 1914 and obtained his M.D. degree from the University of Latvia in 1942. After teaching in Latvia, Germany and England, in 1961 he came to live in the United States.

Peter P. Lejins was made chairman of the board of directors of the National Criminal Justice Educational Development Consortium. Professor Lejins was a past president of the American Latvian Association (1951 to 1970) and the Free World Latvian Federation (1956 to 1970).

1976   MAY 10. A delegation of Soviet clergymen arrived in New York on a ten-day visit during which they hoped to observe religious life in America. The head of the group, Metropolitan Juvenaly of the Russian Orthodox Church, said that the visit should be considered a Bicentennial gift. Included in the group was Archbishop Janis Matulis of the Evangelical Lutheran Church of Latvia.

The *Latvians in Bicentennial America* by Osvalds Akmentins was published by Latvju Gramata of Waverly, Iowa. The book describes in essays, reprints of newspaper and magazine articles and pictures the story of five thousand Latvian immigrants who arrived in the United States from 1905 to 1910 and then recounts a second mass-arrival of forty-five thousand Latvians after the Soviet and Nazi occupation of the Baltic country.

1977 SEPTEMBER 27. Maija Krigena, a mezzo-soprano of the Latvian State Opera, made her American debut at the Carnegie Recital Hall. Ms. Krigena, who presented a program of Latvian art songs, was accompanied on the piano by Peteris Plakidis, a thirty year-old composer who teaches at the Riga Conservatory.

Gunnar Birkerts, the architect who was born in Riga in 1925 and became a United States citizen in 1954, was presented with an award of honor by the Michigan Society of Architects.

Ezekiel Schloss, Latvian-born editor and artist, published *Ancient Chinese Ceramic Sculpture from Han Through T'ang* (a two volume set). Mr. Schloss, who was a student at the Riga Art Academy from 1931 to 1934, came to the United States in 1940 and became a citizen in 1951.

Juris Hartmanis, a Latvian-born mathematician who emigrated to the United States in 1950, was appointed chairman of the department of computer science at Cornell University. Professor Hartmanis had been associated with the university since 1955.

THE
LITHUANIANS
IN AMERICA

1970   JUNE 14. Several hundred Americans of Lithuanian origin
commemorated the Russian persecution of the people of the
Baltic states by holding a protest rally in the Meditation
Garden in Queens, New York. The ceremony marked the anniversary of Soviet deportation and banishment to slave labor camps '
of 700,000 residents of Lithuania, Latvia and Estonia in 1941.

JULY 7. Pope Paul VI consecrated the Lithuanian Chapel,
Mater Miseracordiae, in St. Peter's Basilica at the Vatican. Most
of the contributions for the construction of the chapel came from
Lithuanian Americans.

OCTOBER 18. Demonstrations by Baltic sympathizers took
place in New York City on the occasion of the twenty-fifth anniversary of the United Nations. The purpose of the protest was to draw
attention to the denial of human rights and self-determination in
the Baltic nations. The Baltic Youth for Freedom, an *ad hoc* group
of young Americans of Estonian, Latvian and Lithuanian descent,
staged the demonstrations.

OCTOBER 25. The Baltic Youth for Freedom protested at the
editorial offices of the *New York Times* because of the continued
reticence on the part of New York newspapers to report Baltic events.

NOVEMBER 23. A Lithuanian seaman, Simas Kudirka, defected
from the Soviet trawler, *Sovietskaya Litva* off Martha's Vineyard,
Massachusetts. Mr. Kudirka boarded the adjacent United States Coast
Guard cutter *Vigilant* and asked for political asylum. After eight
hours, the Coast Guard officials, on the advice of the State Department, instructed the cutter to turn Mr. Kudirka over to the Soviets.
A civilian witness, the Latvian American Roberts M. Bieze, was instrumental in bringing the incident to the attention of the American
press. The seaman was subsequently sentenced to ten years of hard
labor in the USSR, but sustained action to secure his release
sponsored by the Lithuanian American Community, Inc. led to his release in August, 1974. The previous month the United States had
ruled that Simas Kudirka was an American citizen by virtue of having
an American-born mother.

---

*The author is indebted to Algirdas Budreckis, the editor of THE LITHUANIANS IN
AMERICA, for his research covering the period 1970 to 1975.*

BATUN organized the Baltic Folk Festival on the Latvian site, Priedaine in Hightstown, New Jersey. This was the first of a series of annual events to provide opportunities for Americans of Baltic descent on the eastern seaboard to strengthen their social and cultural ties.

1971 JANUARY 16. In view of current developments in Soviet-occupied Lithuania, the Council of the Lithuanian American Community Inc., meeting in Philadelphia, decided to become involved in political action. A public affairs council was established under the direction of vice-chairman Algimantas S. Gecys.

FEBRUARY 16. Thanks to the efforts of the Lithuanian American Community Inc. and the Lithuanian American Council, over one hundred legislators spoke in the United States Congress on the occasion of the fifty-third anniversary of Lithuanian Independence.

MARCH 27. The Lithuanian American Community Inc. together with similar Estonian and Latvian organizations sponsored the first Baltic Information Seminar in New York City.

APRIL 26. Representatives of the Lithuanian American Community Inc., joined with Estonian and Latvians to confer with Radio Liberty directors about the possibility of broadcasting in their native languages to the Baltic states.

NOVEMBER 1. Through the initiative of the Lithuanian American Community Inc., shortwave radio broadcasts were transmitted to Soviet fishing vessels off the American shores.

DECEMBER 11. The Lithuanian American Community Inc. sponsored a political studies weekend seminar in Philadelphia. The fourteen speakers addressed themselves to the status of the Baltic question in international affairs.

BATUN delivered a petition with thirteen thousand signatures to the United Nations High Commission for Refugees asking for the release of Simas Kudirka.

The Lithuanian American Community Inc. actively supported Senator Richard Schweiker's Ethnic Heritage Bill that was to provide federal funds for ethnic minority projects. The Lithuanian American Community also participated in the Washington conference of the Confederation of American Ethnic Groups, and established close relations with the National Center for Ethnic and Urban Affairs.

The Institute of Lithuanian Studies, Inc., which was founded in 1951 in Arlington, Massachusetts, first published its proceedings which were entitled *Lithuanistikos Instituto Suvaziavimo Darbai*.

The Lithuanian American Community Inc. organized demonstrations and solicited support for the imprisoned Simokaitis family who had tried to escape from Russia by diverting a plane in November 1970.

1972   FEBRUARY 16. Ninety-two legislators in the United States
Congress spoke on the occasion of the fifty-fourth anniversary of Lithuanian Independence.

MAY 14. Romas Kalanta, a twenty-two year old student, set
fire to himself in Kaunas, Lithuania, crying "Freedom, freedom,
freedom! Freedom for Lithuania!" He committed self-immolation to
draw world attention to Lithuania's plight on the occasion of President Nixon's trip to Moscow.

MAY 18. Demonstrations in protest of religious persecution
were held in Kaunas. Earlier that year a petition signed by 17,054
Catholics of the Prienai region in Lithuania was sent to Leonid
Brezhnev, first secretary of the Communist Party, USSR, and to
Kurt Waldheim, secretary-general of the United Nations. The petition expressed complaints that they were denied religious freedom
and suffered various forms of discrimination in their daily lives.
This action was followed by intensified repression of Catholic bishops and priests in Lithuania.

MAY 31. The Lithuanian American Community Inc. sent a delegation to meet with John Cardinal Krol, president of the National
Conference of Catholic Bishops, and Bishop John J. Dougherty, chairman of the Committee for International Affairs of the United States
Catholic Conference. As a result of this meeting, a joint proclamation was issued by the two prelates which stated: "In view of these
and other equally disturbing reports and in a spirit of brotherly
unity with our fellow Catholics in Lithuania and with the Lithuanian-
American Community we must in conscience censure the suppression of
human rights and freedom in Lithuania and elsewhere. We encourage
our churches in this country to join the Lithuanian-Americans in a
Day of Prayer for the Church in Lithuania on June 18, 1972. We alert
the churches and agencies of the international community to the grave
violations of justice and human rights in Lithuania and encourage
their support of corrective measures in that troubled country and
wherever such violations occur." Similar declarations were issued
by Cardinal Shenan of Baltimore, Bishop McNulty of Buffalo, Archbishop Boland of Newark, Cardinal Cody of Chicago, Bishop Grateman
of Sioux City, Bishop Hogan of Rochester and Bishop Sheenan of Omaha.

JUNE 15. The Lithuanian American Community Inc. declared
it a Day of Mourning for Romas Kalanta.

JUNE 24. Under the sponsorship of the Lithuanian World Community, the Second Lithuanian World Youth Congress was held in the
United States. Two hundred and fifty delegates met in Chicago for
meetings and symposia which lasted until July 16. The Congress voted
to establish a Lithuanian World Youth Federation (Pasaulio Lietuviu
Jaunimo Sajunga), under the aegis of the Lithuanian World Community.
Antanas Saulaitis was elected the first chairman of the executive
committee.

JUNE 26. The fifty-seventh Biennial Convention of the Lithuanian Alliance of America took place in Miami Beach, Florida.

JULY 1. The Fourth Lithuanian Folk Dance Festival, sponsored by the Lithuanian American Community Inc. was held in the Chicago Amphitheater. The First Lady, Mrs. Patricia Nixon, was the
guest of honor, and urged the participants to maintain their culture
"so others could enjoy it".

SEPTEMBER 14. A delegation of the Lithuanian American Community Inc. visited the State Department and lodged a protest against
the visit of United States Consul Culver Glyesteen to Vilnius and
his meeting with "so-called officials of Soviet Lithuania".

OCTOBER. A delegation of the Lithuanian American Community
Inc. was received by Archbishop Luigi Raimondi, apostolic delegate
of the Vatican in Washington, D.C. The archbishop was given a memorandum about religious persecution in Lithuania and asked to intervene with the Holy See for a Day of Prayer for the silent Church in
Lithuania.

NOVEMBER 18. In order to coordinate Baltic political action,
the Supreme Committee for Liberation of Lithuania joined with the
Free World Latvian Federation and the World Estonian Council to form
the Baltic World Conference in New York. Dr. Kestutis Valiunas was
elected the president of the newly-formed organization.

DECEMBER 31. According to the *Fraternal Monitor Yearbook
for 1973*, the status of the three Lithuanian fraternal benefit societies was: Association of Lithuanian Workers, Ozone Park, New York,
with a membership of 3,247 belonging to 100 lodges, insurance in
force, $1,786,479; Lithuanian Alliance of America, New York, with a
membership of 7,710 in 270 lodges, insurance in force, $9,381,045;
Lithuanian Roman Catholic Alliance of America, Wilkes Barre, Pennsylvania, with a membership of 5,138 in 163 lodges, insurance in
force, $4,027,611.

1973 FEBRUARY 15. A delegation of the Lithuanian American Community Inc. met with Michael P. Balzano, special advisor to
President Nixon, and presented him with copies of documents
recording religious persecution in Soviet-occupied Lithuania
for the years 1971 and 1972.

MARCH 4. Boris Lovet-Lorski, a sculptor whose subjects included four American presidents as well as Toscanini and Albert
Schweitzer, died at the age of seventy-eight. The Lithuanian-born
sculptor had studied at the Academy of Art in St. Petersburg and
came to the United States in 1920, becoming a citizen five years
later.

APRIL 24. Dr. Gerald R. Livingston of the National Security
Council received a delegation of the Lithuanian American Community
Inc. at the White House. The delegation delivered a memorandum ad-

dressed to Dr. Henry Kissinger urging that the international status of the Baltic states must not be compromised at the forthcoming European Security Conference by concessions to the Soviet Union.

MAY 26. Jacques Lipchitz, the sculptor who was born in 1891 in Druskieniki, Lithuania, died at the age of eight-one. Mr. Lipchitz, who was one of the first to apply the principles of cubist form to sculpture, became a citizen of France in 1924 but then became a citizen of the United States in 1958.

JULY 1. A nine-man delegation of the Baltic World Conference was in attendance during the European Security Conference in Helsinki, Finland. They were in Helsinki for the purpose of distributing memoranda on the Baltic question to diplomats and journalists.

JULY 5. At the request of the Soviet delegation, the Finnish authorities detained the nine Balts. Estonian, Latvian and Lithuanian political groups immediately took action to secure their release. Following a telephone communique by Secretary of State Rogers to the Finnish foreign minister, the nine were released the following day.

AUGUST 30. The Fourth Congress of the Lithuanian World Community was held in Washington, D.C. Bronius Nainys of Chicago was elected president of the organization.

AUGUST 31. A delegation of the Lithuanian American Community Inc. met with the American Revolution Bicentennial Commission in Washington, D.C. to discuss participation in the Bicentennial celebration The Commission registered the Lithuanian American Community Inc. as the participating Lithuanian organization.

OCTOBER 6. The convention of the Seventh Council of the Lithuanian American Community met in Detroit, Michigan and elected Juozas Gaila as their new president.

NOVEMBER 21. The Second Lithuanian Symposium on Arts and Science was held in Chicago. The sponsoring organizations were the World Lithuanian Association of Engineers and Architects, the Lithuanian American Association of Engineers and Architects, the Lithuanian Studies Institute, the Lithuanian World Doctors Association and similar professional groups.

DECEMBER 28. A meeting of Lithuanian youth leaders was called by the Lithuanian American Community Inc. in Cleveland, Ohio. As a result of these meetings, the Lithuanian Youth Association of America was established for the purpose of organizing students and other young people of Lithuanian descent.

Don Gussow, who was born in Pumpyan, Lithuania in 1907 and became a citizen of the United States in 1923, published a volume entitled *Divorce Corporate Style*.

1974   FEBRUARY 11. Vice President Ford received a delegation of
the Lithuanian American Community Inc. at the White House.
This was the first reception of a Lithuanian civic group on
the anniversary of Lithuanian Independence Day held in the
White House during the Nixon administration.

MAY 16. The Fourth Baltic Studies Conference was held in
Chicago, attended by 360 Baltic scholars. The Association for Advancement of Baltic Studies and the conference was presided over
by Professor Rimvydas Silbajoris, a Lithuanian.

JUNE 5. The Lithuanian American Community Inc., in conjunction with the Lithuanian Youth Association of America, organized visits to 171 Congressional offices, conferring with nine Senators and
nineteen representatives. The Lithuanian delegations sought support
for the resolutions of Congressman Derwinski and Senator Curtis
which upheld the principle of nonrecognition of the incorporation of
the Baltic states into the Soviet Union.

SEPTEMBER 27. The Eighth Lithuanian American Congress was
convened in Chicago to celebrate the continued political action of
the Lithuanian American Council.

OCTOBER 26. The Supreme Committee for Liberation of Lithuania held a conference in White Plains, New York. The conference
rededicated itself to the unequivocal restoration of Lithuanian independence, and reformulated its stand on relations with the occupied homeland.

NOVEMBER 5. Simas Kudirka arrived in New York with his wife,
two children and mother. The Lithuanian American Community Inc. together with the Americans for Simas worked closely with Amnesty International, Congressman Hanrahan and Senator Percy in obtaining
exit visas for Simas Kudirka and his family to come to the United
States.

NOVEMBER 27. The Third Lithuanian Theater Festival was held
in Chicago. The chairman of the Cultural Council of the Lithuanian
American Community Inc., Anatolijus Kairys, directed the series of
dramatic performances.

DECEMBER 7. The annual convention of the Supreme Committee
for Liberation of Lithuania met in Boston, Massachusetts.

1975   JANUARY 5. The first weekly broadcast in Lithuanian was
radioed to Lithuania over the Radio Liberty station in Munich. This was the culmination of efforts of the Lithuanian
American Community Inc. to have one hundred thousand dollars
included in the 1975 fiscal budget of Radio Liberty for Lithuanian
language broadcasts.

MARCH 1. Radio Liberty instituted a daily Lithuanian program. A radio staff under the direction of J. B. Laucka was set up.

JULY 25. President Ford declared that the agreement he was to sign at the Conference on Security and Cooperation in Europe at Helsinki would provide a "yardstick" to guage advances in human rights for subjects of Communist rule in Eastern Europe. Meeting with members of Congress and leaders of emigre organizations, the President asserted that after World War II the United States did not recognize the Soviet annexation of Lithuanian, Latvia and Estonia, and "is not doing so now".

JULY 29. Two American citizens of Baltic descent were detained by the Finnish police at the Helsinki airport. The Finns were afraid that Uldis Grava, head of the Baltic World Conference, and Dr, Joseph Valiunas had come to their country to protest the Soviet take-over of Estonia, Latvia and Lithuania. Mr. Grava called for the signers of the European security charter to recognize "the rights and aspirations of the Baltic peoples."

AUGUST 1. It was reported that thousands of Americans of Lithuanian descent believed that President Ford's signature on a multinational agreement in Helsinki formalized forever the incorporation of their homeland, Lithuania, into the Soviet Union.

Robert Kirsner, a professor of Spanish who was born in Ukmerge, Lithuania and became a citizen of the United States in 1943, published two books, *La Suspension de Mito en Algunas Obras Representatives de la Nueva Novela Hispandamericana* and *Hondradez, Matrimonio y Cortesania en Fortunata y Jacinta*.

1976 MAY 10. A delegation of Soviet clergymen arrived in New York on a ten-day visit during which they hoped to observe religious life in the United States. The head of the group, Metropolitan Juvenaly, of the Russian Orthodox Church, said that the visit should be considered a Bicentennial gift. Included in the group was the Reverend Vladis Rabasauskas, a diocesan chancellor in the Roman Catholic Church of Lithuania.

OCTOBER 2. Jimmy Carter, the Democratic presidential candidate, addressed about a dozen representatives of Pittsburgh's Lithuanian American community, many of whom came to learn his stand on the situation in Eastern Europe.

Charles Bronson (nee Buchinsky) appeared in six major motion pictures including: *Mr. Majestyk, Hard Times, Breakheart Pass, St. Ives, Chino* and *From Noon Till Three*.

Membership of the Lithuanian World Community, Inc. (PLB), which was founded in 1949, reached the half million mark. The organization, through its branches in twenty-three cities, works to preserve the Lithuanian culture, language, literature and history and to support the fight for Lithuanian Independence.

1977 OCTOBER 24. Jacob Robinson, the historian who was born in Lithuania and served in the Lithuanian Parliament from 1922 to 1926, died at the age of eighty-eight. In 1932 he was made legal advisor to the Lithuanian Foreign Office and eight years later, after Lithuania was annexed by the Soviet Union, he and his family settled in New York. Dr. Robinson was the founder of the Institute of Jewish Affairs and was the first director of the World Jewish Congress Institute of Jewish Affairs.

Barnett I. Shur, a Lithuanian-born lawyer who came to the United States in 1908, became vice chairman of the Committee on Governmental Ethics and Election Practices in the state of Maine.

Maurice S. Segal, a Lithuanian-born physician and educator who was associated with Tufts University School of Medicine from 1932, co-authored a volume entitled *Respiratory Care Advances*.

THE POLES IN AMERICA

1970 MARCH 4. The Polish-born leader of the United States Communist Party who was convicted of conspiracy under the Smith
Act of 1953, Betty Gannett (Rifke Yawschewsky), died at the
age of sixty-three. She was an editor of the party's theoretical monthly *Political Affairs*, and a member of the party's national committee.

The Kosciuszko Foundation in New York City initiated a Juni-
or Year Abroad program for students wanting to study at the Jagiel-
lonian University in Cracow, as well as a six-week summer course on
Polish culture at the same university, given in the English language.

The Center for Polish Studies and Culture was established at
Saint Mary's College, Orchard Lake, Michigan. The institute was
founded with the purpose of fostering research in the teaching of
Polish and to provide facilities for a library, an archive, an art
gallery and a museum of Polish Americana.

Thomas Gola assumed the post of City Controller in Philadelphia. He was the first Polish American to hold such a high office
in that city.

Attorney Leon Jaworski of Houston, Texas was named presi-
dent-elect of the American Bar Association.

After several conferences extending back to 1969, a Permanent Committee on Polish-Jewish Relations in the United States was
formed. The Polish National Alliance and the Anti-Defamation League
of B'nai B'rith took the lead in its organization.

Jack Raymond, the Polish-born public relations executive,
was made president of the International Institute on Environmental
Affairs which is based in New York City.

Alexander M. Schenker, a professor of Slavic linguistics at
Yale University, published *Fifteen Modern Polish Short Stories*.
Professor Schenker, who was born in Cracow, came to the United States
in 1946 and was naturalized in 1952. He was also the author of:

The author is indebted to Frank Renkiewicz, the editor of THE POLES IN AMERICA, for his
research covering the period 1970 to 1973.

Polish Declension(1964) and *Beginning Polish, Volume I*(1966) and *Volume II*(1967).

Dr. Hilary Koprowski of Philadelphia, a virologist and director of the Wistar Institute, was awarded a grant of forty thousand dollars by the National Multiple Sclerosis Society to investigate "slow virus".

President Nixon held two meetings at the White House with representatives of Polish American organizations and promised to appoint more qualified Polish Americans to high federal offices. Aloysius Mazewski was named as an alternate member of the United States delegation to the twenty-fifth session of the United Nations General Assembly.

Edmund Muskie's nationally-televised election eve speech on behalf of Democratic congressional candidates provided a strong impetus for his potential candidacy for the presidential nomination.

1971   MARCH 26. The Kosciuszko Foundation awarded medals of recognition for distinguished service to Polish and American culture to Stanislaw Skrowaczewski, music director of the Minnesota Orchestra; and to Maria Kuncewicz, a writer.

APRIL. A three-day congress of Polish American scholars and scientists was held at Columbia University. Damian S. Wandycz, chairman of the meeting, said that its function was twofold: "We think it can be a forum of exchange between men of differing disciplines who share a cultural history and cultural perceptions..and..we think it can show to the world those contributions that Polish thought has made and is making to civilization." About three hundred participants from the United States and Canada attended the conference, which was cosponsored by the School of International Affairs and the Institute on East Central Europe, both divisions of Columbia University.

JUNE. Eugene Kusielewicz, president of the Kosciuszko Foundation, was in Warsaw to negotiate a new student exchange program, a Polish American publishing venture, and to consult with the Polish Academy of Sciences on organizing a separate institute on Polish ethnic studies in the United States.

Cultural exchanges between Poland and the United States included the American tour of the Poznan Boys Choir, an appeal by a Polish committee to Poles everywhere to assist in rebuilding the Royal Castle in Warsaw which was destroyed in World War II, and the inauguration of an educational exchange program between Seton Hall University in New Jersey and the University of Warsaw.

Officials of the Polish American Congress met with federal administrators in Washington, D.C. in a search for fair recognition and equal rights for Polish Americans in all fields of endeavor.

The *Polish Daily News* (Dziennik Chicagoski) of Chicago ceased publication after eighty-one years of business. It was one of several Polish-language newspapers, including the *New World* of New York City, which had closed its offices in the past few years.

Aloysius Mazewski, on behalf of the Polish American Congress, presented Pope Paul with a memorandum which documented the under-representation of Polish Americans in the American catholic hierarchy.

Pope Paul participated in the beatification of Father Maximilian Kolbe, martyred in Poland during World War II. The presence in Rome of over 750 people organized by the Father Justin Rosary Hour was the largest overseas pilgrimage in the history of Polish America.

At its thirteenth General Synod in Toronto, the Polish National Catholic Church elected Bishop T. F. Zielinski as its prime-bishop.

Perspectives: A Polish-American Educational and Cultural Quarterly was first published in Washington, D.C. The magazine, written in English, contains articles on cultural, social and historical events of the Polish American community, past and present.

John Cardinal Krol was chosen president of the National Conference of Catholic Bishops and emerged as an important leader of the World Synod of Catholic bishops.

Adam J. Krakowski, a psychiatrist who was born in Sieciechowice, Poland and who came to the United States in 1949, was made executive director of the Academy of Psychosomatic Medicine.

Nowy Dziennik, a daily newspaper written in Polish, was first published by the Bicentennial Publishing Corporation of New Jersey. It incorporates international, national and local news, but emphasizes Polish American organizations and activities in the eastern part of the United States.

Walter Besterman, who was born in Poland in 1903 and who worked on most of the major immigration legislation in the United States from 1946 to 1970, became overseas director of the Tolstoy Foundation, Inc., a charitable organization active in refugee relief.

Understanding of Polish culture by non-Poles was fostered at a number of levels during the year. The Library of Congress sponsored a successful Polish folklore exhibit organized by Janina Hoskins. The Jurzykowski Foundation of New York City endowed a Chair in Polish Language and Literature to Harvard University, making its first occupant Professor Wiktor Weintraub. The businessman Edward Piszek and the Orchard Lake Schools of St. Mary's College launched a large, well-publicized and well-financed campaign called "Project Pole". It was designed to educate the American public about Poland

and to improve the image and self-image of Polish Americans.

1972   MARCH 21. The Polish National Catholic Church celebrated
it seventy-fifth anniversary. It was in 1897 that a group
of Polish residents of Scranton, Pennsylvania, mostly immigrants, decided to break away from the Roman Catholic Church
seeking to maintain more control over their parish affairs.

SEPTEMBER 10. The President's daughter, Mrs. Edward F. Cox,
attended a Polish American festival at the Shrine of Our Lady of
Czestochowa in Doylestown, Pennsylvania.

SEPTEMBER 13. It was announced that President Nixon had
proclaimed October 11 as a day honoring General Casimer Pulaski.

OCTOBER 7. Vice President Agnew addressed the delegates to
the Ninth Polish American Congress convention. In referring to
President Nixon, Mr. Agnew said: "He stood before the invasion of
domestic chaos in the spirit of John Sobieski (John III, a Polish
king of the seventeenth century) and like Sobieski he has turned
back a movement toward chaos that seemed, only four short years ago,
to be invincible."

DECEMBER 12. Leon Mitkiewicz-Zolltek, who represented the
Polish government in exile for the combined Chiefs of Staff in Washington, D.C. from 1943 to 1945, died in New York City at the age of
seventy-six. He was a colonel in the Free Polish Army and had
served with the Free Europe Committee, Inc.

DECEMBER. It was reported that about five thousand of the
"Polonia" community in the United States had over the years left
this country to resettle in their homeland. Americans who return
to Poland to retire do so because they can live comparatively well
there on what would barely suffice in the United States.
According to Dr. Arnold J. Keen, a former professor of law
and sociology, the main reason Polish Americans return to their
native land is economics, "but there is another enormous attraction
about Poland for the American —in Poland, old people still command
respect. In the United States, the so-called senior citizen is, in
fact, a disenfranchised castout."

The Polish Publication Society of America published *Poland
Discovers America* by Sigmund Uminski. The author looks at the New
World as seen in Polish writings and maps of the fifteenth through
the seventeenth centuries.

Damian S. Wandycz, who came to the United States in 1944
after serving with the Polish government in exile in London, was
awarded the Tadeusz Sendzimip Prize by the Polish Institute of Arts
and Sciences in America of which he was a former director. When he
arrived in the United States, Mr. Wandycz organized the first two
Congresses of American Scholars of Polish Descent. He was also a

former director of the Pilsudski Institute of America.

The American Institute of Polish Culture was established in Miami, Florida. It had formerly been called the Polish-American Cultural Institute. The main objective of the organization was to preserve the Polish heritage in the United States and to foster cultural events to stimulate interest in the Polish American community.

The Polish Museum of America Quarterly, written in English, first appeared. This journal is composed of reports on museum activities, programs, and exhibits and also includes articles on people, places and events of special interest to Polish Americans.

The Polish Cultural Foundations, Inc., was founded in Irvington, New Jersey. The organization planned to operate a Polish Cultural Center consisting of a performing arts theater, classrooms, library archives, a gymnasium and a pool.

Edmund Muskie officially launched his campaign for the Democratic presidential nomination early in the year. Despite considerable support from party leaders, he was unable to win the assistance of labor or reform elements in the party. A lack of support in the presidential primaries caused him to withdraw from active campaigning in April.

A United States Senate subcommittee held hearings on a proposal to convert the last residence of Thaddeus Kosciuszko in Philadelphia into a national historical landmark, further acknowledging Polish participation in American life.

The Polish American Congress joined those forces which sought successfully to continue funding Radio Free Europe over the objections of the Senate Foreign Relations Committee.

Richard Kolm, a Polish-born sociologist at Catholic University in Washington, D.C., was elected president of the National Coordinating Assembly on Ethnic Studies.

1973   AUGUST 5. Charles Rozmarek, honorary president of the Po-
lish National Alliance and the Polish American Congress, Inc., died. Mr. Rozmarek was president of the Polish National Alliance from 1939 to 1967 and was president of the Polish American Congress from 1944 to 1968.

Master of Light: A Biography of Albert A. Michelson by Dorothy Michelson-Livingston was published. It relates the life of the renowned Polish American scientist who first calculated the speed of light and was the first American to win a Nobel Prize in the sciences.

The Immigrant Experience: A Long, Long Journey, a thirty-one minute, 16mm, color and sound film by Linda Gottlieb was released by the Learning Corporation of America. The film focuses on the problems and dreams of newly-arrived immigrants to America by exploring the experiences of an uprooted Polish family.

1974   MARCH. Both the extraordinary sculptures and the drawings by Elie Nadelman were exhibited at the Zabriskie Gallery in New York City.

MAY. Ted Kluszewski, former Cincinnati slugger; Stella Walsh, a one-time track star; and former softball ace, Ed Tyson, were named to the National Polish American sports hall of fame.

AUGUST 4. A celebration commemorating the 200th anniversary of their countrymen's involvement in American history was enjoyed by several thousand Polish Americans who attended the festivities at the Polish Falcon camp near Somerville, New Jersey. The state's division of the Polish American Congress sponsored the celebration and chose Mayor John Jankowski of Perth Amboy as the guest of honor.

AUGUST 22. Jacob Bronowski, author and mathematician who was born in Poland in 1908 and came to the United States in 1964, died. Although he was a mathematician by training, he achieved wide recognition in other fields, especially through his television series *The Ascent of Man*. Among the books Dr. Bronowski authored are: *The Poet's Defence* (1939), *Science and Human Values* (1958), *The Identity of Man* (1965) and most recently, *The Ascent of Man* (1973).

OCTOBER 6. The thirty-eigth annual Pulaski Day Parade up Fifth Avenue was led by Police Officer Anthony Pierzgalski, the parade's grand marshal.

OCTOBER 8. The chief of the Communist Party in Poland and that country's leader, Edward Gierek, made an official visit to the United States. "There has not been a comparable visit in the past by a leader of the Polish People's Republic," said John W. Hushen, the United States deputy press secretary. In meeting with President Ford, both leaders stressed the friendship and friendly ties that have linked the two nations together, created by the emigration of millions of Poles to America.

Tad Szulc, the Polish-born journalist who became a citizen of the United States in 1954, published three books: *The Strange Career of E. Howard Hunt*, *The Energy Crisis*, and *Innocents at Home*.

Samuel Goldwyn was the recipient of the Motion Picture Academy Award for his production of *The Best Years of Our Lives*. Mr. Goldwyn was born in Warsaw in 1882 and came to the United States in 1896.

In order to study the Polish Americans and four other ethnic groups, the Ethnic Heritage Studies Program was founded at Indiana University in South Bend. Funded by the United States Office of Ed-

ucation, the main purpose of the institute is to encourage mutual
awareness and respect, to eliminate myths and recorrect stereotypes
in ethnic relations.

Theodore Roszak had a one-man exhibition of his sculptures
at the Pierre Matisse Gallery in New York City. Mr. Roszak, who
was born in Posen, Poland, came to the United States in 1909 and became a citizen in 1921.

1975   FEBRUARY. The major opening exhibition at Gallery 44 in
    Southampton, Long Island included the paintings of Jerzy
and Bogumila Koss and their children Tomira and Wlodek.
The gallery opened by Barbara B. Dietz-Michniowska was to
be a showplace for the folk art of Poland. Ms. Dietz-Michniowska
remarked that her purpose in opening the gallery was to give Polish
Americans, especially, some feeling of their deep roots.

AUGUST. The first Polish Town (a fifteen block area which
is part of Riverhead, Long Island) Festival and Street Fair drew
approximately sixteen thousand visitors. Shelia Marie Naugles was
chosen Miss Polish Town and was presented with her crown by Denise
Latour.

OCTOBER 5. Polkas, bands and floats, and over 100,000 marchers marked the thirty-ninth annual Pulaski Day Parade up Fifth Avenue,
which was led by this year's grand marshal, Jean Zagurek.

The Polish Museum of America in Chicago published two significant books on the Polish American. The first, a reprint of an earlier edition of *Polish Past in America, 1608-1865* by Miecislaw Hai-
man, is a scholarly look into the early history of the Poles in America, focusing on the period before the mass economic migrations.
The second volume, *Polish American History and Culture: A Classified
Bibliography*, was compiled by Joseph W. Zurawski, and contains 1,700
entries of works available in English. The titles included in the
bibliography are arranged under ninety-seven classifications and
then into fifteen sections.

Mary Anne Krupsak was made lieutenant governor of New York
State. Ms. Krupsak was previously a member of the New York State
Assembly(1968-1972) and was elected to the New York Senate and served
there from 1972 to 1974.

1976   FEBRUARY. An exhibition entitled *Constructivism in Poland,
1923-1936* opened at the Museum of Modern Art in New York
City. The show included works by such noted Polish artists
as Katarzyna Kobro (sculptor), Wladyslaw Strzeminski (painter), Karol Hiller (photographer) and Henryk Stazewski (painter).

FEBRUARY. The Supreme Court refused without comment to listen to a plea made on behalf of Polish Americans to obligate the

television networks to provide them with time to respond to deroga-
tory Polish jokes. This was in response to protests by the Polish
American Congress which for the past three and one-half years had
attempted to make the networks accept responsibility for material
containing Polish jokes.

FEBRUARY. Dr. Paul Wrobel, an anthropologist at the Merrill-
Palmer Institute in Detroit, spoke at the annual meeting of the American Association for the Advancement of Science. His speech summarized the results of his research which appeared in a paper entitled
"Polish-American Men: As Workers, As Husbands and As Fathers."

APRIL. Artur Rubinstein, the eighty-nine year old pianist
who was born in Lodz, Poland, received the Medal of Freedom. In
presenting the nation's highest civilian award to Mr. Rubinstein,
President Ford described the recipient as "One of our national
treasures".

JUNE 22. Ryszard Frelek, chairman of the Polish Parliament's foreign relations committee, presented President Ford with
his country's official Bicentennial gift, a set of gold coins commemorating Casimir Pulaski and Thaddeus Kosciuszko. The two Polish-
born heroes fought the British during the American Revolutionary War.

AUGUST 5. Karol Cardinal Wojtyla of Poland, who was in the
United States attending the forty-first International Eucharistic
Congress in Philadelphia, went to Passaic, New Jersey to rededicate
a plaque at St. Mary's Hospital. The plaque honored Archbishop
John Baptist Cieplak who was imprisoned by the Soviet government
for defying its attempt to prohibit Catholic worship in Russia just
after World War I. The Polish archbishop had died in a room at St.
Mary's Hospital while on a mission to the United States to inform
the American people of the religious persecution in Russia.
      Cardinal Wojtyla was accompanied by fifteen bishops of the
episcopacy of Poland. In addition, more than fifty clergymen and
lay officials from neighboring parishes attended the ceremony.

SEPTEMBER 4. Karol Cardinal Wojtyla, archbishop of Cracow,
was the guest of honor at a reception given by the Polish American
Congress at the Polish Soldier's Home in New York City. That evening, the cardinal visited the Polish Institute of Arts and Sciences
in America and then presented a lecture at the Kosciuszko Foundation.

OCTOBER 3. Thousands attended the fortieth annual Pulaski
Day Parade up Fifth Avenue in tribute to General Casimir Pulaski,
the Polish-born Revolutionary War hero. It is said that the general was the first to organize the American cavalry. He fought battles in Pennsylvania at Brandywine and Germantown, and died in America three days after he was wounded in the battle of Savannah,
Georgia on October 9, 1779.

OCTOBER. Bobby Vinton, the entertainer, set up a scholarship fund for Polish American students at Duquesne University.

DECEMBER. The Polish National Catholic Church reported that it was composed of 150 churches and had approximately 275,000 adherents. "We are a Catholic church following the tradition of Catholicism," said Prime Bishop Thaddeus Zielinski, the third head of the church, "and we give people a democratic form of government."

Samuel H. Reshevsky, the Polish-born chessplayer who came to the United States in 1920, wrote *Spassky-Fischer Games - The Act of Positional Play*. Among his other publications are: *Reshevsky on Chess* (1948), *How Chess Games are Won* (1962) and *Great Chess Upsets* (1975).

1977 AUGUST 27. The third annual Polish Town Fair in Riverhead, Long Island was attended by an estimated fifty thousand people.

OCTOBER. Andrew W. Schally, the fifty year old Polish-born doctor, was informed that he had been awarded a share in the Nobel Prize in physiology and medicine. Dr. Schally, who was affiliated with the Veterans Administration Hospital in New Orleans and with Tulane University, was awarded the prize for his research into the production of peptide hormones in the brain.

NOVEMBER. In order to help fill a void in suitable material to introduce children to Polish culture, Catherine Macaro of Detroit, created the Polish coloring book. The sixty-one page book with a red-and-white cover resembling the Polish flag contains illustrations for children to color plus three pages of footnotes and a brief bibliography for study and research.

DECEMBER 29. President Carter arrived in Warsaw and was greeted by Edward Gierek, Poland's Communist Party leader. The President said: "Relations are changing between North and South, between East and West, but the ties between Poland and the United States are ancient and strong."

DECEMBER 30. While President Carter met with Polish government leaders, Rosalynn Carter and Zbigniew Brzezinski, the President's national security advisor, met with Stefan Cardinal Wyszynski, the primate of Poland's Roman Catholic Church.

Jersy N. Kosinski, the author who was born in Lodz in 1933 and came to the United States in 1957, published *Blind Date*. Among his other works are: *The Painted Bird* (1965); *Steps* (1968); *Being There* (1971); *The Devil Tree* (1973); and *Cockpit* (1975).

THE
PORTUGUESE
IN AMERICA

1970 JUNE. Radio station WGCY of New Bedford, Massachusetts became a full-time Portuguese language broadcaster. Other New England stations with programs in Portuguese include WLYN, WHIL and WUNR of Boston, and WNBM-FM of New Bedford. WTEV television of New Bedford presents a weekly program in Portuguese as well as other programs for the Portuguese community.

George Rogers, a Portuguese American, was made mayor of New Bedford, Massachusetts.

The population of California was 19,957,304, of which 62,857 were native-born Portuguese and 17,805 were foreign-born.

The Right Reverend Monsignor John A. Silvia, a Portuguese American born in Fall River, Massachusetts, died. He was pastor of the Church of St. John the Baptist in New Bedford. During his incumbency, the new St. John's School was built.

1971 MARCH 13. The Uniao Portuguesa do Estado do California (U.P.E.C.) Cultural Center in San Leandro was dedicated. It provided space for the headquarters of U.P.E.C., the J. A. Freitas Library, an auditorium and various conference rooms. The center was the first of its kind in California.

According to the manual of the school committee of the City of New Bedford, there were 281 Portuguese surnamed people on the payroll of the public school system. There was a Portuguese American on the school board, Mrs. Rose Ferreira, first elected in 1952, seven Portuguese surnamed school principals and nine assistant principals. The Portuguese language was offered in the New Bedford High School and in the three junior high schools.

Eugenie Carneiro, a native of Shanghai but of Portuguese descent, died. For many years she was an official of the International Student House in Berkeley, California.

Criancas de Portugal (Children of Portugal) was founded in

The author is indebted to Manoel Cardozo, the editor of THE PORTUGUESE IN AMERICA, for his research covering the period 1970 to 1974.

Honolulu, Hawaii. It is an organization whose membership is limited to children. The purpose of the society is to teach its members Portuguese dances and the history and culture of the Portuguese who came to live in Hawaii.

1972   APRIL 13. By motion of Councilman Manuel F. Neto, a Portuguese American, New Bedford became the "sister city" of
Horta, Faial, the Azores. To further this relationship,
dignitaries of the two cities exchanged visits and on one occasion the Horta soccer team played in New Bedford.

APRIL. Jose Fernandes, who was born seventy-eight years ago on the Island of Madeira, died. He was the founder of the Fernandes supermarket chain.

Passarinho de Portugal (Little Bird of Portugal) was founded in Honolulu. The organization was established for the purpose of teaching its members Portuguese dances and traditions.

Earl J. Dias of Fairhaven, Massachusetts was named chairman of the Department of English at Southeastern Massachusetts University. He had served as a drama and music critic for the New Bedford *Standard Times* since 1947 and was the author of several books and numerous articles.

1973   NOVEMBER 18. The new pavilion at Dighton Rock on the Massachusetts coast near Fall River, was dedicated. About three
thousand people attended the ceremony. A cofferdam was
erected with funds provided by a state grant which raised the rock eleven feet above its original level.

NOVEMBER. The presidential nomination of Stuart N. Scott, the sixty-six year old former president of the New York State Bar Association, to be ambassador to Portugal was announced. He would succeed Ridgeway B. Knight, who was retiring.

Jose S. Silva, a native of Graciosa, the Azores, was the first president of the Portuguese Credit Union in Cambridge, Massachusetts, known as "the bank of the Portuguese in Greater Boston". Mr. Silva was a past president of the Portuguese Cultural Society of Cambridge.

The Luso American Soccer Association was organized in New Bedford.

Our Lady of Fatima Roman Catholic Church was founded as a Portuguese parish in Elizabeth, New Jersey.

Rudolph A. da Silva became mayor of Taunton, Massachusetts.

Edmund Dinis was made treasurer of Bristol County.

1974   MARCH. The gymnasium/auditorium complex of St. Joachim's Church in Haywood, California was completed. The pastor of the church, the Reverend Albano G. Oliveira, is of Portuguese descent.

OCTOBER 1. A new Portuguese radio program, *Portugal-Brazil*, was first broadcast over station KBRO in San Francisco, California.

NOVEMBER. Students registered for a Portuguese class which the Board of Education in Harrison, New Jersey agreed to sponsor.

John M. Arruda, a Portuguese American who served for six years as mayor of Fall River and who was believed to be the first Portuguese American mayor of any American city, became the executive director of the Fall River Housing Authority.

According to a survey conducted by the Brazilian Embassy and the Brazilian American Cultural Institute in Washington, D.C., there were 113 American colleges and universities that offered courses in the Portuguese language.

The first vice consul in the Consulate of Portugal covering all of New Jersey, George Cardiellos, reported that the Portuguese community in Newark had grown from 12,000 in 1965 to 30,000. About 60,000 residents of the state are of Portuguese descent.

Governor Reagan of California signed into law a bill that would henceforth exempt Portuguese fraternal organizations from turning over unclaimed insurance funds to the state government, provided that these proceeds would be placed in trust for scholarship aid to California residents of Portuguese descent.

With the death of Chief Justice Earl Warren of the United States Supreme Court, Council No. 55 of U.P.E.C. in San Leandro, California lost its most distinguished member. Justice Warren joined the Portuguese organization in 1925 when he was district attorney of Alameda County.

According to Manuel Fonseca, the Portuguese vice consul in Waterbury, Connecticut, before this year's revolution "mostly peasants came to this country. Now, all types of Portuguese are coming, hoping to find what they think may be a better life. The Portuguese government is beginning to worry about a brain drain, although no steps have been taken to stop people from coming."

County Commissioner Charles A. Frates of New Bedford, died at the age of eighty-two. The political career of this Portuguese American began in 1938 when he was elected common councilman for the fifth ward of New Bedford.

Belmira E. Tavares, the daughter of Azorean pioneers from Sao Miguel who emigrated to the United States in 1880, authored the volume entitled *Portuguese Pioneers in the United States*.

The first driver's manual to be issued in the Portuguese language in the United States was published by the Department of Motor Vehicles in Rhode Island. There are more Portuguese in Rhode Island in proportion to the total population than in any other state.

During the Nixon administration Ernest Ladeira of Fall River, the son of parents born on Sao Miguel, the Azores, was the most important federal official of Portuguese descent. He served as President Nixon's special advisor on social welfare and then as an assistant to Secretary of Transportation John Volpe.

A committee was organized to revive the traditional festival of the Holy Ghost in Little Compton, Rhode Island. The celebration would take place on August 3, 1975, in connection with the observance of the township's 300th birthday anniversary.

Statistics showed that Portuguese Americans are essential to the milk production of California, accounting for approximately thirty-four percent of all market milk produced in that state. It was reported that there were 1,468 herds owned by the Portuguese in California, amounting to about one-third of a million cows in all. Based on a value of $2,500 per cow, the Portuguese investment amounted to $833,090,000.
. The Portuguese in California are members of and participate in the direction of organizations of milk producers such as: the California Milk Producers Advisory Board of Modesto, the California Manufacturing Milk Producers Advisory Board of Modesto, Associated Dairymen of Lodi, the Producers Market Milk Association of San Jose, Western Dairymen's Association of Merced, the Los Angeles Mutual Cooperative of Montebello and the East-West Dairymen's Association of Newman. In addition, the president of the League of California Milk Producers based in Sacramento was a Portuguese, Albert Soares.

Our Lady of Light Society, a Portuguese benefit association located in Fall River, Massachusetts, reported that it had a membership of five hundred.

1975   MAY. Two Portuguese officials visited Washington, D.C. with the mission of learning something about the United States and explaining something about their own politics. Jorge Correia Jesulno, Portugal's information minister and Jose da Costa Martins, the country's labor minister, were guests of the State Department. Mr. Martins stated that "the United States government has shown real understanding for Portugal. It doesn't intend in any way to become hostile to Portugal. Quite the contrary, the United States' intention is to give us help."

The Portuguese Continental Union of the United States of America, founded in 1925, reported a membership of over nine-thousand. Among the purposes of the Boston-based organization are to provide life insurance benefits for Portuguese Americans, to sponsor cultural activities and to contribute to charitable institutions.

1976   JANUARY 22. Mario Soares, the secretary general of the
    Portuguese Socialist Party, spent three days at Yale Univer-
sity in New Haven, Connecticut as the Chubb Fellow. The
program was established in order to bring notable figures
in politics and public affairs to the university for informal discussions with students and faculty members.

1977   APRIL 18. The prime minister of Portugal, Mario Soares,
    the first government leader to be democratically elected
in his country in almost fifty years, arrived in New York.

APRIL 19. Andrew Young presented Prime Minister Soares
with the Human Rights Prize awarded by the International League
for Human Rights. The inscription on the award read: "By his un-
remitting devotion to democracy and freedom, Mario Soares inspired
his people to redeem their country to the cause of liberty."

Flora Purim, a singer born in Rio de Janeiro, Brazil who
came to the United States in 1967, recorded two solo albums: *Encounter* and *Nothing Will Be As It Was Tomorrow*. She was voted
the number one Established Female Singer by *Down Beat* readers'
poll for the fourth consecutive year.

THE
PUERTO RICANS
IN AMERICA

1970   JUNE 7. Jose Antonio Rodriques, president of the Puerto
   Rican Parade Committee, reported that sixty to seventy thou-
       sand people had taken part in the Puerto Rican Day annual
       march and that approximately four-hundred thousand people
had watched the parade through the streets of New York City.

JULY. New York City's first museum of Puerto Rican culture,
El Museo del Barrio, moved its headquarters to Public School 125 on
West 123rd Street in New York City. The director of the museum,
Robert Ortiz, stated that the museum sought to help Puerto Ricans
develop their cultural identity and a sense of pride in their commun-
ity. Programs at the museum are intended not only to reflect El
Barrio, the Puerto Rican ghetto in East Harlem, but all mainland
Puerto Rican communities.

Puerto Ricans in New Jersey organized a statewide Puerto
Rican Conference as a basis for future political power and influence.
A leading figure in planning and direction of the Conference was
Dr. Hilda Hidalgo, a professor at Livingston College, a division of
Rutgers, the State University of New Jersey.

Eugenio Maria de Hostos Community College was established as
part of the City University of New York. It was founded primarily
to serve the needs of the Puerto Rican community in which it was located. Candido de Leon was appointed president of the college in
1971.

Munoz Marin retired from the Senate.

MIRA, a Puerto Rican revolutionary and pro-independence
group, acknowledged carrying out nineteen terrorist acts since December 1969, including seven which took place in New York City. The
members pledged to continue the attacks.

Governor Ferre and President Nixon formed an *ad hoc* committee
that would discuss the participation of Puerto Rican residents in
United States presidential elections.

*The author is indebted to Francesco Cordasco & Eugene Bucchioni, the editors of THE
PUERTO RICANS IN AMERICA, for their research covering the period 1970 to 1973.*

1971   MARCH. The American Museum of Natural History in New York

City presented an exhibit of Puerto Rican contemporary life.

JUNE 10. At a City Hall ceremony, Mayor Lindsay proclaimed
the period June 7 to 13 to be Puerto Rican Cultural Week in New York
City.

JULY 18. Puerto Ricans in New York City gathered in Central
Park to celebrate the fifty-fourth anniversary of the congressional
act that granted them United States citizenship and to honor Luis
Munoz Rivera, the driving force behind the passage of that act.

AUGUST. Mayor Lindsay proclaimed the week of August 22nd
as Puerto Rican Folklore Fiesta Week. The Commissioner of Relocation, Amalia V. Betanzos, presented the proclamation to the president of the Puerto Rican Folklore Fiesta, Pedro M. Rodriguez, and
other officers in the group.

SEPTEMBER. Cuban representatives to the United Nations proposed a resolution to have United States colonialism in Puerto Rico
debated during future meetings of the United Nations Trusteeship
Council.

SEPTEMBER. Spanish-surnamed Congressmen announced the sponsorship of a National Conference of Mexican-American and Puerto Rican groups to discuss the lack of or inequality of justice over the
past decade.

NOVEMBER. New York City Puerto Ricans celebrated the first
Puerto Rican Discovery Day with a series of events in schools,
churches and community centers.

The United States Postal Service issued a stamp commemorating San Juan's 450th anniversary.

1972   JANUARY. An exhibition entitled *Nine Contemporary Puerto*

Rican Artists opened at the New York headquarters of the
Associated Councils of the Arts. The artists whose works
were being displayed were: Gino Rodriguez, Antonio Bechara,
Ralph Ortiz, Benedict J. Fernandez, Miguel Guzman, Martin Rubio,
Felipe Dante, Angel Franco and Gustavo Candelas.

MAY 22. The Commerce Department reported that the number
of citizens of Puerto Rican birth or parantage living on the mainland rose by fifty-five percent from 1960 to 1970. Although New
York State showed a nine percent drop in residency (63% versus 71%
of the total in 1960), the Puerto Rican population in the state of
New Jersey showed a marked increase over the ten-year period. Illinois ranked third among the states with 87,515 Puerto Rican residents in 1970, more than double the 1960 figure.

In order to establish equal rights for Puerto Rican women

in social, economic and political endeavors, the National Conference of Puerto Rican Women was formed in Washington, D.C.

Roberto Clemente of the Pittsburgh Pirates, the eleventh man in major league history to reach the three thousand hit plateau, died in a plane crash off Puerto Rico. He was on a flight that was transporting supplies to Nicaragua which had been hit by an earthquake.

The Puerto Rican Research and Resources Center opened in Washington, D.C. Its main function was to serve as a general research source on both island and mainland experiences. Antonia Pantoja was named director, and the members of the board of directors included: Blanca Cedena, Hilda Hidalgo, Victor Rivera, Jose Moscoso and Francisco Trilla.

The Popular Democratic Party returned to power in Puerto Rico with the election of Rafael Hernandez Colon as the new governor.

Hernan La Fontaine was appointed director of the New York City Office of Bi-lingual Education by the Board of Education. The Office, operating on a city-wide basis to meet the needs of non-English speaking children, was recommended by a Bi-lingual Commission convened by the chancellor of education, Harvey Scribner, and chaired by Professor Julio Morales.

1973   FEBRUARY 2. Pope Paul VI elevated Luis Aponte Martinez, Bishop of San Juan, to the College of Cardinals.

APRIL 30. In cooperation with the Metropolitan Museum of Art, El Museo del Barrio presented an exhibition entitled *The Art Heritage of Puerto Rico - Pre-Columbian to the Present*. The pieces displayed covered the range of eight hundred years of island history.

JUNE 3. Tens of thousands of marchers and several hundred thousand spectators attended the Puerto Rican Day Parade up Fifth Avenue. The grand marshal of the annual event was Representative Herman Badillo who led hundreds of groups in a parade which lasted nearly seven hours. The parade was dedicated to the memory of Roberto Clemente, the baseball player, and Tito Rodriquez, the bandleader.

JUNE 15. A nine-day fiesta of the Isle's songs and dances, the Salute to Puerto Rico, opened at Carnegie Hall. The tribute was designed to honor the cultural heritage of Puerto Rico and the Puerto Rican community in New York.

JUNE. An exhibition entitled *Puerto Rican Prints*, comprised of approximately fifty graphic works by twenty-five contemporary Puerto Rican artists, was on view at the Exxon Building in New York City.

JULY. Jose M. Lebron, president of the Puerto Rican Day Com-

mittee, stood by as Governor Cahill signed a proclamation designating
July 25 as Puerto Rican Day throughout the state of New Jersey.

A comprehensive bibliography edited by Paquita Vivo, entitled
The Puerto Ricans: An Annotated Bibliography, was published. The
volume, sponsored by the Puerto Rican Research and Resources Center,
included the holdings of the United States Library of Congress, the
University of Puerto Rico Library, the New York Public Library and
other collections.

A thirty-four minute, color and sound 16mm film entitled *Ain't
Gonna Eat My Mind!* by Tony Batten was released by Carousel Films.
The film, in examining the life of Black and Puerto Rican gangs living in the South Bronx area of New York City, documents an attempt
to establish peace and do something constructive for the community.

The Institute of Puerto Rican Unity (IPRU), which was founded
in Los Angeles in 1971, first published its *IPRU Newsletter*.

1974   JANUARY. Boricua College, the only private Puerto Rican col-
        lege on the mainland, and the only fully bilingual college
        in the Northeast, opened in Brooklyn, New York.

JANUARY. An exhibition of Puerto Rican photography called
Dos Mundos was held at the New York Cultural Center. The show was
organized by Geno Rodriguez, director of the Institute of Contemporary Hispanic Art, and was comprised of works by twelve Puerto Rican
photographers.

SEPTEMBER. A Labor Day weekend festival in Branch Brook Park
in Newark, New Jersey, sponsored by the Hispanic organization Focus,
erupted into riots and led to four days of disturbances which included looting, fire-bombing and rock-throwing.

OCTOBER 27. About twenty thousand people attended a rally
for Puerto Rican independence at Madison Square Garden in New York
City. The principal speaker was Juan Mari Bras, the secretary general of the Puerto Rican Socialist party.

NOVEMBER 2. The fifth annual convention of the Puerto Rican
Congress of New Jersey was held in New Brunswick. Governor Byrne
addressed the group, stating that he would press for the establishment of a state office for Hispanic affairs which would "provide
better communication and liaison between the Hispanic community and
the governor's office." The chairman of the convention was Marina
Berkowitz.

NOVEMBER. Approximately five hundred Spanish-speaking psy-
chologists, social scientists, hospital and community workers and
students attended a conference to discuss the difficulties that the
Puerto Rican faces in New York City in obtaining services within the
mental health establishment, especially the strong sense of alienation.

The conference, sponsored by the Association of Puerto Rican Social Service Workers and the National Coalition of Spanish-Speaking Mental Health Organizations, was chaired by J. Julian Rivera.

A collection of essays, mostly written by Puerto Ricans, entitled *Puerto Rican Perspectives*, edited by Edward Mapp, was published by Scarecrow Press. The volume consisted of four parts that presented perspectives from the education, the arts, the community and the individual viewpoint.

A research-political organization, the Puerto Rican Independence, was established in Seattle, Washington. Its primary purpose is to help Puerto Rico gain independence.

Carmen R. Maymi was appointed to the advisory board of the Republican Women's Forum. In 1972 she was made a consultant to the president's Cabinet Committee on Opportunities for Spanish-Speaking people.

1975   MARCH 3. In a weekend conference on the Rutger's Campus in
    Newark, New Jersey, the Puerto Rican Solidarity Day Committee
    was organized into a permanent body. Alfredo Lopez, the executive secretary of the group said: "We must recognize that our strategy is a strategy against the strategies of American imperialism. With this strategy we must unite everyone who can be united around the self-determination of Puerto Rican people."

MARCH. Rafael E. Torregrosa, national director of the Puerto Rican Migration Division located in New York City, reported that the migration of Puerto Ricans to the mainland had reversed during the national recession. The trend reinforced his belief that: "jobs are the magnet that draws our people to the United States mainland."

APRIL 2. Four time-bombs which exploded in midtown Manhattan were claimed as the work of the Fuerzas Armadas de Liberacion Nacional Puertorriquena (the F.A.L.N.). The group was described as a radical organization of Puerto Rican nationalists which had claimed responsibility for several other bombings in New York City, including the June 24 blast at an annex to Faunces Tavern, where four people were killed.

APRIL. The Puerto Rican Family Institute of New York City, sponsored a program called Puerto Rican Family Week, arranging both lectures and workshops around that theme.

JUNE 8. The eighteenth annual Puerto Rican Day Parade, with its Latin music, transformed Fifth Avenue into an extension of El Barrio. Vintin Suarez, the grand marshall of the parade, was one of the founders of the event, back in 1958. City Councilman Ramon S. Velez, the president of the parade committee, estimated that one hundred thousand people had marched in the parade and that several hundred thousand others had lined the parade route.

AUGUST 24. Thousands of Puerto Ricans took part in the tenth annual Puerto Rican Folklore Fiesta in Central Park.

SEPTEMBER 12. The Puerto Rican Statewide Parade of New Jersey organized the first Puerto Rican Heritage Festival, which was held at the Garden State Arts Center in Holmdel.

SEPTEMBER. Oscar Garcia-Rivera, chairman of the board of Aspira and editor of the American Bar Association's juvenile justice project, became the executive director of the Puerto Rican Legal Defense and Educational Fund in New York.

A Survey of Puerto Ricans on the United States Mainland in the 1970's, by Kal Wagenheim, was published. The volume examines the major changes which had occurred in the Puerto Rican community in American during the past three decades. It is arranged in three sections: the first part presents a national profile; the second part considers state and city profiles and concentrates on the Northeast; and the last part looks into the future propects for mainland Puerto Ricans.

1976   JANUARY 16. The National Puerto Rican Forum, Inc., which was founded in 1957, honored Mayor Carlos Romero Barcelo at a banquet at the Americana Hotel in New York City. Mr. Romero was the first Puerto Rican to hold the post of president of the National League of Cities of the United States Conference of Mayors. He had served a one-year term which ended in December.

FEBRUARY. A meeting was held at the Center for Inter-American Relations in New York City to protest the proposed cut in funds for the arts. It was said to be the first meeting devoted to the Hispanic arts which was attended by state legislators, members of the arts council and artists themselves. Among those present were: State Assemblyman Jose E. Serrano; State Senator Robert Garcia; Hiram Maristany of the Museo del Barrio; Marta Moreno Vega, acting executive director of the ten-member Association of Hispanic Arts; and Miriam Colon, the actress who founded the Puerto Rican Traveling Theater and who was also on the board of the arts council.

JUNE 4. A ten-day cultural festival called Fiestas Patronales del Barrio opened in East Harlem. The event coincided with a weekend of much activity surrounding the observance of Puerto Rico Week in the state and the city.

JUNE 16. Mayor Beame officially proclaimed the week of June 20 to be San Juan Week in honor of the Fiesta de San Juan, the traditional Puerto Rican feast day.

JULY. Victor Alicea, the president of Boricua College, the degree-granting Puerto Rican college that had attained an enrollment of almost four hundred students, announced that the school had become a candidate for accreditation by the Middle States Association

Commission on Higher Education.

AUGUST 29. The twelfth annual Puerto Rican Folklore Fiesta was held in Central Park. The festival honored Herman Badillo, the first congressman of Puerto Rican descent; Angel Cordero, Jr., the jockey; and Petra Francis Cintron, the poet and writer,.for their contributions to the Puerto Rican community.

OCTOBER. Manuel A. Bustelo was chosen as the new executive director of the National Puerto Rican Forum. Mr. Bustelo was also general counsel for the New York Federation of Urban Organizations.

1977 JANUARY 28. Freddie Prinze, the twenty-two year old co-star of the popular television show *Chico and the Man*, shot himself and died thirty-three hours later.

MARCH. It was announced that the Puerto Rican Traveling Theater, directed by Mirian Colon and celebrating its tenth anniversary, would move into a permanent home in the Broadway area. Ms. Colon remarked that "the new theater means expanding our outlook in terms of contemporary works by important playwrights and in reaching new audiences, both English and Spanish-speaking."

MAY 27. The Latin music community honored El Padrino (the Godfather) of Latin music, Federico Pagani, with a party on his seventieth birthday.

JUNE. A disturbance errupted in Humboldt Park in Illinois after a Puerto Rican Day demonstration. Two men were shot to death, Raphael Cruz and Julio Osorio, and approximately fifty others were injured.

JUNE. It was estimated that nearly eleven thousand people attended the silver jubilee mass celebrated in Spanish by Terence Cardinal Cooke. Almost one hundred thousand people in all participated in the various activities in celebration of the twenty-fifth annual New York Fiesta de San Juan Bautista. The 1977 fiesta medals were bestowed upon Mirian Colon, director of the Puerto Rican Traveling Theater and Joseph Wiscovitch, an executive with the Banco de Ponce in New York.

JULY 31. The New Jersey Puerto Rican Day Parade was led by Carmen L. Colon, the ceremonial queen of the festivities.

SEPTEMBER. Jorge L. Batista became president of the Puerto Rican Legal Defense and Education Fund, the first organization devoted exclusively to initiating law suits and class actions for Puerto Ricans in such fields as education, housing, migrant labor, employment and the administration of criminal justice, Mr. Batista commented: "We are now taking our efforts a step further and getting the Puerto Rican and entire Hispanic community involved in taking advantage of the rights we have won or are still fighting for."

OCTOBER 30. Nearly one thousand demonstrators marched in front of the White House, demanding independence for Puerto Rico and freedom for four nationalists emprisoned for violent attacks in the 1950s. The march marked the twenty-seventh anniversary of the Puerto Rican nationalist attack at Blair House when President Truman was temporarily living there.

THE
ROMANIANS
IN AMERICA

1970 JANUARY. The United States Information Center was opened in Bucharest, the capital of Romania. The center holds classes in English which are attended by about four thousand people, and presents theater and music performances. Concomitantly, a Romanian government library was opened in New York City.

JULY 30. Ionel Perlea, noted Romanian conductor who made his American debut with the New York Metropolitan Opera in 1949, died in New York City at the age of sixty-nine. Conductor Perlea was on the faculty of the Manhattan College of Music since 1952.

OCTOBER 11. President Nicolae Ceausescu of Romania and his wife visted the United States and met with some of the Romanian American leaders. It was the first visit by a Romanian Communist chief of state to the United States.

The latest United States Census reported that there were 216,803 Romanian Americans. This represented roughly one-tenth of a percent of the total United States population. Native born Romanian Americans numbered 146,116, while 70,687 were foreign born. Of the total number, 56,590 declared Romanian to be their mother tongue.

Marie France Ionesco, daughter of playwright Eugene Ionesco, served on the staff of New York University as a visiting instructor of French.

1971 James C. Augerot and Florea Popescu published *Modern Romanian*, a manual with current methods of language teaching, written for advanced university students. The volume was the product of a joint cooperative effort between an American and a Romanian professor.

Cassius Ionescu Tulcea, a Romanian-born research mathematician who came to the United States in 1957 and became a naturalized citizen ten years later, published two volumes, *Sets* and *Topology*.

The author is indebted to Vladimir Wertsman, the editor of THE ROMANIANS IN AMERICA, for his research covering the period 1970 to 1974.

1972   MARCH 10. Marioara Trifan, a twenty-two year old gifted
    pianist from New Jersey who had graduated from the Julliard
School of Music, made her debut at Carnegie Hall in New York
City. Ms. Trifan held several prizes from international
piano competitions.

DECEMBER 15. Romanian government officials signed a new
cultural exchange program for 1973-1974 with the United States. The
State Department reported that this move reflected "the mutual interest of the United States and Romania in a continued expansion
and improvement of exchanges".

The American Romanian Orthodox Youth (AROY), an organization
that was founded in 1950 in Jackson, Michigan, began publication of
the *A.R.O.Y. Newsletter*

Harry Morgan's Ambassador for Friendship group, consisting
of one thousand American high school students, gave 220 singing concerts in Romania. In return, artistic ensembles from Romania gave
several folk dancing and popular music concerts in the United
States.

Professor George Palade left Rockefeller University to take
over the cell biology section of the Yale University School of Medicine.

A book entitled *Twenty Years in Pictorial Review* was published by the Romanian Orthodox Episcopate of America. The volume included information on the main accomplishments of the episcopate
during two decades, covering the period from 1952 to 1972.

1973   SEPTEMBER 1. A Romanian Folk Ensemble conducted by noted
    artist Gheorghe Zamfir appeared at Carnegie Hall. The en-
semble performed popular Romanian folk tunes on traditional
musical instruments.

DECEMBER 4. President Nicolae Ceausescu arrived in the United States on a nine-day visit for discussions of trade and the Middle East crisis. It was the Romanian President's second visit to
this country.

DECEMBER 8. Romanian tennis player Ilie Nastase won the
Grand Prix of tennis for the third successive year. The twenty-seven
year-old sportsman had accumulated 610 points against 75 competitors
and was considered the number one tennis player in the world.

DECEMBER 27. The Romanian Studies Association of America
(RSSA) was founded by a group of professors during the Modern
Language Association Convention held in Chicago. A scholarly magazine, the *Yearbook of Romanian Studies*, was planned as a possible
publishing venture by the newly-established organization.

Radu Florescu and Raymond T. McNally, two scholars who spent more than ten years investigating Prince Dracula, scientifically reported their results in two books and dispelled all the myths that had accumulated over the centuries since the prince's death. The two books are: *In Search of Dracula: A True History of Dracula and Vampire Legends* (1972) and *Dracula: A Biography of Vlad the Impaler, 1431-1476* (1973).

1974 FEBRUARY 1. The newspaper *Romania* ceased publication, but the editorial board announced to its two thousand readers that if proper financial support were forthcoming, the paper would resume its activities.

MARCH 1. Traian Golea donated books on Romanian studies to 250 academic and public libraries all over the world.

MAY 14. Jacob L. Moreno, the psychotherapist who was born in Bucharest in 1889 and came to the United States in 1925, died. He was widely known as a psychodramatist, sociometrist and group psychotherapist. Among Dr. Moreno's long list of credits, not only did he originate the first living newspaper and invent the concept of psychodrama, he founded the Beacon Hill Sanitorium, the Therapeutic Theatre (the first theater for psychodrama) and the Sociometric and Psychodramatic Institutes. He also started two journals, *Sociometry* and *A Journal of Interpersonal Relations*. In addition, he was the author of many books including: *Group Psychotherapy, A Symposium* (1945), *The Theater of Spontaneity* (1947), *Who Shall Survive?* (1934), *Psychodrama* (two volumes, 1946 and 1959) and *Sociometry and the Science of Man* (1956).

AUGUST 31. The forty-fifth Annual Convention of the Union and League of Romanian Societies of America, the biggest and most influential Romanian organization in the United States and Canada, was held in Akron, Ohio. A new leadership was elected and a special letter of support was sent to President Ford.

OCTOBER 11. Dr. George Palade of Yale University School of Medicine was awarded the Nobel Prize for medicine. Dr. Palade shared the prize with two other scientists who made major contributions to the understanding of the inner workings of living cells. Dr. Palade is credited with discovering the cell's protein factory.

NOVEMBER 7. Alexander M. Bickel, educator and lawyer, born in Bucharest in 1924 and brought to the United States in 1939, died. Professor Bickel, who was on the faculty of the Yale University School of Law since 1956, was the author of *Politics and the Warren Court* (1965) and *Reform and Continuity* (1971), and was a contributing editor to the *New Republic* from 1957 until his death.

DECEMBER 9. At a reception for Nobel Prize winners in Stockholm, Sweden, Dr. George Palade predicted that man would conquer cancer in the near future. According to Dr. Palade: "The problem is how to make the cell defense system more efficient, like we do against bacteria infections."

To promote wider interest in the Romanian heritage in the United States, the Romanian Studies Group was created at the University of Washington in Seattle.

S. G. Theodoru of New York City published a volume entitled *Versuri* (Poems).

John Blebea, an eighteen year old graduate of Alliance High School, was the recipient of the National Youth of the Year Award.

John Houseman, who was born Jacques Haussman in Bucharest in 1902, received the Academy Award for Best Supporting Actor for his performance as Professor Kingsfield in the Twentieth Century Fox production of *The Paper Chase.*

Ioanna Salajan published *Zen Comics*, a collection of Zen stories and koans interpreted through the medium of the comic strip.

1975   FEBRUARY 9. Judge Leon R. Yankwich, who presided over numerous notorious cases, including peacetime espionage, wartime espionage, mineral rights, riparian rights and others, died.
Judge Yankwich, who was born in Jassy, Romania in 1888, emigrated to the United States in 1907 and became a citizen of his adopted country in 1912.

MARCH 18. Michael Gladstone, an assistant United States attorney in Detroit, reported that the government would file suit to revoke the citizenship of the Romanian Orthodox bishop of America, Valerian D. Trifa. This action followed allegations that the sixty year old bishop had played a role in the atrocities which took place in Fascist Romania more than thirty years ago, and that he had misrepresented his record to the immigration authorites. Bishop Trifa became a citizen of the United States in 1957.

JUNE 11. President Nicolae Ceausescu was in Washington, D.C. for meetings with President Ford and members of Congress. His purpose was to persuade the United States representatives that Romania, because it had liberalized its immigration policy, was now eligible for United States trade preferences.

The Acting Company, a national repertory theatre group, was founded by John Houseman who also served as the group's artistic director.

The Romanian Orthodox Episcopate of America reported a membership of almost fifty thousand. The episcopate comprised forty-seven parishes located across the United States.

1976 MAY 12. Toma Ovici, a four-time member of the Romanian Davis Cup tennis team, announced that he was seeking asylum in the United States and that he and his wife wanted to become American citizens.

JUNE 17. It was reported that the Romanian government would be sending a new ambassador to the United States, Nicolae M. Nicolae, a specialist in economics, who was to succeed Corneliu Bogdan in the Washington, D.C. assignment.

DECEMBER 2. Dumitru Udrescu, chief of the film and documentary section of Television Romania, requested political asylum. Mr. Udrescu was in the United States editing the program *Nadia - From Romania With Love*, a television show about Nadia Comaneci, the teenage Romanian olympic gymnast.

1977 FEBRUARY 4. The Romanian Orthodox Church in America suspended Archbishop Valerian D. Trifa from the governing board of the National Council of Churches. The bishop had been accused of Nazi war crimes, allegations which linked him with Nazi atrocities in Romania in the early 1940s.

FEBRUARY. Dumitru Udrescu was granted asylum in the United States. He had defected in December while on an assignment in Los Angeles, California.

DECEMBER 18. Moissaye Marans, a Romanian-born sculptor and art professor at Brooklyn College in New York, died at the age of seventy-five. Professor Marans, who worked mainly with bronze, teakwood and marble, chose religious themes for his subject matter. The artist came to the United States in 1924, but did not become a citizen until fifteen years later.

Eugen Weber, an historian and writer who was born in Bucharest, received the Californian Commonwealth prize for his publication of *Peasants into Frenchmen*(1976). Professor Weber came to the United States in 1955 and had been associated with the University of California at Los Angeles since 1956. In 1976 he was made dean of the School of Social Sciences.

THE RUSSIANS IN AMERICA

1970   FEBRUARY 26. Mark Rothko, the leader of the abstract expressionist movement and co-founder of the influential New York school and discussion center, Subjects of the Artist, committed suicide at the age of sixty-six.

JUNE. Alexander Kerensky, the leader of the first phase of the Russian Revolution and head of the provisional Russian government from July to November 1917, died in New York City at the age of eighty-nine. A funeral service was conducted by the Reverend Alexander Kiselev of St. Seraphim Russian Orthodox Church.

SEPTEMBER 11. A nursing home with ninety-six beds opened on the premises of the Tolstoy Foundation Center in New York.

After an interruption of eleven years, St. Joseph's School of Brooklyn, New York revived publication of *Podsnezhnik* (Snowdrop) which featured the stories, sketches, humor and drawings of students.

Wassily Leontief, noted economist, became president of the American Economic Association. He made several contributions in the field of economics and won international acclaim when he developed the input-output method of analysis used in economic planning and in forecasting output and growth requirements.

Genetics of the Evolutionary Process by Theodosius Dobzhansky was published. Born in Nemirov, Russia in 1900, Professor Dobzhansky emigrated to the United States in 1927 and is presently professor of zoology at the Rockefeller Institute in New York City.

The Russian Orthodox Greek Catholic Church of America was recognized as a fully independent body by the Moscow patriarchate, and changed its name to the Russian Orthodox Church of America. This body, the largest of three Russian Orthodox groups in America, reunited about sixty thousand people, organized under the auspices of 350 churches.

George Vernadsky, who was born in St. Petersburg in 1887 and came to the United States in 1927, published a work entitled *Dictionary of Russian Historical Terms from the Eleventh Century to 1917.* Professor Vernadsky, who taught history at Yale University, was also the author of: *The Russian Revolution* (1932), *Ancient Russia* (1943), *Medieval Russian Laws* (1947), *The Origins of Russia* (1959), *Tsardom of Moscow* (1969) and other scholarly books.

Alexander P. de Seversky, who was born in Tiflis, Russia in 1894 and came to the United States in 1918, was named to the Aviation Hall of Fame. Among his inventions are: the first gyroscopically stabilized bombsight, an in-flight refueling system, the fuel-carrying aircraft wing and a wet-type electrostatic precipitator for air pollution control.

According to the United States Census, 334,615 Americans declared Russian as their mother tongue. Russian Americans enjoyed the availability of thirty-one publications, twenty-five of which were published in Russian.

1971   APRIL. Igor Stravinsky died in New York City at the age of

eighty-nine. He was an active composer and conductor until the end of his life, devoting the last of his years chiefly to chamber music.

JUNE. Naum Gabo, the eighty year old pioneer constructivist sculptor, was made an Honorary Knight Commander of the Order of the British Empire. Mr. Gabo was born in Russia and lived in England for ten years, from 1936 to 1946, before emigrating to the United States. The badge and star of the order were presented to Mr. Gabo by Lord Cromer, the British ambassador, at a ceremony which took place in Washington, D.C.

The United States Bureau of the Census issued a study on self-identification by individuals according to their origin or descent. Among the seven major ethnic groups, families whose head of the household was Russian had the highest median income.

1972   JANUARY 12. An exhibition of Russian folk art opened in

Washington, D.C. On January 24, another exhibition, one centering upon American products, opened in Tbilisi, Russia.
These displays were significant because they marked the resumption of major cultural exchanges between the United States and the Soviet Union.

APRIL 2. M. Knoedler & Co., Inc. announced that a formal agreement on the exchange of art treasures between the Soviet Union and the United States had been signed. The United States would receive an exhibition of forty-two paintings from two Leningrad museums, thirty from the Hermitage and twelve from the Russian State Museum. They were to be shown first at the National Gallery of Art in Washington, D.C. and then to travel to other galleries in America.

JUNE 18. George Balanchine and his friends at the New York City Ballet celebrated Stravinsky's birthday in a week-long festival featuring Stravinsky's works. Stravinsky and Balanchine were close friends for decades and are considered by some the greatest composer and the greatest choreographer of our time.

OCTOBER 26. Igor Sikorsky died in Easton, Connecticut at the age of eighty-seven. Besides his outstanding contributions to American aviation, Sikorsky was also the author of such books as *The Invisible Encounter* and *The Story of the Winged S.*

DECEMBER. Louis Lozowick was honored during his eightieth year with a retrospective exhibition of sixty-four of his lithographs dating from 1923 to 1972. The exhibition of the work of this Russian-born artist took place at the Whitney Museum, New York City.

Vincent Glinsky, the renowned Russian American sculptor, was presented with a Bronze medal by the North American Fellowship of the National Sculpture Society.

A three-volume set entitled *Source Book for Russian History*, edited by the Russian American George Vernadsky, was published.

Louis I. Kahn, born on the Island of Osel, Russia, was awarded the Royal gold medal for architecture by the Royal Institute of British Architects. Mr. Kahn, who arrived in the United States in 1905, was professor of architecture at the University of Pennsylvania. In 1966, he had been appointed the first professor to fill the Paul Philippe Cret chair in architecture, an appointment which he held until 1971, when he was made professor emeritus.

1973   MAY 5. Nicholas Mordvinoff, the Russian-born artist and prize-winning illustrator of children's books, committed suicide at the age of sixty-one.

JUNE 12. The Russian-born composer, musician and arranger, Jacques Belasco, died at the age of fifty-six.

JUNE 12. George Vernadsky, a professor and leading historian on Russia, died at the age of eighty-five. In 1968, Professor Vernadsky was one of ten American academicians chosen to receive a ten thousand dollar award from the American Council of Learned Societies for distinguished accomplishments in the humanities and social sciences.

JUNE 19. With Leonid I. Brezhnev and President Nixon looking on, Soviet and American officials in Washington, D.C. signed four agreements intended to promote Soviet-American cooperation. Foreign Minister Andrei A. Gromyko signed for the Soviet Union and Secretary of State William P. Rogers and Secretary of Agriculture Earl L. Butz signed for the United States. The agreements concerned

sea study, transportation, agricultural research and cultural exchanges.

Artist Boris Anisfeld, professor of advanced drawing and
painting at the Chicago Art Institute from 1928, died. He had emigrated to the United States in 1918.

Eugenie Leontovich, the actress, who was born in Moscow and
graduated from the Moscow Art Theater, founded the Eugenie Leontovich Workshop for actors in New York City.

Michael B. Shimkin was appointed president of the American
Association for Cancer Research. Dr. Shimkin, who was born in Tomsk,
Siberia, came to the United States in 1923 and became a citizen five
years later.

Oscar Bodansky, a pioneer in the use of biochemistry for the
detection of serious diseases, was presented with the Lucy Wortham
James award for clinical investigation in cancer research. Dr. Bodansky, who was born in Elizabethgrad, Russia, became a naturalized
citizen in 1923.

Columbia University in New York City, created a new chair,
the Bakhmeteff Professor of Russian Studies Chair, and M. Raeff
was appointed as the first to hold the position. The chair honors
the late Professor B. Bakhmeteff who established the fund for Russian studies at Columbia.

1974 JUNE 30. Mikhail Baryshnikov, the twenty-seven year old
leading male dancer of the Kirov Ballet Company of Leningrad, defected after appearing with the Bolshoi Ballet
troupe in a performance of *The Nutcracker Suite* in Toronto.
Mr. Baryshnikov was born in Riga, Latvia and was a distinguished
pupil of the late Alexander Pushkin. In 1968 he won the Gold Medal
in the international ballet competition in Bulgaria, and won again
the following year in a similar competition in Moscow.

JULY 27. Mikhail Baryshnikov made his United States debut
at the New York State Theater in the American Ballet Theater's production of *Giselle*. He danced with Natalya Markarova, another former member of the Kirov Ballet Company of Leningrad, who had defected in 1970.

SEPTEMBER. Ilya Bolotowsky, the Russian-born painter, sculptor and muralist, had a major exhibition of his works at the Guggenheim Museum in New York City.

DECEMBER 15. Fifty paintings by twelve non-conformist Soviet artists were exhibited at the Temple Beth El synagogue in New
Rochelle, New York. Many of the works being shown were suppressed
in the violent disruption of an exhibition outside Moscow four
months earlier.

DECEMBER. Naum Gabo, the Russian-born sculptor, took part in a ceremony at Princeton University marking the installation of his *Spheral Theme* among the university's collection of outdoor art. The last of the John B. Putnam Memorial Collection to be installed was this stainless-steel sphere by Mr. Gabo.

The St. Serafimovich Fund of New York City organized a literary evening in honor of the Russian American poet Ivan Elagin.

The Russian American community of St. Petersburg, Florida celebrated the twenty-fifth anniversary of Elena Dolina's artistic activities in the United States.

Sonia Moore, author, director and producer who was born in Gomel, Russia, was the recipient of the John F. Kennedy Library American Heritage Award. In 1964 Mrs. Moore established the American Center for Stanislavski Theatre Art, Inc., and from 1971 acted as the artistic director of the center's repertory company.

Phenomenology and the Theory of Science and *Leibniz Philosophie des Panlogismus*, both by Aron Gurwitsch, were published. The author was born in Wilna, Russia and emigrated to the United States in 1940.

1975   FEBRUARY. New Jersey High School students produced a taped television program in Russian so effective that other schools were using it to teach foreign languages. The program, called Gorki after the world famous Russian writer Maxim Gorki, was patterned after the televison program *Sesame Street*.

MARCH 10. The noted sculptor Gleb Derujinsky died in New York City at the age of eighty-six. During the last years of his life, Mr. Derujinsky received the Therese Richard Award of the Allied Artists of America, the Anna Hyall Huntington Award of the American Artists' Professional League, and the Pauline Law Prize. Some of his works were acquired by the Metropolitan Museum of Art.

MARCH 19. Vincent Glinsky, sculptor, born in Russia in 1895, died. He had been a professor at New York University from 1950.

MARCH 28. David Lloyd Kreeger, president of the National Symphony Association, announced that the Russian cellist Mstislav Rostropovich was to be the new music. director and conductor of the National Symphony Orchestra, beginning with its 1977-1978 season.

MARCH 29. Pinhas Pierre Delougaz, educator and archeologist, who was born in Russia in 1901 and came to the United States in 1938, died. From 1969 he was the director of the Museum of Cultural History at the University of California, Los Angeles.

MARCH. The Russian society Rodina of Lakewood, New Jersey, exhibited a collection of paintings and sculptures by noted Russian

American artists as well as by representatives of promising young talent. The first prize was awarded to Igor Redkin, a nineteen year old sculptor.

APRIL 1. Alexandra Sannikova of New York City, widow of the late General A. S. Sannikov, celebrated her 100th birthday. She settled in the United States in 1955.

APRIL 19. One hundred and eighty objects, many in gold, *From the Lands of the Scythians*, made up an exhibition of ancient art from the Eurasian Steppe, which opened at the Metropolitan Museum of Art.

APRIL. The International League for the Rights of Man presented its Human Rights award to Mstislav Rostropovich and his wife, Galina Vishnevskaya, "for their courageous stand for artistic freedom".

MAY 8. In an editorial, the newspaper *Novoye Russkoye Slovo* voiced support for President Ford's plan for resettling about 130,-000 South Vietnamese refugees. It urged Russian Americans to sign a petition of support which should be sent to President Ford.

MAY 13. The thirtieth anniversary of the Allied victory in World War II was marked by the entrance of two Soviet guided missile destroyers into Boston harbor. At the same time, two American warships were sailing into Leningrad harbor.

MAY 18. A group of musical students enrolled in a studio conducted by Elena Volonsky gave a successful concert in Steinway Hall, New York.

MAY. The Russian American organizations celebrated the 175th birthday anniversary of Alexander Pushkin, the famous Russian classic poet. The New York Public Library organized a special exhibit of rare books and illustrations by Pushkin, or in his honor.

JULY. Russian exile writer Alexander Solzhenitzyn, a Nobel Prize winner and one of the most talented literary figures of our time, made an extensive trip to the United States, visiting several Russian American communities. He received a warm reception from many Russian American organizations as well as American academic circles. Mr. Solzhenitzyn's works, ranging from *One Day in the Life of Ivan Denisovich*, his first book, to *Gulag Archipelago*, were translated and published in the United States. Before his visit, the Congress of Russian Americans urged all Russian Americans to sign a petition and support a bill authorizing President Ford to declare Mr. Solzhenitzyn an honorary United States citizen.

SEPTEMBER. Alexander Filipov, a favorite ballet dancer of Pittsburgh, Pennsylvania, born in Russia and formerly with the Moiseyev Youth Company, joined the Pittsburgh Ballet Theatre as a principal dancer. He had been a guest artist in residence with the company for several years, and had also danced with the American

Ballet Theatre, San Francisco Ballet and Pittsburgh Ballet Theatre.

SEPTEMBER 28. Avrahm Yarmolinsky, author, editor and translator of many books dealing with the Russian language and its literature, died at the age of eighty-five. Included among his works are:
Russian Americana(1943), *A Treasury of Russian Verse*(1949), *A Russian's American Dream*(1965) and *The Russian Literary Imagination*
(1969). The last book he published was an edited volume in 1973 entitled *Letters of Anton Chekhov.*

DECEMBER 19. Professor Theodosius Dobzhansky, recipient of
the 1964 National Medal of Science award and the 1969 Distinguished
Achievement in Science award presented by the American Museum of
Natural History, died.

DECEMBER. An exhibition entitled *Russian Emigre Artists* was
held at the Andre Emmerich Downtown Gallery in New York City.

Kaleriya Fedicheva, a leading ballerina of the Kirov Company,
left her native land to join her American husband, a former dancer
with the Maryland Ballet Company.

John Shahovskoy, a Russian-born clergyman, wrote *The History
of Russian Intelligencia.*

The Russian American Youth Theater, founded by Tamara Levit-
skaya in 1968, celebrated its seventh anniversary. The group presented several plays by classic Russian and noted Western playrights.

Marc M. Szeftel, a professor of Russian and Slavic history,
wrote *Russian Institutions and Culture up to Peter the Great.* Professor Szeftel was born in Starokonstantinov, Russia in 1902 and
came to the United States in 1942.

A special memorial award was given in honor of the work of
Gleb W. Derujinsky by the North American members of the National
Academy of Fine Arts-National Sculpture Society.

The American Council of Learned Societies, the United States
Social Science Research Council and the Soviet Academy of Science
reached an agreement establishing the first cooperative venture in
the social sciences and the humanities. John Richardson, Jr., assistant secretary of state for education and cultural affairs, stated
that it was "in keeping with the kind of joint endeavors taking place
under the various specialized cooperative agreements signed between
our two governments and adds another dimension to our efforts to improve relations."

Boris Yavitz, born in Tblisi in 1923, was appointed Dean of
Columbia University's Graduate School of Business.

The Russian American Congress held its bi-annual convention.

Ilya Bolotowsky, the Russian-born artist and educator, had a one-man show at the National Collection of Fine Arts of the Smithsonian Institution in Washington, D.C., at the Schloss-Remseck Galerie in Stuttgart, Germany and at the Basel Art Fair in Switzerland. Mr. Bolotowsky, who was born in St. Petersburg, came to the United States in 1923 and became a citizen six years later.

The Russian Orthodox Church in America announced that it would publish a book entitled *Orthodox America: 1794-1976*. The book was to be produced as a tribute to America's Bicentennial and was to reflect the history and achievements of the Russian Orthodox Church in America.

Victoriya Feodorova, a leading Soviet movie star, came to the United States to visit her father Admiral Jackson R. Tate of Lantana, Florida for the first time in her life. During her visit, Ms. Feodorova married an American pilot, became a United States resident, and settled in the United States.

1976   FEBRUARY. The Feldman Gallery in New York City held the first exhibition of dissident Soviet art called "Sots". The works of Vitali Komar and Aleksandr Melamd reveal a type of Pop art which parodies the propaganda posters and street banners designed by Russian officialdom for public consumption. The works were smuggled out of Russia where they had been officially disapproved.

APRIL 30. The House of Representatives unanimously approved a resolution which urged the Soviet Union to permit free emigration of Jews and other citizens wishing to leave.

MAY 8. Marc Slonim, the Russian-born American critic, author and internationally-recognized expert on European literature, died at the age of eighty-two. Mr. Slonim, who was born in Novgorod-Severski in 1894, did not come to the United States until 1941 and only received his citizenship in 1957. Among his published works are: *The Epic of Russian Literature* (1950), *Soviet Russian Literature* (1964) and *Russian Theatre: From the Empire to the Soviets* (1961).

MAY 10. A delegation of Soviet clergymen arrived in New York on a ten-day visit in which they hoped to observe religious life in the United States. The head of the group, Metropolitan Juvenaly of the Russian Orthodox Church, said the visit should be considered a Bicentennial gift. Sponsored by the Appeal of Conscience Foundation, a private interfaith organization, the delegation also included: Rabbi Yakov Fishman of Moscow; Archbishop Janis Matulis of the Evangelical Lutheran church of Latvia; Bishop Nereses Bozabalian of the Armenian Apostolic church; and the Reverend Vladis Rabasauskas, a diocesan chancellor in the Roman Catholic church of Lithuania.

MAY 12. Mirra Komarovsky, the Russian-born professor who served as chairman of Barnard College's sociology department from 1948 to 1962, was presented with the Barnard Alumnae Association's highest award.

AUGUST 6. Gregor Piatigorsky, the Russian-born cello virtuoso and teacher, died at the age of seventy-three. Mr. Piatigorsky, who became an American citizen in 1942, was said to be one of the three greatest cellists of the twentieth century.

1977 JANUARY 21. Alexander I. Solzhenitzyn announced that he would start a non-profit publishing business in Vermont that would distribute works on Russian culture, history and religion in the United States and abroad.

FEBRUARY 5. President Carter responded to Andrei Sakharov's letter of January 28. In his letter to the Soviet Union's leading dissident, Mr. Carter said "the American people and our government will continue our firm commitment to promote respect for human rights not only in our own country but also abroad." It was the first time a Western leader had personally communicated with a Soviet dissident.

FEBRUARY. An exhibition of photographs, programs, books and art objects of Anna Pavlova was held at the Norman Crider Gallery.

MARCH 1. Exiled Soviet dissident, Vladimir Bukovsky, met with President Carter and Vice President Mondale at the White House, in a reception meant to symbolize Carter's commitment to human rights.

MARCH 22. President Carter sent a message to Congress recommending a substantial increase in the government's capacity to transmit radio broadcasts to the Soviet Union via Radio Liberty.

MARCH 27. Will Herberg, the Russian-born writer, scholar and educator whose views evolved from those of an American Communist Party leader in the 1930s to those of a religious conservative and social philosopher of contemporary American life, died at the age of seventy-five.

APRIL 24. A new chamber orchestra, Strings in Exile, also known as the New Russian Chamber Orchestra, gave its first public performance in New York. The group, composed of fifteen Soviet-Jewish emigres, was organized in 1976 by its director and conductor, Joel Spiegelman.

JULY 2. Vladimir Nabokov, the American novelist whose mastery of language, word-play and cultivated humor made him one of his generation's most recognized literary figures, died at the age of seventy-eight. He came to the United States in 1940 and was naturalized five years later. Among his better-known works are: *Laughter in the Dark* (1938), *Bend Sinister* (1947), *Lolita* (1958), *Nabokov's Quar-*

tet(1966), *Ada*(1969), *Transparent Things*(1972) and *A Russian Beauty and Other Stories*(1973).

JULY 7.   *Highlights of the Russian Dance Festival* was presented on NBC televison as a United Euran program filmed in association with Gosconcert, USSR.

AUGUST 23.   Naum Gabo, the Russian-born sculptor who founded constructivism, died at the age of eighty-seven. His theories were based on the concept of space as a structural element possessing material characteristics. He influenced other creative movements such as Pop and kinetic art.

SUMMER.   Leonid Dervbinsky, a twenty-one year old native of Odessa, slashed his way past 144 competitors in a Portland, Oregon tournament to become the national fencing champion of the United States.

OCTOBER 6.   Bishop Innocent, who served in Alaska in the nineteenth century and is identified with American orthodoxy, was canonized as a saint in Russia.

OCTOBER 25.   Bishop Theodosius of Pittsburgh was selected as the first American-born metropolitan of the million-member Orthodox church in America at a convention in Montreal.

NOVEMBER 24. Alexander Keller, the son of a Russian immigrant, found among his father's papers three letters written by Catherine the Great, the eighteenth century Empress of Russia. He also discovered thrity-four letters which were written by Nikolai Mikhailovich Karamzin, the Russian historian and literary figure who wrote an eleven-volume *History of the Russian State* in 1824.

DECEMBER 4.   Andre Eglevsky, often acclaimed as the greatest male classical dancer of his generation, died at the age of sixty. The Russian emigre who performed with the American Ballet, Ballet Russe de Monte Carlo, the American Ballet Theater, Ballet International and the Grand Ballet du Marquis de Cuevas, joined the New York City Ballet in 1951. He stayed with the New York City Ballet for seven years, the longest period he spent with any troupe in his career. In 1961 he formed the Eglevsky Ballet.

DECEMBER 13.   W. Michael Blumenthal, the secretary of the treasury, was the principal speaker at a fund-raising dinner for the Citizen Exchange Corps, an international exchange organization that arranges visits to the Soviet Union by Americans and to the United States by Soviet citizens.

THE
SCANDINAVIANS
IN AMERICA

1970   APRIL 14. President Nixon received Premier Hilmar Bauns-
        gaard of Denmark in the East Room of the White House. The
        President described the Danish leader, who was in the United
        States on a two-day visit, as a representative of "the pro-
gressive characteristics of Denmark."

        JUNE 4. Premier Olof Palme of Sweden began a nine-day visit
to the United States, a trip aimed at convincing Americans that although his country was opposed to the war in Vietnam, he and the Swedish people were not hostile to the United States. "We maintain
quite honestly," Mr. Palme stated, "that we maintain very good relations with the United States. Over the whole period since 1783,
there have been no bones of contention. In many respects, we are
the most Americanized country in Europe."

        John E. Kirk, professor of medicine at Washington University
in St. Louis, was the recipient of the Wisdom Award of Honor. Professor Kirk, who was born in Kallundborg and educated in Copenhagen,
emigrated to the United States in 1947.

        Edvard Hambo, Norwegian ambassador to the United Nations,
was the guest of honor and principal speaker at ceremonies following
the Norwegian Day Parade which has been held annually in Brooklyn's
Bay Ridge section since 1952.

1971   FEBRUARY 14. Theodore Jorgenson, a professor who was born
        in Narvestad, Norway in 1894 and came to the United States
        in 1911, died. He had been a professor of Norwegian history
        and literature at St. Olof College since 1925. Among the
studies that he published are: *The Cultural Development of the Norwegian People*(1930), *History of Norwegian Literature*(1933) and
American Ibsen Journal(1953).

        MAY 17. A parade to mark Norway Day took place in the Bay
Ridge section of Brooklyn. Bay Ridge, with its thirty thousand Norwegians, is the largest Norwegian community in the United States
and is sometimes referred to as the fourth largest city of Norway

(following Oslo, Bergen and Stravanger). About twenty bands, sixty marching units and twenty-five floats took part in the celebration. The keynote address was delivered by Joe Foss, a former governor of South Dakota who is the son of Norwegian immigrants.

SEPTEMBER 2. Oskar J. W. Hansen, the Norweigian-born sculptor who specialized in heroic and religious art themes, died at the age of seventy-nine. Mr. Hansen is probably best known in his a- dopted state Virginia for his 100-foot high figure of *Liberty*, a Yorktown landmark which commemorates George Washington's victory over Lord Cornwallis and his British forces. The piece that earned him the President's Medal of Merit for artistic achievement, however, was his *Winged Figures of the Republic* at Boulder Dam which is reputedly the largest single-cast bronze in the world.

R and E Associates of San Francisco reprinted a volume entitled *The Scandinavian-American* by Alfred A. Fonkalsrud. The book was first published by the K. C. Holter Publishing Company in 1915.

Arvid Paulson, the actor, author and translator who was born in Helsingborg, Sweden, presented his collection of Strindberg first editions to New York University. His translations of Strindberg plays as well as works by Ibsen and other Scandinavian playwrights have been performed in university, college and community theaters throughout the United States.

The Norweigian-American Historical Association of Northfield, Minnesota published *A Voice of Protest: Norwegians in American Politics, 1890-1917* by John Wefald. The author examines the political involvement of this ethnic group on local, state and national levels and compares differences in attitudes as revealed in the Norwegian American press versus "Yankee" newspapers.

 1972   OCTOBER 28. Her Royal Highness Princess Christina of Sweden attended a formal dinner party in the SoHo area of New York City. The party was given in her honor by Robert Rauschenberg, the artist. Earlier in the day, the Princess had attended another reception, where the New York art collection destined for Sweden's Moderna Museet was unveiled.

The Norwegian Society of Washington, D.C., which was founded in 1902, began publication of its monthly, *The Norwegian Society Newsletter*.

 1973   JANUARY 9. Eugenia Sodeberg, the Swedish-born novelist and journalist who came to the United States in the late 1930s, died at the age of sixty-nine.

JULY 1. Roy F. Lawson, the architect-planner who designed Independence Mall in Philadelphia, died at the age of eighty. Mr. Lawson was a past president of the American Swedish Historical Foun-

dation and Museum and had been made a Knight of the Royal Order of Vasa of Sweden.

OCTOBER 17. Colonel Bernt Balchen, USAF, retired, the aviator and explorer who was the chief pilot on Admiral Richard E. Byrd's first flight over the South Pole in 1929, died at the age of seventy-three. During World War II, the Colonel, who was born in Tveit, Norway, aided the Norwegian underground by flying from Sweden with agents, arms, medicine and radio equipment.

Laurence Melchoir, the world famous Wagnerian tenor who came from a Danish-Jewish family, died.

Victor Borge, the pianist and humorist who was born in Copenhagen in 1909 and emigrated to the United States in 1940, was awarded the Royal Norwegian Order of St. Olav, Knight First Class. He had previously been honored by King Frederik IX of Denmark who dubbed him Mr. Borge, Knight of the Royal Order of Dannebrog, and by being decorated with the Order of Vasa, Sweden.

1974 FEBRUARY 12. Arne Domerus and his seven-piece jazz group made their debut in the United States, performing at the Swedish Church on East 49th Street in New York City. Mr. Domerus and his band had long been recognized as the best brass band in Sweden, an unusually jazz-conscious country.

MARCH 21. After a fifteen-month diplomatic freeze between Stockholm and Washington, D.C., it was decided by the two countries to re-establish normal relations. President Nixon named Robert Strausz-Hupe to be the new United States ambassador to Sweden. At the same time, Premier Palme named Count Wilhelm Wachtmeister as the new Swedish ambassador to Washington. Commenting on his latest assignment, Count Wachtmeister said that he was eager to rebuild associations at all levels in Washington and especially to renew ties with Swedish Americans.

MAY 19. The annual Norwegian Day Parade in the Bay Ridge section of Brooklyn hailed the 160th anniversary of the Eidsvoll Constitution which set up Norway's legislative assembly. More than 5,000 marchers from 115 lodges, churches and civic groups participated in the event.

NOVEMBER 3. A week-long cultural festival celebrating the rich heritage of the Scandinavians began at the Brooklyn Public Library in New York City. The festival was sponsored by the library and the Peoples Bicentennial Committee and included 175 Scandinavian community organizations in the New York metropolitan area.

DECEMBER. Elsa de Brun, the seventy-eight year old Swedish-born artist known professionally as Nvala, was awarded the Royal Order of Vasa, First Class, by the King of Sweden.

Arnulf Muan, professor of geochemistry at Pennsylvania State
University since 1955, was chosen president of the Mineralogy Society of America. Professor Muan was born in Lokken Verk, Norway in
1923, came to the United States in 1952 and became a citizen of his
adopted country ten years later.

1975   APRIL. Queen Margrethe of Denmark had a birthday party in
    absentia when almost three hundred Danish Americans cele-
brated her thirty-fifth year at the Center for Inter-American Relations in New York City. The president of the Danish
American Society, Jorgen Kolding, announced that the royal couple
would visit the United States during the Bicentennial.

MAY 12. Niels C. Klendshoj, M.D., the Danish American bio-
chemist who was the co-discoverer of blood substances B and D and
who in general researched the practical application of specific
blood factors in transfusions, died.

JUNE 21. The Senate adopted a resolution calling on President Ford to designate October 9, 1975 as Norwegian American Day.

JUNE 26. It was announced that King Olav of Norway would
visit the United States in October to commemorate the 150th anniversary of the first organized Norwegian immigration to America.
The seventy-two year old monarch was scheduled to arrive in New York
on October 4, to visit the Norwegian community of Bay Ridge and
to address the United Nations. From New York, the King was expected
to visit Minneapolis, Chicago, Seattle, San Francisco, Los Angeles
and Anchorage before returning home on October 29th.

JUNE. Arthur O. Davidson, president of Wagner College and
chairman of the national coordinating committee, arranged for many
Norwegian Americans to travel to Stravenger, Norway. The travelers
returned to their native land to attend ceremonies on July 4 that
would commemorate the 150th anniversary of the departure of the
passanger sloop *Restoration* which brought forty-six immigrants to
New York on October 12, 1825. Among those who attended the ceremony in Stravenger were: Senator Hubert H. Humphrey, whose mother
was born in Tveit; Senator Walter F. Mondale, whose grandfather was
Norwegian; and Senator John C. Culver, who is a Swede but whose
wife's family is Norwegian.

JULY 25. The ninth annual Decorah, Iowa Nordic Fest was
held. It was estimated that fifty thousand people would attend the
various functions in an area where the Norwegian immigrants settled
almost 150 years ago. Decorah became a cultural center for Americans of Norwegian descent, who founded Luthor College in 1861 and
the Norwegian-American Museum in 1877.

JULY. Norway issued two commemorative stamps marking the
150th anniversary of the start of Norwegian immigration to America.
The 150-ore stamp depicted a family of settlers outside their

first home in the United States, a peat house that was the usual
Norwegian immigrants' home on the woodless prairie. The other
stamp, of 140-ores, depicted a watercolor of Cleng Peerson, who was
so active in the movement that he was called the "father of immigration".

AUGUST. Governor Wendell R. Anderson of Minnesota was received by King Carl XVI Gustaf as the Swedish American of the year.
The ceremony took place in the seventeenth century palace in Stockholm.

AUGUST. In commemoration of the one hundredth year since
the death of Hans Christian Andersen in Copenhagen, the New York
Public Library put on a display of illustrated editions of his stories and prepared a program showing film adaptations of some of these
works.

OCTOBER 7. King Olav V, celebrating the 150th anniversary
of organized immigration of Norwegians to the United States, visited
the Statue of Liberty. He unveiled a four-and-one-half foot wood
and stone inverted lectern depicting the sloop *Restoration*. The
monument was designed by Rolf Fredner in the United States, but was
executed in Norway. King Olav V was the first foreign head of state
to donate an object to the American Museum of Immigration which
opened three year ago.

OCTOBER 7. King Olav V attended ceremonies at the Biltmore
Hotel, during which a room in the Wings Club was dedicated to Bernt
Balchen, a Norwegian American pioneer aviator.

NOVEMBER 13. Prime Minister Anker Jorgensen of Denmark met
with President Ford at the White House. He later announced that
Queen Margrethe II and her husband, Prince Henrik, would pay a Bicentennial visit to Washington, D.C., New York and other cities in
May 1976.

Letters From the Promised Land: Swedes in America, 1840-1914
edited by H. Arnold Barton was published by the University of Minnesota Press. The historical events which most affected the Swedish
settlers from 1840 to 1914 are reflected in the letters they wrote to
the people back in Sweden.

1976   APRIL 19. The Swedish branch of the Vasa Lodge of America
selected Ewald B. Nyquist, New York state commissioner of
education, as the Swedish American of the Year.

APRIL. The King of Sweden, Carl XVI Gustaf, was in Washington, D.C. attending a debate between Swedish and American industrial-
ists. The conference was co-sponsored by the Swedish Federation of
Industries and the Work in America Institution.

APRIL. King Carl XVI Gustaf visited Jamestown, New York,
where forty-five percent of the population is of Swedish descent.

While there, the King awarded Roger T. Peterson the highest award
of the Swedish Academy of Science. Mr. Peterson, the "modern Audu-
bon" is the artist-writer of the popular series of field guides
about birds and other animals, as well as plants.

MAY 10. Queen Margrethe and Prince Henrik of Denmark arrived in New York City for a month-long visit to the United States
marking the Bicentennial.

MAY 12. Consul General Erik Krog-Meyer presented both Mayor
Abraham Beame and Public Events Commissioner Angier Biddle Duke with
the decoration of the Danish rank of Commander in the Order of Dannebrog. Decorated as Knights of Dannebrog were: Walter Terry, the
dance critic, for his longtime coverage of Danish ballet; John Heis-
tein, a Norwegian who was the North American president of Scandinavian Airlines; and Jens Rommerdahl, a Danish-born American who was
the director of the new passenger terminal on the West Side piers
in New York City.

MAY 17. Queen Margrethe and Prince Henrik attended a lunch-
eon at the Museum of the City of New York where they were given the
opportunity to see an exhibition of photographs of the Lower East
Side slums of New York taken at the turn of the century. The photographer whose works were being exhibited was the Danish-born
Jacob Riis.

JUNE 15. Harald T. Friis, a pioneer in several branches of
radio communications who was born in Naestved, Denmark in 1893, died
at the age of eighty-three. He came to the United States in 1919
and very soon was awarded a fellowship from the American-Scandinav-
ian Foundation that allowed him to study at Columbia University. He
became a citizen of the United States in 1925.

JULY 3. Crown Prince Harald of Norway presented President
Ford with his country's Bicentennial gift, a check for $200,000 that
was to be used to build a sports center in Minnesota. The Prince
commented that the gift reflected the close ties between Norway and
the United States, including his own education in America.

1977   MAY 15. The 163rd anniversary of the Norwegian constitution
was celebrated by thousands of Norwegian Americans who watched Liv Ullmann, the actress and author from Norway, and thousands of other marchers wind their way up Fifth Avenue in the
Bay Ridge section of Brooklyn.

JULY 29. The eleventh annual Nordic Fest took place in Decorah, Iowa. The Norwegian-American Museum in the town, founded in
1877, had a special exhibit of costumes, furnishings, tools and folk
arts recounting the story of the Norwegian immigrants in America.
The town puts on the festival annually to celebrate the community's
ties with Scandinavia.

SEPTEMBER 24. Andrew G. Hagstrom, founder and president of Hagstrom Map Company, died at the age of eighty-seven. Mr. Hagstrom, who was born in Sweden, came to the United States in 1909 and in 1916 founded the map concern which in 1968 became a subsidiary of the Macmillan Company.

Bo Svenson, the Swedish-born actor who came to the United States in 1958, starred in *Our Man in Mecca.*

David Abrahamsen, a psychiatrist, published *Nixon vs. Nixon: An Emotional Tragedy.* His brother, Samuel, an educator and director of the Norseman's League, was appointed to the advisory board of the Ibsen Sesquicentennial Symposium. Both were born in Trondheim, Norway and came to the United States in 1940.

THE SPANISH
IN AMERICA

1970   JULY. The National Urban League convention approved a resolution supporting equal opportunity for Spanish-speaking Americans.

AUGUST. President Nixon proclaimed September 13 to be the
start of National Hispanic Heritage Week.

The New York City Hispanic-American Dance Company, which
would later be renamed the Ballet Hispanico of New York, was organized by Tina Ramirez. Ms. Ramirez, the daughter of a Puerto Rican
mother and a Mexican father who was a bullfighter, trained in ballet
and Spanish dances in New York and at the age of fourteen joined the
Spanish dance troupe of Federico Rey.

Jose Luis Sert, professor of architecture and city planner,
was the recipient of the Thomas Jefferson medal in architecture a-
warded by the University of Virginia. Professor Sert, who was born
in Barcelona, came to the United States in 1939 and became an American citizen in 1951.

President and Mrs. Nixon invited the popular Mexican American singer Vikki Carr to entertain at a White House state dinner in
honor of President Rafael Caldera of Venezuela.

Official estimates from the 1970 census showed the following
numbers of Spanish-speaking immigrants in New York City: Cubans,
60,043; Dominicans, 51,231; Columbians, 22,581; Ecudorians, 16,075;
Peruvians, 3,814; Mexicans, 3,541; Venezuelans, 2,246; Bolivians,
956 and other South Americans, 8,647.

1971   FEBRUARY. A. F. Rodriquez was appointed executive director
  of the Cabinet Commission on Opportunities for the Spanish
Speaking.

OCTOBER 17. The seventh annual United Hispanic-American Parade took place in New York City. The Fifth Avenue parade, with fifteen thousand participants, honored Columbus Day as La Dia de la Raza

---

*The author is indebted to Arthur A. Natella, the editor of THE SPANISH IN AMERICA, for his
research covering the period 1970 to 1974.*

(the Day of the Hispanic Race) and the Spanish discovery of America. The marchers paraded under the flags of Puerto Rico, Mexico, Spain, Argentina and several Central American countries in what was said to be "a tribute to the twenty-two million Spanish-speaking Americans."

Lee Trevino teamed up with Jack Nicklaus to win the sixty-eighth national World Cup Golf Tournament at Palm Gardens.

Baseball player Joe Torre received the National League's most valuable player of the year award.

Samuel Z. Montoya was appointed justice of the New Mexico Supreme Court.

The Spanish Heritage in the United States, by Dario Fernandez-Flores, was published by Publicaciones Espanolas in Madrid.

1972   JANUARY. Officials of San Diego State College announced that Desi Arnaz had agreed to lecture on studio production of movies and acting.

JANUARY. The Institute of Contemporary Hispanic Art was founded by Gino Rodriguez and others to encourage development and awareness of the works of the Spanish-speaking artists in New York.

FEBRUARY 23. The National Conference of Christians and Jews announced that it would focus its "brotherhood committment emphasis" for 1972 on the Spanish-speaking minority in the United States. The two co-chairmen of the conference were Dr. Pascual Sanchez and Mrs. Grace Olivarez.

MAY 24. Dr. Felix Marti-Ibanez, a Spanish-born American psychiatrist, publisher and author, died at the age of sixty. Dr. Marti-Ibanez founded MD Publications, Inc. in 1950 and in 1957 began publication of the *MD Medical News-Magazine*, an unusual blend of medicine and culture.

JULY. The *New York Times* reported that according to the 1970 Bureau of the Census statistics, fifteen percent or 1,202,208 people living in New York City were Spanish-speaking. Of this number, 811,843 were identified as Puerto Ricans and 390,438 were reported to be of another Hispanic extraction.

OCTOBER 14. Emilio Bacardi, son of the founder of the Bacardi rum industry and the last surviving ranking officer of Cuba's war of independence with Spain, died at the age of ninety-five. Mr. Bacardi was born in Santiago de Cuba and fled his homeland in 1961 after Fidel Castro came into power.

DECEMBER. An exhibition of recent sculptures by Jose de Creeft was held at the Kennedy Galleries in New York City.

Romana Acosta Banuelos was named treasurer of the United States.

1973   FEBRUARY 21. Standing ovations greeted Andres Segovia's
▓▓▓   eightieth birthday recital at New York's Philharmonic Hall.
        During intermission, the Spanish guitarist was presented
        with the Lincoln Center Medal, a bronze award struck in
1972 in honor of the arts center's tenth anniversary and periodically bestowed upon distinguished artists.

   Chile, Peru and the California Gold Rush of 1849, by Jay
Monaghan, was published by the University of California Press.

   Argentine musician Gato (Leandro) Barbieri established himself in the United States as a popular composer and musician.

   Phillip Victor Sanchez was named United States ambassador to
Honduras.

   The Spanish government established a fund of $587,000 to be
used to aid the completion of a one million dollar, 140-yard Spanish-
style plaza in New Orleans. The plaza was suggested by Luis Aparicio,
the Spanish consul in New Orleans, as a commemoration of Spain's part
in the history of Louisiana.

   Golfer Chi Chi Rodriquez won the Greensboro Open golf tournament.

1974   FEBRUARY. An exhibition entitled *Latin American Prints From
▓▓▓   the Museum of Modern Art* was held at the Center for Inter-
        American Relations in New York City. The one hundred prints
        being shown represented a broad and diverse survey of the
graphic styles of Latin American artists from the beginning of the
century to the present.

   NOVEMBER. In celebration of the five hundredth anniversary
of the birth of Bartolome de las Casas, the Princeton University Library organized an exhibition of his books and related writings from
the period. Don Casas, a friend of King Ferdinand and Queen Isabela,
was an anthropologist-jurist-missionary-theologian-conquistador-
writer-historian who defended the rights of the American Indian in
Spain.

   The Forum of National Hispanic Organizations, which is composed of professional, community service, business and research
groups in the Hispanic community, was founded.

   Fernando E. C. de Baca, western regional director of the United States Department of Health, Education and Welfare, was named
special assistant to President Nixon for Hispanic affairs.

Reverend Robert F. Sanchez was appointed archbishop of the diocese of Santa Fe, New Mexico.

Jose Quintero, the director, producer and actor who was born in Panama City, received both the Antoinette Perry (Tony) award and the Drama Desk award for his direction of the play *A Moon for the Misbegotten.*

The first Cuban-owned and Cuban-operated bank in the United States, the Continental National Bank, opened in Miami, Florida. Charles Dascal, a Cuban American businessman who organized the bank's founders, was made chairman of the new association.

Angel J. Valbuena-Briones, an educator and author who was born in Madrid, published *Primera Parte de Comedias de Pedro Calderon de la Barca.*

1975   JUNE. The first National Hispanic Arts Conference took place in Washington, D.C. The acting executive director of Hispanic Arts, Inc. (the sponsoring organization of the nine-member group), Marta Vega, commented that they were "trying to get to the people who make decisions for support, by showing everything we do."

JULY 4. The National Basque Festival in Elko, Nevada was attended by some ten thousand Basques from all over the West. The weekend of activities which included a parade, a mass celebrated in Basque and a gigantic outdoor barbecue was highlighted by strength contests held at the Elko Fairgrounds.

DECEMBER 7. Representatives from Wisconsin, Iowa, Ohio, Kansas, Washington and California attended a meeting in Lincoln, Nebraska and voted to form a national organization to lobby the federal government on behalf of Spanish-speaking citizens. The group, called the Association of State Officers for Spanish-Speaking Affairs, elected Stan Porras of the Nebraska Mexican-American Commission as its first president. The members were particularly concerned about questions dealing with unemployment, migrant labor, voting rights and education.

DECEMBER 12. A meeting of the Forum of National Hispanic Organizations was held in Washington, D.C. Its members expressed their concern over "the President's lack of responsiveness to the particular problems, concerns and needs" of the nation's fifteen million Hispanic residents.

Emilio Gonzalez, a professor of Spanish who was born in La Coruna, Spain and came to the United States in 1939, published *El Teatro Infantil de Benavente.* Among his other published works are: *The Theory of Crime* (1931), *Grandeza y Decadencia del Reino de Galicia* (1957), *Bajo la Doble Aquila* (1970), *Spanish Cultural Reader* (1970) and *El Aguila Gala y el Bubo Gallego* (1974).

Maria Cellario, who was born in Buenos Aires, made her Broadway debut in *The Royal Family*.

Juan Gomez-Quiroz, a painter born in Santiago who has taught and exhibited his work in the United States, became a naturalized American citizen.

Jose de Creeft was awarded the Gold Medal of Honor by the National Arts Club in New York City. The Spanish-born sculptor came to the United States in 1929 and became a citizen in 1940. In 1974 the New School for Social Research Art Center mounted a one-man retrospective of his works, and in 1972 a book of his sculpture was published called *The Sculpture of Jose de Creeft*.

1976   APRIL. In honor of the United States Bicentennial, the Spanish government announced that it would loan the National Gallery of Art in Washington, D.C. eight paintings by Francisco de Goya including the famous naked and clothed *Majas*. The paintings were chosen to show the full range and variety of Goya's work, covering the years 1779 to 1822.

JUNE 2. A formal state dinner was given at the White House in honor of King Juan Carlos I and Queen Sophia of Spain. Their visit to this country marked the first official visit to the United States of any Spanish head of state.

JUNE 3. King Juan Carlos I and Queen Sophia spent a busy day in Washington, D.C. opening Bicentennial exhibitions and presenting Bicentennial gifts. They opened a Christopher Columbus exhibition at the Smithsonian Institution's Museum of History and Technology. Many of the things being displayed were lent to the Smithsonian by Spanish museums and included the first letter written by Columbus from the Americas dated January 4, 1493. The royal couple then dedicated an equestrian statue of Bernardo Galvez which stands in front of the State Department building. Galvez led two thousand Spanish soldiers in American revolutionary battles which resulted in the defeat of the British in western Florida in 1781. Afterwards, the King and Queen attended the unveiling of a sixty-ton statue of Don Quixote designed by Arelio Teno. The statue stands in front of the Kennedy Center for the Performing Arts.

JUNE 4. An exhibition of paintings and sculpture portraying impressions of New York by a group of Hispanic American artists opened at the Museum of the City of New York. The show included works by: Miguel A. Guzman, Lorenzo Pacheco, Felix R. Cordero, Ivonne Villaquiran, Jose Carabello, Domingo A. Pouble and Carlos Nevedo.

JUNE 16. President Ford signed into law a bill that directed federal agencies to keep more and better statistics on Americans of Spanish origin in order to help them "achieve a better life." The bill required the Labor and Commerce Departments and the Office of Management and Budget to collect additional data in order to "promote the improvement and expansion of social and economic statistics relating to Americans of Spanish origins."

JULY 2.   Leopold Badia, the Spanish-born actor who made his Broadway debut in 1927 in *Speakeasy*, died at the age of seventy-four.

JULY 11.   The Association of Hispanic Arts presented a program of Spanish music and drama at Lincoln Center for the Performing Arts.   The festival, made possible by a grant from the New York State Council of the Arts, was to take place annually.

JULY.   The White House announced the nomination of Ignacio E. Lozano, Jr., to replace James F. Campbell as the ambassador to El Salvador.   Mr. Lozano was the publisher of the Los Angeles Spanish-language daily *La Opinion* from 1953 onwards.

NOVEMBER.   An exhibition of photographs, slides, films, video-tapes and recording commemorating the one hundredth anniversary of Pablo Casals' birth opened at the International Center of Photography in New York.   The show, *Remembering Casals*, included recordings of music played and conducted by the cellist.

George Deloy, a Uruguayan-born actor, made his Broadway debut in *The Robber Bridegroom* playing the part of Kyle Nunnery.

1977   JANUARY 14.   President Carter named Joseph W. Aragon, a thirty-six year old California lawyer who was director of voter registration and Hispanic affairs for the Democratic National Committee, as special assistant to the president and White House ombudsman.

JANUARY 16.   Members of the Association of Hispanic Arts met to discuss what they considered to be inequalities in the distribution of support for the arts from the New York State government.   A representative of the Hispanic cultural center and theater, International Arts Relations, summarized the feelings of the group when he said: "The survival of Hispanic arts in the United States is intimately linked to the development of more adequate levels and a pattern of funding from governmental and private sources.   The State Council developed special programs to provide an outlet for funding. It ultimately segregated Hispanic and other non-mainstream art forms, limited their funding and by now has become a straitjacket preventing further development."

JANUARY.   The Spanish poet, Jorge Guillen, who has lived in the United States in voluntary exile since the Spanish Civil War, was awarded the Cervantes Prize, the highest literary award of the world's Spanish-speaking countries.   In 1955, Mr. Guillen won the Award of Merit of the American Academy of Arts and Letters and in 1976 he was named the first recipient of the Bennett Award, a new literary prize established by The Hudson Review.   Among his published works are: *Garden of Melibea*(1954), *Maremagnum*(1957), *Living and Other Poems*

(1958), *Language and Poetry* (1962) and *Affirmation: A Bi-lingual Anthology, 1919-1966.*

FEBRUARY 25.   Secretary of State Vance met with seven Cuban exile leaders who claimed to represent a substantial number of the Cuban Americans.   They told the secretary of state that they were unanimously opposed to any United States negotiations with the Cuban government of Fidel Castro.

MARCH 1.   President Carter met with five members of the Congressional Hispanic Caucus who urged the president to make more Hispanic appointments and to support legislation that would benefit the nation's Spanish-speaking population.   The group revealed to President Carter that he had only made four Hispanic appointments which did not include any Puerto Ricans, while President Ford had made fifty-two Hispanic appointments during his administration.

MAY 30.   The United States and Cuba agreed to exchange diplomats by establishing "interest" offices in each other's capitals.

MAY 30.   Rosalynn Carter began her trip to seven countries in the Caribbean and Latin America, a tour that combined gestures with substantive political and economic discussions.   During her two-week trip, she would make stops in Costa Rica, Ecuador, Peru, Colombia and Venezuela.

MAY 31.   Three Spanish-speaking priests who for many years had been involved in Hispanic affairs were named as auxiliary bishops of the New York archdiocese by Pope Paul VI.   Of the three, two were born in New York, Monsignors Theodore E. McCarrick and Austin B. Vaughan, and the third, Reverend Francisco Garmendia, was born in Spain and came to the archdiocese as a parish priest in 1964.

JUNE 4.   Two thousand marchers followed a color guard of Latin American flags during a demonstration in New York.   The marchers were voicing their support of amnesty for the millions of aliens living illegally in the United States.

JUNE 27.   President Carlos Andres Perez of Venezuela visited the United States for consultations with President Carter and business leaders in New York and Chicago.

JULY 1.   President Perez was in Philadelphia to dedicate a statue of Francisco de Miranda, a hero of Venezuela's revolutionary war and a fervent supporter of the American Revolution.

AUGUST 20.   After an interval of five years, the second national meeting of Hispanic-American Catholics took place in Washington, D.C.   It was said that the attendance by more than forty bishops reflected the growing political power of Hispanics within the church.   The Hispanic-American Catholics who account for nearly one-third of the fifty million American Catholics were concerned about representation in the church hierarchy, said Paul Sedillo, Jr., the

Secretariat for the Spanish-speaking. Hispanic groups which had
been fragmented regionally, Puerto Ricans in the North, Cubans in
the Southeast, Chicanos in the West, were becoming organized. According to Father Frank Ponce, the coordinator of Segundo Encuentro,
there was a growing "sense of Hispanics as a mosaic. We make each
other whole."

SEPTEMBER 20. Thousands of people participated in a March
for Freedom in Miami, Florida. Most of the marchers were Cuban exiles who protested the limited resumption of United States relations
with Cuba. The demonstration was organized by the Bay of Pigs Brigade 2506 and was supported by some sixty other exile organizations.

NOVEMBER 15. Santiago Carillo, the Spanish Communist Party
leader, began an eleven-day speaking tour of the United States at
Yale University in New Haven, Connecticut.

NOVEMBER. Felipe Gonzalez, the leader of Spain's Socialist
Workers Party, was in Washington, D.C. to meet with government officials including Vice President Mondale and Secretary of State Vance.

DECEMBER. The classical music monthly *Musical America* chose
Alicia de Larrocha as the Musician of the Year. The Spanish-born
pianist, presently in her fiftieth year on the concert stage, has
been acclaimed for her interpretations of Spanish music as well as
her mastery of the classic keyboard literature.

Federal government statistics revealed the strong influence
of the Hispanic culture in the United States. There were about twenty million Spanish-speaking people living in America who supported
nearly sixty Spanish newspapers and magazines. In addition, there
were about 450 radio and television stations that had at least some
Spanish-language programming.

David D. Sabatini, a cell biologist who was born in Buenos
Aires, Argentina in 1931 and received his MD from the University
Litoral in 1954, was made president of the American Society of Cell
Biology.

THE
UKRAINIANS
IN AMERICA

The author is indebted to Vladimir Wertsman, the editor of THE UKRAINIANS IN AMERICA, for his research covering the period 1970 to 1975.

1970   JANUARY 22. Governor William Cahill declared the day to
    be Ukrainian Independence Day in New Jersey, and urged all
        citizens in the area to observe the occasion. For fifty-
two years, Ukrainians throughout the world had been commemorating the day, on January 22, 1918, when after almost two hundred
years of foreign domination, Ukrainians proclaimed to the world
that the "Independent National Republic of Ukraine is hereby established on all Ukrainian territories". Governor Cahill made his
proclamation "in order that encouragement shall be given to these
brave people by the people of America, and that Ukrainians and Americans of Ukrainian descent be afforded the opportunity of formally
commemorating the significance of this memorable day throughout the
State of New Jersey."

JULY 1. Representative Kleppe introduced House Resolution
No. 1127 requesting that the President be authorized to issue a
proclamation designating January 22 of each year as Ukrainian Independence Day. Almost two months later, on August 25, Senator
Schweiker introduced Senate Resolution No. 455 making the same request. Both resolutions were referred to the Committee of the Judiciary.

The Ukrainian Academy of Arts and Sciences in the United
States started publishing *Visti Uvan* (News of the Academy), reflecting the academy's activities and disseminating short biographies,
bibliographies and other news.

The semiannual journal *Recenzija* was first published by the
Harvard Ukrainian Research Center. Written in English, the journal
serves as a source of reviews of scholarly materials published in
the Soviet Ukraine.

The Federation of Ukrainian Students Organizations of Mich-
novsky in Detroit, Michigan started publishing *Soniashnyk* (Sunflower),
a quarterly covering political and cultural aspects of the Ukrainian
Americans.

Walter Tkaczuk and Dave Balon, both players for the New York Rangers, were members of the National Hockey League's highest scoring line during the 1969-1970 season.

The library of the Ukrainian archeologist Jaroslaw Pasternak was donated to the Ukrainian collection at Harvard University.

1971   MARCH. Dr. Jurij Bojko-Blochyn of the Ludwig-Maximillian

University in Munich, Germany participated in the Harvard University Ukrainian Studies Program. The professor delivered a series of lectures on the life and works of the poetess Lesja Ukrajinka.

MAY 3. Metropolitan John Theodorovich, the spiritual leader of the 200,000-member Ukrainian Orthodox Church of the United States, died in Philadelphia at the age of eighty-three.

Roman Kupchynsky of New York City started a monthly publication, *Kryza* (The Crisis), advocating the creation of a Ukrainian Catholic patriarchate in the United States.

The Shevchenko Scientific Society of New York City, in cooperation with the Ukrainian Library Association, started issuing *Ukrainska Knyha* (The Ukrainian Book), a bibliographical quarterly covering literature, history and other pertinent topics of interest to the Ukrainian American community.

Lemkovina (Lemko Land), a monthly publication dealing with political, social and other aspects of the Lemko Ukrainians in the United States and Poland as well as the Ukraine, was started by the Lemkovina Press in Yonkers, New York.

Johnny Bucyk, a prominent player for the Boston Bruins, was selected for the National Hockey League's 1971 All-Star team. Mr. Bucyk, together with Vic Stasiuk and Bronko Horvath, formed the famous "Uke" line in national hockey during the 1950s.

The Association of Ukrainian Theater Artists, which was originally founded in 1946 and reactivated this year, began publication of *Actor's Voice*.

1972   FEBRUARY 23. Peter Pucilo, supreme treasurer of the Ukrainian National Association, died at the age of fifty-eight. Mr. Pucilo was also the treasurer of the Ukrainian Congress Committee of America and secretary-treasurer of the Ukrainian National Urban Renewal Corporation.

SEPTEMBER. The Beryozka Dance Company, directed by Nadezhda Nadezhdina, performed for two weeks at the New York City Center before embarking on a tour of other United States cities.

Professors' News, a quarterly publication of the Ukrainian American Association of University Professors (UAAUP), was first published.

1973   JUNE. Joseph Cardinal Slipyi arrived in New York City and received a very warm reception from Ukrainian Catholics. Cardinal Slipyi was a prominent leader and fighter for a Ukrainian Catholic patriarchate in the United States, but his views were not accepted by the Vatican.

JUNE. The Harvard Ukrainian Research Institute was established. The main objective of the institute is to conduct basic research projects and to provide annotated bibliographies and teaching materials for the three major Ukrainian disciplines: language, literature and history.

DECEMBER 23. Philip Rahv, who was born in Kupin, the Ukraine in 1908 and came to the United States in 1922, died in Cambridge, Massachusetts. In 1934 he became, with William Phillips, the founding co-editor of *Partisan Review*. After a brief period of suspended publication, the magazine reappeared dissociated from the Communist Party and was devoted to "the modern sensibility in literature and the arts and to a radical consciousness in social and political matters." Mr. Rahv stayed with the *Partisan Review* until 1969; in the following year he founded the quarterly *Modern Occasions*.

The Shevchenko Scientific Society of America celebrated a century of creative existence, prolific publishing activity, and useful exchange of ideas and experiences with three sister societies: the Shevchenko Scientific societies of Canada, Europe and Australia. The society, whose headquarters are in New York City, is headed by Matthew Stachiw, president, and Joseph Andrushkiw, first vice president.

During the academic year, the Ukrainian language was accepted as a subject to be studied for credit towards graduation from high school by the Maryland State Department of Education. The drive to receive accreditation for Ukrainian in the Baltimore area was led by Wolodymyr C. Sushko, assistant principal of the School of Ukrainian Studies-Ukrainian Congress Committee of America, who was also an instructor in the Baltimore school system.

1974   FEBRUARY 22. The Ukrainian National Association (UNA), the oldest and most influential of the Ukrainian American organizations, celebrated its eightieth anniversary. In celebration, the association's newly constructed fifteen-story skyscraper, named the "Ukrainian Building", was dedicated in Jersey City, New Jersey. The UNA embraces Ukrainians of all walks of life, of all ages, professions and religious faiths. The association has grown to include 460 branches in twenty-eight states of this country and seven provinces of Canada, with a total membership of 90,000.

MARCH. Professor Peter Reddaway of the London School of
Economics and Political Science, Professor Thomas E. Bird of Queens
College and Professor Alexander Yesenin-Volpin of Boston University
participated in seminars on Ukrainian studies at Harvard University.
Their discussions and debates examined the political and religious
aspects of the dissident movement in the Soviet Ukraine.

JUNE 23. The Ukrainian Congress Committee of America, in an
open appeal, urged the American people to show concern and to ask
President Nixon to intercede on behalf of persecuted Ukrainian political prisoners. The appeal stated that "Ukrainian political prisoners are not criminals - they are patriots who love their country and
are resisting the alien yoke of Communist Russia! They protested
against discrimination of the Ukrainian language, Russification of
Ukrainian culture and gross violations of human rights in Ukraine."
The members of the organization asked that "If you are a believer
in the principles of freedom and justice, demand that these victims
of Soviet Russian tyranny be released forthwith." A list of seventy
Ukrainians being persecuted, with a short biographical sketch of
each, closed the appeal.

JUNE 29. This day and the following day were declared Ukrainian Pioneers Days in North Dakota in honor of the first Ukrainian
American settlers in that state. About 2,500 Ukrainian Protestant
families of the Stundinsts sect first settled in Virginia in 1890
but later moved to North Dakota and founded a community which they
called Kiev, named after the capital of their native country.

SEPTEMBER 7. Katherine Hupalo, who for more than forty years
was a leading actress with the American Ukrainian Art Theater, died
at the age of eighty-five.

SEPTEMBER 30. Over two thousand Ukrainian Americans singing
the pre-Soviet Ukrainian national anthem and carrying Free Ukraine
flags, marched down Fifth Avenue to protest the treatment of Ukrainian Nationalist intellectuals. After rallying in Bryant Park, the
protestors held a demonstration on East 47th Street, near the United
Nations.

The Ukrainian National Women's League of America presented
a collection of books on Ukrainian Americans to the American Museum
of Immigration located beneath the Statue of Liberty in New York City.

Ukrainian publishers, bookstore owners and librarians from
the United States and Canada established a Ukrainian bookstore center
with the purpose of fostering the development of Ukrainian publications and popularizing and disseminating Ukrainian books in the free
world.

The Ukrainian Research Foundation, Inc. located in Englewood,
Colorado was created. The primary function of this organization is
to foster scholarly research and writing concerning the Ukraine and
Eastern Europe.

The Federation of Ukrainian Student Organizations of America (SUSTA), which was established in Washington, D.C. in 1953, first published its monthly newsletter entitled *Prism*.

The Ukrainian Research and Information Institute of Chicago published its second edition of *Ukraine: Selected References in the English Language* by Roman Weres. This bibliography lists about two thousand annotated entries for books, monographs, articles and dissertations in English about the Ukraine and Ukrainians.

1975 JANUARY. An exhibition of paintings, including some by Taras Shumilovich of New York City, opened in the Providential Savings Bank in New York City.

FEBRUARY. The Bronx Society of Engineers honored George Golovchenko for his outstanding professional activities and contributions to the development of the society.

APRIL. Dr. Michael Yarymovich of College Park, Maryland was appointed assistant administrator for laboratory and field coordination of the Energy Research and Development Administration. Dr. Yarymovich, a prominent scientist, had previously served as assistant director for the Apollo Flight Systems.

SEPTEMBER 21. More than a thousand Ukrainian Americans marched down Fifth Avenue to celebrate the American Bicentennial as well as the 100th anniversary of Ukrainian settlement in the United States. Senator James L. Buckley, who addressed the group in Bryant Park said: "I can think of no other people who came here more for their freedom than the Ukrainians. Too many people in this country want to hide from the fact that there is a new wave of repression in the Soviet Union." After the parade, the group gathered at Dag Hammarksjold Plaza at the United Nations to protest what they described as violations of human rights and the imprisonment of Ukrainians, particularly women, in Soviet jails.

Basil W. Steciuk, who was born in Hnylyiczky, the Ukraine in 1910 and became a citizen of the United States in 1955, died. He was a professor of classics at the Ukrainian Technological Institute in New York City from 1951 to 1961 and belonged to the Ukrainian Teachers Association.

The United Committee of Ukrainian Organizations of New York and the Ukrainian Bicentennial Committee of America published and distributed a pamphlet entitled "Ukrainians Salute the Bicentennial of the American Revolution." The brochure presented an historical retrospective of the Ukrainian experience in America and a description of the Ukraine. In closing, the Ukrainian organizations expressed the following sentiments: "Ukrainian Americans salute the Bicentennial of the American Revolution with pride and gratitude for the freedom and opportunities they have found here.
"They believe the same freedom and opportunities should be

enjoyed by their kin in captive Ukraine, and are striving to help them in achieving these goals... Ukrainian Americans say, 'Thank you, America' - may you grow and prosper for long ages to come! Mnohaya lita!"

1976   MAY 14. The first Ukrainian Street Fair on East Seventh Street, New York City opened its week-long celebration with a benediction by the Very Reverend Volodymyr Gavlich, who also recited a prayer in Ukrainian.

1977   FEBRUARY. An exhibition of Ukrainian American art, organized by the Newark chapter of the Ukrainian National Women's League, was held at the Newark Museum. Among the works being displayed, were pieces by Alexander Archipenko, Jacques Hnizdovsky and Michael Chershniovsky.

SEPTEMBER 18. After participating in a march organized by the Ukrainian Organizations of New York, two thousand young Ukrainian Americans left the rally to demonstrate in front of the Soviet Mission to the United Nations. A disruption broke out and a number of demonstrators as well as policemen were reported injured. The latter march was organized by the Ukrainian Student Organizations.

SEPTEMBER 19. Borys Martos, who headed an independent Ukrainian government in Kiev in 1919 to 1920 before the Bolshevik takeover, died at the age of ninety-eight. In 1917, after the overthrow of the Czar, Mr. Martos had become a member of the Central Rada, a Ukrainian Nationalist legislative group, and served during 1918 as the minister of agriculture and the treasury. In 1919 he became prime minister of the Ukrainian National Republic. Mr. Martos emigrated to the United States in the late 1940s.

SEPTEMBER 21. The Ukrainian Dance Company Yatran made its debut performance in North America as part of the Radio City Music Hall Pop Festival. Anatoly Krivokhiza was the artistic director and chief choreograher for the fifty-plus member dance group.

DECEMBER 1. Joseph Schmondiuk was installed as the Ukrainian Catholic archbishop of Philadelphia.

Haym Kruglak, who was born in Dneprodzerzhinsk, the Ukraine in 1909 and came to the United States in 1927, received a Distinguished Service citation from the American Association of Physics Teachers.

Lester Velie, a Ukrainian-born editor associated with Reader's Digest since 1953, authored the book *Desperate Bargain: Why Jimmy Hoffa Had to Die*.

DOCUMENTS

The article and charts that follow have been included in this volume to help the reader understand American immigration policy and how it bears directly on the different ethnic groups. Charles B. Keely, the author of the research report which was prepared for the Commission on Population Growth and the American Future, emphasizes the point that immigration policy cannot be considered outside the context of its historical, political and social implications. He believes, as do other scholars in the field, that Americans are either immigrants or descendants of immigrants and that the question of immigration policy has always and still continues to affect us all.

Immigration: Considerations on Trends, Prospects, and Policy *

INTRODUCTION

Contexts

Immigration to the United States is a theme as old as the Republic. Thus, in considering current immigration and its effects on America's population growth and future, the historical context should be taken into consideration. We are all immigrants and the children of immigrants. From the plains Indians to the latest plane of Cuban refugees landing in Miami, Americans have come from migrating peoples. The European colonization and the post-revolutionary periods of the United States are even more clearly affected by the impact of immigration.

Immigration, therefore, is part and parcel of what we have been and have become as a nation. The conception of the nation as a refuge, as a land of opportunity, and as a country made great by the contributions of many groups of people is deeply imbedded in our self-image. Despite their dubious accuracy, concepts and symbols like the "melting pot" and the Statue of Liberty sum up an ideal of humaneness characteristic of American society.

Immigration has been a major contributor to growth and development in the United States. The population, our cities, the economy, scientific endeavor, the arts, and American life and culture itself have been formatively influenced by immigration. Immigration has in turn been incorporated in the ideals and self-image of the country.

Immigration has another historical role in the United States which is important in considering immigration policy. Choosing and excluding immigrants has been

* The article, by Charles B. Keely, appeared in *Demographic and Social Aspects of Population Growth* edited by Charles F. Westoff and Robert Parke, Jr.; U.S. Bureau of The Census, 1974 pp. 179-204. A small section of the text has been deleted as have the footnotes.

an historical approach to solving domestic problems. Immigration restriction is often proposed as a solution to recessions in the economy, rapid growth of cities, and conflicts of religious and political values. The restrictionist response itself seems an almost institutionalized political response to a host of internal issues.

While, history should neither restrict our perception nor determine our response, historical roles should not be overlooked when evaluating the place of immigration in population policy. The country's openness to and faith in the immigrant have been repaid handsomely. Our image of ourselves as a society, our ideals and goals, include the humanity, openness, and trust necessary for the acceptance of the foreign-born into our society and culture. And policy considerations should also proceed with a clear recognition of the sometimes scapegoating role of restrictionist policies in solving domestic problems.

In addition to the historical context, immigration takes place in a contempory political context of some complexity. In Congress, legislation on immigration is presided over by subcommittees of the Committee on the Judiciary in each of the houses. In addition, the Senate has a Subcommittee on Refugees and Escapees. Appropriate committees on finance, labor, and foreign relations also take an interest in immigration matters. Within this committee structure, Congress handles both public and private legislation. In addition, Congress exerts informal influence on immigration matters by giving opinions on interpretation and intention to Executive departments.

The Executive Branch is represented in immigration matters by parts of the Departments of State, Justice, and Labor. Due to the strong assertion by Congress of its rights over immigration, the Executive has most carefully tried to avoid Congressional disfavor on the subject. The amount of interaction and the care involved in drafting and administering immigration law has meant the investment of many hours and much patience by members of both branches of government. The result is an extremely complex operation. It would be surprising if major changes did not quite naturally (although not necessarily rightly) result in hesitation and outright opposition from legislators and officials who administer immigration law.

Immigration issues draw much attention from well-organized interest groups. There does not now exist a documented history of the development of the coalition which lobbied for and was successful in repealing the national origins quota system. Those who have followed the events know that the change had both powerful support and opposition from nongovernmental groups.

Since the Immigration Act of 1965, nongovernmental groups have shown continued interest both in further changes in the law and in its administration. Much of this interest has centered around the question of labor certification. (For an explanation of this program, see section on "Problem Areas.") Policy alternatives must take into account the influence of these various groups.

There is a final aspect affecting the political context of immigration. The impact of immigration on the labor force is a variable of deep interest to supporters and opponents of any immigration issue. It is now axiomatic that there must be a careful and special appraisal of the effects of any change of immigration policy on the work force.

In addition to the historical and political contexts, what may be called the social context should also be clearly in mind when considering immigration. This "social context" is more diffuse and cannot be as clearly explicated as the previous two contexts, but it is nonetheless real and important.

Immigrants are not just numbers. (Of course, one can say the same of newborn children when considering fertility.) Deeply held values can affect immigration legislation just as they affect fertility patterns. Immigration policy gives priority to the *reunion* of families, as was the clear intention of Congress. Altering immigration policy, therefore, affects the established relationships within the families of citizens and permanent residents. Immigration is not the indiscriminate entrance of unsocialized people without a past history. Even the nonrelative groups of immigrants do not come indiscriminately. They must pass difficult barriers to gain entrance. Their contribution to the economy in terms of the cost of their training and experience, as well as their subsequent contributions, may well be needed by the country. The example of foreign doctors is a case in point.

The social context includes knotty questions of cultural pluralism and cultural contribution. The cultural admixture generated by immigrants has at times been looked on with fear, it is true. Nevertheless, the contributions of immigrants are enormous. For example, try to conceive of the history of the United States after 1940 without the relatively small but extraordinary group of scientists who fled Germany and Austria in the thirties and were by-and-large received at some personal expense and inconvenience by their American colleagues.

In sum, the following considerations and any consideration of immigration policy should be made within the context of the historical, political, and social implications. To neglect these may lead to old mistakes, to politically impractical suggestions, or to a violent wrench to our cherished values and ideals as a people.

Definition

The term "immigration" is used to describe various statistical categories. The concept, as used in the Commission consultants' reports and by the Census Bureau, generally refers to net civilian immigration. This category includes net alien immigration—the figures being those reported by the Immigration and Naturalization Service (INS) and adjusted by the Census Bureau—net arrivals from Puerto Rico, net arrivals of civilian citizens, conditional entrants, and emigration. The data on these components, however, are not equally reliable.

Net civilian immigration is a useful concept. It is a measure of the number of arrivals from beyond our political boundaries who plan more or less permanent residence. It is, therefore, a more accurate base than simple alien immigration is for projections of population and resource needs. There are, however, two problems with the concept. The first is the misinterpretation of the concept's empirical referent. The second problem is that the concept as defined by the Census Bureau does not include all groups of persons who enter the country annually and are thus a part of the migration factor in population growth.

The danger of misinterpretation stems from shortening the phrase "net civilian immigration" to just "immigration" in narrative. (The Commission's interim report did exactly that.) One possible result is that the impact of net civilian immigration may be seen as the result of only alien immigration. If the impact is judged negatively, the reaction is to alter alien immigration policy and to ignore the other components of net alien immigration.

Although the Commission and its staff are aware of this possible tendency, not everyone is. The response of others, influenced by the interim report, is perhaps not so discerning as the Commission's. In recent testimony before the House Subcommittee on Immigration and Naturalization (Subcommittee No. 1 of the House Committee on the Judiciary), the Honorable Barbara Watson, Administrator of the Bureau of Security and Consular Affairs of the Department of State, was asked by a subcommittee member what her bureau (which controls the issuance of visas) planned in the way of alternative suggestions and procedures in light of the Commission's interim report.

Two recent articles in the *New York Times* mention the 20 percent figure as immigration's contribution to population growth in a context which clearly implies alien immigration and not net civilian immigration. To a certain extent the amount of research time and space limitations in a newspaper do not allow for the extended discussion of a research report. Nevertheless, such newspaper accounts by themselves may be misleading. Journalistic concern over immigration was reflected in another recent article in the *U.S. News and World Report*. That article is full of egregious errors.

The importance of these reports is that they elicit and form public opinion and reaction. The interpretations of statistics concerning net civilian immigration have resulted in presentations which clearly indicate misunderstanding of the category. The possible result is misinformed public pressures. Parenthetically, a consequence of current statistical categories is the attention given to racial change in alien immigration. Such emphasis can result in additional public pressure for various alternatives to shift racial characteristics. (See section below on "Present Policy Assumptions and Goals.")

In addition to the misinterpretation of "net civilian immigration," a second problem is that the concept is too narrowly defined for an accurate measure of the immigration component of population growth. If net civilian immigration is a factor to be considered in discussions of resource need, labor force participation, and population growth, to name but a few topics, additional components should perhaps be included within the net civilian immigration category.

Each year numerous temporary workers are admitted as nonimmigrants, but their length of stay and their participation in the labor force clearly does not make them tourists. In FY 1970, 11,096 persons of extraordinary or "star" calibre, 69,288 temporary workers, and 5,304 trainees were admitted into the United States with H1, H2, and H3 visas respectively.

Foreign students and their dependents received 67,205 visas to come to the United States. The foreign student population is a constant and growing group, with changing individual members, but still a permanent part of the population physically present in this country. It is true, as will be detailed below, that many adjust status to permanent resident, but those who do so are here for years because they are counted in the net civilian immigration. Of course, not all foreign students settle in this country.

There were approximately 60,000 exchange alien visas issued in 1970. In the same year, there were also 9,501 visas issued to treaty traders (businessmen admitted under reciprocal arrangements for substantial time periods) and 2,731 visas issued to foreign media representatives.

Besides the above uncounted residents of some duration (who are nonimmigrants), there are a number of quasi-legals. This category includes all those persons in the country who are fighting deportation, trying to adjust status, or are the object of a private Congressional bill. The Immigration and Naturalization Service, for example, reported about 32,000 more deportable aliens apprehended (383,557) then expelled (351,463) in 1969. These aliens are in the United States before they surface in the alien immigrant or deportation statistics.

Another group of persons excluded from the net civilian immigration category are commuters. Commuters, also known as Green Card commuters, have obtained immigrant visas but continue to reside in Mexico or Canada and commute to a job in the United States. Although such persons do not affect population growth estimates and are therefore beyond the scope of the net civilian immigration concept in that particular respect, they do affect the labor force and make regular demands on United States resources. The omission of this category from the net civilian immigration total is misleading for certain kinds of estimates based on civilian immigration. Although the INS reports 47,876 Green Card commuters from Mexico and 10,688 from Canada, there is difficulty in getting an exact count of these workers and a tendency to underestimate them. One well-informed source on immigration labor matters estimates the total number of Green Card commuters at 75,000. It should be noted that the same source estimates that 30,000 United States citizens commute to jobs in the United States from Canada and Mexico.

A final category of which many are aware but which does not show up in the net civilian immigration statistics is the illegals. The INS apprehended an estimated 345,000 deportable aliens in 1970. The actual number of illegals living in the United States has been estimated as three times the number of illegals captured.

It is clear from this description that additional categories of persons are physically present in the United States (some of which, admittedly, overlap) who are not counted in net civilian immigration. These persons reside here for various periods (some for many years) before they appear in alien immigrant categories, and their presence and effects are frequently never acknowledged in the net civilian immigration category.

In summary, "net civilian immigration" is a phrase with a quite specific meaning. The shortening of it to "immigration" can lead, and has led, to imputing the effects of net civilian immigration to alien immigration. To so misconstrue the situation can result in unwarranted conclusions and pressures. Secondly, the concept "net civilian immigration" does not include a rather large group of nonimmigrants whose presence can appreciably affect some population situations of importance to the Commission, including resources, the labor force, and population dispersion.

Present Policy Assumptions and Goals

The goals of American immigration policy as enunciated in Congress are fairly clear. The major goals include family reunion, protection of American labor, avoidance of brain drain, lack of discrimination on a nationality basis, and humanitarianism, especially in regard to refugees. These goals are not equally valued by all. In considering the impact of present policy and alternatives, these goals and their achievement obviously play an important part. What needs to be emphasized is not the substance of each goal; this can be presented rather briefly. The difficult problem results from the fact that the goals themselves or the legislative and administrative measures taken to achieve them can and do contradict one another. This working at cross purposes to achieve conflicting ends produces much of the dissatisfaction and frustration over immigration. There should, therefore, be an awareness of this problem in considering immigration goals and their achievement.

The family reunion goal is a major purpose of the 1965 amendments to the Immigration and Nationality Act. Not only was this clearly stated in the reports on the bill from both houses, but the very structure of the law itself makes it clear. The exclusion of certain members of the immediate family from any ceilings and the assignment of 74 percent of available visas to preference categories reserved for family members underlines the family reunification goal. (See Appendix.)

The protection of the American labor market is a second goal of the country's immigration policy. There is wide agreement that opening our doors to those born elsewhere should not be at the expense of our current work force. The labor certification program was aimed at providing that kind of protection. There is debate whether labor certification performs this task adequately. (Some of this discussion will be summarized below.) What is of importance is that any consideration of immigration policy must include both the short-term and long-term impact on the labor market.

An additional factor in labor considerations is that they are not unrelated to the country of origin of immigrants. The historical origin of Oriental exclusion from the United States was, to a large extent, labor market impact. More recently, labor certification was specifically singled out as a mechanism intended to help control the amount of Latin American immigration by Congressman Michael E. Feighan (then Chairman of the House Subcommittee on Immigration) during debate on the 1965 Immigration Act. Labor protection and the labor certification program as the mechanism for the implementation of that policy are interrelated with other aspects of immigration policy.

The problem of a brain drain was allied to the labor question and an issue in its own right during debate on the 1965 Act. The avoidance of a brain drain was clearly the intention of Congress. While Congress did not want to decrease the quality of immigration, it did not wish to encourage the emigration of highly skilled aliens from precisely those countries which could least afford their loss. The complex debate continues on what constitutes a "drain," the value of international mobility of trained manpower, and related issues. It is nonetheless clear that since the 1965 amendments, the proportion of professional level immigrants to the United States has increased slightly, while the absolute number has increased considerably. Even more to the point, there has been a decided shift in country of origin of professional workers to lesser developed nations.

Equal treatment regardless of country of origin is also another goal of the law. The most glaring exception here is the different provisions for Western and non-Western Hemisphere natives. A few examples are the separate hemisphere ceilings, the lack of both a preference system and a per-country limit for the Western Hemisphere, and differences in exemptions from labor certification based on relationship.

The equal treatment within the limitations of a ceiling is related to the larger area of humanitarian concern. This humanitarian goal is also apparent in the special attention paid to refugee matters in relation to immigration. The separate preference for refugees and the parole power granted the Attorney General under Section 212 (d)(5) of the 1965 Act are clear evidence of this concern.

It should be clear that the various goals of present immigration policy can contradict one another. The matter is further complicated by the administrative machinery needed to realize these goals in practice. It is not necessary to go into detail here on this point, however.

There is, nevertheless, one aspect of these conflicts in realizing policy goals which will be of importance to the Commission. This problem is a glaring contradiction which is hardly ever referred to in discussions of policy. It is taken as a given that there must be an annual ceiling on immigration. It is presupposed that there will be more applicants than the country can handle. The present ceilings are arbitrary from the point of view that they are unrelated to a conscious policy of population growth, labor force absorption, or any similar policy. There is no policy or reliable data to justify a ceiling of 170,000 and 120,000 immigrants from the Eastern and Western Hemispheres respectively.

Although the size of our ceiling should probably be related to a national population policy, let us suppose that the 290,000 total worldwide ceiling is acceptable. The anomaly is that although the need for a ceiling is accepted, whenever backlogs arise there is usually a movement to clear them away. Some seem unwilling or unable to accept the fact that if demand is greater than we can accommodate, there will of necessity be backlogs. Some will have to wait, and some may never be able to emigrate to America. Some current proposed legislation to guarantee a larger supply of visas for certain northern European countries adversely affected by the implementation of the 1965 amendments is but one case in point.   The use of special immigrant visas to reduce various backlogs has had a major effect on immigration totals since the 1965 Act. This tendency to want to reduce backlogs clearly conflicts with the need to control immigration. The solution is not simple. The consistent pursuit of the control goal to the exclusion of humanitarian considerations (or vice versa) is perhaps appealing but politically impractical.

PRESENT TRENDS AND IMMINENT PROSPECTS

Size

To speak of clear trends in the size of net civilian immigration and its component parts is misleading. The various components used by the Census Bureau, with the exception of emigration, all show fluctuations which indicate no clear upward or downward trend. The single exception of emigration is based on admittedly fragmentary data. In addition, the decrease in American military involvement in the Republic of Vietnam may result in some reversals in emigration trends.

The major component of net civilian immigration, alien immigration, cannot be said to have established a verifiable pattern as yet. To begin with, the period between December 1, 1965, and June 30, 1968, was a period of transition from the McCarran-Walter Act provisions to the revisions in the Act of October 3, 1965. During this period, each country retained its national quota but the unused visa numbers from the previous fiscal year were put in a visa pool to be used by preference immigrants. The 170,000 ceiling on visa issuance for those fiscal years (1966-1968) was, therefore, a combination of visas issued under the national origins quota system, which was being phased out, and the visa pool, which was a foreshadowing of the first come—first served process mandated by the 1965 Act. Visa issuance in FY 1969 and 1970 has been solely under the requirements of the new system (including the addition of the 120,000 ceiling for the Western Hemisphere commencing in FY 1969). Since visa data is available for only two full years under the new system, one cannot say whether a trend is being set. What data there is, however, indicates a decrease in visa issuance. (See Table 1.) Annual visa issuance may be more significant than alien immigrant entries for gauging the future amount of growth in alien immigration. This is so since actual entrants may have received visas in a previous fiscal year. Thus, visa issuance can be a more accurate indication of future immigration. This is so since actual entrants may have received visas in a previous fiscal year. Thus, visa issuance can be a more accurate indication of future immigration. As pointed out above, the lack of experience with the current law, as well as new legislation which can change the current statutes, makes any firm conclusions on trends impossible.

The various ceilings in the present law and the proposed legislation (discussed below) are often looked upon not only as ceilings but as targets to be reached. There is considerable pressure on the State Department, directly from groups interested in what is usually called a "liberal immigration policy" and indirectly through Congress, to use up the total number of visas available each year. There is also agreement with this attitude in the Executive. If it is sensible to make available a specified number of visas for persons who can be absorbed or are even needed in this country, we should make every effort to use the visas. Nevertheless, any suggestion to change or lower the qualifications just to reach current ceilings on visa numbers should be carefully scrutinized. Such scrutiny is especially advisable at this time since the ceilings of 170,000 and 120,000 are ultimately arbitrary figures. If ceilings were related to population and labor force needs and capaci-

Table 1.—Immigrant Visas Issued, Fiscal Years 1963-1970

Year	Immigrant visas issued
1963	286,252
1964	271,030
1965	280,212
1966	289,472
1967	294,250
1968	349,486
1969	313,632
1970	309,701

Source: U.S. Dept. of State, Bureau of Security and Consular Affairs, *Report of the Visa Office*, 1967 and 1970.

ties, in accordance with political and social values acceptable to the nation and reflective of what we stand for as a society, the effort to use all visa numbers would make greater sense than it does now.

In sum, trends in the alien immigration component of net civilian immigration are not clear. There has not been a long enough time series under the full provisions of the 1965 amendments to determine clear trends. In addition, the direction of a trend will depend in part on the persistence or decline of the attitude concerning the use of all available immigrant visa numbers annually. Trends in the other components of net civilian immigration are equally unclear.   Both the reliability of the data and the fluctuations apparent in almost every component lead to the conclusion that the use of 400,000 for various projections is a *very* round figure.

The discussion above concerning the exclusion from the net civilian immigration category of such groups as temporary workers, foreign students, exchange aliens, treaty traders, commuters, and quasi-legal and illegal residents adds further weight to the hesitation about the 400,000 figure and all the projections based on it. It is not certain how inaccurate that estimation may be. What is clear is that the current basis for that estimation, recent net civilian immigration, is suspect for two reasons. First, available data on net civilian immigration, as currently defined, do not really support a conclusion of a trend of approximately 400,000. The data do not supply a clear and definite *trend*, and past experience with changes in immigration law would make projections based on such trends suspect. Second, as currently defined, "net civilian immigration" excludes many components which affect population projections, labor force estimates, and estimates of resource needs and allocations.

There is one final point to be made about current immigration size and trends. There are a number of bills now in Congress (to be discussed below in some detail) which would make major alterations in immigration law. It seems that, for the near future and perhaps for some time to come, Congress will continue to modify immigration law. Such changes will make the task of divining trends and projecting effects next to impossible. Our current immigration law and process is cumbersome, contradictory (see above), and not particularly related to population policy or manpower needs.

Labor Force

The Immigration Act of 1965 has not adversely affected the skill level of immigrants to the United States. Rather, on the macro-level, the proportion of immigrants with high-level skills has increased slightly.

In certain fields (for example, medicine) the contributions of immigrants in meeting the needs of the United States are large indeed.

The current provisions of the law and suggested revisions before Congress do not give any indication that there will be a radical down-swing in immigrant skill level. (See below.) If anything, the suggestions to omit married brothers and sisters from the fifth preference and to reduce backlogs for third preference by enlarging the number of visas available will most likely result in an even larger proportion of higher skill levels. (See Appendix.) As Irwin has indicated in his report to the Commission, the present skill distribution of immigrants compares favorably with the country's labor force, particularly in the professional and technical category.

In terms of absorption into the labor force, immigration does not seem to present a problem on the macro-level. The average annual increase in the labor force between 1966 and 1970 was 1.3 million. These new workers were being absorbed by a work force of 83,000,000.   In FY 1967-1970, an average of 168,725 immigrants entered the United States with work experience.   This is a small addition to the overall work force but represents about 13 percent of the annual growth in the labor force for the roughly comparable period.

It should be pointed out, however, that the labor certification program, which is meant to be a check on labor skill levels, affected only a small number of the immigrants with work experience. The annual average of certification holders for the 1967-1970 period was 68,026 or about 5 percent of the annual average labor force increase.   This situation points to some problems with the labor certification program which will be discussed below.

Before leaving the macro-level impact, it might be well to point out that the figures cited do not represent the total impact of aliens on the work force. Many of the persons who do not show up in net civilian immigration figures are in the American work force. It is difficult to measure both the numbers involved and the annual increase, but there is reason to believe the numbers are substantial. A listing of the categories of aliens (in addition to permanent immigrant workers and parolees in the work force) will lend weight to this suspicion. The list includes temporary workers (H1, H2 and H3 visas, totaling 85,688 in FY 1970), foreign students who usually work part-time, exchange visitors and spouses, visitors for business, treaty traders, foreign media representatives, fiancees, foreign executives of American firms, commuters, quasi-legals, and illegals. One source estimates the number of these nonimmigrant aliens in the work force at 650,000 for 1970.

For the foreseeable future, immigration will continue to affect the labor force in ways similar to its present impact. Nevertheless, according to a recent assessment of manpower needs for the decade of the 1970's, the nation· could well have a shortage of manpower at all levels. Our problem is that we do not have at present the kind of express goal priorities presupposed by that study; therefore, projections seem to be more on the order of guesses than true estimates.

The more immediate prospect for alien immigration is that it will continue with a similar proportionate distribution of skills, including a high ratio of professional and technical level workers. Thus, on the macro-level, immigration does not seem to be a threat to the country's labor force now or in the near future. Rather, immigration makes important contributions, as Fortney has pointed out.

On the micro-level of labor impact, three topics have been chosen from many possible areas of discussion. These areas are discussed because they are embodiments of larger issues of population and immigration policy which are of interest to the Commission. The three topics are agricultural labor on the Mexican border, dispersion of labor certification holders, and the live-in maid controversy.

When the 1965 amendments to the Immigration and Nationality Act were passed, the experience of the bracero program was fresh in the minds of Congress and organized labor. The labor certification program was viewed as a precautionary measure against exploitation of aliens and depressing wages and working conditions for Americans. In practice, it has been extremely difficult for an alien to receive labor certification for an agricultural occupation, except for the most exotic jobs. There have not been any complaints registered, to the author's knowledge, of *labor certification* leading to the depressing of wages or working conditions for the United States work force.

Nevertheless, there remains a major problem in both the agricultural work sector and the work force in general on our southern border. The problem seems to lie partially with our legislation on alien commuters (people who live in Mexico but are legally "resident aliens") and INS's interpretation of those statutes. Whatever the causes, the resulting conditions are poor both for the commuters and for other workers in competition for jobs with commuters in the high unemployment border area. It would seem that a unified policy could resolve some of the severe and grinding conditions which arise out of using legal technicalities to make a person residing in Mexico (or Canada) a "permanent resident alien" of the United States.

The selective dispersion of immigrants and of labor certification holders is indicated in Table 2. The impact of approval rates by regional offices of the Labor Department, shown in Table 3, generally strengthens this interpretation of Table 2. These data underline the fact that there is a heavy concentration of immigrants (and labor certification holders) in our most populous states. (See Table 4.) However, the data raise an additional question. In analyzing Table 2, it is apparent that the states with high certification holder preference rates are generally states with the strongest unions and very high labor standards. These conditions pre-date the labor certification program, so the program did not cause the conditions. The immigrants gravitate to the prosperous areas. This raises a question about allocation of resources. Should the country have a program to inspect aliens coming to areas where conditions are good and organized labor is strong, or should we turn our attention and resources to the control of legal and illegal aliens where laborers are especially disadvantaged? We are *de facto* doing the former. Realigning programs would not be easy if we were to change priorities, but that should hardly be the deciding factor.

The live-in maid situation also caused something of a furor after passage of the 1965 Act. One problem is possible fraud, that is, using the live-in maid occupation as a vehicle of entry and then switching jobs. Live-in maids are usually desired in the metropolitan areas, and thus the concentration of population is exacerbated that much more. In 1967, 37 percent of the 93,324 immigrants approved for permanent employment were in the service category and 85 percent of those service workers were live-in. From the Western Hemisphere, 59 percent of the 34,440 approvals were for service workers and 95 percent of them were live-ins.

A final question, which is related to the live-in maid problem and presents many difficulties, is whether rare visa numbers ought to be used to fill what are basically private needs. Involved here, of course, is public surveillance of the labor certification and visa approval systems. At present they are not very public and are handled like private negotiations. There is probably an element of proletarian resentment against pampering the affluent. Nevertheless, there is a question of using a scarce document for the private needs of the relatively well-off, especially since the procedure may lend itself to fraud.

Political and Legislative Prospects

Three major bills aimed at the revision of American immigration policy are presently before Congress (92nd Congress, 1st session). In addition, there are a number of other bills before Congress which are intended by their sponsors to clear up problems in the operation of the country's immigration procedures. Areas of agreement in legislative change will be fairly clear but differences (and at times contradictions) in basic attitudes and approaches will also be highlighted. It is obvious from the analysis below that there is no Congressional unanimity on immigration law.

H.R. 2328: The Administration Bill

The Administration bill was introduced in the 92nd Congress by Rep. William M. McCulloch (Ohio), ranking Republican on the House Judiciary Committee. The law makes a number of changes in hemispheric ceilings, the preference system, adjustment of status, naturalization, deportation, and punishment of employers of aliens ineligible to work.

H.R. 2328 proposes that the Western Hemisphere ceiling be changed from 120,000 to ceilings of 35,000

Table 2.—States Ranked by Preference of Labor Certification Holders (LCH) and Settlement Preference of Immigrants

State	Percent of population 1970 Census	Percent of LCH's 1969 approvals	Preference rate (col 2 ÷ col 1)	Percent of admitted immigrants 1969	Rank	Preference rate (col 4 ÷ col 1)
1. District of Columbia	.37	2.22 (2,289)	6.00	.84 (3,012)	4	2.27
2. Maine	.49	1.95 (2,008)	3.98	.39 (1,391)	14	.80
3. New York	8.98	24.52 (25,248)	2.73	26.33 (94,403)	2	2.93
4. New Hampshire	.36	.59 (602)	1.64	.29 (1,046)	13	.81
5. New Jersey	3.54	5.61 (5,771)	1.58	5.28 (18,935)	8	1.49
6. Hawaii	.37	.58 (592)	1.57	1.45 (5,199)	1	3.92
7. Massachusetts	2.81	4.08 (4,201)	1.45	5.31 (19,043)	6	1.89
8. California	9.84	12.56 (12,935)	1.28	19.85 (71,183)	5	2.02
9. Illinois	5.48	6.41 (6,603)	1.17	5.70 (20,420)	11	1.04
10. Connecticut	1.49	1.68 (1,728)	1.13	2.32 (8,332)	7	1.56
11. Missouri	2.32	2.55 (2,623)	1.10	.62 (2,207)	35	.26
12. Rhode Island	.46	.48 (493)	1.04	1.06 (3,802)	3	2.30
13. Maryland	1.93	1.89 (1,945)	.98	1.30 (4,650)	17	.67
14. Florida	3.33	3.21 (3,300)	.96	3.84 (13,783)	9	1.15
15. Washington	1.67	1.39 (1,433)	.83	1.21 (4,321)	16	.72
16. Vermont	.22	.16 (166)	.73	.14 (513)	18	.64
17. Michigan	4.38	2.99 (3,080)	.68	2.62 (9,407)	19	.60
18. Nevada	.24	.15 (158)	.63	.19 (682)	15	.79
19. Pennsylvania	5.83	3.54 (3,642)	.61	2.80 (10,041)	21	.48
20. Utah	.53	.28 (291)	.53	.21 (769)	25	.40
21. Delaware	.27	.14 (139)	.52	.12 (424)	23	.44
22. Idaho	.35	.18 (183)	.51	.12 (430)	28	.34
23. Virginia	2.27	1.14 (1,170)	.50	.84 (3,010)	27	.37
24. Ohio	5.27	2.60 (2,674)	.49	2.35 (8,434)	22	.45
25. Oregon	1.03	.50 (519)	.49	.45 (1,602)	24	.44

26. Nebraska	.73	.35	358)	.17	.48	601)	36	.23
27. Alaska	.15	.07	70)	.05	.47	196)	29	.33
28. Colorado	1.10	.52	536)	.42	.47	1,499)	26	.38
29. Minnesota	1.88	.89	915)	.51	.47	1,837)	33	.27
30. Texas	5.49	2.52	2,597)	4.95	.46	17,739)	12	.90
31. Arizona	.87	.37	376)	.98	.43	3,501)	10	1.13
32. Louisiana	1.78	.66	675)	.50	.37	1,787)	31	.28
33. Kansas	1.11	.36	365)	.24	.32	868)	37	.22
34. Indiana	2.57	.65	672)	.73	.25	2,614)	32	.28
35. Montana	.34	.08	84)	.07	.24	249)	38	.21
36. Wisconsin	2.18	.52	538)	.58	.24	2,065)	34	.27
37. Iowa	1.39	.31	314)	.29	.22	1,042)	39	.21
38. New Mexico	.50	.11	109)	.27	.22	982)	20	.54
39. Oklahoma	1.25	.25	259)	.21	.20	758)	43	.17
40. Georgia	2.24	.38	388)	.44	.17	1,571)	40	.20
41. South Dakota	.33	.05	46)	.05	.15	186)	45	.15
42. North Carolina	2.48	.33	340)	.41	.13	1,477)	44	.17
43. South Carolina	1.26	.17	172)	.17	.13	601)	46	.13
44. Tennessee	1.92	.25	255)	.23	.13	927)	47	.12
45. West Virginia	.85	.11	111)	.15	.13	535)	42	.18
46. Wyoming	.16	.02	52)	.05	.13	163)	30	.31
47. Kentucky	1.58	.14	140)	.18	.09	631)	48	.11
48. Mississippi	1.08	.10	103)	.10	.09	370)	49	.09
49. Alabama	1.68	.11	114)	.14	.07	499)	51	.08
50. North Dakota	.31	.02	52)	.06	.06	207)	41	.19
51. Arkansas	.94	.03	27)	.08	.03	292)	50	.09
52. U.S. possessions and territories	...	3.47	3,566)	2.15	...	7,704)	...	...
53. Region unknown	...	5.76	5,926)	.18	...	639)	...	...
Total	100.0	100.0	(102,953)	99.99		(358,579)		

Source: U.S. Dept. of Labor, Manpower Administration, *Alien Workers: A Study of the Labor Certification Program*, by David S. North (Washington: Trans-Century Corp., 1971), Table X.

each for Canada and Mexico and 80,000 for the rest of the hemisphere (excluding Cuban refugees). The non-Western Hemisphere ceiling would remain at 170,000. This has the effect of raising the ceiling worldwide from its present 290,000 to 320,000 (plus Cuban refugees). The law also proposes to increase the ceiling of a dependent possession from 200 to 600 and to charge the allowance against the limitation for the hemisphere in which the dependent territory is located rather than against the mother country's hemisphere.

Major changes in the preference system are also proposed. First, the preference system is to be applied to the Western Hemisphere (except Canada and Mexico, which are to remain without a preference system) as well as to the Eastern Hemisphere. The preference system is to be applied separately to the two hemispheres under their respective ceilings.

The preference system itself is also altered. (See Appendix.) Briefly, these changes include a decrease in the current first preference and an extension in the eligibility for second preference to include parents of adult resident aliens. The third preference would be increased by five percent and permits unused visas from the first two categories to "fall down" and be used by the third preference. This would probably increase appreciably the third preference (highly skilled, often professional level) immigrant population. The fifth preference would be reduced from 24 percent to 20 percent, and married brothers and sisters would be excluded from eligibility for a fifth preference. (There is a savings clause for currently qualified fifth preference petitioners on a waiting list who would be excluded in the future.) The sixth preference is increased from 10 percent to 15 percent and may also benefit from the "fall down" of unused visas, unlike the present system. The refugee preference is increased from 6 percent to 10 percent. The effect of these changes is to put more emphasis on preferences related to labor skills and to de-emphasize family relationships slightly.

The law also proposes to permit the adjustment of status to permanent resident by Western Hemisphere natives. However, natives of Canada, Mexico, and the adjacent islands (except some classes of immediate relatives) are excluded from such adjustments. The provision will make it possible for persons physically present in the United States who are natives of this hemisphere to apply for a change of status from nonimmigrant without leaving the country. (See below on change of status.)

The Administration bill also changes naturalization provisions to conform with recent court rulings. These changes are mainly technical and, while generally liberalizing, do not change the basic orientation contained in the McCarran-Walter Act. A statute of limitations on the grounds of ineligibility which could lead to deportation proceedings is proposed by H.R. 2328. The absence of such limitations has been criticized for many years.

The Administration bill provides for criminal penalties for hiring persons in the country illegally or here temporarily without permission to work. This provision has received support as a possible means of remedying exploitation, particularly in the Southwest. Others, however, criticize it, since employers cannot possibly know all the ramifications of the immigration laws, and thus may be afraid to hire aliens who do have the right to work. The onus of proof is on the employer. Enforcement is also at the peril of the employer and not the government. One alternative suggestion is to provide penalties for employers who, in the pattern of their business practice, knowingly and ordinarily employ aliens in violation of their status.

The effects of this law would probably include an increase in the size of alien immigration and in the proportion of the highly skilled (at least in the short run, given current third preference backlogs and the suggested preference changes). Thus, present patterns of countries of origin of professional level immigrants would probably be reinforced. The refugee provisions are slightly liberalized by increasing the size of the preference. However, the definition of refugee was changed to exclude explicitly from the refugee category an alien firmly resettled in another country. In addition, there is no provision for paroling refugees in emergency situations. The Attorney General is empowered in a limited way under Section 212(d)(5), but the use and interpretation of this provision has been a bone of contention for some Congressmen.

H.R. 1532: The Rodino Bill

Peter W. Rodino (N.J.), Chairman of the House

Subcommittee on Immigration and Naturalization, introduced H.R. 1532 on January 25, 1971. The bill is
substantially the same as one introduced in the last
session (H.R. 17370). The bill proposes three major
modifications in current law relating to a worldwide
ceiling, the preference system, and refugees.

H.R. 1532 proposes a worldwide ceiling of 250,000,
excluding immigrants from Canada and Mexico and
some immediate relatives who, for the most part, have
previously enjoyed a status outside all ceilings. There is
no limit provided for Canadian and Mexican immigration, but labor certification is required for immigrants
entering on the basis of labor skill and not family
relationships. In addition, the ceiling on any individual
country is raised from 20,000 to 25,000 annually. The
Rodino bill also provides for adjustment of status by
persons from Western Hemisphere countries, excluding
natives of Canada, Mexico, and the adjacent islands.

The Rodino bill introduces a major change in the
preference system. This system is to be applied on a
worldwide basis except Canada and Mexico. (See Appendix.) The system de-emphasizes family relationships by
reducing the number of visas reserved and by omitting
certain relatives from visa preferences. It should be
noted, however, that the Rodino bill contains a savings
clause for the beneficiaries of current fifth preference
(brothers and sisters of a United States citizen) who filed
applications prior to July 1, 1968.

The Rodino preference system increases preference
visas for professional and skilled workers (50 percent
total). However, unskilled workers in short supply in the
United States (current sixth preference) are left out of
the preference categories. The effect would probably be
to maintain or increase the skill levels, but the per-
country limitation for the second preference ought to
stem some criticisms of brain drain. However, this could
result in large backlogs of second preferences which may
lead to pressure to reduce the backlog and, thus, defeat
the per-country limitations.

A final innovation of note in the H.R. 1532
preference system is the reservation of 2.5 percent of the
total visas as part of the nonpreference category for
persons under 25 years old at the time of visa application; these younger immigrants would be exempted from

labor certification. While many applaud this provision of visas for younger "new seed" immigrants, it may lead to large backlogs due to demand.

The Rodino bill mandates two major changes in regard to refugees. First, the definition is broadened to include not only those who have fled a Communist or Communist-controlled country, but also refugees who have fled and are unwilling to return to *any* country owing to a well-founded fear of persecution. Second, the mechanism for entry to the United States is altered. There are no preferences for refugees. Rather, they are to be admitted subject to the determination of the Attorney General after consultation with the Department of State. Such parolees are allowed retroactive adjustment of status after two years. The Attorney General is directed to report to Congress semi-annually on the use of this authority. Either house may terminate this authority within 60 days by passage of a resolution to that effect. The refugee sections are an attempt to introduce flexibility into refugee policy, settle controversy over the interpretation and use of Section 212(d)(5), and yet maintain congressional power over and review of all immigration matters.

The effects of H.R. 1532 would probably be to moderately increase alien immigration as a result of (1) the new ceiling, (2) the special immigrant status (not covered by the ceiling) accorded to natives of Canada and Mexico, and (3) the refugee provisions. Skill levels will probably rise slightly under the new preference system with the retention of labor certification. The origins of the highly skilled may be affected; and an additional result might well be the build up of a backlog of professional applicants in some underdeveloped countries, possibly creating pressure to reduce those backlogs.

S. 1373: The Kennedy Bill

On March 24, 1971, Senator Edward M. Kennedy (Mass.) introduced S.1373, a bill almost identical to S.3202-H.R. 15092, introduced in the previous session and referred to as the Kennedy-Feighan bill. S.1373 proposes changes in the ceilings, preference system, refugee policy, commuter system, hiring of illegals, adjustment of status, and deportation and appeals of visa decisions.

The Kennedy bill proposes a worldwide ceiling of 300,000. This ceiling would go into effect on July 1,

Table 3.—Labor Certification Approval Rates by Region, 1970

Region	Approval rate
1. Region unknown	89.9%
2. Region V (Chicago)	86.9
3. Region VII (Kansas City)	85.1
4. Region X (Seattle)	84.5
5. Region VIII (Denver)	82.2
6. Region III (Philadelphia)	81.8
7. Region IV (Atlanta)	81.0
8. Region II (New York)[a]	77.4
9. Region I (Boston)	75.4
10. Region VI (Dallas)	69.3
11. Region IX (San Francisco)	62.1

[a]Includes Virgin Islands.
Source: See source, Table 2, Table XXII.

1974. In the meantime, the Eastern Hemisphere would continue with a ceiling of 170,000 and the Western Hemisphere ceiling will be 130,000. There would be a 20,000 per country limitation except for Canada and Mexico, which would be limited to 35,000 each. The preference system would apply to both hemispheres during the interim. Cuban refugees adjusting status would be outside the ceilings. Dependent area quotas would also be raised from 200 to 600.

The Kennedy bill would also modify the present preference system. (See Appendix.) In brief, the changes are the same as those proposed in the Administration bill; the bill also includes a savings clause for married brothers and sisters of United States citizens who applied for visas prior to the Act. The refugee definition, however, is expanded in a manner similar to the Rodino bill. In addition to the 10 percent of the visas reserved for refugees (seventh preference), the bill provides flexibility in refugee matters by amending Section 212(d)(5) to stipulate specifically that the Attorney General may parole refugees into the United States at his discretion for emergent reasons or in the public interest, irrespective of numerical limitations. Such parolees would be eligible to adjust status. It should also be pointed out that refugees entering under the seventh preference need not be conditional entrants as they are now but could receive immigrant visas.

S.1373 would modify the commuter system by requiring each alien commuter to be certified every six months by the Department of Labor that his presence does not adversely affect wages or working conditions. The bill does not provide any transition period or specify any remedial action for the probable rush, especially into the Southwest, which would strain governmental and private services and the job market. The Kennedy bill, like the Administration bill, provides penalties for employers of aliens ineligible to work. The Kennedy bill, however, limits these penalties to employers of five or more aliens. Neither this bill nor the Administration bill mandates easily recognizable identification for such determinations by employers.

Table 4.—Volume of Certifications, Preference Rates, Labor Certification Holders (L.C.H.) Preference Rank, and Settlement Preference Rank, Selected States, 1969

State	Number of certifications	L.C.H. preference rate	L.C.H. preference rank	Settlement preference rank
New York.	25,248	2.73	3	2
California	12,935	1.28	8	5
Illinois	6,603	1.17	9	11
New Jersey	5,771	1.58	5	8
Massachusetts	4,201	1.45	7	6
Pennsylvania	3,642	.61	19	21
Florida	3,300	.96	14	9
Michigan	3,080	.68	17	19

Source: See source, Table 2, Tables X and XI.

The Kennedy bill provides for adjustment of status by a nonimmigrant except for all natives of Canada, Mexico, and adjacent islands. At present, Western Hemisphere natives are not afforded this privilege. A statute of limitations is also mandated, as well as a Board of Visa Appeals to review denials by American Consuls of immigrant visas to relatives of United States citizens or permanent resident aliens. S.1373 contains additional provisions pertaining to naturalization, including creation of a Select Commission to study the country's naturalization law and procedures.

There are additional bills in Congress that would

affect various aspects of the law. For example, Senator James O. Eastland's (Miss.) S.1500 would transfer the visa function from the State Department to the Immigration and Naturalization Service of the Justice Department. There are also numerous bills dealing with topics like Cuban refugees, commuter aliens, labor certification procedures, and so on.

Table 5 summarizes the major provisions affecting population characteristics in the bills discussed above. Such legislation contains other provisions (for example, naturalization, due process, and so on) which only indirectly affect population characteristics. The presence of such matters, however, cannot be ignored since they are part of the warp and woof of immigration policy and can figure prominently in Congressional deliberation and compromise.

The foregoing analysis of major immigration legislation before Congress highlights areas of both agreement and disagreement. It is widely accepted that there are inequities between Eastern and Western Hemisphere procedures. A worldwide ceiling and a universal preference system scheme both receive broad, but obviously not unanimous, support. Canada and Mexico are seen as special cases and a number of alternatives for dealing with contigious countries are in evidence. There is no significant movement for repealing labor certification although there is much opposition to it. The change to a worldwide preference system may reduce that part of the opposition which is due to the different treatment of the Western Hemisphere in regard to labor certification.

The operation of the preference system has also been an object of concern. There is broad support for omitting married brothers and sisters from the system and increasing preferences for workers. Congressman Rodino's bill also attempts to lessen the possibility of brain drain by limiting the second preference (roughly equivalent to present third preference) visas available to a country and blocking the use of other preference system categories by persons eligible for his bill's second preference.

There is wide agreement about the need for a generous and flexible refugee program. This is reflected in the three bills reviewed. The variety of alternatives are not very different with one exception. The exception is

Table 5.—Changes Proposed by Major Immigration Bills, 92nd Congress, 1st Session

Major provisions	Present law	Administration H.R. 2328	Rodino H.R. 1532	Kennedy S. 1373
A. Numerical limitation	Eastern Hemisphere 170,000 Western Hemisphere 120,000 Worldwide 290,000	Eastern Hemisphere 170,000 Western Hemisphere 80,000 Canada 35,000 Mexico 35,000	World 250,000 Canada No limit Mexico No limit World 250,000+	World 300,000 July 1, 1974 Interim Eastern Hemisphere 170,000 Western Hemisphere 130,000
B. Excluded from limit	Immediate family	Immediate family and Cuban refugees adjusting status	Immediate family Cuban refugees, Canadian & Mexican natives	Immediate family and Cuban refugees adjusting status
C. Per country limitation	Eastern Hemisphere 20,000 Western Hemisphere None	20,000 Canada 35,000 Mexico 35,000	25,000 Canada None Mexico None	20,000 Canada 35,000 Mexico 35,000
D. Preference system[a]	Eastern Hemisphere - Emphasis on family relationships (74%) Western Hemisphere None	Same for Eastern & Western Hemisphere but applied separately. Modified to emphasize labor more, esp. by falldown. Not applied to Canada or Mexico	Worldwide, except Canada & Mexico. Emphasizes skills more	See Administration bill. Does apply to Canada and Mexico
E. Refugees & Parolees	Reference - 7th pref. - 6% Parolees at Att'y Gen.'s discretion	Reference - 7th pref. - 10% Parolees, no change	References not in pref. system. Paroled at Att'y Gen.'s discretion but reports to Congress. Broader definition	Reference - 7th pref. Parolees, no change but Sec. 212(d)(5) clarified. Broader definition
F. Labor certification	Eastern Hemisphere - required of 3rd, 6th and non-preference. Western Hemisphere - required of all covered by numerical limitation	Eastern Hemisphere system made worldwide	Worldwide, 2nd, 3rd, non pref. (except new seed) incl. Mex. & Can. natives who would have been in those categories	Eastern Hemisphere system made worldwide

[a]See Appendix.

a major point of difference even now, and so a central issue regarding refugee policy is unsolved. That issue is the use of the parole power of the Attorney General under Section 212(d)(5) of the Immigration and Nationality Act.

The Kennedy bill addresses itself to the commuter problem. Commuters have been of concern to Congress and there have been and are bills which address it specifically. The parameters of a future policy and its enforcement, however, are far from clear.

In sum, the legislation reviewed would probably lead to a slight increase in alien immigration with a distribution of occupational skills similar to the current distribution, including a high proportion of professionals. None of the bills views immigration in the wider perspective of population policy or manpower needs and

PROBLEM AREAS...

Ethnic Change

The 1965 amendments to the Immigration and Nationality Act shifted the distribution of countries of origin of immigrants. There have been some studies of various groups whose numbers have increased. However, no reports have come to the author's attention suggesting that the changed ethnic patterns have caused any major animosity or problems within the United States. It is true, though, that such could be developing now and that major problems may result within or among groups. For example, an Associated Press report of May 13, 1971 describes some difficulties in the school situation and between old and young in San Francisco's Chinatown area.

At the opposite end of the country, the Spanish speaking in the New York area present an interesting case. The city's major Spanish group, the Puerto Ricans, show no signs of cooperation or coalition formation with other Spanish-speaking groups. Apparently, they are not interested in any united front generally. Other Spanish speakers, notably the Cubans and Dominicans, stay to themselves, by and large, and there is no evident tension. For example, Rogg's study of Cubans in West New York, New Jersey, across the Hudson River from New York, showed marked adjustment in the economic sphere and found employment success the major factor in adjustment and contentment.

New York data on Spanish-speaking nationality groups concerning some indicators of adjustment problems (like welfare, mental illness, or drug addiction) could not be located. Apparently these groups are as yet unexplored in terms of their cultural and social structural adjustment.

In short, with the exception of continuing problems on the southwest border which antedate the 1965 Act, immigrant group adjustment does not present major problems which are currently clearly identifiable. To be sure, adjustment most likely presents many personal and family difficulties. However, group dislocation, enmity, and massive value and interest conflict does not appear to be characteristic of the settlement of recent immigrants. The change in the national origins of immigrants does not appear at this time to have produced major ethnic strains in addition to the inherent difficulties of uprooting and resettlement in a foreign land.

Settlement Patterns

There are two elements to settlement patterns, the area of intended residence of each year's immigrants and the distribution of the total alien population. As Table 6 points out, New York and California have traditionally accounted, and still do account, for a lion's share of annual immigration settlement. In 1969, 46 percent of the immigrant aliens intended to reside in these states. Particular nationality groups favored these states also:

In 1969, a predominant number of immigrants from Mexico, Canada and the Far East chose to live in California. One out of every two Mexicans made this choice, as did 13 per cent of the Canadians, 39 per cent of the Filipinos, and 36 per cent of the Chinese. Some 20 per cent of all new Portuguese immigrants chose to reside in California.

Also, in 1969, 44 per cent of all arriving Italian immigrants planned to reside in New York, as did 36 per cent of the Poles, 25 per cent of the Chinese, and 18 per cent of the Cuban and British nationals.

Table 6.—Immigrant Aliens Admitted by Selected States of Intended Residence and Percent of Total Admissions: 1940, 1950, 1960, and 1969

States of intended residence	1940		1950		1960		1969	
	Total admitted	Percent of total	Total admitted	Percent of total	Total admitted	Percent of total	Total admitted	Percent of total
Total	70,756	100.00	249,187	100.00	265,398	100.00	358,579	100.00
Arizona	199	.28	950	.38	3,129	1.18	3,501	.98
California	5,714	8.07	20,428	8.20	61,325	23.11	71,183	19.85
Connecticut	1,099	1.55	6,282	2.52	5,769	2.17	8,332	2.32
Florida	657	.93	2,980	1.20	10,713	4.04	13,783	3.84
Illinois	3,629	5.13	18,673	7.49	15,132	5.70	20,420	5.69
Massachusetts	2,755	3.89	10,443	4.19	11,953	4.50	19,043	5.31
Michigan	3,190	4.51	14,681	5.89	8,271	3.12	9,407	2.62
Minnesota	433	.61	5,287	2.12	1,970	.74	1,837	.51
New Jersey	3,001	4.24	13,349	5.36	13,611	5.13	18,935	5.28
New York	36,494	51.58	68,944	27.67	60,134	22.66	94,403	26.33
Ohio	1,773	2.51	9,829	3.94	6,829	2.57	8,434	2.35
Pennsylvania	2,641	3.73	15,268	6.13	7,933	2.99	10,041	2.80
Rhode Island	315	.45	1,288	.52	1,578	.59	3,802	1.06
Texas	1,421	2.01	6,385	2.56	12,992	4.90	17,739	4.95
Washington	842	1.19	3,825	1.53	3,897	1.47	4,321	1.21
Wisconsin	447	.63	5,776	2.32	2,504	.94	2,065	.58
All others	6,146	8.69	44,799	17.98	37,658	14.19	51,333	14.32

Source: Marvin Gibson, "Alien Population in the United States: Changing Residence Patterns," *Immigration and Natural-* *ization Reporter,* October 1970, Vol. 19, No. 2, Table 2, p. 24.

Table 7.—Comparisons of Aliens Registered, by Selected States, 1940 vs. 1969

States of residence	1940		1969		Increase or decrease in registrations 1940 vs. 1969	
	Number of aliens registered	Percent of U.S. total aliens registered	Number of aliens registered	Percent of U.S. total aliens registered	Actual	Percent
Arizona	31,954	0.6	50,151	1.2	+18,197	+56.9
California	524,464	10.8	944,149	23.7	+401,685	+80.0
Connecticut	158,128	3.2	96,274	2.4	−61,854	−39.1
Florida	41,327	0.8	267,360	6.8	+226,033	+546.9
Hawaii	91,447	1.8	49,642	1.2	−41,805	−45.7
Illinois	325,070	6.5	239,705	6.0	−95,365	−26.3
Massachusetts	364,421	7.3	160,048	4.0	−204,373	−56.1
Michigan	303,103	6.1	149,099	3.7	−154,004	−50.8
Minnesota	61,433	1.2	21,755	0.5	−39,678	−64.6
New Jersey	279,199	5.6	219,406	5.5	−59,793	−21.4
New York	1,257,501	25.1	740,369	18.5	−517,132	−41.1
Ohio	203,038	4.1	95,958	2.4	−107,080	−52.7
Pennsylvania	370,020	7.4	107,303	2.7	−262,717	−71.0
Rhode Island	52,570	1.0	23,301	0.6	−29,269	−55.7
Texas	213,898	4.3	249,735	6.2	+35,837	+16.8
Washington	81,636	1.6	49,150	1.2	−32,486	−39.8
Wisconsin	75,127	1.5	34,016	0.8	−41,111	−54.7

Source: Marvin Gibson, "Alien Population in the United States: Changing Residence Patterns," *Immigration and Naturalization Reporter*, Oct. 1970, Vol. 19, No. 2, Table 1, p. 23.

Registered alien population in selected states is indicated in Table 7. The data show shifts in the states where aliens have resided over the past 30 years. Nevertheless, nearly 82 percent of the registered aliens in 1969 lived in 11 states: California, Connecticut, Florida, Illinois, Massachusetts, Michigan, New Jersey, New York, Ohio, Pennsylvania, and Texas. These states accounted for nearly 75 percent of the alien population in 1940. Also, since 1962 (when INS first obtained Alien Address Report data broken down by state of residence and nationality) nearly two-thirds of the registered permanent resident aliens were natives of 10 countries: Mexico, Canada, United Kingdom, Cuba, Italy, Germany, Poland, Philippines, China, and Portugal.

In interpreting this data, two facts should be kept in mind. First, it is natural for immigrants to settle near relatives, and this is usually in cities in our most populous states. These same states are highly industrialized and contain the most job opportunities. (See data on areas of settlement of labor certification holders and on labor certification rates in Tables 2 and 3, respectively.) Since our policy is based on family reunion and labor qualifications, we should expect immigrants to gravitate to where their families are and where job opportunities are. Both of these are in our most populous states and in our larger cities.

Second, we have no reason to expect immigrants to settle in smaller proportions than the general population does in cities. Even if family relationships and labor certification were not factors in residential settlement, there should be no surprise that the alien population behaves in the manner of the native born. Therefore, efforts to disperse the general population might have some impact on the alien population also. Unless we radically alter our priorities on family reunion and skill levels, no forced dispersion of immigrant arrivals seems possible.

POLICY CONSIDERATIONS

It seems difficult to imagine that the United States would accept a policy of no immigration. Aside from historical, political, and social considerations, it seems impossible that this country should as a matter of policy forbid a husband, for example, to be joined by his foreign-born wife. The contribution and importance of immigrants in the economy also seems to mitigate against a policy of exclusion even from the point of view of absolute self-interest. Humanitarian values also seem to impel us to be open to accepting the stranger, especially those in need. While it is true that meeting all these goals and adhering to the values underlying them frequently involves problems and conflicts, such tension need not be destructive. It can be creative for the nation to try to be true to its values even though this takes time and effort.

Now that the nation is at least tentatively facing up to the question of a national population policy, we should bear in mind the role of immigrant restriction as a scapegoating mechanism for domestic problems. Given the historic and contemporary role of and need for immigration, perhaps an alternative to exclusion ought to be sought. One possibility is to continue immigration. As the society moves on in its journey toward a stable population, immigration would be accepted as a contributor to the replacement, and admittedly in the short run, to the growth of population. As population growth levels off, replacement of population would be then accomplished by fertility and immigration. There would be a tendency to want to delete immigration if we fail to control fertility. The cost of such a move might be dear, indeed, despite its seeming simplicity. It should be noted that a policy of continuing immigration as a component in efforts leading to a stable population need not be any less generous than is current immigration policy.

On the question of dispersion of immigrants, perhaps the wisest course is to include resident aliens in any dispersion policy along with the native-born population. Restricting residential or occupational mobility of aliens runs into serious Constitutional questions of equal protection and involuntary servitude. Since immigrants seem to gravitate toward relatives and jobs, dispersing the general population and/or economic development should affect both the immigrant and the native.

A policy which might help disperse future immigrants would be to reward going to less populated areas with some sort of preference. Canadian immigration selection, based on a point system, might serve as an example. In Canada, the selection of immigrants is based on a system of points which are awarded for various desired characteristics (relationships, education, skills, place of intended residence, etc.). The current preference system, population dispersion, and labor certification functions could all be included in the point system. While such a system might aid in distributing the immigrant population more widely, that alone may not be justification for such a radical alteration of current procedures.

A second program which may aid in wider diffusion of immigrants would be some form of assisted migration to areas needing particular skills. The Cuban refugee program, with its efforts at relocating Cubans by means of a system heavily financed by the Federal Government and administered through the cooperative efforts of Federal, state, and local governments and private voluntary agencies, provides a model for this kind of program. However, such a program would be costly, and there may be some severe economic and political problems in justifying doing this for nonrefugee immigrants.

Labor aspects of current immigration policy have aroused the most opposition and create many thorny problems. The current preference system, while not necessarily encouraging the immigration of professional and technical personnel, does single out such persons who have decided to become immigrants for special treatment over other workers. In one sense, this preference does not produce the demand for entrance by the highly skilled; it rather selects and rewards the more highly skilled among the applicants. Abolishing such a preference or combining all occupations into a single preference category (needed professional, technical, skilled, and semi-skilled workers) would probably not appreciably reduce the demand for visas by the more highly skilled and would not reward or encourage the highly skilled more than other needed workers.

Such a combination of all needed occupations into a single preference category would open the way for useful modifications in the labor certification system. More energy could be expended in drawing up lists of more and less needed and unneeded occupations. Labor Department machinery could be geared for producing lists of needed and unneeded skills and for checking out unusual situations. This would reduce the necessity for many individual certifications. Individual certifications might even be done away with except in cases where a single employer hired a large number of workers or where a large number of like qualified workers entered for settlement in a confined area. Such a procedure should result in data more conducive to a rational manpower policy than the present individual review of whomever happens to apply for certification.

The combining of occupational preferences and the realignment of labor certification could also lead to the alleviation of any current or future brain drain problems. The absence of a preference which encourages skilled persons to move, along with the ability to identify needed skills and to be more selective than we are now in giving blanket coverage, for example, to all Ph.D's (or alternately requiring individual review of each case), might be a plus on a number of levels. The brain drain question, foreign policy, internal manpower policy, and immigration policy could all be positively affected by this sort of approach.

Another labor-related policy which could well hold tremendous potential in terms of population questions is the support of adequate enforcement programs concerning illegals and visa violations in regard to working. The number of illegals is obviously large and the investment might be well made, especially if coupled with a development program with Mexico on our southwest border.

Finally, in regard to labor-related questions, the use of adjustment of status by nonrelatives and nonrefugees as a means of obtaining immigrant visas might also be worth attention. The large number of adjustments of status and labor certifications for persons in the country seems to be circumventing exchange and student programs.

There is one last policy area which should be mentioned, that of refugees. The world's refugee problem is enormous and no one country can solve it. The provision of relief in the form of money and material is one part of this country's efforts at coping with this problem. But we have been a haven also. For a period longer than the history of our nation, the United States and the colonies before them have provided a new home for those driven by war, disaster, and political and other oppression. This traditional American role has been the source of tremendous growth and pride for the nation. However, perhaps the most compelling reason to be open to receiving our fellow men in distress is that it is morally right.

In sum, I would make the following suggestions and conclusions for consideration by the Commission:

1. To think that immigration can simply be stopped now or in the forseeable future is politically naive. It may also not be in our best interests. As an alternative, immigration can continue, along with fertility, as a component of population growth in the United States. Immigrants, of a fixed or variable number, would enter the population as we strive for and after we achieve a stable population. Such an approach need not be any less generous than current policy. The influx of new ideas, training, and so on may well be worth the effort of reducing fertility slightly more, if our past history as a nation of immigrants is used as an indicator.

2. Efforts at dispersion of the general population ought to affect alien settlement patterns due to the close relationship of immigration to family relationships and job opportunities. Incentives for dispersion, such as assisted migration or extra points in a point system of immigrant selection, might also be considered.

3. Combining labor preferences and modifying the labor certification system may lead to a more rational manpower policy and one which is coordinated with immigration policy. Such an approach would assure greater ability to react to brain drain problems which may require future government action. These suggestions should neither reduce the desire of the trained and skilled to enter the country nor encourage and reward them to the detriment of their countries of origin or of other petitioners.

4. More support for vigorous enforcement programs, combined with area development on a binational level in the southwest, may have the greatest proportionate payoff in terms of population pressures.

5. Special consideration should be given to the place of refugees in our total immigration and population policy.

APPENDIX
PREFERENCE SYSTEMS
PREFERENCE SYSTEM, IMMIGRATION AND NATIONALITY ACT OF 1952
(McCarran-Walter Act)

1. First preference: Highly skilled immigrants whose services are urgently needed in the United States and the spouse and children of such immigrants.

   50 percent plus any not required for second and third preferences.

2. Second preference: Parents of United States citizens over the age of 21 and unmarried sons and daughters of United States citizens.

   30 percent plus any not required for first and third preferences.

3. Third preference: Spouse and unmarried sons and daughters of an alien lawfully admitted for permanent residence.

   20 percent plus any not required for first or second preference.

4. Fourth preference: Brothers, sisters, married sons and daughters of United States citizens and an accompanying spouse and children.

   50 percent of numbers not required for first three preferences.

5. Nonpreference: Applicants not entitled to one of the above preferences.

   50 percent of numbers not required for first three preferences, plus any not required for fourth preference.

PREFERENCE SYSTEM, IMMIGRATION ACT OF 1965

1. First preference: Unmarried sons and daughters of United States citizens.

   Not more than 20 percent.

2. Second preference: Spouse and unmarried sons and daughters of an alien lawfully admitted for permanent residence.

   20 percent plus any not required for first preference.

3. Third preference: Members of the professions and scientists and artists of exceptional ability.

   Not more than 10 percent.

4. Fourth preference: Married sons and daughters of United States citizens.

> 10 percent plus any not required for first three preferences.

5. Fifth preference: Brothers and sisters of United States citizens.

> 24 percent plus any not required for first four preferences.

6. Sixth preference: Skilled and unskilled workers in occupations for which labor is in short supply in the United States.

> Not more than 10 percent.

7. Seventh preference: Refugees to whom conditional entry or adjustment of status may be granted.

> Not more than 6 percent.

8. Nonpreference: Any applicant not entitled to one of the above preferences.

> Any numbers not required for preference applicants.

PREFERENCE SYSTEM, H.R. 2328, ADMINISTRATION BILL

Same as preference system for Immigration Act of 1965 with the following exceptions:

1. First preference: Not more than 10 percent.
2. Second preference: Add parents of permanent resident aliens over 21 years of age.
3. Third preference: 15 percent plus any not required by the first two preferences.
4. Fourth preference: No change.
5. Fifth preference: Unmarried brothers and sisters of United States citizens.

> 20 percent plus any not required for first four preferences.

6. Sixth preference: 15 percent plus any not required for the first five preferences.
7. Seventh preference: 10 percent.

PREFERENCE SYSTEM, H.R. 1532, RODINO BILL

1. First preference: Not to exceed 25 percent of the total. Includes the spouse, or unmarried son or daughter of an alien lawfully admitted to the United States for permanent residence, or the married son

or daughter of a citizen of the United States, or the unmarried brother or sister of a citizen of the United States.

2. Second preference: Not to exceed 25 percent. Includes any qualified immigrant who is a member of the profession, or who because of his exceptional ability in the sciences or the arts will substantially benefit prospectively the national economy, cultural interests, or welfare of the United States. Labor certification required. Under this preference no more than 2,500 numbers may be made available to natives of any single state.

3. Third preference: 25 percent and any numbers not used in the first and second preference. Includes qualified immigrants who by training or experience are capable of performing specified skilled labor not of a temporary or seasonal nature, for which a shortage of employable and willing persons exists in the United States. Labor certification is required.

4. Fourth preference: 15 percent and any numbers not used in the previous preferences. Includes:

    • aliens who continuously for at least two years immediately preceding the time of application for a visa and for admission to the United States have been engaged solely or principally by any religious denomination having a bona fide organization in the United States and who are seeking admission to the United States to perform duties which are related to the religious objectives of such denomination;

    • aliens who affirmatively establish that they will not seek employment in the United States and will not have to earn a living;

    • aliens seeking to enter the United States to engage in a commercial or agricultural enterprise in which they will invest a substantial portion of the capital, commodities, services, patents, processes, or techniques.

5. Nonpreference: The remaining 10 percent and any numbers not used for the preferences, shall be allocated in the chronological order in which immigrants qualify, except that within this group, 25

percent (2.5 percent of the total) shall be available for persons under 25 years of age at the time of application for a visa; and such persons shall not be subject to labor certification. Spouses and children accompanying or following to join have the same immigrant status. Labor certification is required except for those specifically exempted.

PREFERENCE SYSTEM, S.1373, KENNEDY BILL

See H.R. 1532, Administration Bill above.

Origins of U.S. Immigrants, 1965 and 1974

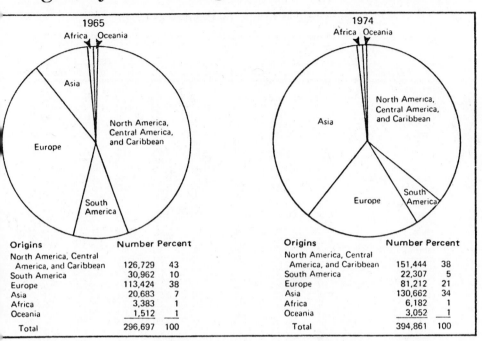

1965 Origins	Number	Percent
North America, Central America, and Caribbean	126,729	43
South America	30,962	10
Europe	113,424	38
Asia	20,683	7
Africa	3,383	1
Oceania	1,512	1
Total	296,697	100

1974 Origins	Number	Percent
North America, Central America, and Caribbean	151,444	38
South America	22,307	5
Europe	81,212	21
Asia	130,662	34
Africa	6,182	1
Oceania	3,052	1
Total	394,861	100

Immigrants Admitted to the United States

Total	Annual average
1931-1940 528,431	52,843
1941-1950 1,035,039	103,504
1951-1960 2,515,479	251,548
1961-1965 1,450,312	290,062
1966-1970 1,871,365	374,273
1971-1974 1,550,087	387,522

Source: U.S. Bureau of Immigration and Naturalization 1974 Annual Report

Fiscal year data

Immigration to U.S. by Country of Origin

(Figures are totals, not annual averages, and were tabulated as follows: 1820-67, alien passengers arrived; 1868-91 and 1895-97, immigrant aliens arrived; 1892-94 and 1898 to present, immigrant aliens admitted. Data before 1906 relate to country whence alien came; since 1906, to country of last permanent residence.)

Countries	1977	1820-1977	1961-70	1951-60	1941-50	1931-40	1921-30	1820-1920
Europe: Albania[1]	51	2,515	98	59	85	2,040	—	
Austria[2]	459	4,314,512	20,621	67,106	24,860	3,563	32,868	3,626,110
Belgium	531	201,807	9,192	18,575	12,189	4,817	15,846	137,542
Bulgaria[3]	98	67,692	619	104	375	938	2,945	61,973
Czechoslovakia[1]	273	136,591	3,273	918	8,347	14,393	102,194	3,426
Denmark	403	363,761	9,201	10,984	5,393	2,559	32,430	300,036
Estonia[1]	1	1,122	163	185	212	506	—	
Finland[1]	227	33,128	4,192	4,925	2,503	2,146	16,691	756
France	2,651	747,683	45,237	51,121	38,809	12,623	49,610	532,765
Germany[2]	7,414	6,970,176	190,796	477,765	226,578	114,058	412,202	5,495,691
Great Britain: England	12,579	3,163,576	174,452	156,171	112,252	21,756	157,420	2,462,015
Scotland	884	819,108	29,849	32,854	16,131	6,887	159,781	567,106
Wales	139	94,993	2,052	2,589	3,209	735	13,012	72,647
Not specified[4]	438	804,468	3,675	3,884	—	—	—	793,741
Greece	7,792	647,892	85,969	47,608	8,973	9,119	51,084	370,405
Hungary[2]	475	—	5,401	36,637	3,469	7,861	30,680	442,693
Ireland	967	4,722,621	37,461	57,332	26,967	13,167	220,591	4,358,350
Italy	7,369	5,287,386	214,111	185,491	57,661	68,028	455,315	4,195,880
Latvia[1]	8	2,539	510	352	361	1,192	—	
Lithuania[1]	11	3,822	562	242	683	2,201	—	
Luxembourg[1]	27	2,843	556	684	820	565	—	
Netherlands	1,039	358,459	30,606	52,277	14,860	7,150	26,948	219,661
Norway[5]	344	856,046	15,484	22,935	10,100	4,740	68,531	731,584
Poland[6]	3,331	510,001	53,539	9,985	7,571	17,026	227,734	169,995
Portugal	9,977	434,837	76,065	19,588	7,423	3,329	29,994	222,721
Romania[7]	1,506	169,263	2,531	1,039	1,076	3,871	67,646	85,428
Spain	5,568	255,285	44,659	7,894	2,898	3,258	28,958	137,907
Sweden[5]	576	1,271,281	17,116	21,697	10,665	3,960	97,249	1,116,239
Switzerland	812	348,243	18,453	17,675	10,547	5,512	29,676	260,492
U.S.S.R.[8]	5,443	3,368,637	2,336	584	548	1,356	61,742	3,280,249
Yugoslavia[3]	2,315	111,322	20,381	8,225	1,576	5,835	49,064	1,888
Other Europe	340	55,198	4,203	8,155	3,983	2,361	22,983	10,716
Total Europe	74,048	36,126,807	1,123,363	1,325,640	621,124	347,552	2,463,194	29,658,016
Asia: China[9]	12,513	513,272	34,764	9,657	16,709	4,928	29,907	347,338
India	16,849	144,553	27,189	1,973	1,761	496	1,886	7,491
Japan[10]	4,545	401,938	39,988	46,250	1,555	1,948	33,462	242,181
Turkey	991	384,533	10,142	3,519	798	1,065	33,824	326,347
Other Asia	115,944	1,165,868	315,688	88,707	11,537	7,644	12,980	22,915
Total Asia[11]	150,842	2,610,164	427,771	150,106	32,360	16,081	112,059	946,272
America: Canada and Newfoundland[12]	18,003	4,081,362	413,310	377,952	171,718	108,527	924,515	1,972,686
Central America	16,892	292,382	101,330	44,751	21,665	5,861	15,769	27,524
Mexico[13]	44,645	2,031,045	453,937	299,811	60,589	22,319	459,287	296,649
South America	33,671	670,944	257,954	91,628	21,831	7,803	42,215	71,284
West Indies	109,959	1,599,084	470,213	123,091	49,725	15,502	74,899	356,570
Other America[13]	4	109,424	19,630	59,711	29,276	25	31	—
Total America	223,174	8,784,241	1,716,374	996,944	354,804	160,037	1,516,716	2,724,713
Africa	9,612	121,723	28,954	14,092	7,367	1,750	6,286	18,024
Australia and New Zealand	2,544	115,843	19,562	11,506	13,805	2,231	8,299	44,002
Pacific Islands[14]	195	24,434	1,769	4,698	5,437	780	427	9,938
Countries not specified[15]	1,900	280,311	3,884	12,493	142	—	228	253,838
Total all countries	462,315	48,063,523	3,321,677	2,515,479	1,135,039	528,431	4,107,209	33,654,803

1. Countries established since beginning of World War I are included with countries to which they belonged. 2. Data for Austria-Hungary not reported until 1861. Austria and Hungary recorded separately after 1905. Austria included with Germany 1938-45. 3. Bulgaria, Serbia, Montenegro first reported in 1899. Bulgaria reported separately since 1920. In 1920, separate enumeration for Kingdom of Serbs, Croats, Slovenes; since 1922, recorded as Yugoslavia. 4. United Kingdom not specified; for 1901-51, included in "Other Europe." 5. Norway included with Sweden 1820-68. 6. Included with Austria-Hungary, Germany, and Russia 1899-1919. 7. No record of immigration until 1880. 8. From 1931-63, the U.S.S.R. was broken down into European U.S.S.R. and Asian U.S.S.R. Since 1964, total U.S.S.R. has been reported in Europe. 9. Beginning in 1957, China includes Taiwan. 10. No record of immigration until 1861. 11. From 1952, Asia included Philippines. From 1934-51, Philippines were included in Pacific Islands; before 1934, recorded in separate tables as insular travel. 12. Includes all British North American possessions, 1820-98. 13. No record of immigration, 1886-93. 14. Included with "Countries not specified" prior to 1925. 15. Includes 32,897 persons returning in 1906 to their homes in U.S. *Source:* Department of Justice, Immigration and Naturalization Service.

BIBLIOGRAPHY

The selected bibliography that follows suggests the vast amount of literature on ethnic communities in America which is available to the ardent researcher. The list, which covers books and audio-visual material dealing with broad groupings and comparative studies (but not single ethnic groups), is not comprehensive; rather it is intended as a starting point for students who wish to examine the development of ethnic pluralism in the United States.

The first section lists approximately twenty comprehensive bibliographies of single and multi-ethnic group studies. Certain of these, notably the Miller and Wynar volumes, were of particular value in researching the chronology for *Ethnic America*.

The second section notes several classic works on the melting pot and other sociological theories, as well as a number of more recent multi-ethnic studies. The last section directs the reader to pertinent audiovisual material, including films, cassettes and recordings.

bibliographies

American Bibliographical Center. *The Emerging Minorities in America: A Resource Guide for Teachers*. Santa Barbara: Clio Press, 1972.

Baden, Anne L. *Immigration in the United States: A Selected List of Recent References*. Washington, D.C.: Library of Congress, 1943.

Bengelsdorf, Winnie. *Ethnic Studies in Higher Education: State of Art and Bibliography*. Washington, D.C.: American Association of State Colleges and Universities, 1972.

Bruno, Louis. *Preliminary List of Resource Materials on Minority Groups*. Olympia, Washington: State Department of Public Instruction, 1968.

Buttlar, Lois, and Wynar, Lubomyr R. *Building Ethnic Collections: An Annotated Guide for School Media Centers and Public Libraries*. Littleton, Colorado: Libraries Unlimited, Inc., 1977.

Jakle, John, and Jakle, Cynthia. *Ethnic and Racial Minorities in North America: A Selected Bibliography of the Geographical Literature*. Monticello, Illinois: Council of Planning Librarians, 1973.

Johnson, Harry A., ed. *Ethnic American Minorities: A Guide to Media and Materials*. New York: R. R. Bowker Company, 1976.

Kinton, Jack F. *American Ethnic Groups: A Sourcebook for the 1970's*. Des Moines, Iowa: University of Iowa Press, 1970.

Kolm, Richard, ed. *Bibliography of Ethnicity and Ethnic Groups*. Washington, D.C.: United States Government Printing Office, 1973.

Miller, Wayne Charles, ed. *A Comprehensive Bibliography for the Study of American Minorities*. New York: New York University Press, 1976.

Oaks, Priscilla S. *Minority Studies: An Annotated Bibliography*. Boston: G. K. Hall & Company, 1976.

Prichard, Nancy S. *A Selected Bibliography of American Ethnic Writing and Supplement*. Champaign, Illinois: National Council of Teachers of English, 1969.

Prpic, George J. *General Bibliography of Immigration and Related Problems*. Cleveland, Ohio: John Carroll University, 1972.

United States Department of Commerce. *Directory of Minority Media*. Washington, D.C.: United States Government Printing Office, 1973.

Wasserman, Paul, and Morgan, Jean, eds. *Ethnic Information Sources of the United States: A Guide to Organizations, Agencies, Foundations, Institutions, Libraries and Museums, Etc.* Detroit, Michigan: Gale Research Company, 1976.

Weed, Perry L. *Ethnicity and American Group Life: A Bibliography*. New York: Institute of Human Relations, 1972.

Wynar, Lubomyr R. *Encyclopedic Directory of Ethnic Newspapers and Periodicals in the United States*. Littleton, Colorado: Libraries Unlimited, Inc., 1972.

_____. *Encyclopedic Directory of Ethnic Organizations in the United States*. Littleton, Colorado: Libraries Unlimited, Inc., 1975.

multi-group studies

Abbot, Edith. *Historical Aspects of the Immigration Problem: Selected Documents*. Chicago: University of Chicago Press, 1926; reprinted New York: Arno Press, 1969.

Abramson, Harold J. *Ethnic Diversity in Catholic America*. New York: John Wiley & Sons, Inc., 1973.

Adamic, Louis. *From Many Lands*. New York: Harper & Row Publishers, Inc., 1940.

Appel, John J. *The New Immigration*. Englewood, New Jersey: Jerome S. Ozer, Publisher, 1971.

Baltzell, E. Digby. *The Protestant Establishment*. New York: Random House, Inc., 1964.

Baroni, Geno C., ed. *All Men Are Brothers*. Washington, D.C.: United States Catholic Conference, 1970.

Barron, Milton. *American Minorities*. New York: Alfred A. Knopf, Inc., 1967.

Bell, Wendell, and Freeman, Walter E., eds. *Ethnicity and Nation-Building: Comparative, International, and Historical Perspectives.* Beverly Hills, California: Sage Publications, Inc., 1974.

Bennett, Marion T. *American Immigration Policies.* Washington, D.C.: Public Affairs Press, 1963.

Bernard, William S., ed. *Americanization Studies: The Acculturation of Immigrant Groups into American Society.* Montclair, New Jersey: Patterson Smith Publishing Corp., 1971.

_____, ed. *Immigrants and Ethnicity: Ten Years of Changing Thought.* New York: American Immigration and Citizenship Conference and National Project on Ethnic America, 1972.

Brody, Eugene B., et al. *Minority Group Adolescents in the United States.* Baltimore: Williams and Wilkins Co., 1968.

Bromwell, William J. *History of Immigration to the United States.* New York: Redfield Publishing, 1856; revised 1966.

Brown, Francis J., and Roucek, Joseph S., eds. *Our Racial and National Minorities: Their History, Contributions and Present Problems.* New York: Prentice-Hall, Inc., 1937.

Commager, Henry Steele, ed. *Immigration and American History: Essays in Honor of Theodore C. Blegen.* Minneapolis, Minnesota: University of Minnesota Press, 1961.

Dinnerstein, Leonard, and Jaher, Frederick C., eds. *The Aliens: A History of Ethnic Minorities in America.* New York: Appleton Century-Crofts, 1970.

Dinnerstein, Leonard, and Reimers, David M. *Ethnic Americans: A History of Immigration and Assililation.* New York: Dodd, Mead & Co., 1975.

Duncan, H. G. *Immigration and Assimilation.* Boston: D. C. Heath & Co., 1933

Eiseman, Alberta. *From Many Lands.* New York: Atheneum Publishers, 1970.

Eisenstadt, S. N. *The Absorption of Immigrants.* Glencoe, Illinois: Free Press, 1955.

Elazar, Daniel, and Friedman, Murray. *Moving Up: Ethnic Succession in America.* New York: Institute on Pluralism and Group Identity, 1976.

Engel, M. H. *Inequality in America.* New York: Thomas Y. Crowell Co., 1971

Enole, Cynthia. *Ethnic Conflict and Political Development.* Boston: Little Brown & Co., 1973.

Fallers, L. A., ed. *Immigrants and Associations.* New York: Humanities Press, Inc., 1968.

Feinstein, Otto. *Ethnic Groups in the City: Culture, Institutions, and Power.* Lexington, Massachusetts: D. C. Heath & Co., 1971.

Fellows, Donald K. *A Mosaic of America's Ethnic Minorities.* New York: John Wiley & Sons, Inc., 1972.

Field, Harold. *The Refugees in the United States.* New York: Oxford University Press, 1938.

Fishman, Joshua A. *Language Loyalty in the United States: The Maintenance and Perpetuation of Non-English Mother Tongues by American Ethnic and Religious Groups.* The Hague: Mouton Press, 1966.

Franklin, Frank G. *The Legislative History of Naturalization in the United States: From the Revolutionary War to 1861.* Chicago: University of Chicago Press, 1906; reprinted New York: Arno Press, 1969.

Freedman, Morris, and Banks, Carolyn. *American Mix: The Minority Experience in America.* Philadelphia: J. B. Lippincott Co., 1972.

Fuchs, Lawrence, ed. *American Ethnic Politics.* New York: Harper & Row Publishers, Inc., 1968.

Garis, Roy L. *Immigration Restriction: A Study of the Opposition to and Regulation of Immigration into the United States.* New York: The Macmillan Co., 1928.

Glazer, Nathan, and Moynihan, Daniel P. *Beyond the Melting Pot.* Cambridge, Massachusetts: M. I. T. Press and Harvard University Press, 1963.

_____, eds. *Ethnicity: Theory and Experience.* Cambridge, Massachusetts: Harvard University Press, 1975.

Grear, Collin, ed. *Divided Society: Ethnic Experience.* New York: Basic Books, Inc., 1974.

Greeley, Andrew M. *Ethnicity.* New York: Seabury Press, Inc., 1977.

_____. *Why Can't They Be Like Us? America's White Ethnic Groups.* New York: E. P. Dutton & Co., 1975.

Greenleaf, Barbara Kaye. *America Fever: The Story of America's Immigration.* New York: Four Winds Press, 1970; reprinted New York: New American Library, 1974.

Hall, Prescott F. *Immigration and Its Effects on the United States.* New York: Holt, 1906.

Handlin, Oscar. *A Pictorial History of Immigration.* New York: Crown Publishers, 1972.

_____. *The Uprooted.* Boston: Little Brown & Co., 1951.

_____, ed. *Immigration as a Factor in American History.* Englewood Cliffs, New Jersey: Prentice-Hall, Inc., 1959.

Hawkins, Brett W. and Lorinskas, Robert A., eds. *The Ethnic Factor in American Politics.* Columbus, Ohio: Charles E. Merrill Publishing Co., 1970.

Herzog, S. J. *Minority Group Politics.* New York: Holt, Rinehart & Winston, 1972.

Howard, John, ed. *Awakening Minorities: American Indians, Mexican Americans, Puerto Ricans.* Chicago: Aldine Press, 1970.

Hudson, Winthrop S. *Nationalism and Religion in America.* New York: Harper & Row, 1970.

Hughes, Helen M., ed. *Racial and Ethnic Relations.* Boston: Halbrook Press, Inc., 1972.

Hutchinson, E. P. *Immigrants and Their Children, 1850-1950.* New York: John Wiley & Sons, 1956.

Hutchmacher, Joseph J. *A Nation of Newcomers: Ethnic Minority Groups in American History.* New York: Delacorte Press, 1967.

Katz, William Loren. *Minorities in American History: Early America, 1492-1812.* New York: Franklin Watts, Inc., 1974.

Kennedy, John F. *A Nation of Immigrants.* New York: Harper & Row, Inc., 1964 revised edition.

Kramer, Judith R. *The American Minority Community.* New York: Crowell Co., 1970.

Kraus, Michael, ed. *Immigration: The American Mosaic.* New York: Van Nostrand Reinhold Co., 1966.

LaGumina, Salvatore J., and Cavaioli, Frank J. *The Ethnic Dimension in American Society.* Boston: Holbrook Press, 1974.

Leinwand, Gerald. *Minorities All.* New York: Washington Square Press, 1971.

Levy, Eugene, and Renaldo, John. *America's People.* Glenview, Illinois: Scott, Foresman & Co., 1975.

Levy, Mark R., and Kramer, Michael S. *The Ethnic Factor: How America's Minorities Decide Elections*. New York: Simon & Schuster, Inc., 1972.

Litt, Edgar. *Ethnic Politics in America*. Glenview, Illinois: Scott, Foresman & Co., 1970

Maisel, Albert Q. *They All Chose America*. New York: Nelson Publishers, 1957.

Mann, Arthur. *Immigrants in American Life*. Boston: Houghton Mifflin Co., 1974.

Marden, Charles F., and Meyer, Gladys. *Minorities in American Society*. New York: Van Nostrand Reinhold Co., 1968.

Mindel, Charles H., and Habenstein, Robert W. *Ethnic Families in America: Patterns and Variations*. New York: American Elsevier Publishing Co., 1976.

Myers, Robert. *Education and Emigration*. New York: David McKay Co., Inc., 1972.

Neuman, William M. *American Plualism: A Study of Minority Groups and Social Theory*. New York: Harper & Row, Inc., 1973.

Novak, Michael. *The Rise of the Unmeltable Ethnics: Politics and Culture in the Seventies*. New York: The Macmillan Co., 1971.

Park, Robert E. *The Immigrant Press and Its Control*. New York: Harper & Row, Inc., 1922.

Patterson, Orlando. *Ethnic Chauvinism: The Reactionary Impulse*. New York: Stein & Day, 1977.

Seabrook, William. *These Foreigners*. New York: Harcourt, Brace, Inc., 1938.

Schneider, Mark. *Ethnicity and Politics: A Comparative State Analysis*. Chapel Hill, North Carolina: University of North Carolina, Institute for Research in Social Science, 1978.

Seller, Maxine. *To Seek America: A History of Ethnic Life in the United States*. Englewood, New Jersey: Jerome S. Ozer, Publisher, 1977.

Shuval, Judith. *Immigrants on the Threshold*. New York: Atherton Press, Inc., 1964.

Smith, William C. *Americans in the Making: The Natural History of the Assimilation of Immigrants*. New York: Appleton-Century, 1939.

Stephenson, George M. *A History of American Immigration 1820-1924*.

Boston: D. C. Heath, Co., 1926; reprinted New York: Russell & Russell, 1970.

Tomasi, Lydio F. *The Ethnic Factor in the Future of Inequality*. Staten Island, New York: Center for Migration Studies, 1972.

Van Doren, Charles, et. al. *Makers of America*. New York: Encyclopedia Britannica, 1971.

Walsh, James P. *Ethnic Militancy*. San Francisco: R & E Research Associates, 1972.

Weiser, Marjorie P. K., ed. *Ethnic America*. New York: The H. W. Wilson Company, 1978.

Wheeler, Thomas C., ed. *The Immigrant Experience: The Anguish of Becoming American*. New York: Dial Press, Inc., 1972.

Wood, Leonard C., et. al. *America: Its People and Values*, second edition. New York: Harcourt Brace & Jovanovich, Inc., 1975.

Wright, Kathleen. *The Other Americans: Minorities in American History*. Greenwich, Connecticut: Fawcett Publications, 1973.

Yinger, J. Milton, and Simpson, George. *Racial and Cultural Minorities*. New York: Harper & Row, Inc., 1972.

Znaniecki, Florian. *Immigrant Backgrounds*. New York: John Wiley & Sons, 1927.

audio-visual materials

Accent on Ethnic America. Six filmstrips, six records or cassettes, six teacher guides. Chicago: Multi-Media Publications, Inc.

The American People: A Nation of Minorities. Four filmstrips, four cassettes. Stamford, Connecticut: Educational Dimensions Group, 1974.

Celebrating the Peoples of the U.S.A. One filmstrip, one disc, one manual. Friendship Press.

Ethnic Heritage: A Living Mosaic. One filmstrip, one cassette, a workbook and teacher's guide. J.C. Penney Company-Educational and Consumer Relations Department, 1973.

Ethnic Studies: The Peoples of America. Four filmstrips, two cassettes; eighteen cassettes. Educational Resources Division-Educational Design.

The Huddled Masses. 16mm film with teacher's guide. Time-Life Films, 1972.

Immigrants in the City. 16mm film. Films, Inc., 1972.

Immigrants in the 19th Century. 16mm film. Films, Inc., 1972.

Immigration in America's History. 16mm film. Coronet, 1960.

Immigration in the 20th Century. 16mm film. Films, Inc., 1972.

Land of Immigrants. 16mm film. Churchill, 1966.

Minorities-USA. Eight filmstrips, eight phonodiscs or cassettes. Globe Filmstrips, 1975.

Minority Groups: Development of a Nation. One cassette. Education Unlimited, 1972.

Nation of Immigrants. 16mm film. Metro-Media Producers Corp.

Our Ethnic Heritage: Immigration, Migration, and Urbanization. Six filmstrips, six cassettes and a teacher's guide. Current Affairs Films, 1975.

They Chose America. Six filmstrips, six cassettes and one listener's guide. Audio Visual Education Corp., 1975.

NAME INDEX

The names listed in the cumulative index are keyed to the chronology section of ETHNICS IN AMERICA, 1970 TO 1977 and to the chronologies of the thirty previous volumes in the series. References in italics are to entries in this volume: the index listing *Bancroft, Anne, 138,* for example, means that the actress is mentioned on page 138. If an italicized name and page number is then followed by roman numerals, the person is referenced both in this volume and in one or more of the other books. The roman numerals give the volume number of the relevant book in the series: the full titles and respective volume numbers are listed immediately following the Index. In the case of *Kerensky, Alexander, 229;* XXIV: 15, 24, a reference to the statesman will be found on page 229 of this volume and on pages 15 and 24 of volume XXIV, THE RUSSIANS IN AMERICA. Individuals whose names are not italicized are to be found elsewhere in the series; the volume numbers are given in roman numerals. The entry Tyler, John, II: 14; XXX: 6, should lead the reader to page 14 of THE BLACKS IN AMERICA (the second book in the series) and to page 6 of THE GREEKS IN AMERICA (the thirtieth book in the series).

b

i

$\mathcal{M}$

O

Valdsaar, H., XVII: 59
Valenta, Frantisek A., XXVIII:
   11
Valenti, Jack, 146
Valentino, Rudolph, IV: 13
Valera, Eamon de, 132-133; X:
   24, 25, 26
Valerian, (Archbishop), 226
Valerianos, Apostolos, XXX: 1
Valgemae, Mardi, 86, 87; XVII:
   63, 66, 68
Valgemae, P., XVII: 41
Valiant, F., XVII: 59
Valim, Joao C., XXII: 41, 55
Valiukas, Leonard, XXI: 52
Valiunas, Joseph, 90, 189, 197
Valiunas, Kestutis, 194; XXI:
   49, 63
Vallas, Anthony, XVIII: 16
Valle, Marta, XI: 15
Valle, Ole, VI: 20, 23
Vallens, Dagmara, XIII: 66
Valles, Joao B. de, XXII: 54
Valletutti, Joseph, 145
Vallot, E., XVII: 48
Valters, Arturs, XIII: 39
Valters, Kristaps, Jr., XIII:
   42
Valtman, E., XVII: 48, 49
Vanagaitis, Antanas, XXI: 27, 31
Van Altena, C.G., V: 29
Van Boven, Jan, V: 31
Van Braam Hockgeest, Andre E.,
   V: 13
Van Brugh family, V: 8
Van Buren, Martin, V: 12; VIII:
   29
Vance, Cyrus, 24, 178, 253, 254
Van Curler, Arend, V: 5
Van Courtlandt family, V: 8, 9
Vancouver, George, XXII: 21
Van Dam, Heiman, 83
Van Dam family, V: 8
Van de Luyster, Jannes, V: 18
Vandenberg, Arthur, IX: 29
Van den Bosch, Koene, V: 19,
   27
Van den Broek, Theodorus, V:
   19, 21, 27
Van den Heuvel, Gerhard, V: 21,
   27
Vanderbilt, Cornelius, V: 11
Van der Casteele, Eduard, V:
   30
Van der Donck, Adriaen, V: 4, 5
Van der Heyden family, XXVIII:
   3

Van der Kemp, Francois, V: 11,
   13
Van der Meulen, Cornelius, V:
   18
Vanderryn, Jack, 84
Van der Wall, Giles, V: 29
Van der Werp, Douwe, V: 29
Van Doren, Charles, 144
Vanik, Charles, XXVIII: 62
Van Lieuwen, John, V: 36
Van Noppen, Leonard, V: 34
Van Peyma, Worp, V: 23
Van Raalte, Albertus, V: 15,
   16, 17, 18, 19, 25, 27, 29
Van Rensselaer, Jan, V: 4
Van Rennselaer, Kiliaen, V: 2,
   4
Van Tongeren, Jan, V: 19
Van Twiller, Wouter, V: 1
Van Velzen, Simon, V: 15
Vanzetti, Bartolomeo, 147; IV:
   22
Vapheiadakes, K., XXX: 17
Vaporis, N. Michael, 117; XXX:
   54
Varandian, Emmanuel, XXVII: 13
Vardys, Vytautas, XXI: 45
Varick, James, II: 4
Varkala, J.P., XXI: 30
Varleth, Joan, XXVIII: 2
Varna, Leons, 188; XIII: 90
Varnagiris, Antanas, XXI: 9,
   14
Varona, Francisco, XXIII: 35,
   38, 39
Vartan, (Saint), XXVII: 24
Vartanian, Aram, XXVII: 22
Vartanian, Vahan, XXVII: 24
Vasar, J., XVII: 38, 40
Vasconcellos, John, XXII: 84
Vasiliu, Mircea, XIX: 22, 24
Vaska, L., XVII: 54
Vaska, V., XVII: 47
Vaskys, Justinas, XXI: 37
Vasquez, Tiburcio, XXVI: 2
Vasquez de Ayllon, Lucas, XII:
   1
Vasquez de Coronado, Francisco,
   XII: 2; XXII: 7
Vassar, Matthew, XX: 90
Vassardakis, Cleanthes, XXX:
   37
Vassilakakis, L., XXX: 24
Vasu, Gloria, XIX: 16
Vasvary, Edmund, XVIII: 29
Vasylivska, Zhenia, XXV: 24
Vasys, Antanas, XXI: 51

the ethnic chronology series

I. The American Indian, 1492-1976, 2nd edition. H. Dennis, 1977.

II. The Blacks in America, 1492-1977, 4th edition. I. Sloan, 1977.

III. The Jews in America, 1621-1977, 2nd edition. I. Sloan, 1978.

IV. The Italians in America, 1492-1972. A.F. LoGatto, 1972.

V. The Dutch in America, 1609-1970. P. & J.W. Smit, 1972.

VI. The Scandinavians in America, 986-1970. H.B. Furer, 1972.

VII. The British in America, 1578-1970. H.B. Furer, 1972.

VIII. The Germans in America, 1607-1970. H.B. Furer, 1973.

IX. The Poles in America, 1608-1972. F. Renkiewicz, 1973.

X. The Irish in America, 550-1972. W.D. Griffin, 1973.

XI. The Puerto Ricans in America, 1493-1973. F. Cordasco, 1973.

XII. The Spanish in America, 1513-1974. A.A. Natella, Jr., 1975.

XIII. The Latvians in America, 1640-1973. M. Karklis, 1974.

XIV. The Chinese in America, 1820-1973. W.L. Tung, 1974.

XV. The Japanese in America, 1843-1973. M. Herman, 1974.

XVI. The Koreans in America, 1882-1974. H. Kim, 1974.

XVII. The Estonians in America, 1627-1975. J. Pennar, 1975.

XVIII. The Hungarians in America, 1583-1974. J. Szeplaki, 1975.

XIX. The Romanians in America, 1748-1974. V. Wertsman, 1975.

XX. The French in America, 1488-1974. J.S. Pula, 1975.

XXI. The Lithuanians in America, 1651-1975. A.M. Budreckis, 1976.

XXII. The Portuguese in America, 590B.C.-1974. M. Cardozo, 1976.

XXIII. The Filipinos in America, 1898-1974. H. Kim, 1976.

XXIV. The Russians in America, 1727-1975. V. Wertsman, 1977.

XXV. The Ukrainians in America, 1608-1975. V. Wertsman, 1976.

XXVI. The Chicanos in America, 1540-1974. R.A. Garcia, 1977.

XXVII. The Armenians in America, 1618-1976. V. Wertsman, 1978.

XXVIII. The Czechs in America, 1633-1977. V. Laska, 1978.

XXIX. The Scots in America (still to come)

XXX. The Greeks in America, 1528-1977. M. Hecker & H. Fenton, 1978.

XXXI. The Arabs in America, 1492-1977. B. Mehdi, 1978.